THE NEW
UN PEACEKEEPING

THE NEW UN PEACEKEEPING

BUILDING PEACE IN LANDS OF CONFLICT AFTER THE COLD WAR

STEVEN R. RATNER

ST. MARTIN'S PRESS
NEW YORK

COUNCIL ON
FOREIGN RELATIONS

THE NEW UN PEACEKEEPING
Copyright © Steven R. Ratner, 1995, 1996.
All rights reserved. Printed in the United States of America.
No part of this book may be used or reproduced in any manner
whatsoever without written permission except in the case of
brief quotations embodied in critical articles or reviews. For information,
address St. Martin's Press, 175 Fifth Avenue, New York, N.Y. 10010.

ISBN 0–312–16448–3 (pbk.)

Library of Congress Cataloging-in-Publication Data

Ratner, Steven R.
    The new UN peacekeeping : building peace in lands of conflict
after the Cold War / Steven R. Ratner.
        p. cm.
    Includes bibliographical references and index.
    ISBN 0–312–12415–5   (cloth) ISBN 0–312–16448–3 (pbk.)
    1. Security, International.   2. Peace.   3. United Nations
4. United Nations—Armed Forces.   I. Title.
JX1953.R34 1995
341.5'8—dc20   94-35326
                                                                      CIP

Interior design by Harry Katz

First published in hardcover in the United States of America in 1995
First St. Martin's paperback edition: December, 1996
10 9 8 7 6 5 4 3 2 1

*To my parents
and Nancy*

C·O·N·T·E·N·T·S

PART I: CONSTRUCTING THE NEW PARADIGM

PART II: A LOOK BACK

L·I·S·T O·F T·A·B·L·E·S

A map of Cambodia appears on page 136.

L·I·S·T O·F A·C·R·O·N·Y·M·S

ACABQ	Advisory Committee on Administrative and Budgetary Questions
ASEAN	Association of Southeast Asian Nations
CIVPOL	Civilian Police Component of the United Nations Transitional Authority in Cambodia
CGDK	Coalition Government of Democratic Kampuchea
CPP	Cambodian People's Party
DPA	United Nations Department of Political Affairs
DPKO	United Nations Department of Peacekeeping Operations
ECOWAS	Economic Community of West African States
FMLN	Frente Farabundo Martí para la Liberación Nacional (El Salvador)
FUNCINPEC	United National Front for an Independent, Neutral, Peaceful and Cooperative Cambodia
ICAO	International Civil Aviation Organization
ICRC	International Committee of the Red Cross
ITU	International Telecommunication Union
JIM	Jakarta Informal Meeting
KPNLF	Khmer People's National Liberation Front
MICIVIH	International Civilian Mission in Haiti
MINUGUA	United Nations Human Rights Verification Mission in Guatemala
MINURSO	United Nations Mission for the Referendum in the Western Sahara
NAM	Non-Aligned Movement
NGC	National Government of Cambodia
OAS	Organization of American States
ONUC	United Nations Operation in the Congo
ONUCA	United Nations Observer Group in Central America
ONUMOZ	United Nations Operation in Mozambique
ONUSAL	United Nations Observer Mission in El Salvador
ONUVEH	United Nations Observer Group for the Verification of Elections in Haiti
ONUVEN	United Nations Observer Mission to Verify the Electoral Process in Nicaragua
PCC	Paris Conference on Cambodia
PLO	Palestine Liberation Organization
PRK	People's Republic of Kampuchea
SNC	Supreme National Council of Cambodia
SOC	State of Cambodia
SWAPO	Southwest Africa People's Organization
UNAMIC	United Nations Advance Mission in Cambodia
UNAMIR	United Nations Assistance Mission for Rwanda
UNASOG	United Nations Aouzou Strip Observer Group

UNAVEM	United Nations Angola Verification Mission
UNCIP	United Nations Commission for India and Pakistan
UNCOK	United Nations Commission on Korea
UNCURK	United Nations Commission on the Unification and Reconstruction of Korea
UNDOF	United Nations Disengagement Observer Force (Golan Heights)
UNDP	United Nations Development Programme
UNEF	United Nations Emergency Force (Sinai)
UNFICYP	United Nations Peacekeeping Force in Cyprus
UNGOMAP	United Nations Good Offices Mission in Afghanistan and Pakistan
UNHCR	United Nations High Commissioner for Refugees
UNICEF	United Nations Children's Fund
UNIFIL	United Nations Interim Force in Lebanon
UNIIMOG	United Nations Iran-Iraq Military Observer Group
UNIKOM	United Nations Iraq-Kuwait Observation Mission
UNIPOM	United Nations India-Pakistan Observation Mission
UNITA	National Union for the Total Independence of Angola
UNITAR	United Nations Institute for Training and Research
UNMIH	United Nations Mission in Haiti
UNMO	United Nations Military Observer
UNMOGIP	United Nations Military Observer Group in India and Pakistan
UNOGIL	United Nations Observation Group in Lebanon
UNOMIG	United Nations Observer Mission in Georgia
UNOMIL	United Nations Observer Mission in Liberia
UNOMSA	United Nations Observer Mission in South Africa
UNOMUR	United Nations Observer Mission Uganda-Rwanda
UNOSOM	United Nations Operation in Somalia
UNOVER	United Nations Observer Mission to Verify the Referendum in Eritrea
UNPROFOR	United Nations Protection Force (Former Yugoslavia)
UNSF	United Nations Security Force (West Irian)
UNTAC	United Nations Transitional Authority in Cambodia
UNTAG	United Nations Transition Assistance Group (Namibia)
UNTCOK	United Nations Temporary Commission on Korea
UNTEA	United Nations Temporary Executive Authority (West Irian)
UNTSO	United Nations Truce Supervision Organization (Middle East)
UNV	United Nations Volunteer
UNYOM	United Nations Yemen Observation Mission
WFP	World Food Program
WHO	World Health Organization

A·C·K·N·O·W·L·E·D·G·M·E·N·T·S

This study was born of a unique opportunity presented to me early in my professional life as an international lawyer: to serve as the legal adviser to the U.S. delegation to the Paris Conference on Cambodia during the final years of the Cambodia peace negotiations. The process that I witnessed was one of an amalgam of global powers and regional actors, motivated by intentions both self-serving and beneficent, groping to solve a seemingly intractable conflict—one the Cambodian political factions themselves seemed unwilling or unable to end. Their decision to attempt a novel and risky UN-dominated solution struck me then as perhaps the beginning of a new place for the United Nations in the peaceful settlement of disputes. From that springboard, I determined to explore this new genre of peacekeeping in detail.

My first expression of gratitude thus goes to my former colleagues at the United States Department of State for giving me the chance to participate in that special assignment—in particular, Jamison Borek and Elizabeth Verville of the Office of the Legal Adviser; and Richard Solomon, David Lambertson, Kenneth Quinn, and Charles Twining of the Bureau of East Asian and Pacific Affairs. This outstanding group of seasoned and savvy foreign policy professionals welcomed me as a full member of their team, and I will always remember their show of confidence at that important time.

My formal work on this study began during a year as an International Affairs Fellow at the Council on Foreign Relations. The year at the Council, and its funding of various research trips, provided the environment and time needed to initiate this undertaking. I greatly appreciate the Council's support, and, in particular, that of Enid Schoettle, Senior Fellow for International Organizations and Law; Alton Frye, Vice-President; Kempton Dunn, Director of Membership and Fellowship Affairs; David Kellogg, Director of Publications; and Lawrence Hamlet, Research Associate, all of whom convinced me of the worthiness of this project and offered the encouragement needed to press on. The United States Institute of Peace also gave me substantial financial assistance for this work in 1993.

Many professional colleagues provided critical comments on early drafts of the text. Through the generous support of the Ford Foundation, the Council on Foreign Relations organized an author's review group in the fall of 1993, thus providing me with an unparalleled opportunity to receive suggestions from a large group of distinguished cognoscenti. I benefited enormously from the views of all those who participated: Michael Doyle,

Lawrence Finkelstein, Thomas Franck, Leon Gordenker, John Hirsch, Richard Lillich, Gene Lyons, Fred Morrison, Anne Richard, James Schear, George Sherry, Louis Sohn, James Sutterlin, Francesc Vendrell, Rick Waddell, Ruth Wedgwood, and David Wippman. I am especially thankful to Paul Szasz, who found time during his service as Legal Adviser to the International Conference on the Former Yugoslavia to provide an exacting commentary on the entire text.

At the University of Texas School of Law, where I began teaching in the fall of 1993, I thank Hans Baade and Douglas Laycock for their many helpful suggestions, as well as John Robertson for his warm friendship. Dean Mark Yudof provided additional financial assistance for travel and books associated with this study. My research assistant, Gregory Naarden, helped immeasurably in locating and checking sources during 1993 and 1994, as did Diane Pearson and Brett Swanson during the final months of the project. My secretary, Cheryl Harris, incorporated countless changes in draft upon draft, and her extraordinary competence was exceeded only by her consistently good cheer. At the Tarlton Law Library, I greatly appreciate the assistance of David Gunn and Jonathan Pratter, who searched far and wide for so many secondary sources.

Elsewhere, Georges Abi-Saab and Victor-Yves Ghébali of the Institut Universitaire de Hautes Études Internationales in Geneva provided useful insights for this work during its early stages. Later, they kindly invited me to present parts of this book to their International Colloquium on New Dimensions of Peacekeeping, held in Geneva in March 1994. Anna Ascher of *The American Journal of International Law* and Charles William Maynes of *Foreign Policy* offered assistance in completing two articles that are reflected, in one fashion or another, in parts of this book. Ambassador Gerald Helman proved a constant source of fresh ideas on the United Nations. The Carnegie Endowment for International Peace included me in its May 1994 U.S.-Japan Conference on UN Peace Efforts and U.S.-Japan Relations, offering yet another set of perspectives on the subject. I also thank the staff of the League of Nations collection at the United Nations library in Geneva and of the libraries of the Carnegie Endowment for International Peace, the Council on Foreign Relations, the United Nations Information Center in Washington, and the American Society of International Law.

My appreciation is also extended to the many persons interviewed for this project, whose names appear at the end of the book, especially the men and women of the United Nations Transitional Authority in Cambodia. During my research in Southeast Asia, I received extraordinary assistance from Yasushi Akashi, Special Representative of the Secretary-General for Cambodia, and Mary Fiske of UNTAC Headquarters in Phnom Penh; Gregory Fergin of the United States Embassy in Jakarta, Indonesia; and Mark Storella of the U.S. Mission in Phnom Penh. Hédi Annabi of the UN Department of Peacekeeping Operations and James Schear of the United Nations Office in Washington kindly helped keep me up to date on some of UNTAC's less publicized activities during the mission; Frank Januzzi of the U.S. Department of State's Bureau of Intelligence and Research assisted with the map that appears in Chapter 6.

Finally, I owe an eternal debt of gratitude to Leon Gordenker and W. Michael Reisman for their invaluable intellectual insights and constant encouragement over the past thirteen years. One could not ask for teachers more committed than they to understanding and conveying the dynamic processes of international organization and law.

Steven R. Ratner
AUSTIN, TEXAS
DECEMBER 1994

Introduction:
A New Generation of Peacekeeping

As the United Nations passes its fiftieth anniversary, it is witnessing a sea change in the nature and purposes of peacekeeping, one of the UN's most cherished inventions. Envisioned at its creation as a stop-gap measure to preserve a cease-fire between two hostile armies, peacekeeping has, since the end of the Cold War, come to include something vastly different—the employment of UN operations to implement an agreed political solution to the underlying conflict between antagonists. Since the late 1980s, the UN has inserted itself with regularity into the domestic arena of war-torn states. In the process, it has treaded down rough paths with regard to elections, human rights, governmental administration, and economic recon- struction. And it has seen an exponential rise in the number of such missions, with 12 established in the UN's first 40 years and as many as 25 since 1989.

This study attempts to understand this new peacekeeping by offering a comprehensive framework for scholars, policymakers, and an informed pub- lic confronted with these operations and the choices of whether to deploy or support them. It views peacekeeping as an instrument of international orga- nization and law—a way of and process for securing important, shared val- ues. While the earlier missions primarily sought to minimize external conflict by monitoring cease-fires, the latest efforts strive to advance more fundamental goals: civil order and domestic tranquillity; human rights, from those most basic to human dignity to those empowering a people to choose its govern- ment; and economic and social development.

Yet as the international community has only begun to experiment with the new dimensions of peacekeeping, scholarly treatment has been scant, and pol- icymaking necessarily ad hoc. The UN's members, in particular the United

States, are grappling with vexing issues that only rarely engaged them for the first generation of peacekeeping. Some are inherently political, such as how to gain and maintain the support of the parties for a durable settlement, or how to respond should it disappear. Others qualify as more managerial, such as how to organize the underfinanced UN to oversee a proliferating number of missions. Each conflict has brought new challenges to the Organization, and the lessons of each conflict often appear overtaken by the sui generis aspects of the next crisis. The results, after five years, are not in all ways encouraging for the future.

In providing such a framework of analysis for these events, I begin where all peacekeeping operations must, with the consent of the parties to the UN's presence. This consent is the first principle of all peacekeeping, and that which distinguishes it from a wholly different, and until recently, relatively unknown exercise—nonconsensual peace enforcement, in which the UN imposes a solution on unwilling combatants. This consent, however, has many dimensions, both formal and substantive, which determine its genuineness and durability. When it begins to decay, as has become all too common in peacekeeping operations around the world, decision makers must react in a way that makes neither too much nor too little of the parties' original bargain, but takes account of the realities on the ground.

From this basis of consent, the processes involved in the new peacekeeping can be constructed. I view the Organization as engaging in three primary political roles—as administrator, mediator, and guarantor of peace agreements, with each operation entailing a different breadth and depth of UN involvement in pursuing these roles. Harmonious, simultaneous performance of these three functions, however, is hardly guaranteed; indeed, they have inherent incompatibilities that are exacerbated if the parties begin to withhold their cooperation from the UN. Eroding consent can also undermine the other revered tenet of peacekeeping, namely the UN's quest for impartiality, or at least the appearance of it.

To comprehend the processes inherent in responding to consent and undertaking these roles, one must peer within and outside the Organization and examine the multitude of actors responsible for the new phenomenon. The three principal components of the UN—the Security Council, the General Assembly, and the Secretary-General—have begun to carve out areas of competence over the new peacekeeping. Despite often obscure legal bases in the United Nations Charter and the relatively simple tasks in the earlier peacekeeping missions, each now has an important part to play, though with greater risk than in the past of stepping on each others' toes or speaking with dissonant voices. The Secretary-General, in particular, as the manager of these missions, has had to adopt the mechanisms of the earlier operations to the new challenges. Outside the UN, donor states, regional organizations, nongovernmental entities, and other participants are now playing significant parts alongside, if not always in support, of the peacekeeping operation.

Elaboration of the underlying principles and identification of the pertinent actors permit the next phase of scrutiny—appraisal of the case law of the new peacekeeping. As with most of the development of international law and organizations, peacekeeping must be viewed historically, as an accretion of precedents whose underlying circumstances must be analyzed. In fact, this case law began long before the birth of the United Nations, as its oft-maligned predecessor, the League of Nations, undertook many of the same endeavors we would today regard as second-generation peacekeeping. And the UN itself, even during the decades in which it appeared paralyzed by the Cold War, was able to lay the groundwork for the new peacekeeping in a few unusual early operations in the Congo and Western New Guinea, as well as through its important responsibilities for the decolonization process during the 1950s, 1960s, and 1970s.

With the late 1980s, the new peacekeeping arrived on the international scene on a more regular, seemingly permanent basis. Beginning with the UN's operation in Namibia, the transformed operations took hold as a core function of the United Nations in the area of international peace and security. Over the next three years, the UN deployed more missions, especially in Latin America, that challenged the prevailing legal and practical assumptions about the UN's role in the internal affairs of states as well as the military-centered nature of peacekeeping. Some seemed clear successes for the UN, others obvious failures, but the general tendency showed the Organization enlarging its horizons regarding both the targets and mandates of peacekeeping.

This trend reached a high point in 1992, with the establishment of the UN's Cambodia operation, in whose formation this author was privileged to play a small part. The United Nations Transitional Authority in Cambodia (UNTAC) represented the most ambitious of the new peacekeeping operations completed to date. It undertook daring, and only partially effective, efforts at UN involvement in the civil administration of a UN member state, conduct of elections, protection of human rights, law and order, refugee repatriation, and economic rehabilitation. While earlier second-generation operations moved the UN forward to a degree, the sheer comprehensiveness of UNTAC's mandate makes it unique in offering insights critical to a full understanding of the genre. Equally important, as a completed mission, UNTAC is ripe for analysis, unlike the ongoing operations in Yugoslavia, Somalia, and elsewhere.

The case study of UNTAC seeks to give a sense of the workings of such a complex operation and the continuous challenges second-generation missions can face, as viewed through the conceptual lenses posited earlier in the study. It thus represents an application of the more theoretical parts of the study through a realistic scenario. In UNTAC's case, the lack of cooperation from the key belligerents led to immediate and significant challenges to the UN's roles as administrator, mediator, and guarantor of the Paris peace accords, as well as its attempts at impartiality.

In evaluating UNTAC's performance as a precedent for future missions, the challenge of the observer is to filter out those exogenous factors beyond the control of the Organization as well as those unique to the endless, intractable conflict in that country. In addition, the predilection of decision makers to label a mission as a success or failure and seek immediate lessons yields an instrument too blunt for productive analysis.

Finally, with the UN likely to encounter more conflicts in the future that suggest the application of enhanced forms of peacekeeping, its members must make coherent decisions on when to deploy these missions and grapple with improving the Organization's capacity to carry them out. In this context, they must begin to rectify structural shortcomings within the Secretariat, assume greater leadership roles over peacekeeping operations, confront concerns that the UN decision making does not legitimately reflect the views of member states, and address the ongoing financial crises of the United Nations. And if peacekeeping operations continue to take place in situations where consent is less than ideal, as seems inevitable, member states must be prepared for a more assertive new starting point that tolerates violations of peace agreements less than in the past.

The observational standpoint underlying this book is thus that the emergence of the new operations is a positive development in international relations and law, and that a better understanding of the phenomenon can contribute to its improvement over time. In a world where the twin goals of global order must remain the minimization of armed conflict and promotion of human welfare, political settlements terminating interstate and intrastate disputes contribute to those ends. The compliance with those settlements and the establishment of conditions to prevent recurrence of conflict remain, in the first instance, the responsibilities of the effective decision makers and communities closest to the dispute, the leaders and citizens of a particular country. The historic patterns, however, have suggested that a diffuse desire for peace rarely serves to guarantee it. The resources offered by outside actors have become essential to preserving the peace, a hardly novel idea and one clearly reflected in the United Nations Charter.

The new peacekeeping continues a long, slow trend of decision by states in allowing the United Nations to provide those resources and thereby advance the values in the Charter. It thus shows the possibility of assistance to those communities seeking to end strife by the one universal international organization currently dedicated to the promotion of key public order values. Although the resource commitments to this endeavor are likely to be high, the rewards in terms of conflict minimization and advancement of human dignity are likely to be far greater. It thus seems most beneficial if this new phenomenon continued to emerge as a core function of the United Nations.

This study also assumes that peacekeeping, rather than nonconsensual peace enforcement, has the brighter future for the UN and the greater potential contribution to public order and human welfare. Clearly, nonconsensual approaches may be appropriate for a limited number of conflicts with an identifiable aggressor or other targets, and a foreseeable nexus between any forcible measures and a desired outcome. This was the case with the Korean War, the Persian Gulf War, and the delivery of food to the starving people in Somalia in 1992 and 1993, where the UN's members, principally the United States, used force on its behalf.

But while peace enforcement may ease the most dire crises in a conflict, such as hunger or mass killings, the vast majority of interstate and internal conflicts cannot be genuinely solved by imposing a fighting vanguard of Blue Helmets on a country, and the international community's tolerance for enforcement measures is not limitless. Rather, as Javier Perez de Cuellar admonished in his 1991 Annual Report on the United Nations—written in the wake of the Persian Gulf War, the most successful use of force in the Organization's history—the UN's greatest promise is not as a forum for litigation and a "negative verdict" against one side, but for mediation and promotion of "just and honorable settlements."[1] It is as a novel instrument for advancing and carrying out such settlements that the new peacekeeping now deserves our attention.

This book is structured in four parts. Part I provides the underlying conceptual basis for the new peacekeeping. Chapter 1 addresses the transformation of peacekeeping from the first generation to the second, including the proximate causes and the distinguishing features of the new missions. Chapter 2 examines the underlying political and legal bases for the new peacekeeping, the UN's depth and breadth of involvement, and its political roles. Chapter 3 examines the key participants in the process of creating, overseeing, managing, and supporting new peacekeeping missions.

Part II comprises two chapters. Chapter 4 considers the precedents for the new peacekeeping in the League of Nations and the United Nations through the 1960s, including actual and aborted cases of involvement by these international organizations in implementing solutions to interstate conflicts. Chapter 5 begins with the first of the true second-generation missions, in Namibia, and reviews the operations established through 1991.

Part III provides the central case study on UNTAC. Chapter 6 describes the negotiating process leading up to UNTAC and the powers the international community gave it to oversee the Cambodia settlement agreements. Chapter 7 provides a detailed examination of UNTAC's work from its arrival until its departure. And Chapter 8 evaluates UNTAC's performance as a second-generation operation, appraising both internal management and political matters.

Part IV contains policy prescriptions and conclusions. Chapter 9 posits a series of issues for decision makers to consider in determining whether to establish a second-generation mission and how to oversee it, as well as proposals for the UN's members to make these missions more effective at reaching the international community's goals. Chapter 10 reflects on the new phenomenon's course in the future.

Part I

■

Constructing the
New Paradigm

.1.

An Old Word, A New Meaning
[or Some Very New Wine in Old Bottles]

A BIRTH IN THE DESERT, BUT WHEN?

The ongoing experiment of the international community in peacekeeping through the United Nations has followed a long and inconstant course through the Organization's history. The uncertainty surrounding its launch date seems emblematic of the many turns the phenomenon has taken. To most historians of the United Nations, it began on November 4, 1956, when the General Assembly, meeting in emergency session after the outbreak of war in the Sinai, endorsed Canadian foreign minister Lester Pearson's initiative and asked Secretary-General Dag Hammarskjold to plan for the deployment of "an emergency international United Nations Force to secure and supervise" a cease-fire between the Egyptian and Israeli armies.[1] Three days later, the Assembly created the United Nations Emergency Force, which quickly deployed on Egyptian territory near the international border with Israel, interposing itself between the two adversaries. UNEF stood between the warring armies until May 1967, when Egypt demanded its withdrawal.

Peacekeeping may, however, have begun nearly a decade earlier. Although UNEF represented the Organization's first deployment of a multinational military force, with the consent of the parties, to help maintain or restore international peace to an area of conflict, the UN had already dispatched military observers—under UN command, but not in an organized force—on two prior occasions. During and after the previous Arab-Israeli war in 1948, the UN had stationed a small number of military personnel to monitor the tenuous cease-fires between Israel and her Arab neighbors. By 1949, the UN Truce Supervision Organization (UNTSO) was observing the armistice agreements signed by Egypt, Jordan, Lebanon, and Israel, maintaining a presence that still stands today. And several time zones away in Kashmir, the United Nations sent military men in February 1949 to watch over the cease-fire between India and Pakistan. This operation, the United Nations Military Observer Group in India and Pakistan (UNMOGIP), set itself up along the frontier in Kashmir, where it has remained despite wars between the two countries in 1965 and 1971.[2]

Whenever it commenced, during the UN's first 40 years, participants in and observers of the UN seemed to agree on peacekeeping's definition and essential attributes—the stationing of UN military personnel, with the consent of warring states, to monitor cease-fires and dissuade violations through interposition between competing armies. New acronyms proliferated with more operations: observer groups—the UN Observer Group in Lebanon (UNOGIL); the UN Yemen Observation Mission (UNYOM); and full-fledged forces—the UN Peacekeeping Force in Cyprus (UNFICYP), the Second UN Emergency Force in the Sinai (UNEF II), the UN Disengagement Observer Force in the Golan Heights (UNDOF), and the UN Interim Force in Lebanon (UNIFIL).[3] (See table 1.1)

Apart from a few unusual operations in the Congo and Western New Guinea (more about this later), none succeeded in doing more than freezing conflicts in place, although that itself represented an accomplishment given the tensions between the belligerents. And rather than "keeping" that peace, they limited their role to observing it.[4] Perhaps peacekeeping was supposed to create the conditions for peace, but rarely did this appear to happen. Indeed, the UN's presence may well have prolonged the underlying conflict by removing any incentives to settle it.[5]

By the mid-1980s, this paradigm for peacekeeping seemed well ensconced. The UN created no new operations, and none of the interstate disputes requiring the existing missions seemed capable of any political settlement: the Kashmir front patrolled by UNMOGIP remained tense; UNFICYP monitored a Cyprus still divided into Greek and Turkish zones; Syria and Israel seemed uncompromising on the Golan Heights; and UNIFIL had to stand by and watch while Israelis and Palestinians fought battles in Lebanon. UN Assistant Secretary-General George Sherry was prompted to say that the UN could engage in little more than "impasse management" in the field of international peace and security.[6]

TABLE 1.1

First-Generation United Nations Peacekeeping Operations: 1948–94

MISSION	DURATION	PRIMARY MANDATE
UN Truce Supervision Organization (UNTSO)	1948–	Supervise Israel-Arab truces
UN Military Observer Group in India and Pakistan (UNMOGIP)	1949	Monitor India-Pakistan truce in Kashmir
UN Emergency Force I (UNEF I)	1956–67	Supervise Israel-Egypt truce in the Sinai
UN Observation Group in Lebanon (UNOGIL)	1958	Monitor Lebanon-Syria border
UN Operation in the Congo (ONUC)*	1960–64	Ensure Belgian withdrawal/end secession/restore law and order/ technical assistance
UN Yemen Observation Mission (UNYOM)	1963–64	Monitor Yemen-Saudi Arabia–Egypt truce
UN Peacekeeping Force in Cyprus (UNFICYP)	1964–	Supervise Cypriot truce
UN India-Pakistan Observation Mission (UNIPOM)	1965–66	Monitor India-Pakistan truce (except in Kashmir)
UN Emergency Force II (UNEF II)	1973–79	Supervise Israel-Egypt truce in the Sinai
UN Disengagement Observer Force (UNDOF)	1974–	Supervise Israel–Syria truce in the Golan Heights
UN Interim Force in Lebanon (UNIFIL)	1978–	Monitor truce in South Lebanon, assist Lebanese government—de facto monitor of hostilities
UN Good Offices Mission in Afghanistan and Pakistan (UNGOMAP)*	1988–90	Monitor USSR troop withdrawal from Afghanistan and non-interference pledges
UN Iran-Iraq Military Observer Group (UNIIMOG)	1988–91	Supervise Iran-Iraq truce
UN Operation in Somalia I (UNOSOM I)	1992–93	Monitor cease-fires; failure to prevent widespread starvation leads to U.S.-led force (UNITAF), then UNOSOM II
UN Observer Mission in Georgia (UNOMIG)	1993–	Monitor government-Abkhazia cease-fire and Commonwealth of Independent States force

* includes traits of second-generation missions

SOURCES: United Nations, *The Blue Helmets: A Review of United Nations Peace-Keeping* (New York: United Nations, 1990), UN Sales No. E.90.I.18; United Nations Peace-Keeping Operations, Information Notes, 1993 Update No. 2, UN Doc. DPI/1306/Rev.2; Gareth Evans, *Cooperating for Peace: The Global Agenda for the 1990s and Beyond* (St. Leonards: Allen & Unwin, 1993), p. 101; various reports of UN Secretary-General.

In 1988, however, two new military operations were born. One, to monitor a cease-fire between Iran and Iraq at the end of their exceptionally bloody eight-year war, seemed reminiscent of the past missions. Several hundred UN military personnel under the United Nations Iran-Iraq Military Observer Group (UNIIMOG) deployed along the Iran-Iraq border; the political talks to end the conflict foundered until Iraq's invasion of Kuwait in 1990 forced it to sue for peace with Iran.

The other peacekeeping force, however, made a cautious step forward. That operation, with the innocuous name of the United Nations Good Offices Mission in Afghanistan and Pakistan (UNGOMAP), followed the signature in April 1988 of agreements among Afghanistan, Pakistan, the Soviet Union, and the United States calling for the withdrawal of Soviet troops from Afghanistan and an end to outside assistance to the Afghan factions.[7] This agreement was not merely a cease-fire, but an attempt to terminate a significant, festering international dispute arising out of the Soviet invasion of Afghanistan in 1979. While leaving much of the future of Afghanistan undecided, the accords definitively resolved the question of Soviet combat forces in Afghanistan by mandating their speedy withdrawal. UNGOMAP observed this withdrawal from monitoring points and reported to the UN on the progress of the troop movements northward. (UNGOMAP had little success with its other task, namely monitoring the cessation of outside military aid and the return of refugees, because of the continued war within Afghanistan even after the withdrawal of Soviet troops.)

With UNGOMAP, the UN had taken off in a new direction. It was now supervising the execution of a type of political settlement. But even that step proved modest, as the 1988 accords did not seek to terminate armed conflict within Afghanistan. Indeed, war still waged between the government and the opposition mujahideen (and, later, among the mujahideen themselves) years after the Soviet troops left. More important, peacekeeping still lived in a well-defined military box characteristic of most of the UN's first 40 years.

But then peacekeeping underwent a revolution. Since 1989, the United Nations has authorized or deployed a host of new missions still popularly called peacekeeping operations, as well as several smaller monitoring and assistance missions (see tables 1.1 and 1.2). Seven were approved for Latin America—the UN Observer Mission to Verify the Electoral Process in Nicaragua (ONUVEN); the UN Observer Group in Central America (ONUCA); the UN Observer Group for the Verification of Elections in Haiti (ONUVEH); the UN Observer Mission in El Salvador (ONUSAL); the International Civilian Mission in Haiti (MICIVIH), jointly staffed with the Organization of American States; the UN Mission in Haiti (UNMIH); and the UN Human Rights Verification Mission in Guatemala (MINUGUA).

Thirteen missions were dispatched to Africa—the UN Transition Assistance Group in Namibia (UNTAG); the UN Angola Verification Missions (UNAVEM I and II); the UN Mission for the Referendum in the Western Sahara (MINURSO); the UN Operations in Somalia (UNOSOM I and II); the UN Operation in Mozambique (ONUMOZ); the UN Observer Mission in South Africa (UNOMSA); the UN Observer Mission to Verify the Referendum in Eritrea (UNOVER); the UN Observer Mission Uganda-Rwanda (UNOMUR); the UN Observer Mission in Liberia (UNOMIL); the UN Assistance Mission for Rwanda (UNAMIR); and the UN Aouzou Strip Observer Group (UNA-SOG). The UN deployed two in Europe—the UN Protection Force in the former Yugoslavia (UNPROFOR) and the UN Observer Mission in Georgia (UNOMIG); and one in the Persian Gulf area—the UN Iraq-Kuwait Observation Mission (UNIKOM). And two were sent to Cambodia—the UN Advance Mission in Cambodia (UNAMIC) and the UN Transitional Authority in Cambodia (UNTAC).

Most of these missions had, in various ways, novel mandates compared to the earlier group. UNIKOM monitors a demilitarized zone established between Iraq and Kuwait at the end of the 1991 Persian Gulf War, but, unlike other operations based on consent, was essentially imposed upon Iraq by the Security Council as part of Iraq's surrender. UNOMIG attempts to supervise a cease-fire within a UN member state, the Republic of Georgia, between governmental and Abkhazian secessionist forces. UNPROFOR has struggled to separate warring combatants in Croatia, ensure delivery of humanitarian relief to civilians suffering in Bosnia-Herzegovina, and prevent the expansion of the conflict into Macedonia. UNOSOM I, deployed to supervise a cease-fire among Somali clans after the country's government collapsed, proved powerless against them; after the U.S.-led humanitarian relief mission, UNOSOM II assumed a similar humanitarian relief mission and a mandate to help build governmental institutions in that shattered country.

Others primarily addressed matters of self-determination, either transitions to independence or to democracy, which usually entailed an active role in trying to establish domestic conditions for fair polling: UNTAG for Namibia, ONUVEN in Nicaragua, ONUVEH in Haiti, MINURSO in the Western Sahara, UNOVER in Eritrea, and UNOMSA in South Africa. ONUCA supervised complex demobilization of guerrillas in several Central American states as part of a regional peace plan, and UNOMUR tried, with limited results, to monitor a 1993 pledge by Rwanda's then-rebel movement not to receive arms from Uganda. To differing degrees, and with vastly varying efficacy, UNAVEM II in Angola, UNAMIC and UNTAC in Cambodia, ONUSAL in El Salvador, ONUMOZ in Mozambique, UNOMIL in Liberia, and UNMIH in Haiti were or are responsible for overseeing the implementation of comprehensive accords to end domestic strife among factions warring for power. UNAMIR received a new, humanitarian-centered mandate in 1994 after Rwanda's peace accord collapsed and genocidal slaughter between its two main ethnic groups left hundreds of thousands dead and displaced much of the country's population.

Still other missions seemed quite sui generis. MICIVIH, the civilian mission in Haiti, was first sent to that island to monitor human rights conditions during negotiations for the return of deposed President Jean-Bertrand Aristide. It was supposed to assist the larger mission, UNMIH, upon President Aristide's return. UNASOG monitored Libya's withdrawal from a strip of Chadian territory under the terms of an International Court of Justice ruling. And MINUGUA was dispatched to Guatemala in 1994 to verify the implementation of a set of human rights agreements between the government and guerrilla opposition as part of a complex process to end that country's long civil war. All these operations placed the United Nations in untidy political situations between and within member states in ways sharply at odds with most of the prior missions.

CONDITIONING FACTORS

It is nearly conventional wisdom that the proximate cause for both the vastly increased number of peacekeeping operations as well as their new scope lay in the change in the international order resulting from the end of the Cold War. This simple explanation, however, obscures the strands of change from the late 1980s that fostered conditions favorable to the new peacekeeping. First, the decline in the U.S.-Soviet superpower rivalry rendered a number of "proxy wars" that had festered during the Cold War amenable to settlement—most importantly, those in Cambodia, Central America, Angola, and Mozambique. In addition, the end of the Cold War facilitated settlements of conflicts that were long-standing items on the agenda of the developing world by removing from them the distortions caused by the spheres of influence inherent in the East-West rivalry. These included the decolonization of Namibia and Western Sahara, and the introduction of majority rule in South Africa. The United Nations became the instrument for concluding and overseeing these settlements.

Second, a contrary trend was visible in the increased number of states falling victim to domestic violence, often ethnically based, as the superpower support that had buttressed their governments and suppressed internal divisions dried up.[8] In extreme cases, this has led to the breakup of states. Thus, the end of the Cold War directly contributed to the strife in the former Yugoslavia, Somalia, Georgia, and elsewhere, as well as the somewhat more peaceful secession of Eritrea from Ethiopia. These crises have flooded the Organization, forcing its members to contemplate new responses, but underscoring the enormity of resources required to terminate many such conflicts.

Third, with the collapse of communism in Eastern Europe and the Soviet Union and the fading of the UN's decolonization agenda into history, the Western states began to assert more forcefully, and in a more balanced way, their own doctrinal commitment to political and civil rights generally, and democracy and free elections in particular. In documents such as the 1990 Charter of Paris that affirmed the right to democratic government in all European states,[9] in policies that tied economic assistance to democratization efforts, in the dispatch of nongovernmental missions to assist and monitor elections, the developed world sought to focus the world's attention on free and fair elections as a fundamental element of self-determination.

In so doing, it challenged the assumption of many developing states that the internal political construction of a member state was not appropriate for international scrutiny (for example, as discussed in chapter 2, through claims of sovereignty), and invited new controversies into the arena of the United Nations. But despite these disagreements, the Western states that dominated much of the decision making related to peacekeeping insisted that respect for human rights and free and fair elections were indispensable elements for political settlements to end conflicts.

As these three trends transformed the agenda of the United Nations by opening up seemingly insoluble wars for settlements, adding new conflicts to the brew, and directing attention to domestic governance issues, the end of the Cold War began to influence the political organs of the United Nations responsible for peacekeeping. During the last years of the Soviet Union, its leaders put forth rather innovative proposals for UN roles for the peaceful settlement of disputes, at odds with its prior skeptical view.[10]

The most significant development proved to be the cooperation among the superpowers and the other members of the Security Council in responding to Iraq's invasion of Kuwait in August 1990, after which the Council imposed previously unimaginable sanctions on an aggressor state, approved a military action to liberate Kuwait, and forced a hard peace on the vanquished Iraq. Although the 1991 Persian Gulf War hardly ended all divisions within the Council, it did emerge more united than before on a greater range of issues, more along the model that the founders of the Organization had envisioned.

These trends flowing from the end of the Cold War have thus led the UN to alter both the targets and instrumental purposes of peacekeeping. Both the old and the new conflicts would be addressed through comprehensive solutions, not simply observations of cease-fires, and those solutions would transcend military issues to others directly affecting the welfare of the people of these states. The result was a proliferation of missions, seizing and creating new opportunities for the Organization but also portending a different set of dangers and mishaps—from political overextension to serious financial difficulties, to new tensions regarding the legitimacy of UN decisions.

THE DEFINITIONAL WRANGLE

But are these new undertakings even peacekeeping? What has become of that term and can it be employed responsibly to describe this latest round of UN operations? The definitional quandary requires attention before any analysis can begin of the nature of the new activities, their legal bases, their precedents, and future prospects. The analytical exercise becomes more complex by the confusing and inconsistent use in diplomatic and popular circles of the term *peacekeeping* and two related and now equally murky concepts, *peacemaking* and *peace-building*. Scholars and diplomats have groped for definitions with varying levels of success.

The current UN Secretary-General, Boutros Boutros-Ghali, first offered his views on this question in his seminal 1992 report, *An Agenda for Peace: Preventive diplomacy, peacemaking and peace-keeping.* [11] There he defined peacekeeping as "the deployment of a United Nations presence in the field, hitherto with the consent of all parties concerned . . . that expands the possibilities for both the prevention of conflict and the making of peace." Peacemaking is "action to bring hostile parties to agreement," as foreseen in Chapter VI of the UN Charter. Peace-building, a term given its diplomatic debut in *An Agenda for Peace,* was defined as "efforts to identify and support structures which will tend to consolidate peace and advance a sense of confidence and well-being among people." [12]

While introducing the important concept of peace-building, these definitions still seemed hostage to the older forms of peacekeeping. These missions would freeze a conflict in place in order to permit peacemaking, namely the use of diplomatic intervention and other instruments, to bring parties to a political settlement. Under this two-phase approach, peacekeeping and peace-making occur before settlements and peace-building can begin after them.

This dichotomous view proves anachronistic in light of the complexities of the modern operations. Today's peacekeeping operations combine elements of *peacemaking* and *peace-building,* as the Secretary-General defines those terms, as well as aspects of preventive diplomacy to avoid spreading of conflict. In his 1993 Annual Report, Boutros-Ghali retained his definitions from *An Agenda for Peace,* but recognized that the lines between these UN endeavors had faded, noting that "peacekeeping has to be reinvented every day . . . [and] there are as many types of peace-keeping operations as there are types of conflict."[13] Today, the United Nations and member states employ the term *peacekeeping* for missions that do far more than manage conflicts.

So the term endures, yet calls out for reappraisal, or at least division into discrete categories. This study adopts a generational approach—to speak of first-generation peacekeeping operations and second-generation or new peace-keeping operations.[14] This perspective highlights the important distinctions between most (but not all) of the peacekeeping operations undertaken during the UN's first 40 years and most (but not all) begun since the Namibia mission in 1989. First-generation operations represent those where a political organ of the UN deploys a military force between two or more armies, with their consent, pending, and in the absence of, a political settlement. Second-generation operations, or "the new peacekeeping," are best defined as *UN operations, authorized by political organs or the Secretary-General, responsible for overseeing or executing the political solution of an interstate or internal conflict, with the consent of the parties.*

The term *generation* focuses upon the changing nature of the operations, not only the time period in which they commenced. It points to a clear shift in the purpose of the operations—from provisional to permanent peace, and from primarily military-centered missions to predominantly political ones. As will be elaborated later, some second-generation missions were created during the first era of peacekeeping. Today we witness both the continuation of older first-generation missions as well as the establishment of new ones. Moreover, a given operation can evolve from one to the other over time as the competing parties move toward or away from a peace settlement. And, although most second-generations operations are multifaceted in mandate and composition, they can, as dictated by the terms of the underlying peace accord, fall along a range from exclusively military to exclusively civilian.[15]

At the same time, the use of the same word—peacekeeping—to describe these operations highlights their critical common trait: the consent of the parties to the operation. As discussed further in the next chapter, the principle of consent, first stated by Dag Hammarskjold in his 1956 report to the General Assembly on the Sinai operation,[16] serves to differentiate peacekeeping from the emplacement of UN personnel in conflict situations without the parties' consent under Chapter VII of the UN Charter, what is best termed peace enforcement.[17] A given operation can change over time from peacekeeping to peace enforcement (or vice versa), or act on both mandates simultaneously with regard to different subject areas in the same overall conflict, depending upon the extent of the consent of the parties to the presence of the UN. But consent remains the sine qua non of peacekeeping, and any mission that includes war-fighting by the Blue Helmets is operating under a different set of conceptual and practical assumptions and constraints.[18]

As set out in table 1.2, despite their variegated mandates and the crises that brought them about, whether decolonization and Cold War mop-ups or post–Cold War fractionating states, most of the operations established since 1989 fall under the rubric of second-generation peacekeeping. All were undertaken as part of attempts at a long-term solution to a conflict, most transcending the observation of the military aspects of an accord to include functions such as electoral and human rights monitoring, public order oversight, and assistance to refugees.

TABLE 1.2

Second-Generation United Nations Peacekeeping Operations: 1962–94

MISSION	DURATION	PRIMARY MANDATE
UN Temporary Executive Authority and UN Security Force (UNTEA/UNSF)	1962–63	Governmental administration in West Irian during transition to Indonesian rule
UN Angola Verification Mission I (UNAVEM I)	1989–91	Monitor Cuban troop withdrawal as part of Namibia independence process
UN Transition Assistance Group (UNTAG)	1989–90	Supervise transition to independence in Namibia
UN Observer Mission to Verify the Electoral Process in Nicaragua (ONUVEN)	1989–90	Monitor elections
UN Observer Group in Central America (ONUCA)	1989–92	Monitor arms flows, force movements, cease-fire, and contra demobilization
UN Observer Group for the Verification of Elections in Haiti (ONUVEH)	1990	Monitor elections
UN Angola Verification Mission II (UNAVEM II)	1991–	Supervise peace accords; peacemaking mission after war resumes
UN Observer Mission in El Salvador (ONUSAL)	1991–95	Supervise peace accords
UN Mission for the Referendum in the Western Sahara (MINURSO)	1991–	Supervise peace plan, particularly referendum on future status
UN Advance Mission in Cambodia (UNAMIC)	1991–92	Supervise cease-fire before UNTAC

MISSION	DURATION	PRIMARY MANDATE
UN Transitional Authority in Cambodia (UNTAC)	1992–93	Supervise peace accords
UN Operation in Somalia II (UNOSOM II)	1992–95	Construct civil institutions, disarm for food relief—includes peace enforcement
UN Operation in Mozambique (ONUMOZ)	1992–95	Supervise peace accords
UN Observer Mission in South Africa (UNOMSA)	1992–94	Confidence-building, monitor elections
International Civilian Mission in Haiti (MICIVIH)	1993–	Monitor human rights conditions
UN Observer Mission to Verify the Referendum in Eritrea (UNOVER)	1993	Monitor elections on establishment of independent state of Eritrea
UN Observer Mission Uganda–Rwanda (UNOMUR)	1993–94	Monitor cross-border military assistance (began as first-generation mission)
UN Observer Mission in Liberia (UNOMIL)	1993–	Supervise peace accords; de facto monitor of hostilities
UN Mission in Haiti (UNMIH)	1993–	Supervise governmental transition
UN Assistance Mission for Rwanda (UNAMIR)	1993–94	Supervise peace accords; new mandate after civil war resumes
UN Aouzou Strip Observer Group (UNASOG)	1994	Monitor Libyan withdrawal from territory pursuant to World Court decision
UN Human Rights Verification Mission in Guatemala (MINUGUA)	1994–	Verify implementation of human rights agreements

Other Operations

MISSION	DURATION	PRIMARY MANDATE
UN Iraq-Kuwait Observation Mission (UNIKOM)	1991–	Supervise truce—nonconsensual mission
UN Protection Force (UNPROFOR)**	1992–	Monitor truces/humanitarian relief/ protect "safe areas" in Croatia and Bosnia-Herzegovina; preventive diplomacy in Macedonia —includes nonconsensual enforcement
UN Assistance Mission in Rwanda (UNAMIR)	1994-	Humanitarian protection/return of refugees—includes nonconsensual enforcement

** includes traits of first-generation missions

SOURCES: United Nations, *The Blue Helmets: A Review of United Nations Peace-Keeping* (New York, United Nations, 1990), UN Sales No. E.90.I.18.; United Nations Peace-Keeping Operations, Information Notes, 1993 Update No. 2, UN Doc. DPI/1306/Rev.2; Gareth Evans, *Cooperating for Peace: The Global Agenda for the 1990s and Beyond* (St. Leonard's: Allen & Unwin, 1993), p. 101; various reports of UN Secretary-General.

Two forces the UN has deployed since 1989 clearly do not meet this definition: the Iraq-Kuwait border mission (UNIKOM), forced upon Iraq under the
terms of the Security Council resolution ending the 1991 Persian Gulf War;[19]
and the observer mission in the former Soviet republic of Georgia (UNOMIG),
which follows a traditional first-generation model by monitoring a cease-fire
between the Georgian army and Abkhazian separatists in the absence of a final
peace. And the holdovers from the first generation in Cyprus (UNFICYP),
Lebanon (UNIFIL), the Golan Heights (UNDOF), and Kashmir (UNMOGIP)
do not join the ranks of new peacekeeping simply by virtue of their longevity.

Peacekeeping has, however, metamorphosed too much for overly neat clas-
sifications, as demonstrated by the evolving missions in the former Yugoslavia
and Somalia. Both the mandate and the basis for the presence of the UN
Protection Force in the former Yugoslavia have changed since its initial
deployment. Initially an approximation of a first-generation peacekeeping
mission to separate warring groups within Croatia, UNPROFOR later took on
untraditional mandates, including a humanitarian relief mission in Bosnia-
Herzegovina and a conflict prevention role in Macedonia. Moreover, in 1993,
as fierce fighting continued, the Security Council reauthorized part of its work
in Croatia and Bosnia as a peace enforcement action.[20]

As for the Somalia operation, UNOSOM I began as a type of first-generation mission, but after the U.S.-led humanitarian relief mission handed operations back to the UN in March 1993, UNOSOM II was permitted to use force
to disarm the Somali factions and maintain law and order.[21] It was also
intended to help Somalis carry out a set of agreements on national reconciliation signed by factional leaders in Addis Ababa in January and March 1993,
but effectively ignored by Somali leaders ever since. To the limited extent the
Somalia mission has assisted the parties to implement the Addis Ababa
accords, it has resembled a second-generation mission. However, much of its
work has taken place as peace enforcement, independently or in the absence
of any peace accord, without the consent of the parties.

At the other extreme, peacekeeping should not be so broad as to encompass
low-level operations by the Organization involving technical assistance, even
if that aid serves to help a state implement some type of solution to a conflict.
The dispatch of a group of experts to advise on elections or delimit a boundary
does not typically constitute a separate UN operation, but rather application of
existing assistance programs to benefit a member state. Peacekeeping operations
will thus usually have certain formalities that are lacking in more routine technical assistance, such as high-level oversight, separate budgets, reports by the
Secretary-General, and acronyms. The lines here, however, are not clear either,
and the transition from small operations—such as the 1990 and 1993-94 Haiti

election and human rights missions (ONUVEH and MICIVIH), the 1993 Eritrea election mission (UNOVER), and the Guatemala human rights mission (MINUGUA)—to technical assistance is best viewed as a graduated one. Indeed, it can be argued that the exclusively nonmilitary mandate and composition of these missions places them outside a workable definition of peacekeeping.

But a terminological obstacle still looms. Although the first-generation operations undertook solely to "keep" (that is, observe) the "peace" in the sense of deterring armed conflict, the second generation strives for much more. Why not then, entirely dispense with the term peacekeeping for the newer missions, and refer to them as peace-building or peace-execution? Three reasons suggest retention of the term peacekeeping, albeit prefaced by new, second-generation, enhanced, or some other appropriate adjective.

First, although some theorists might enjoy propagating yet another "peace-something" to describe the new peacekeeping more precisely, diplomats have become used to the term peacekeeping to encompass a wide range of UN deployments. (Indeed, some overuse the term to include peace enforcement missions.) Second, the phrase "second-generation peacekeeping" recognizes the link with the old operations, some of whose underlying principles, such as consent, remain central to recent operations. It also acknowledges that these new operations grew out of traditional peacekeeping, not spontaneously at the end of the Cold War.

Finally, and most pragmatically, no new term seems better than the old one. Boutros-Ghali's term, *peace-building,* could be redefined, but the term *building* suggests a long-term process that precludes some of the short-term goals of the new peacekeeping, such as conduct of elections. Peacemaking already has a generally accepted and distinct meaning, namely the diplomatic process of bringing the sides to a conflict together toward a settlement (both before and after the signature of any peace agreement). Some might label these missions peace-execution, but that phrase has overtones of nonconsensual enforcement activity antithetical to peacekeeping. So, unless the international community is ready for the hypersyllabic term *peace-implementation,* the old word, with its new modifiers, remains the lingua franca for these new undertakings.

THE OLD VS. THE NEW: AN OVERVIEW

The attributes that first- and second-generation operations share, such as the consent of the parties to the operation, should not overshadow their differences or suggest that the UN can effortlessly adapt old structures to this new paradigm. As addressed in further detail in the ensuing chapters, the following general distinctions should be noted across the generations.

• *Second-generation operations aim primarily at assisting a state or group of states in executing an agreed political solution to a conflict.* During the Cold War, the UN and its member states seized upon peacekeeping as a way to preserve a truce, while assuming that other mechanisms would be employed to settle the underlying issues. As first elucidated by Hammarskjold in his pathbreaking 1960 Annual Report, peacekeeping formed part of the preventive diplomacy function of the United Nations. It aimed to prevent conflicts in the Third World outside the immediate spheres of interest of the United States and Soviet Union from escalating into superpower confrontations.[22] (This definition of preventive diplomacy continues to be used today, though it is divorced from earlier fears of escalation of conflict to the superpower level.) The latest first-generation missions, such as the original deployment of UNPROFOR to Croatia and the sending of observers to Georgia (UNOMIG), followed this pattern of truce supervision.[23] The new peacekeeping rejects this limitation. By working from the starting point of a political settlement, it seeks to end the underlying dispute, not simply avoid its aggravation. It is thus directed more at the long-term than the immediate goal of termination of armed hostilities.

• *Second-generation peacekeeping operations are not limited to an exclusively military mandate, but can have (and usually have had) a substantial or predominantly nonmilitary mandate and composition.* First-generation missions were limited to military matters, and the classic studies of first-generation peacekeeping operations addressed almost solely military functions.[24] The mandate of the new missions will depend directly upon the nature of the dispute among the parties. While some (ONUCA in Central America and UNOMUR along the Rwanda-Uganda border) only supervised cease-fires, arms cutoffs, and demobilizations, most others have conducted numerous nonmilitary activities. The new peacekeeping missions thus require substantial investment of civilian personnel with expertise in areas such as elections, human rights, public administration, and economics. Military issues remain important, as an end to fighting will usually prove a prerequisite to the successful deployment and functioning of the nonmilitary components. But unlike first-generation peacekeeping or peace enforcement, the military acts in an essentially supportive role, even if troops comprise a large portion of the total mission strength.

• *Second-generation peacekeeping has complex agendas.* These new agendas follow directly from its primary goal of helping the parties execute a political settlement of their differences. The new peacekeeping includes the broad notion of peace-building, namely creation of conditions for the long-term preservation of the peace brought about by the settlement. This peace-building entails promotion of reconciliation among the former combatants and assisting them in identifying and responding to the longer-term needs of the nation.[25]

Fulfilling these agendas has thus far meant that the new peacekeeping undertakes the following nonmilitary functions: verification, supervision, and conduct of elections; supervision of civil administration; promotion and protection of human rights; supervision of law and order and police activities; economic rehabilitation; repatriation of refugees; humanitarian relief; de-mining assistance; public information activities; and training and advice to governmental officials. Components within operations must coordinate and even synchronize their efforts.

• *The new peacekeeping is as likely to respond to an ostensibly internal conflict as to an interstate conflict.* First-generation peacekeeping operations were and are primarily deployed in situations of international conflict. During the Cold War, first-generation operations were generally deployed only where two or more states were identified as the principal antagonists (one exception being the Congo operation, where the boundaries between the internal and international elements were quite blurred), as governments were reluctant to countenance the entry of the UN into their domestic disputes without a political settlement. Missions did, however, deploy uniquely on the territory of one state where the underlying dispute was interstate in nature, such as UNFICYP in Cyprus and UNIFIL in Lebanon.

The new peacekeeping responds to both domestic conflicts and international ones. It reflects the realization that separation of and distinction between the two is anachronistic, as most civil wars are both fueled by foreign supporters and have ramifications beyond a state's borders. The UN's horizon of attention has thus fundamentally expanded. Operations can take place in the context of termination of colonial situations, such as Namibia or the Western Sahara, disputes between factions in one state, such as Haiti or Liberia, and wars with a significant interstate dimension, such as Cambodia or Central America. The competing parties will seek out the United Nations to provide international legitimacy to their peace settlement and assistance in implementing it.[26] As instruments for settling internal conflicts, second-generation peacekeeping operations are intertwined with the domestic political situation and do not stand apart from it as would the typical first-generation mission.

Indeed, the dissolution of barriers between internal and external conflicts has had important ramifications on the scope of *first*-generation missions as well. No longer limited to classic interstate conflicts, these operations now appear after states invite peacekeepers into their territory to deter factional violence in the absence of a peace accord. This occurred in the original deployment of UNPROFOR to Croatia (whose "internal" dispute concerned the Croatian government and the Serb minority and whose interstate dimension involved the emergence of new states among the former Yugoslav republics). It also materialized with the Georgian government's invitation to UNOMIG (addressing a dispute affecting both the breakaway province of Abkhazia and relations between Georgia and Russia).

• *Second-generation peacekeeping operations involve numerous types of actors.* First-generation operations engaged primarily two sets of participants: military personnel under UN auspices—the Blue Helmets—and states, principally the combatants and a handful of others, such as troop donors and members of the Security Council. The new peacekeeping includes those two groups, but also the following: guerrilla movements; domestic political parties; regional organizations; nongovernmental organizations (for example, in the fields of economic development, human rights, and humanitarian relief); civilian participants in the mission, whether from within the Organization or seconded from governments; international financial institutions; specialized and technical agencies of the United Nations; private foundations; foreign investors; academic institutions; and even domestic criminal organizations. Each has demands and expectations regarding the operations, and can thereby aid or aggravate the UN's work. Those in charge of the new peacekeeping can ill-afford to limit their dialogue to traditional state actors.

• *The new peacekeeping is a fluid phenomenon.* The paradigmatic first-generation operations tended to have one mandate that scarcely changed over time. The new peacekeeping is, however, inherently mercurial and versatile. The UN may adjust the mandate of an operation to respond to the political situation on the ground, adding or eliminating tasks at the behest of the parties and the international community. It may include within the operation a peace enforcement component, as in Somalia, or even a first-generation component for those aspects of the conflict not yet ripe for settlement.

Moreover, groups deployed before a settlement is reached may later receive a new mandate to help implement the settlement, as the civilian mission in Haiti (MICIVIH), originally sent in 1993 to oversee human rights conditions pending a final settlement, is supposed to work with the follow-on mission, UNMIH, in second-generation peacekeeping. Contrariwise, a second-generation operation may metamorphose if a settlement collapses. UNAVEM II became a small peacemaking mission after Angola returned to civil war following UN-monitored elections in 1992, and UNAMIR belatedly engaged in humanitarian protection following Rwanda's collapse into chaos.

Second-generation peacekeeping thus stands at the edge of an inviting, yet hazardous frontier for the United Nations—the insertion of the Organization into the process of building lasting peace in areas devastated by civil and international conflict. This new initiative represents a by-product of the end of the Cold War but has a heritage dating to an era of lesser expectations and more limited capabilities of the United Nations. After barely five years, the new project is still in its infancy, with the long-term prognosis far from clear.

.2.

Setting the Scene: The Conceptual Underpinnings of the New Peacekeeping

I n 1956, in a report written hurriedly in the midst of the Suez Crisis, Dag Hammarskjold defined the essential principles of the peacekeeping that would dominate the United Nations through the late 1980s: (1) its emplacement and operations would require the consent of the parties and not constitute enforcement action against any member state; (2) it should not influence the military or political balance of power among the parties; and (3) the mission would be temporary in duration.[1] These tenets formed the legal and political bases for the UN's first full-fledged peacekeeping force, UNEF I. That operation, and all the first-generation operations that followed, had a relatively simple mandate: to secure and supervise the cessation of hostilities according to a truce accord.

The new peacekeeping, however, has a broader purpose—creation of long-term peace through implementation of political settlements. Such a goal demands a reappraisal of the precepts of peacekeeping.[2] This chapter begins by reassessing the first principle of all peacekeeping, the consent of the parties, exploring its form and substance, the legal and political constraints on the Organization in responding to it, and the results if consent begins to decay. From this consensual starting point, I discuss the processes inherent in the new peacekeeping. After considering several dimensions from which to view the UN's efforts, I suggest the UN is performing three core political functions—

administrator, mediator, and guarantor of political settlements. The chapter concludes by analyzing the implications of the simultaneous conduct of these roles for a core principle of peacekeeping—the impartiality of a UN operation.

FIXING A STARTING POINT: THE CONTOURS OF CONSENT

The new peacekeeping, like the old, must start with the consent of the parties to the conflict. They have always represented the most significant actors in all forms of peacekeeping. Without their approval, the UN is imposing its policy through peace enforcement. Consent appeared to operate somewhat mechanically in the era of first-generation operations: the UN would call on the warring parties to stop fighting, and, when the parties tired of war, the subsequent cease-fire would include provisions for a peacekeeping force. The United Nations might officially create the force before the parties formally agreed to the cease-fire (as occurred in the Suez Crisis) or afterward (as occurred in the Golan Heights in 1973). The means to achieve that consent, the relationship between consent and the UN's competence in establishing new missions, and the legal limitations upon the Organization deriving from consent, raise important questions for the new peacekeeping, as they did for the old.

1. Gauging Consent: Forms and Qualities of Agreement

a. Matters of Form

The written international agreement, signed by all the adversaries, represents the most formal method of a political settlement and consent to a UN presence. If concluded between states alone, the accord is, under international law, a treaty, which is binding and must be observed in good faith (*pacta sunt servanda*).[3] The likelihood that second-generation peacekeeping operations will address conflicts with a strong internal dimension, even if they also involve international disputes, means that the signatories to settlements will include nonstate actors, whose centrality to the process of conflict resolution is now an axiom of international relations and law.[4] When nonstate actors sign these agreements, the presumption is that *pacta sunt servanda* applies to them as well: a nonstate party that acts in contravention of an agreement it has signed is considered to be violating international law.[5]

Agreements to end armed conflict may be developed by the parties alone or with the assistance of the UN or other intermediaries (the classic peacemaking process), and carried out by the parties alone or with UN assistance. For example, the UN had only a marginal involvement in the termination of French involvement in Indochina after the Viet Minh's siege of Dien Bien Phu and in the execution of the 1954 Geneva accords on Indochina.[6] The *Rainbow Warrior* dispute between France and New Zealand over the former's sabotage of a Greenpeace ship ended under a plan offered by the Secretary-General, but later implemented by the parties alone.[7] For all second-generation operations, the UN has provided substantial aid in both formulating and executing settlements. (The fourth iteration, agreements developed solely by the parties but implemented by the United Nations, seems unlikely in light of the active involvement of the Organization in peacemaking when the outcome envisages a substantial UN presence.)[8]

The treaty offers not only a legally binding form of consent, but formality and clarity. Formality appears through impressively organized preambles, articles, paragraphs, and concluding sections that announce to the parties and the international community the seriousness with which the signatories are assuming their obligations. Clarity results from the craftsmanship of the treaty drafter in distinguishing between legally binding obligations and hortatory expressions. The content of the binding commitments, however, may prove quite vague, especially if the parties use ambiguous language to achieve a compromise. The treaty then serves as a departure point for future interpretive disputes.[9]

In the context of second-generation peacekeeping, the agreement will contain two types of obligations: those *inter se,* among the state and nonstate parties, with the obligations comprising the core of the settlement; and those between the signatories and the United Nations that (a) describe the operation that the disputants foresee for the successful execution of their settlement, and (b) obligate them to allow the UN to implement it.

Agreements do not constitute the only bases for consent. The parties may issue a paper or memorandum outlining the settlement, while not committing themselves in any strictly legal terms to its implementation. The political weight of such a document may render its lack of "legal" force of only academic relevance.[10] The parties can more likely concur upon a political statement than a legal instrument, and the former entails less precise drafting, important advantages if the parties need to design a solution without the aid of legal experts. Second-generation operations can build upon this form of accord, as long as the political commitments are reasonably clear (allowing for the inevitable ambiguities in all settlements) and the consent to the presence of the UN bona fide. A recent example of this form of consent is the Esquipulas II accord and subsequent agreements that have served as the basis for several UN missions in Central America beginning in 1989 (ONUCA, ONUVEN, and ONUSAL).[11]

One permutation of this nonlegal form of consent is the acquiescence by the parties to a settlement plan developed by the United Nations itself. Here the

Secretary-General, pursuant to his peacemaking responsibilities, prepares a report suggesting a settlement and a proposed UN mission. The parties would accept the plan in writing, for example, by signing it or through correspondence with the Secretary-General. Perez de Cuellar sought this type of consent during his negotiations with the parties to the conflict in the Western Sahara in 1990 and 1991.[12] (Subsequent disagreements between the two main protagonists, the Government of Morocco and the Polisario Front, over the meaning of certain elements of the plan thereafter stymied the settlement.)

Moreover, regardless of the nature of the underlying settlement, the UN usually concludes a legal agreement directly with the parties—the Status of Forces Agreement. While principally concerned with the privileges and immunities to be afforded UN personnel in the host country, this agreement also serves as another layer of consent to the presence of the UN mission.[13]

As the new peacekeeping evolves in the decades ahead, decision makers will develop other formulae for consent in response to the needs of the antagonists. The parties to an international arbitration or a case in an international court, over, for example, disputed territory, could jointly ask the United Nations to assist in executing the award. This occurred when Libya and Chad accepted UN monitors to observe Libya's withdrawal from the Aouzou Strip in northern Chad after the World Court found it belonged to Chad.[14] Ultimately, the form becomes less important than the key elements of substance—a clear description of the settlement, including the extent of UN involvement in it, and the agreement of the parties for the UN to carry out its mission.

b. Qualities of Consent

Beyond form issues, those appraising or participating in the new peacekeeping must decipher the nature of the consent behind the operation. The parties may have tired of their conflict and agreed upon a reconciliation plan that takes account of the respective power capabilities of the adversaries and that they are ready to implement in good faith. Equally possible is a political settlement that the antagonists enter into grudgingly, with arms twisted by outside sponsors or local constituents. Furthermore, settlements may be negotiated by the immediate parties (willingly or under duress), or brokered by others. They may also ignore the interests of some actors that did not actively contribute to the negotiation process due to lack of internal or external power bases, odious personalities or policies, or other reasons.

Indeed, these settlement accords raise the question of whose consent is legally necessary to invite the UN to conduct the mission. The traditional law of treaties, with its focus upon states, does not provide a satisfactory answer.[15] Clearly, consent demands a settlement with the concurrence of the principal holders of effective power in the affected state or states. However, political calculations among domestic and foreign participants as to the feasibility of the operation in the absence of support of all nonstate actors will greatly influence the recognition and inclusion of such groups and the necessity of incorporation of other power centers.

As a result, different settlement plans, and the peacekeeping operations derived from them, will evince more or less firm, durable consent and engender varying risks of decay over time. Without attempting to posit any overall theory of the durability of such peace accords, it would seem that those negotiated directly by all the parties representing effective sources of power in the conflict, out of a genuine spirit of reconciliation, are most likely to lay the groundwork for smooth, though hardly incident-free, second-generation peacekeeping missions. In the absence of such attributes, those working within or supporting the new operations will have to employ a range of resources and strategies to maintain the underlying consent. As will be seen in later chapters, this distinction proves important in comparing, for example, the Namibia operation (UNTAG) with the Cambodia one (UNTAC).[16]

In certain situations, the preferred opening positions regarding the form and quality of consent may not square with reality. For states in the midst of civil collapse, such as Somalia in 1991–93, the indigenous sources of power may well be unable to agree on any type of peace plan, or may even lack internal organization themselves. Here, the UN lacks guidance from the parties (if it can identify them) on a settlement and the peacekeepers' mandate. It thus may have to devise its own proposal for a peacekeeping mission, seek the consent of the relevant actors for its deployment, and then fill in the details of a settlement simultaneously with its new peacekeeping responsibilities. Indeed, the UN may not succeed in obtaining even oral approval in situations of anarchy.

The international community may have to interpret the absence of resistance or simple acquiescence as a form of consent, and seek more explicit forms after the operation is in place. The normative and practical questions associated with such an approach to these scenarios are daunting: who must acquiesce? how? for how long? Such a path risks stretching the notion of consent beyond reason and effectiveness. Thus, in anarchical states, the UN could abandon any pretense of consent and establish a presence in the country through enforcement action under Chapter VII of the Charter, as occurred in Somalia beginning with the U.S.-led mission in December 1992. Over time, the operation could then negotiate with the antagonists on a settlement that would permit the operation to transform itself into one based upon consent.[17]

2. Responding to Consent: Basic Legal Competence of the Organization

UN peacekeeping operations, old or new, do not materialize by virtue of settlement accords alone.[18] Regardless of the consent or request of the parties to
a UN role in ending their conflict, the Organization can only act according to
the Charter, the key backdrop for all its missions.[19] The Charter, however,
nowhere mentions peacekeeping as a function of the UN. But the UN and its
members have never interpreted the Charter so narrowly, searching for a specific authorization for each new activity. Rather, seeing it as a dynamic, *constitutive* instrument, they have asked whether a proposed activity for the UN
is consistent with the principles and purposes of the UN and is nowhere pre-
cluded.[20] This approach was endorsed by the International Court of Justice
early in the UN's history in the *Reparation for Injuries* case. In an opinion
whose holding now seems inescapable, the Court held that the UN could
make a compensation claim against Israel for the murder of the UN's mediator for Palestine, Count Folke Bernadotte, despite the absence of any Charter
provision permitting the UN to assert such claims.[21]

By this measure, the UN as an organization of states has demonstrable legal
competence for the new peacekeeping. Article 1 lists the first purpose of the
Organization as "maintain[ing] international peace and security," including
through "bring[ing] about by peaceful means . . . adjustment or settlement of
international disputes or situations which might lead to a breach of the
peace."[22] This core UN function mirrors an obligation upon all states to "settle
their international disputes by peaceful means in such a manner that international peace and security, and justice, are not endangered."[23]

Chapter VI of the Charter elaborates the UN's role in the peaceful settlement of disputes, in requiring parties to a dispute to seek a solution through
one of a number of peaceful means, and continuing with provisions for
involvement of the Security Council, the General Assembly, and the
International Court of Justice. Chapter VI thus invokes responsibility for the
Organization and its members in the settlement of disputes. The UN has
repeatedly claimed an ability and duty to help states in this area through resolutions of the General Assembly and other authoritative means.[24]

Other provisions in the Charter grant the Organization additional competence over the new peacekeeping. Article 1 says the UN should "achieve
international co-operation in solving international problems of an economic,
social, cultural, or humanitarian character, and in promoting and encouraging
respect for human rights and for fundamental freedoms for all . . . ." Chapter
IX expands upon this, requiring the UN to promote higher standards of living,
solutions to social and economic problems, and "universal respect for . . .
human rights and fundamental freedoms. . . ."[25]

The new peacekeeping thus aims to fulfill the principles and purposes of the Charter in several key subject areas; in so doing, it constitutes a new instrument for the peaceful settlement of disputes in furtherance of the Charter. While the individual capabilities of each organ of the UN raise a number of important questions (discussed in the following chapter), the legal competence of the Organization as a whole for these operations is beyond serious question.[26]

3. Limitations upon Consent-Based Peacekeeping

The consent of the parties to the UN and the UN's legal ability to respond to it represent only the beginning of the inquiry regarding the UN's competence. Does the consent of the adversaries allow the UN to undertake whatever they seek or whatever the UN's members or officials wish? The legal landscape includes some warning signs for the UN, although some hazards prove to be more mirages than actual restraints.

a. Article 2, Paragraph 7 of the Charter

The Charter's principal textual restriction on the activities of the United Nations appears in Article 2(7), which prohibits the Organization from "interven[ing] in matters which are essentially within the domestic jurisdiction of any state," except when the UN is applying enforcement measures—those, by definition, not based upon the consent of the parties. The drafters of the Charter believed this clause expressed an inherent limitation upon any international organization. They were especially concerned that an organization with responsibilities in economic, social, and cultural affairs not have the power to intervene directly in the internal governance of a state (except when executing enforcement measures like economic sanctions).[27]

Because peacekeeping does not include enforcement measures (even if it may coexist with, or evolve to or from them), the limitations in Article 2(7) remain pertinent to the new peacekeeping as much as they did to the old. Indeed, Article 2(7) would present, prima facie, a significant obstacle to the new peacekeeping as so many of the UN's recent undertakings in the areas of civilian administration, economic reconstruction, election supervision, and otherwise appear to fall within the "domestic jurisdiction" of a member state. Derek Bowett, for example, one of the original scholars of UN forces, wrote that Article 2(7) bars peacekeeping operations primarily directed at restoring internal order, regardless of the consent of the parties to the conflict.[28]

The trends of decision in international law have, however, sharply curtailed, if not eliminated, Article 2(7) as a bar to the new peacekeeping. First, the concept of matters "essentially within the domestic jurisdiction of any state" has changed over time. As early as 1923, the Permanent Court of International Justice, in interpreting a similar phrase in the League of Nations Covenant in the *Nationality Decrees Issued in Tunis and Morocco* case, stated with great foresight and a hefty dose of legal realism:

> The question whether a certain matter is or is not solely within the jurisdiction of a State is an essentially relative question; it depends upon the development of international relations.[29]

As most carefully chronicled by Rosalyn Higgins, the political organs of the UN have narrowly interpreted Article 2(7) since the earliest days of the Organization. Beginning as soon as 1946, in deciding to investigate conditions within Generalissimo Franco's Spain, the UN's organs have developed the position that, as long as a matter was of "international concern," they could competently undertake nonenforcement action. Nearly all states now accept that the United Nations may concern itself with internal human rights questions notwithstanding Article 2(7).[30]

But have "international relations developed," to quote the Permanent Court, enough to permit the intrusive types of peacekeeping characteristic of the second-generation operations? The signs to date, while hardly uniform, suggest an affirmative answer. The emergence with the end of the Cold War of a greater degree of consensus and objectivity in securing compliance with human rights norms and in encouraging democratization processes has significantly eroded the areas covered by Article 2(7). The authority of the United Nations to assist a people in freely exercising its choice of a government is gaining acceptance, even if many member states remain undemocratic.[31]

The acquiescence to, at a minimum, and active support of, in many cases, the missions in Namibia, Haiti, Nicaragua, Angola, El Salvador, Cambodia, Somalia, and Mozambique also suggest that the international community sees the UN as competent for these matters under the Charter. This practice by states holds great interpretive weight for understanding the contemporary meaning of Article 2(7).[32] Yet UN member states' reluctance to address the fissures within Yugoslavia until it approached dissolution, and in Rwanda despite the genocide of 1994, demonstrates a continued political aversion, difficult to extricate from legal concerns, to delve into many internal conflicts.[33] And, as discussed later, invocations of a broad view of sovereignty continue to emanate from many developing nations.

A second factor also mitigates arguments that Article 2(7) bars the new peacekeeping. Article 2(7) prohibits the Organization from "interven[ing]" in domestic affairs. The plasticity of the term *intervention* is apparent, as has only been confirmed by overly broad UN resolutions that purport to define and proscribe it.[34] Does it extend to diplomatic discussions, radio broadcasts, foreign aid, or trade policy? But whatever the precise meaning of intervention, the new peacekeeping, by definition, flows from the consent of all the parties to the conflict, including all the relevant factions in an internal conflict. This precludes its characterization as "intervention" in the internal affairs of a state.[35] This consent serves as both a source of authority for the new peacekeeping and a limitation on it. Thus, the consent permits the UN to act in domains that states might genuinely regard as "essentially within the domestic jurisdiction" of a country, as in oversight or management of its economy. Obtaining and appraising that consent may prove frustrating; but the UN must rely upon it if the Organization is to enter fields traditionally seen as off-limits, without repeatedly seeking recourse to peace enforcement measures.

b. Claims Regarding Sovereignty

A related impediment often proclaimed as a limitation upon the new peacekeeping centers around the amorphous concept of sovereignty. As the argument goes, certain forms of extensive UN activity could impinge upon the sovereignty of a state. Examples might include close oversight of a state's governmental administration. This argument retains great appeal among many states in the developing world, which remain distrustful of any use of the UN to impose the policies of the large, powerful countries upon small, weak ones. For example, in recent years the General Assembly has apparently welcomed the promise of UN involvement in electoral conduct within states by passing a resolution entitled "Enhancing the effectiveness of the principle of periodic and genuine elections;" yet it has also approved a resolution entitled "Respect for the principles of national sovereignty and non-interference in the internal affairs of States in their electoral processes."[36] The latter attempts to counterbalance the former by emphasizing that UN electoral assistance must fully take account of "national sovereignty" and adopts a strongly pro-government position on the ability of people to vote upon their future. At the Assembly's autumn 1993 session, 51 states, most of them established or newly emerging democracies, opposed the resolution as inimical to promotion of democratic processes.

Invocations of sovereignty as a barrier to the new peacekeeping simply highlight the instrumental, and ultimately circular, definition of that term. (Sovereignty should not be confused with territorial integrity or political independence, two cornerstones of modern international law with clear meanings.) International lawyers have recognized that uncertainty for many years. Despite attempts to define the term, many scholars avoid its use in serious discussion.[37] J. L. Brierly, in his influential treatise, referred to it as "merely a term which designates an aggregate of particular and very extensive claims that states habitually make for themselves in their relations with other states."[38] Yet governments of UN member states have asserted it for the proposition that certain governmental activities of states per se remain matters of internal concern beyond the scrutiny of international law or organizations.

Indeed, the International Court of Justice endorsed this position in its 1986 opinion in the *Military and Paramilitary Activities in and Against Nicaragua* case, stemming from Nicaragua's suit against the United States for the latter's support of the contras and other acts against the Sandinista government. There it defined sovereignty as including "the choice of a political, economic, social and cultural system, and the formulation of foreign policy."[39] (Does this render the use by a state of its foreign policy to influence another state's foreign policy a violation of the latter's sovereignty?) Under this view, by which the Court found the United States to have violated Nicaragua's sovereignty, it would appear that some natural limit exists beyond which outside states or organizations may not seek to affect the policy of a state.

The practice of the UN, its members, multilateral agencies, and nongovernmental organizations has discredited this position.[40] Among the numerous indicia of this trend of decision are: provisions in key human rights instruments (Article 21 of the Universal Declaration of Human Rights [41] and Article 24 of the International Covenant on Civil and Political Rights[42]) suggesting that a state must have a democratic political system; the narrow interpretation of Article 2(7); the emergent views on the appropriateness of international scrutiny of human rights practices in member states; the International Monetary Fund's policy of "conditionality," whereby a country must restructure its economy to be eligible for favorable loans from the Fund; and the proliferation of international regimes on environmental matters that require states to modify their economic conduct. Most significantly, the General Assembly, itself a bastion of pro-sovereignty forces, has challenged old notions of sovereignty by passing a resolution endorsing the idea that humanitarian relief operations need not have the consent of the government of the affected state.[43]

Secretary-Generals Perez de Cuellar and Boutros-Ghali, while defending the need for respect for the fundamental sovereignty of the state (out of deference to the Third World majority), have noted key changes in the concept. Perez remarked in his 1991 annual report: "[Sovereignty] would only be weakened if it were to carry the implication that [it] . . . includes the right of mass slaughter or of launching systematic campaigns of decimation or forced exodus of civilian populations in the name of controlling civil strife."[44] Boutros-Ghali, in *An Agenda for Peace,* commented that "[t]he time of absolute and exclusive sovereignty . . . has passed; its theory was never matched by reality."[45] Even Salim Salim, the Secretary-General of the

Organization of African Unity, long a stronghold of the more extreme positions on sovereignty, has stated:

> It would be a wrong approach to start from the premise that by getting involved in an attempt to resolve a conflict, you are infringing on the sovereignty of a given country. . . . Nobody can suggest to me that one can invoke sovereignty and argue against a collective decision to put an end to the misery, anarchy, chaos, and mayhem that, for example, is taking place in Somalia.[46]

Continuing assertions of sovereignty in the face of international peacekeeping proposals stem almost exclusively from fears by entrenched elites in the target states and others that might find themselves similarly situated, rather than from any coherent legal position. The concerns of the developing world regarding the encroachment of Western parochial interests may, in certain cases, prove well-grounded. The international community will have to consider the views of the developing world in order to derive appropriate constraints on the formation of new, more assertive peacekeeping operations. But reciting the mantra of sovereignty to suggest a clear line beyond which the Organization may not tread subverts candid debate.

c. Settlements in Violation of International Law

Though the legal limits upon the Organization's ability to respond to the parties' consent are not as vast as proponents of strict sovereignty assert, the UN is constrained by principles of international law both reflected in and beyond the Charter. Article 1(1) of the Charter requires the Organization to act "in conformity with the principles of justice and international law." Thus, a settlement agreement that deprived part of a population of civil rights, forcibly repatriated refugees, permitted rigged elections, or the like could not be a candidate for UN support. Indeed, settlements that override key norms of international law (*jus cogens*), such as the non-use of force or universal human rights protections, are legally void *ab initio,* regardless of the consent of the warring factions.[47] Of course, the interpretation of these norms remains with the UN's members. One should not be surprised to see the UN's political organs endorse all sorts of seemingly obnoxious settlement accords, even those that effectively ratify illegal acts such as invasions or mass murder.

4. The Critical Constraint: Political Will

If the claims based on invocations of noninterference and sovereignty ultimately fail as arguments precluding consent-based operations, the UN's ability to mount these missions faces its most pertinent challenge from the member states that comprise it. For the new peacekeeping derives not only from the consent of the belligerents, but from the consent of all the participants in the undertaking. Acting formally through the vote of a political organ or through more informal methods, the key member states (including the Permanent Five, large financial contributors, and important developing world nations) must concur upon the necessity of the mission. Moreover, the international community should have an active interest in supporting directly and sustainedly the peace process in the affected state or states.

But the consent of the immediate parties and political will of the UN's membership are not wholly independent determinants of whether the UN will or should launch a peacekeeping mission. Rather, strong evidence of consent will itself contribute to the requisite political will to set up an operation. Despite diffuse concerns by UN participants and observers that the Organization is engaging in too much peacekeeping, its members have not categorically refused a request for involvement in implementing a peace accord when the consent is steadfast enough to suggest a successful final outcome to the UN's mission. Durable, strong consent has been and should remain a sufficient touchstone for member states' decisions to create new operations. This precept could change if the UN receives a large number of requests, backed by firm consent, for new peacekeeping missions and lacks the human and financial resources to respond to all of them. Until then, the UN need not select among bona fide entreaties from groups that have chosen to end their dispute and seek UN help in carrying out those promises, especially as the UN could oversee many peace accords with only a modest presence coupled with assistance from regional organizations.

But is a durable peace accord a *necessary* factor to create political will? Will states be prepared to approve missions only if they are confident of such consent? The answer appears to be no. UN member states, in particular the larger states, will at times evince the readiness to create peacekeeping operations even in the absence of ideal consent. Their secondary criterion appears to be the extent to which the conflict threatens international peace and security, the preservation of which is the UN's first-listed purpose in the Charter. While states have so broadly interpreted that phrase that it offers little practical guidance to decision makers, it does summarize the idea that, in the case of conflicts presenting immediate dangers to key shared public order and human rights values, states will show flexibility in the type of consent they demand before deploying a mission. Such threats include proliferation of violence, refugee flows, gross violations of human rights, or humanitarian disasters. The level of importance that the conflict maintains to states will directly affect the quality of consent they demand to approve the operation as well as their reactions in the event of decay.

No strict formula can be devised to determine the traits of a conflict that render it sufficiently important to justify a lesser degree of consent in establishing an operation. Rather, the two determinants, consent and the degree of threat to international peace, operate along a spectrum. At one end, members will and should find the political will to create an operation if consent is ideal, even if the conflict seems somewhat localized and controllable. Here the peacekeeping mission might be quite small, with a limited military component. The 1989–90 Nicaragua or 1993 Eritrea election missions represent examples of this case. At the other end, members have acted if consent is tenuous but the conflict assumes greater international importance. This occurred in the decision to establish UNTAC for Cambodia.

The UN's members have even moved off the spectrum entirely, acting in the absence of consent in truly exceptional situations, through peace enforcement in Somalia and Bosnia. But the reluctance to engage in peace enforcement remains profound, as seen by the limited mandates given the Blue Helmets in Somalia and Bosnia and the refusal to send peace enforcers to Rwanda and elsewhere.

Across this range, the commitment of member states will reflect the views of domestic constituencies, especially in states donating personnel or contributing large shares of an operation's budget. These constituencies might well be willing to deploy personnel or devote money in low-risk, high payoff situations of durable consent, but only favor expenditure of personal and financial resources in chancier situations if they saw a peace settlement as most directly advancing the national interest. That determination of the national interest will vary across states, with some more concerned with humanitarian questions and others focused on physical threats to their own security. In the case of Cambodia, again, much of the global commitment was based on the desire to end the human suffering of the Cambodian people (prompted by guilt over the fate of Cambodia during the Vietnam conflict). Cambodia's neighbors had less altruistic motives.

5. When Consent Decays: To Retreat or Advance?

a. Defining the Problem

If the new peacekeeping stems from a prior invitation by the parties to the dispute to the United Nations, what happens if that consent is withdrawn in some manner? For example, the signature of contending parties to some type of settlement accord will not always translate into cooperation with the UN.

The sides may commit outright violations of the accords, or may in good faith implement them inconsistently with the modus operandi of the peacekeeping mission. They could revoke their consent explicitly or through their actions. And the often nonexistent or at least indecipherable chain of authority within some nongovernmental actors can mean that violations occur beyond the control of a party's leadership.

This issue is not new to the second generation. The United Nations confronted it in May 1967, when Egypt, which had agreed in 1956 to the stationing of UNEF I on its territory in the Sinai desert, demanded its immediate withdrawal as a prelude to war with Israel. Secretary-General U Thant tried to persuade Egypt to change its mind and to convince Israel to station UNEF I on its soil, but when both sides refused, he quickly withdrew UNEF I, justifying the move on the fundamentally consensual nature of peacekeeping.[48]

The 1967 UNEF I pullout remains pertinent for the new peacekeeping. In responding to the Egyptian demand, U Thant concluded that, because UNEF had been established through nonenforcement measures (the Uniting for Peace Resolution, about which more will be said later), its presence depended wholly upon the consent of the territorial state, Egypt. U Thant rejected arguments that Egypt had somehow limited its ability to revoke its consent when it accepted the stationing of UNEF I. Historians have questioned this position, asserting that it is not evident that Egypt preserved for itself in 1956 the right unilaterally to demand UNEF's withdrawal, or that at least Egypt accepted that such a move triggered consultations with the United Nations.[49]

More important, however, than the disagreement between U Thant and others about the scope of Egypt's consent is the important point on which they agreed—that Egypt *could* have constrained its right to rescind consent, and that evidence that Egypt had done so would have affected the reaction of the United Nations to any request for withdrawal. (The controversy centered on whether Egypt constrained its right, not the effect of any limitation.) Similar issues plagued the Congo operation (discussed in chapter 4), where Hammarskjold interpreted the Congo's original invitation and consent to the UN operation as a mandate to act, if needed, against the immediate wishes of the government.

The new peacekeeping can find itself in precisely the situation U Thant faced if the parties that invite it to conduct its operations then refuse to cooperate with it. One or more adversaries could explicitly denounce the settlement or indicate their dissatisfaction through actions alone. Does the former grant of consent allow the UN to execute its mandate notwithstanding obstructionist moves by the parties, through force if necessary? In other words, is consent irrevocable and any UN use of force to be characterized as merely

legitimate defense of the mission? At the other extreme, must the mission perform its job only if it maintains the complete ongoing consent of the parties,
such as to necessitate withdrawal or a switch to peace enforcement in the
absence of complete cooperation?[50] Or is an intermediate position possible?
These questions have proved far from hypothetical during nearly all second-
generation operations, most notably in Cambodia, El Salvador, and Somalia,
as well as within the former Yugoslavia.

The form of the consent hardly disposes of these issues. If the parties have
concluded the settlement in a treaty that permits no renunciations, they must,
under international law, fulfill their obligations. Lack of cooperation constitutes not simply bad faith, but unlawful behavior. But parties surely do commit illegal acts, and withholding cooperation to a peacekeeping operation
despite signature of an agreement can and will happen. Equating the mere fact
that the belligerents once signed a legal document with a carte blanche to the
UN to force compliance upon an uncooperative party (in the absence of
authority to engage in peace enforcement) would completely blur the distinction between peacekeeping and enforcement. While a solemn undertaking
by a belligerent to cooperate with the UN will give peacekeepers some additional flexibility in the face of violations, it cannot, on its own, as a legal or
political matter, countenance a battle by the Blue Helmets with a recalcitrant
participant under the guise of peacekeeping and self-defense.

b. A Framework for Decision

Consideration of the quality of the consent may open the door to a process of
appraisal. If the overall consent appears durable, reflecting a bona fide commitment by all the relevant parties to solve the conflict, then small deviations
ought not to halt the process. The operation risks almost immediate paralysis
if it interprets consent so strictly as to freeze or retrench after even minor
infractions by a party and then pin its hope on negotiation for compliance to
resume. The extreme (if principled) positions of irrevocable and fully revocable consent thus appear easily dismissed, for they risk either turning peacekeeping into enforcement or paralyzing the new peacekeeping.

The options facing the new peacekeeping when consent is withdrawn must
rather turn upon factors related to the *context* of the noncooperation. Primary
among these will be the interest of key states in the resolution of the conflict
according to the settlement plan. The attitude of the UN's members, especially
donors of personnel and key actors in the political organs, may exhibit great
patience toward decaying consent, a desire to take decisive measures, or a readiness to abandon a mission when consent fades. Through a political process,
they will determine malleability of consent—a malleability that has no clearly

marked limits short of its extremes. They will also make an implicit decision as to the importance of this operation compared to other commitments.

This evaluative process will occur continuously, although the member states have also created a more formal procedure through the use of sunset provisions for most operations. By explicitly limiting missions' durations, the UN can conduct a periodic reappraisal of the consensual basis of the mission and its progress. Missions are typically authorized for three- to six-month intervals.

Directly affecting the position of member states will be those determinants grounded in the situation on site. Such factors would include: (a) the degree of resistance of the noncooperating party (for example, is the noncooperation approved at senior levels or simply the frustration of rogue elements; how strongly does the recalcitrant party voice its opposition); (b) the range of options available to a UN operation facing noncompliance to continue with its mandate (as in, will ignoring the noncooperating party work, or is its active support required; can the UN act without recourse to arms); and (c) the likely reaction of the recalcitrant party to action by the United Nations to attempt these options. These factors will suggest the possibilities for continuing the mission in a peacekeeping role.

In each operation, and, indeed, for each episode of noncooperation, various actors will weigh the determinants differently. In some situations, the UN might hold the parties to their word and proceed with implementation through assertive, or perhaps coercive, measures. In others, the operation might cease to perform all or part of its mission, as consent has evaporated. Or the UN could switch to peace enforcement, with its greater risks to UN personnel and the local population. Under a middle alternative, the UN could muddle through, making necessary compromises in its mandate along the way.

On the ground, the line between peacekeeping and peace enforcement can prove very thin. A UN mission may well engage in small-scale responses to lack of cooperation and still act within the parameters of peacekeeping. Peacekeepers could drive through a poorly defended roadblock, conduct an unexpected search of a faction's office, or publicly expose classified documents, and still not cross the line to peace enforcement. But at a certain point, these responses become more hazardous, peacekeeping has given way to peace enforcement, and the operation must obtain a new source of authority from the UN's political organs.

Eventually these claims and responses to decaying consent will yield a process of authoritative decision. Evaluating those outcomes will enable future observers to discern the contours of international law on the question of the limits of peacekeeping.[51] At this early stage of the new peacekeeping, it would appear that the international community is prepared to characterize an operation as peacekeeping and continue with its implementation as long as most of the principal actors within the affected states voice their commitment to the process and do not so interfere with it as to render it a mere farce. This admittedly loose view of consent has permitted the UN to pursue new peacekeeping operations (as in Angola, Cambodia, and El Salvador) despite eroding cooperation. It reflects an implicit choice by member states that they will neither insist upon enforcement authority from the Security Council to respond to many types of violations nor demand the termination of missions facing lack of compliance.

On the other hand, member states do not seem prepared to countenance more than a bare minimal use of force to preserve an operation facing truly recalcitrant parties. If force seems the only resort, key member states will likely insist upon withdrawal, as occurred in October 1993 when the United States turned around a ship transporting the first elements of the UN Mission in Haiti after Haiti's military government sent armed bands to intercept it at the dock. In exceptional instances, they will approve peace enforcement, as in Croatia, Bosnia, Somalia, and, by 1994, in Haiti as well.

THE PROCESSES OF THE NEW PEACEKEEPING: IDENTIFYING THE UN'S MISSIONS

Consent defines the starting point for the new peacekeeping, for it determines the role the UN will play in executing a political settlement. Continued cooperation represents an ongoing requirement, furthering or constraining the operation's effectiveness in performing its missions. The missions themselves may be viewed through at least three lenses. (See table 2.1.)

TABLE 2.1
The Missions of the New Peacekeepers

Breadth of the Operation

1. Military matters	6. Refugees
2. Elections	7. Humanitarian relief
3. Human rights	8. Governmental administration
4. National reconciliation	9. Economic reconstruction
5. Law and order	10. Relationships with outside actors

Depth of the Operation

1. Monitoring	4. Conduct
2. Supervision	5. Education—Technical Assistance and Public Information
3. Control	

Political Functions of the Operation
1. Administrator (Executor)
2. Mediator
3. Guarantor

1. Breadth of Responsibility

The subject areas of settlement accords, envisaging eventual UN involvement, have thus far typically fallen into ten major categories.

(1) *Military matters*: cease-fires; withdrawal of foreign forces and termination of foreign military assistance; cantonment, disarmament, and demobilization of forces; custody of weapons; transition to civilian jobs for demobilized or unacceptable members of armed forces; creation of new national armed forces;

(2) *Elections*: election of a constituent assembly or new government after civil strife; decisions on independence for non-self-governing territories; referenda on status of disputed territories;

(3) *Human rights*: improvement in existing conditions; promotion of long-term awareness; appropriate disposition of past offenders;

(4) *National reconciliation*: cooperation between rival factions and interest groups through sharing of power, joint projects, and other means; preparation of new constitutions;

(5) *Law and order*: maintenance of civil peace; improvement in conduct of police forces; elimination of vigilante groups; creation of new police forces;

(6) *Refugees*: return of refugees from abroad and resettlement of internally displaced persons;

(7) *Humanitarian relief*: alleviation of human distress through receipt and distribution of food, medicine, clothing, and shelter; clearance of mines; natural disaster relief;

(8) *Governmental administration*: fair and effective functioning of the civilian governing apparatus of the country or territory;

(9) *Economic reconstruction*: priorities for reconstruction (food cultivation, public works projects, and so on); campaigns for and subsequent use of foreign assistance; land reform; rebuilding of infrastructure; and

(10) *Relationships with outside actors*: foreign policy (including military relations with other states); relations with nongovernmental organizations.

2. Depth of Responsibility

A second perspective invites a deeper level of inquiry, addressing the extent of intrusion or involvement of the UN during the execution of the peace accords. This depth moves along a spectrum from the UN's acting as a mere witness to the process of settlement to one of direct authority over the aspects of the peace plan.[52] Along that scale, the UN can engage in a four levels of responsibility over each of the ten subject areas.[53]

(1) *Monitoring*: observation of a situation to confirm that certain behavior conforms to that previously accepted by the parties, but without a mandate to

influence directly the actors involved. This could include observation of an electoral process, verification that a cease-fire is holding, or examination of a particular human rights practice. Monitoring will typically include investigation. But while the UN can prepare reports that might influence the actors, it would have no authority to demand modifications of the situations witnessed. A variation of monitoring would include investigation of past practices, such as earlier human rights abuses.

(2) *Supervision*: oversight over situations with a mandate to request changes in the behavior of actors, but not to order those actors directly to correct their behavior. For example, if the UN were supervising an election, it could request senior officials in the host state to modify the actions of subordinates that subverted the process. For a human rights matter, it would ask the superiors of an offender to end the abuse and remove the guilty party.

(3) *Control*: direct line authority over the pertinent domestic actors. If the UN "controlled" the disbursement of foreign assistance, it could order officials to channel the money for a certain purpose.

(4) *Conduct*: authority to perform certain tasks directly, with or without the assistance of local authorities and notwithstanding their views on those matters. If the parties asked the UN to conduct an election, it would have plenary authority to make all decisions regarding the election and employ its own personnel to run it.

Finally, standing next to this spectrum are two other degrees of involvement for the UN that it can execute along with the other four. Together, they represent the UN's involvement in an *educational* role in the settlement.

Technical assistance: conduct of programs to train local personnel in specialized areas reflecting the needs of the country, such as training of government bureaucrats, armed forces, and police; and

Public information: dissemination through public media of information regarding the process and the substance of the settlement, such as campaigns to explain voting procedures and to foster consciousness of human rights.

3. Political Functions

A final, more conceptual perspective focuses on the political functions of the new peacekeepers. First-generation operations helped fulfill the Organization's mandate in the Charter to maintain international peace and security through the peaceful settlement of disputes. They represented a significant breakthrough for the UN because they demonstrated that, as an organization, it could actively contribute to managing conflict. The UN would this serve as more than an arena where states assert their positions and negotiate.[54]

As noted in chapter 1, peacekeeping represented one of two activities directed at convincing (not forcing) countries to resolve their differences. The other was peacemaking, namely the use of the resources, personnel, and political influence of the Organization to bring parties towards a settlement. Peacemaking included both active third-party intervention by UN officials and passage of resolutions by the political organs that express the opinion of states on a means to resolve a conflict. This latter function was best summed up by the Irish writer and sometime diplomat Conor Cruise O'Brien as "the feeling that the thing feared may be averted, and the thing hoped for to be won, by the solemn and collective use of appropriate words."[55] Peacemaking and peacekeeping were supposed to complement each other, with the UN simultaneously preserving the peace and promoting a solution, thus moving beyond the limited functions of the League of Nations.

But within this complementarity lay mutual exclusion. During the first generation, peacekeeping and peacemaking operated on distinct tracks—in different arenas (demilitarized zones in deserts for peacekeeping, conference rooms in Geneva for peacemaking); with different participants (armies vs. diplomats); and different goals (freezing conflict vs. settling it). Peacekeeping and peacemaking did not interact with each other as effectively as the UN preferred; and the UN had a better record with peacekeeping than peacemaking.[56]

This distinction loses its validity for the new peacekeeping, which integrates these concepts into one operation. As practiced by the UN and envisaged by parties inviting in the new peacekeepers, the Organization performs three interrelated functions in second-generation missions: administrator (or executor), mediator, and guarantor.

a. The United Nations as Administrator

The primary task of the UN in second-generation operations involves the conduct in an executive capacity of specific tasks requested of it in the settlement, with varying degrees of involvement in the full range of subject areas. Although execution of the mission's mandate includes the managerial and bureaucratic legwork inherent in organizing a complex operation, it also encompasses political duties, involving utilization of appropriate skills by the UN to guide the settlement forward. This political dimension requires the new peacekeepers to galvanize and maintain outside support (diplomatic, financial, and other) for the settlement and push the parties along during the process. For example, supervision of an election will demand both enormous logistical talent, such as planning the observation of polling, as well as political effort, such as maintaining the trust of the parties. The UN undertakes this administrative function in three general loci.

First, the UN may execute aspects of the *settlement* itself. In the typical second-generation mission, the accords make the UN an integral part of the solution to the conflict.[57] Administration of a settlement includes observation of compliance, response to actions inconsistent with the settlement, establishment of fora and facilities for certain aspects of the operation (for example, an ombudsman for human rights complaints, a polling station, or a collection point for weapons), and dissemination of information related to the settlement to the parties, the public, and other actors. The mission ideally works from the script written by the parties and with additional guidance prepared by the UN's overseeing organs.

At a second level, the United Nations may administer aspects of the *governance of the state* or states that are the subject of the settlement. The UN may take charge of governmental functions normally within the province of states if the parties ask it to do so in the settlement. These would include distribution of foreign economic assistance, police work, electoral conduct, provision of technical experts, and powers over the civilian administration.

Finally, the United Nations may execute *tasks outside the settlement proper.* For instance, other actors in the international community may make additional demands upon the operation. Such actors include states that authorize and pay for the mission and nongovernmental organizations that request the assistance of the peacekeeping operation. The assignments must complement the settlement and receive some type of consent of the immediate parties, so as to avoid any conflicting duties and ensure that the activity remains part of peacekeeping. Examples of such roles include certain humanitarian functions (as in distribution of medicine and disaster relief) not contemplated in the settlement. These ancillary activities become integrated into the overall settlement process, although they originate from outside the immediate disputants.

The administrative function of the United Nations is not new, as it formed the essence of first-generation operations. There, the UN would execute observation duties contemplated in the truce. The United Nations developed administrative practices for peacekeeping, such as rules for recruitment of military personnel (such as asking donor states to send a self-contained contingent, rather than mixing nationalities throughout the force); procurement and logistics; chain of command; and relations with UN Headquarters. But in first-generation peacekeeping, the breadth of tasks was narrow and depth of administration shallow, and the bureaucratic and managerial aspects of execution took on greater importance than the political aspects. Today, the UN must both adapt its managerial practices and develop the political tools needed to serve the new missions.

b. The United Nations as Mediator

Intertwined with the UN's executive duties are mediation responsibilities. In mediation, a third party inserts itself diplomatically, with the consent of the parties, into a conflict to serve as a source of ideas, incentives, and pressures to move the parties toward agreement. It constitutes the most active form of third-party intervention to contribute to the resolution of conflict.[58]

The role of the UN as mediator proceeds from the incorporation of peacemaking into the new peacekeeping. It also continues a tradition of mediation, albeit with a mixed record of success, performed outside the ambit of first-generation operations.[59] For the signature of a settlement is only one point in the process of settling conflict. Its significance lies in offering prima facie evidence that the parties have resolved the basic differences between them and will cooperate on implementation. Once the parties accept the settlement, then the terms of the debate shift to its meaning, even if the arguments harken back to their original differences.

Settlements resonate well within the UN due to its long preoccupation and reliance upon texts. Texts in general, and legal texts in particular, have a special significance for international organizations. They view them as the only "objective" standard for action; without a legal starting point, all decisions become mere politics.[60] Although the Charter represents an outer limit governing all peacekeeping operations, the settlement plan serves as a more immediate and relevant text for the second generation. It forms the new standard for the UN, whose officials will dissect it to seek support for action they contemplate to further the settlement.

Yet, as seen in the discussion of decaying consent, the agreement on a settlement does not conclusively prove that the parties will cooperate on implementation. One or more may have penned their names in bad faith, or each may attach such conflicting interpretations to the same words that their original approval becomes a mere gesture, postponing resolution of the hardest questions for the implementation phase. Furthermore, even if the parties appear ready to end their major disputes and share a general view on the implementation, conflicts over the execution will inevitably arise and require resolution. Settlement plans thus contain areas of clear agreement, deliberate ambiguities (as well as unintended ones), and lacunae reflecting topics where the parties remained at odds.

Consequently, the UN must help the parties adhere to their promises and reach new agreements on areas unresolved from the negotiations. Mediation and execution are thus not hermetically separable, as the political work in encouraging the parties to comply can quickly transform into a mediation role when they resist. And mediation may be used as a substitute for execution to encourage the parties to carry out part of the settlement themselves (for example, organization of debates during a campaign), rather than having the UN perform the task. Mediation will prove especially challenging where the parties seek not merely to advance their interpretations of vague or unsettled areas, but to renegotiate parts of the accord that appeared clear from the start.[61] And in those unusual situations where the UN acts in the absence of any political settlement (such as Somalia), it will have to mediate to craft the original peace accord.

In mediation, the intermediary serves not simply as a channel of communication (a good offices role), an investigator of facts (the process of enquiry), or an encouraging facilitator of compromise or soother of differences (the essence of conciliation).[62] When faced with a disagreement, the mediator proposes solutions and uses tools to convince the parties to accept them or other possible compromises. Of the possibilities for third-party intervention available, mediation most accurately describes the actual and desired role of the United Nations in the new peacekeeping for several reasons.

(1) *Time pressures*: once implementation of a settlement has begun, the UN cannot afford, financially or politically, a prolonged period of uncertainty and lack of direction when disagreements arise. The entity in charge of the settlement must seize each moment of difficulty and forcefully advance ideas to move the parties back together.

(2) *Credibility*: because the parties have asked the UN to assist them in implementing their solution, the UN officials involved need not tread slowly in establishing their credentials. They are familiar with the actors, who have accepted them as the appropriate mediators. An unfamiliar intervenor might have to limit its role to good offices or conciliation.[63]

(3) *Expertise*: new peacekeeping operations will ideally include persons familiar with the conflict and the frictions left unsettled by any peace accords, as well as an intelligence-gathering capability (if only through staff meetings and situation reports). The UN thus immediately can use those resources to devise compromises when difficulties arise.

(4) *Tools of persuasion*: the tricks of the trade of the mediator are incentives and pressures, also known as carrots and sticks.[64] Because it simultaneously operates as administrator of the settlement, the UN can push, convince, or cajole parties toward a compromise by linking progress with further implementation of the settlement. For example, the UN could refuse to move forward on an electoral timetable until the parties have settled their differences on demilitarization. In extreme situations, it could threaten to withdraw from the operation, or to begin enforcement action under Chapter VII, if the parties did not solve a dispute. This double identity offers the UN powers that other

intermediaries lack, and which the UN itself often finds wanting when it mediates before the conclusion of a settlement.[65]

During the new peacekeeping operations, the UN performs the following critical mediation roles:

• *Face-saving and escape routes*: The UN officials in charge of a mission can propose solutions to impasses that neither party could on its own, offering a way for one or both sides to back down in a graceful way.[66]

• *Redefinition of issues*: The United Nations may be able to characterize the divisive issue completely differently from the parties, and thereby contribute to its resolution. The mediator can bring in additional issues to be traded against one another or propose a "win-win" solution.[67]

• *Containment of disputes*: If the mediator believes that a certain issue cannot be satisfactorily resolved, it can attempt to define common ground and leave resolution until later.[68] The success of this mediation technique depends upon both the amenability of the parties to "agree to disagree" and the UN's ability to undertake its administrative function in the absence of agreement on the matter under dispute.

• *Follow-through on resolution*: Because of the two hats of the UN, it can exert its influence to ensure that the parties comply with their bargain, enhancing its credibility as a mediator.[69]

Finally, the UN's role as mediator does not preclude other third-party intermediary roles in carrying out a peace plan. It can engage in good offices by passing information between the parties; enquiry by investigating disputes; and conciliation as well. Moreover, as administrator of the settlement, it can act as arbitrator or umpire. If the parties accept, in the settlement accords or later on, the UN's authority to resolve interpretive or other disputes definitively, it acts in a traditional arbitration mode, though without the procedural obstacles of arbitrations involving states or corporations. However, if the parties do not cooperate with the UN, it may have to impose its decision, risking the slide from peacekeeping to peace enforcement. Alternatively, it could try to convince the parties to go along with its solution, and compromise with them as necessary.

c. The United Nations as Guarantor

From the perspective of diplomatic history, a guarantor has been regarded as a powerful actor, usually a state, that agrees to undertake its best efforts to preserve a political situation involving other actors. One state may guarantee the borders of another or the security of an entire region from outside invasion, the outcome of a peace treaty, or the neutrality of another state. States often concluded treaties that purported to guarantee a certain result, such as the pre–World War II treaties among the Western European allies, or issued unilateral guarantees, such as the Monroe Doctrine.[70] As discussed in chapter 4, the United Nations even moved close to assuming guarantee commitments toward Trieste and Jerusalem in the immediate postwar years.

Such a guarantee, legal or otherwise, cannot ensure that the guarantor will actually take all available means to achieve the intended result; nor does it imply that, even if the guarantor(s) do what they pledge, the desired result will occur. Legal guarantees of the old sort are thus increasingly rare. (One remarkable recent exception to this pattern occurred in the Security Council's decision after the 1991 Persian Gulf War to "guarantee the inviolability" of the Iraq-Kuwait boundary.[71]) Rather, today the term stands for a promise by a group of states that, if observed uniformly, would entail a certain outcome, coupled with pledges to respond, if only through consultations, to a violation of the agreement. It literally guarantees nothing, but has political significance and some legal content. Recent examples include the U.S.-Soviet guarantee of the 1988 Afghanistan accords,[72] the U.S. guarantee of the 1979 Egypt-Israel peace treaty,[73] and the multilateral guarantee of the Cambodian settlement.[74]

The settlements that form the starting points for the new peacekeeping may have individual guarantors in the noted sense, that is, states that commit themselves, politically or legally, to preserve the settlement and respond in some way to violations. But for most disputes, outside states will abstain from the significant political commitment required of a guarantor. Their foreign policy priorities and national capabilities will not permit them to guarantee settlements in poor, strategically insignificant areas trying to end internal conflicts—places such as Somalia, El Salvador, Cambodia, or others in which they lack a clear national interest. The burden thus falls on the Organization to serve as the most immediate guarantor of the solution by continually engaging in its execution on the ground and at Headquarters. Member states remain secondary guarantors, insofar as they have pooled their human, financial, and political resources to establish and maintain the peacekeeping operation.

The UN fulfills its guarantor function in two senses: First, by virtue of the operation's mandate, the international community has entrusted the Organization with representing member states' commitment (but not too much commitment, as noted earlier) to see the settlement work, and the conflict ended. It observes and verifies compliance; when the parties disagree, when violations occur, or when the process seems to be breaking down, UN officials are supposed to take the first step and push the process and the parties along. The deployment of large numbers of UN personnel in the country as virtual hostages to the peace process will add to the UN's attention to the conflict. The Organization is dedicated to making the settlement work, independently of the outlook of the parties. In principle, its first loyalty belongs to the settlement it must implement.

Second, the UN represents a guarantor due to its presence alone. This psychological effect of peacekeeping missions changes the political landscape in the affected state.[75] Parties will more likely comply with their obligations or address any violations, and the populace will feel somewhat more secure about the prospects for a settlement. The UN may represent one of the few entities within the country that the society's weak elements regard as untainted and interested in their welfare, or a place to which they can complain about corruption or violence without fear of retribution.[76] In this sense, the United Nations does not directly advance the implementation of the settlement; rather it acts as a confidence-builder.[77]

The UN's role as guarantor, like its function as administrator and mediator, can cross the line from peacekeeping to peace enforcement. If the Security Council orders the operation to guarantee part of the settlement in the literal sense of that word, then it must be prepared to move beyond a mission based upon consent. This type of strict guarantee will likely remain rare, for as most new peacekeeping operations address conflicts beyond the immediate national interests of the United States and other powerful member states, they remain unwilling to commit military forces to preserve those accords. A different answer might apply for missions in more strategic areas, such as the Middle East.

The UN's three political functions thus form a web of responsibility for the Organization. Each role can complement the others. Its administrative functions give it leverage as mediator; and its mediation position can facilitate the administration of the mediated outcome. The executor role also renders the UN the most direct guarantor of the process; and as guarantor, it promotes a perception among the parties of the UN's integrity during the administration phase. The mediation and guarantor tasks are also linked: its continuous mediation of disagreements helps guarantee the accord, and its guarantor role enhances its respect and credibility as a mediator.[78]

Yet the three functions may also work at cross-purposes. Mediation is a lengthy process; and the UN's participation as mediator may lend legitimacy to a violator of the accord and lead local factions and outside states to question the UN's determination to proceed with the administrative duties. Moreover, the UN's determination to administer or guarantee the process according to its own interpretations of the settlement and the ongoing situation may cause some local elites to regard it with mistrust, as a foreign overlord uninterested in local views. These tensions form part of a larger dilemma facing the UN in second-generation missions.

NEUTRALITY AND IMPARTIALITY: OLD TENETS AND NEW DILEMMAS

1. Hammarskjold's Principles

In carrying out its three political functions, the UN adheres to several core operating principles. At a minimum, the Organization must comply with the Charter, which governs the UN's activities as a whole and the competence of the individual organs. Second, it must act with the original consent of the parties and follow their peace plan, although any subsequent noncooperation raises complex questions about the limits of peacekeeping. The UN has also endorsed a third principle for peacekeeping, though two different terms have, unfortunately, been used interchangeably to describe it—*impartiality* and *neutrality*.

Hammarskjold inaugurated this principle in his November 4, 1956, report to the General Assembly on the establishment of UNEF I. The Secretary-General noted that the peacekeeping force would be recruited from states other than the permanent members of the Security Council and that this force would take no position on the merits of the underlying conflict.[79] Hammarskjold and his aides clarified this concept several years later in various reports issued during the Congo operation, in which they asserted that the United Nations Force in the Congo would maintain an attitude of "strict neutrality" and thus abstain from interfering in the internal political struggle in the Congo or influencing its outcome.[80]

Since that time, the UN and observers typically speak of the peacekeeping force as "neutral," "disinterested," "impartial," or "unbiased."[81] States have seen the UN as the best institution for peacekeeping not only because of its institutional expertise, but because they viewed it as impartial compared to any alternative. The competing interests of states would be factored into any decisions of the political organs, and the multinational nature of the bureaucracy, required by Article 101 of the Charter, would ensure their implementation in an impartial manner. This "UN way" contrasts with the stance of regional organizations or sui generis peacekeeping forces, more vulnerable to pressure from powerful members and not sufficiently distant from a conflict to be neutral as peacekeepers.[82]

In the context of peacekeeping operations, impartiality suggests that the UN has no initial bias toward either side and acts independently of their gains and losses.[83] Neutrality would encompass a more expansive concept: it could mean that the United Nations is and should be indifferent to whether the parties even solve their differences (not simply who wins and loses in that outcome). But although this conforms with a literal reading of the term neutrality, it runs contrary to the purposes of the Organization. The UN is never neutral in this sense, as it has a primary mission to facilitate the peaceful settlement of disputes.[84] A better concept of neutrality would regard the United Nations as unable (as opposed to unwilling) to affect the outcome of the conflict with regard to the parties' relative positions.[85]

In the era of traditional peacekeeping, the United Nations sought impartiality, and, due to the limited nature of its mandate, usually achieved it. It often proved not neutral, in that the presence of a force had effects upon the parties, for example, tending to solidify one side's gains by creating de facto accretions of territory. But the UN officially regarded itself as neutral (as well as impartial), as its officials stated categorically that its presence would not affect the merits of the conflict, other than to promote some peaceful solution.

2. The Contemporary Challenges

The new peacekeeping affords no such simple positions. Because the UN acts as administrator, mediator, and guarantor, it is pulled by forces not present in the earlier operations. The intrusive nature of the new peacekeeping prevents the Organization from acting as a neutral player in the sense of having no effect on the ultimate resolution of the dispute. Whether through supervision of elections or oversight of human rights conditions, the UN's actions are bound to—and, indeed, are supposed to—have some impact on the country generally and the disputants in particular. Implementation of the settlement inevitably affects the relative power of the belligerents. It also changes the polity through the effects of peace-building.

Regarding impartiality, the new peacekeepers will and should continue to abstain *ab initio* from favoring one side or the other in interpreting and executing a settlement. Because the entire operation occurs as a nonenforcement measure tied to a negotiated solution, the UN avoids blaming one party as responsible for the conflict.[86] (This contrasts with peace enforcement, where the UN typically identifies one party as at fault.) Moreover, as Hammarskjold pointed out in a 1961 speech at Oxford University, those implementing the accord must act independently of any national or parochial concerns.[87] Thus, the UN must interpret and implement the accord based on criteria independent of any preferences regarding the final balance of power. These standards include UN policies regarding human rights or fair elections, canons of treaty interpretation, logistical constraints, and budgetary considerations.

Yet this impartiality can be threatened in a number of ways. First, when consent decays and violations of a settlement occur, the UN must take a position against the violator. Such responses could occur through actions of the peacekeepers in the country or the political organs (through resolutions or sanctions to press the recalcitrant party toward compliance). Their reactions do not per se compromise the principle of impartiality, because the UN is only taking a stance vis-à-vis one party in response to specific action, rather than through any predisposition.[88] As Hammarskjold stated in his Oxford speech, "[T]he international civil servant cannot be accused of lack of neutrality simply for taking a stand on a controversial issue when this is his duty and cannot be avoided."[89]

But the violating party may well perceive the Organization as partial, and a perception of favoritism can undermine the UN's role as mediator and executor. The UN thus faces a core dilemma: if it relies heavily upon mediation to resolve implementation disputes, the parties may regard it as weak; if it attempts to proceed with its executive function, the recalcitrant party may see it as biased.

This quandary becomes even more severe if an operation combines mandates of peacekeeping, with its requirement of impartiality, and peace enforcement, which lacks any such stricture. In principle, peace enforcement can be conducted in an impartial way, such as by using force against all sides violating a truce. But in practice it has targeted only one side, as was evidenced in the Somalia and Yugoslavia missions in 1993 and 1994.[90] The UN's decision to respond to violations of Security Council resolutions through peace enforcement and the eventual use of force caused the violators, namely the clan of Mohammed Aideed and the Bosnian Serb forces, respectively, to label the UN as a party to the dispute rather than an impartial peacekeeper. This combination of conceptually dissimilar tasks required the key actors within the operation and the Council to predict whether such force would undermine the UN's credibility as a fair mediator or, conversely, would push the violating side to return to the bargaining table. The on-again, off-again nature of the peace talks in both Somalia and the former Yugoslavia belied any simple causal relationships between UN actions and the reactions of the combatants.

Second, as with any mediator, the UN's self-interest may cause it to favor one party over another.[91] If the Organization senses that one side acts more constructively or politely, or somehow can advance other UN agendas in the long run, the operation may in subtle ways prove more sympathetic to its positions than to those of the other side. Incumbent governments may be the recipient of favorable treatment due to pre-existing ties to UN officials. As holders of power, they will be able to influence events in their country more readily than opposition groups.

In addition, because the UN wishes to see an operation regarded as a "success," it could downplay certain violations of the accords. If the settlement has implementation phases, these pressures may lead the UN to oversee a new phase before conditions have ripened for it. Or it could minimize electoral irregularities in a desire to declare an election "free and fair."[92] The quest for success may also lead the UN to act more sympathetically to an incumbent government since its continued governance may lead to the fewest disruptions in the future.

Third, Hammarskjold's dictum notwithstanding, the interests of individual states become intertwined in the peacekeeping process. In first-generation operations, the limited nature of the mandate and the policy of deploying no contingents from the five permanent members of the Security Council helped counteract trends toward bias. Today, interested states seek incorporation of their views in resolutions passed by the political organs during the execution phase or place pressure directly on the Secretary-General. They can influence the operation from within by seconding personnel sympathetic to national concerns or even exercising continual control over seconded officials in violation of Article 100 of the Charter.[93]

This issue is of greater import today as nationals of powerful states routinely participate in senior positions. The presence of these nationals is now viewed as a means of demonstrating political support for the operation, rather than undermining it. National biases also pose a more significant threat today because of the large civilian presence in peacekeeping operations. These personnel do not operate in a chain of command under a UN force commander, and their political duties leave room for more discretion and susceptibility to outside influence than military personnel would ordinarily have.

New peacekeeping operations thus confront a continuous challenge to their impartiality. Although a mediator alone need not always be an impartial third party,[94] the United Nations also serves as an executor and guarantor of the underlying settlement. To best fulfill all three political functions, the United Nations should thus at least be perceived by the parties as not predisposed to an outcome in the settlement process that favors one side or the other.[95] The credibility of the operation in the eyes of the immediate parties and outside actors depends upon preserving this appearance of impartiality while not hesitating to respond to violations. Walking this thin line will often prove hazardous, for once one party regards the UN as partial, its trust may be lost irrevocably.

.3.

The New Peacekeepers: UN Organs and Supporting Participants

T he new peacekeeping, like its predecessor, builds upon the acceptance of a UN role by the interested parties and relevant outside participants. From that basis, the UN performs the political functions of administrator, mediator, and guarantor, with varying depth and breadth in its involvement in the conflict. But within the Organization, the UN's main political bodies that represent the views of member states—the Security Council and the General Assembly—must join forces with the Secretary-General, the UN's chief executive officer, from the conception of an operation until its termination. This joint involvement, however, invites new intra-Organizational tensions. Moreover, the organs of the UN are hardly the only outside participants in the new peacekeeping. States, acting individually or jointly, UN agencies, and other public and private organizations are also critical players, whose degree of support for an operation can determine many of the final results.

This chapter thus analyzes the roles of these new peacekeepers within and outside the Organization. For each of the UN's principal organs, its legal, political, and administrative capabilities and limitations are appraised in the context of the generational transformation of peacekeeping, and its operative functions for the new peacekeeping described. Particular attention is given to the Secretary-General and those working for him. In addition, the various potentials for conflict, accommodation, and cooperation among the organs are considered. Finally, the spate of supporting actors outside the UN are identified and discussed.

THE SECURITY COUNCIL

During the first 40 years of peacekeeping, the Security Council served as the principal organ by which states created and oversaw operations. All the first-generation missions, except for UNEF I (Sinai) and UNTEA (West Irian), have originated in Security Council resolutions. Of the second-generation operations, all but the Nicaragua, Haiti, and Eritrea election missions (ONUVEN, ONUVEH, and UNOVER) and the human rights missions in Haiti (MICIVIH) and Guatemala (MINUGUA), have been explicitly authorized by the Council.

1. The Council's Competence:
Legal and Political Authority over the New Peacekeeping

a. Legal Competence: The First Generation

As the organ endowed by the Charter with "the primary responsibility for the maintenance of international peace and security,"[1] the Security Council has a constitutionally mandated special competence in the establishment of old and new peacekeeping missions.

For many years, legal scholars searched for a textual basis in the Charter allowing the Council to dispatch first-generation missions to supervise truces. Attention focused upon a number of Charter provisions, in both Chapters VI ("Pacific Settlement of Disputes") and VII ("Action with Respect to Threats to the Peace, Breaches of the Peace, and Acts of Aggression"). (See appendix I.) Within Chapter VI, Article 36 allows the Council to "recommend appropriate procedures or methods of adjustment" of any dispute referred to it that could endanger international peace and security; some scholars saw a peacekeeping operation as part of such an adjustment.[2]

Others focused upon Article 40, which allows the Council, in the event of a threat to or breach of the peace, to "call upon the parties concerned to comply with such provisional measures as it deems necessary or desirable . . . without prejudice to the rights, claims, or position of the parties concerned."[3] Under this view, the peacekeeping force served as the mechanism created by the Council for verifying the compliance with the "provisional measures" that the Council demanded, in this case, the cease-fire and disengagement of forces. The precise legal effect of such measures (obligatory vs. recommendatory) was unclear from the Charter, although the UN and its followers seemed to agree that the Council could enact them as decisions binding on member states.[4]

Yet both diplomats and legal scholars recognized that neither Charter section quite captured the essence of peacekeeping, which is never mentioned by name in the Charter. Reliance upon Article 36, and Chapter VI in general, may have suggested that the Security Council's decision to establish a mission was simply a suggestion for the settlement of the conflict that parties could accept or reject at their leisure.[5] Article 40 and Chapter VII suggested that the missions were part of a coordinated UN response that might lead to nonconsensual enforcement action; but peacekeeping was, in fact, a holding action at best. Moreover, as Council decisions under Article 40 are binding, its invocation may have undercut the premise that peacekeeping could only operate with the consent of the parties. Hammarskjold seemed to sum up the limits of textual exegesis in his now oft-quoted quip that the Security Council created peacekeeping missions under Chapter "VI$\frac{1}{2}$."[6]

Their differing views on the precise constitutional bases for peacekeeping aside, both the critical decision makers within and observers of the UN could agree on several legal underpinnings of peacekeeping. First, it did not constitute nonconsensual enforcement action under the Charter. Chapter VI action is per se not enforcement action; and although Article 40 is found in Chapter VII, the UN's power to enforce its resolutions appears in Articles 41–50, especially Articles 41–42 on economic sanctions and military measures. Accordingly, the parties' consent to the operation remained a prerequisite to its emplacement. If a state refused to comply with the Council's decision creating the mission, for instance by refusing to disengage its forces to allow the peacekeepers to deploy, the UN would have to switch from a peacekeeping mode to enforcement measures in order to impose the force. This rarely, if ever, took place during the first thirty years of peacekeeping.[7]

Second, the constitutional basis of the operations in Articles 36 or 40, or any other nonenforcement provisions of the Charter, formed the legal foundation for the ideal of an impartial and neutral force. Article 36 suggests that the UN is merely facilitating the parties to solve their dispute; Article 40 requires explicitly that the Council's action not prejudice the rights of the parties. Although the UN would usually posit political, rather than strictly legal, reasons for its impartiality and neutrality, the Charter appeared to serve as a constraining influence in limiting peacekeeping to observation and deterrence (necessitating new legal arguments for more assertive missions such as the Congo operation).

Finally, because peacekeeping was not enforcement action, the Security Council was bound by the prohibition in Article 2(7) on intervention "in matters . . . essentially within the domestic jurisdiction of [a] state." Yet as noted earlier, the practice of the United Nations revealed a great reluctance to allow that article to prevent it from responding to internal situations that have aroused international concern.

The first thirty years of peacekeeping thus led to an abandonment of a search for particular Charter provisions to justify peacekeeping. Instead, the international community came to recognize the constitutive nature of the Charter. It thereby accepted the necessity for the Council to have broad discretion to act in furtherance of the principles and purposes of the Organization, as long as the Charter does not explicitly preclude such action. Thus has emerged the doctrine of implied powers of the various organs.[8] It reflects the expectations of critical decision makers regarding the appropriate extent of the authority of the Council and the other organs. The constitutive process of interpreting the Charter produced an expansive scope of authority for the organs: that which is not prohibited is permitted. This ended most debate over the Council's competence to create first-generation missions.

b. Legal Competence: The Second Generation

For the new operations, a search for a specific Charter reference for the Council's power in Chapters VI and VII proves equally frustrating. Within Chapter VI, Article 36, as well as Article 38 (allowing the Council, "if all the parties to any dispute so request, [to] make recommendations . . . with a view to a pacific settlement of the dispute") could cover the second-generation missions established at the request of the parties, although the drafters intended these articles to describe a peacemaking role for the Council prior to a settlement.[9]

In Chapter VII, action under Article 40 is meant "to prevent an aggravation of the situation [before the Council]"—to freeze a conflict in place. The drafters of the Charter saw Article 40 as limited to the first line of action by the Council to respond to breaches of the peace.[10] The new peacekeeping, however, aims for a definitive settlement. As a result of these textual gaps, the Council has acted under a broad construction of Chapters VI, "VI$\frac{1}{2}$," and VII, usually without identifying individual authorizing articles.

This pattern of deliberate ambiguity may be changing, however, especially when peacekeeping gives way to peace enforcement. In February 1993, the Council specifically cited Chapter VII as a basis for UNPROFOR's duties in Croatia and Bosnia-Herzegovina.[11] According to the resolution's French sponsor, this invocation was not meant to convert the operation to peace enforcement, but rather to strengthen its traditional right of self-defense after the deaths of French and other peacekeepers in hostilities.[12]

By June 1993, the Council decided to convert part of UNPROFOR's work in Croatia and Bosnia-Herzegovina—such as protection of "safe areas"—into peace enforcement that would not depend on the parties' consent; in so doing, it invoked Chapter VII again.[13] But this invocation did not per se turn all of UNPROFOR's duties into peace enforcement. Indeed, much of its work remained based solely on consent. The mission thus includes enforcement duties as well as consent-based peacekeeping. The references to Chapter VII in these resolutions may permit UNPROFOR to switch to peace enforcement in those matters where it was engaged in peacekeeping, but they do not require it.[14]

To step out of the confines of Chapters VI and VII, however, it seems inescapable that the constitutive nature of the Charter, including the doctrine of implied powers, that legally justifies the first-generation operations also undergirds the Council's role in the new missions. As a first principle, the Organization has a clear responsibility under Articles 1 and 55 for the promotion of peace and the improvement of human welfare. The Council, under Article 24, has primary responsibility for realizing the first of these, and its competence thus extends to those aspects of the new peacekeeping most directly related to ending armed hostilities.

For other aspects of the new mandates, such as human rights and elections, the Council has sufficient authority for its current activities. First, the improvement of the dignity and welfare of individuals in states experiencing conflict contributes directly to the restoration of peace and the furtherance of the Council's primary responsibility. As President Kennedy said at his 1963 American University speech, "[I]s not peace, in the last analysis, basically a matter of human rights . . . ?"[15] Free and fair elections, protection of human rights, development of an economic infrastructure, and preservation of law and order, while not absolute prerequisites for either domestic tranquillity or international peace, are sufficiently tied to it for the Council to assume functions in these areas. Moreover, twentieth century history has provided empirical support for Immanuel Kant's thesis that liberal states will be less inclined to go to war against each other.[16] As the post–Cold War international community searches for a peace beyond the absence of war, its views on the desiderata of peacekeeping and the concomitant authority of the Security Council have evolved.[17]

Second, the clear practice of the UN's members in permitting the Council to establish most second-generation operations with broad mandates suggests an accommodation within the UN on the appropriateness of Security Council action.[18] Indeed, the emphasis by developing countries on democratization of the Council, discussed in chapter 9, implies an acceptance and expectation by them that the Council will remain the lead organ for setting up and overseeing peacekeeping operations.

The Council's legal authority is not without limits, however. It could act *ultra vires* by undertaking action within the sole authority of another organ (more a theoretical possibility than a real one) or, conceivably, by taking action that violates supreme norms of international law *(jus cogens)*. This last possibility appeared to be more of a legal scholar's issue than one of practical import until recently, when two states upon which economic sanctions have been imposed under Chapter VII instituted proceedings in the International Court of Justice to nullify those Council actions.

Libya, the target of sanctions due to Western dissatisfaction with its level of cooperation in the Pan Am 103 and UTA 772 bombing investigations, and Bosnia-Herzegovina, under an arms embargo imposed on all of the former Yugoslavia, have each argued that the Council deprived them of fundamental rights that even the Charter cannot deny to states. The World Court's rulings on the merits of these disputes may help clarify the margins of lawfulness of certain Security Council decisions.[19] Yet while these decisions may affect the Council's authority over the new peacekeeping, the consent of the parties to second-generation missions (clearly lacking in the Libya and Bosnia economic sanctions cases) may limit the practical effect of the Court's ruling.

c. Political Bases of Power

The Council's Charter-assigned preeminence over maintaining international peace and security undergirds the unique political characteristics that render it the organ to which states repair for the formation of most second-generation enterprises. First and foremost, the constant participation and required concurrence of the five permanent members in any Council resolution reflects the political reality that they support, or at least do not oppose, the operation. The local actors should thus know that the mechanism deployed represents the only one that major sources of global power are supporting. Their backing of the initiation and continuation of the mission signifies a vote of confidence in the process of peacemaking inherent in the operation.

With the endorsement of these powers comes the potential, though sometimes not the reality, that they will employ diplomatic and economic tools to reward compliance and penalize violations. Thus the operations set up by the Council have political weight behind them. Further, its decisions are legally binding upon member states under Article 25. This causes the belligerents and other states to take them more seriously, though often not seriously enough, than actions by the Assembly or the Secretary-General alone.

Finally, the Council's historic involvement in the first-generation operations has created an institutional momentum in its favor and inertia against primary reliance on any other organ. Its permanent members have developed expertise on peacekeeping since the 1950s: they perforce understand the costs, logistics, and other aspects of the operations better than other states (with the exception of a handful of longtime important troop donors, such as Canada, Pakistan, India, and the Scandinavian countries). With large permanent missions in New York and foreign and defense ministries at home, they can intelligently review draft mandates prepared by the Secretary-General. And the Council's relatively small size of fifteen members renders it more collegial and efficient than the General Assembly at making decisions and following up on them.

2. A Typology of the Council's Responsibilities

The Council's contribution to the new peacekeeping begins well in advance of its approval of a particular operation. As an organ, it can help lay the groundwork for new peacekeeping operations. Through the traditional tools of peacemaking, including mediation, it can push the parties toward a settlement. Common methods used in the past include issuance of recommendations or decisions to the parties that they settle the conflict according to certain basic principles. The Council has issued these types of resolutions since well before the days of second-generation peacekeeping. Examples over the years include Resolution 47 (1948) on Kashmir; Resolutions 242 (1967) and 338 (1973) on the Arab-Israeli conflict; and Resolution 598 (1987) on the Iran-Iraq War.[20] As the new peacekeeping emerged, those resolutions endorsed substantial UN involvement and thus presaged the creation of large forces. For instance, Resolutions 435 (1978) on Namibia, 621 (1988) on Western Sahara, and 668 (1990) on Cambodia all called for UN operations to implement the settlement endorsed by the Council. Thus, as a forerunner to peacekeeping operations that integrate peacemaking, the Council has engaged in the presettlement phase of peacemaking that contemplates peacekeeping.

The Council's role once the parties have reached a political settlement has two stages. First, it establishes the operation by a formal vote, requiring nine affirmative votes out of fifteen members, including nonopposition from each of the permanent members. The resolutions typically will approve a detailed report prepared by the Secretary-General that includes the mandate of the proposed operation; formally create the force and specify its duration; call on the belligerents and other parties to take various actions to make the operation work; and ask the Secretary-General to implement the decision and keep the Council apprised of developments. All of the second-generation missions created by the Council since 1988—in Namibia, Central America, Angola, El Salvador, Western Sahara, Cambodia, Somalia, Mozambique, South Africa, Uganda-Rwanda, Liberia, Haiti, Rwanda, and Chad—have passed by unanimous votes.[21] The original authorizing resolutions become critical, as they can grant the mission a broad mandate for responding to the exigencies on the ground. This mandate can legally be constricted only by a subsequent vote of the Security Council.[22]

Second, the Council oversees the execution process. Whereas, for first-generation operations, the Council typically did little more than reauthorize the operation or terminate it, second-generation missions demand its constant attention. The Council will need to make follow-up decisions based on the progress of the settlement. It could pass further resolutions approving the work of the mission and urging various parties to cooperate with it. These demonstrate to the antagonists, especially in the face of violations, the strength of international support, providing a sort of political ammunition for the new peacekeepers.[23] The Council may also have to adjust the mandate of the operation or issue new instructions to the Secretary-General as demands increase. In extreme cases, it may have to take enforcement action, such as economic sanctions, in response to violations as it aims to fulfill the UN's role as guarantor of the settlement.

The Council as a whole or its members can also carry out a mediating function without passing resolutions, through quiet diplomacy.[24] For example, consultations among the five permanent members, the nonaligned members, or other groups may result in a consensus over a question of implementation that they can gently urge upon any allies among the combatants.[25] At the same time, the prior settlement means that many critical issues have already been decided by the parties, with the Council supporting the agreement. In cases like Somalia, where no settlement exists, the Council engages in a fundamentally different process, and is forced to address a new range of issues to promote a settlement.

To oversee these missions, the Council needs access to information. Much will be provided by the Secretary-General from his subordinates in the operation and in the Secretariat. The Secretary-General will typically issue periodic official reports on the progress of the operation. These reports, however, destined for public consumption, have traditionally had an unfortunate tendency to accentuate the positive elements of the mission and avoid candid assessments of blame for its shortcomings, though this problem is now much improved. UN members will also need to rely upon private briefings from Secretariat officials.

The larger states on the Council, including the permanent members, will also rely upon national sources, such as diplomats stationed in the area, covert intelligence-gathering (through human or electronic means), and reports from visits of official and unofficial delegations. Such intelligence proves more important than it did for first-generation missions because the Council needs to follow political developments, not merely the number of truce violations. Moreover, the settlement usually concerns the entire country, not only a secluded cease-fire zone.

THE GENERAL ASSEMBLY

The Assembly, the only UN organ containing all the Organization's members, has largely been eclipsed by the Security Council in the formation of first- and second-generation peacekeeping missions. It has created only six operations since the dawn of peacekeeping: the first Sinai mission (UNEF I), the West Irian operation (UNTEA), the 1990 electoral and 1993 civilian missions to Haiti (ONUVEH and MICIVIH), the Eritrean electoral mission (UNOVER), and the 1994 human rights mission to Guatemala (MINUGUA), although it also played a significant part during the Congo mission when the Soviet Union vetoed action by the Council. The Assembly nevertheless remains relevant for the new peacekeeping by virtue of its special powers under the Charter and its political authority.

1. The Limits of the Assembly's Authority over the New Peacekeeping

a. The Assembly's Prerogatives

Chapter IV of the Charter contains the germ of the Assembly's powers over peacekeeping, new and old. Article 10 gives it the authority to discuss *any* matter within the scope of the Charter and make recommendations to the member states and the Security Council, unless the Council is "exercising . . . the functions assigned to it" on the same matter. Articles 11(2) and 14 specify that these may include recommendations related, respectively, to "the maintenance of international peace and security" as well as any other situation "which it deems likely to impair the general welfare or friendly relations among nations."[26] Article 13 extends this power to recommendations on economic, social, cultural, educational, health, and human rights matters. And Article 22 allows it to create subsidiary bodies. (See appendix I.) The UN's members have at times viewed these general grants of authority in conjunction with the implied powers of all the organs as providing the Assembly sufficient legal competence to set up peacekeeping operations.

Thus the Assembly created the first true UN military force, UNEF I. In that episode, the Assembly acted after the Council utilized the procedures of the Uniting for Peace Resolution, the pivotal 1950 Assembly resolution under which the Council, if paralyzed by a veto, could transfer matters of peace and security to the Assembly for recommendations regarding collective action.[27]

In 1956, after Britain and France vetoed two draft Council resolutions on the Suez Crisis, the Council transferred the matter to the Assembly, which established UNEF I.[28] (The Uniting for Peace Resolution was only the procedural means for Assembly action, not the constitutional basis for UNEF, which was found in the Charter.) The resolution has not been used since the Congo crisis to move a peacekeeping matter from the Council to the Assembly, although it remains a legal option should a permanent member block action in the Council.

Beyond establishing missions, the Assembly retains unique competence under Article 17 of the Charter to approve the budget of the UN. As long as a peacekeeping operation incurs the official expenses of the Organization, it ultimately faces some type of approval by the Assembly.[29] The Assembly's budgetary power constitutes a critical source of influence over the Security Council and the Secretariat. Although the Assembly is unlikely to make fundamental changes to the budget proposed by the Secretary-General, it will work with planners in the Secretariat and the Security Council to scrutinize and adjust it.

The length of the budget review process and the timing of the disbursements all affect the ability of the Secretary-General to recruit staff, procure supplies and transportation, and begin moving people onto the site. Moreover, the Assembly's power to approve the budget permits UN members not on the Council to ask questions about the expenditures and the mission. The vast majority of the Assembly's members will not, however, follow the budgetary deliberations closely, as they cumulatively pay a mere fraction of the costs of peacekeeping. Approximately three-quarters of the peacekeeping budget is assessed against the United States, Russia, Japan, Germany, France, and Britain.[30]

b. The Assembly and the Council

The Charter thus establishes a potentially dynamic relationship between the two central political organs, with separate spheres of competence (such as the Assembly's budget power) and overlapping jurisdictions (for instance, to discuss issues and create operations). Proponents of Assembly power can justifiably point out that although the Assembly's resolution establishing a peacekeeping operation legally constitutes only a recommendation, this lack of strictly legal force has no practical significance, as any peacekeeping operation requires the consent of the parties to its presence. Moreover, the Charter's requirement in Article 12 that the Assembly defer to the Council when the latter is "exercising . . . the functions assigned to it" in the Charter has been completely eviscerated in practice.[31]

Yet, the Assembly's powers do face a Charter-based limitation in Article 24, which grants the Council the "primary responsibility" for the maintenance of international peace and security. As long as peacekeeping, even with its non-military tasks, continues to be viewed as related to maintaining international peace, claims regarding the comparative competence of the two organs to establish missions will continue to be resolved in favor of the Council in most cases.

Beyond the question of Charter-based competence, other factors suggest a continued secondary role for the Assembly. The Security Council's historical assertion of power will prove difficult to budge, especially if a peacekeeping operation has any military component. Equally important, the Assembly's enormous size has made fast, operational decisions impossible. Consultations among members on the details of a mandate prove more cumbersome than in the Council, with increased risk that some states will seek to bring extraneous issues into the debate.

The Council will, however, have to take account of the Assembly's views in the creation and oversight of new peacekeeping operations. Beyond budgetary matters, the Assembly's members will pass on their views to sympathetic (and unsympathetic) members of the Council, individually or through regional and other groupings, via formal consultations or hallway diplomatic intercourse. Thus, if a significant group of states within the Assembly had a strong opinion about the desirability or organization of a particular mission, the Council would not ignore those sentiments.

Moreover, at least two trends point to the potential for more active Assembly participation in future missions. First, if many developing states continue to regard the Security Council as controlled by the larger states, and reform of the Council does not address these concerns sufficiently, the Assembly will demand a larger say in establishing operations. As a condition to budgetary approval, it could insist upon more complete consultations during the design and implementation of the operation, so the Security Council does not become the only organ to whom the Secretary-General reports.[32] These could include meetings between representatives of states or regional groupings and members of the Security Council and the Secretariat.

Second, member states could agree that the Assembly would assume more responsibility over the nonmilitary aspects of second-generation operations. The Security Council's historic preeminence in approving traditional military peacekeeping missions is not inconsistent with a leading role for the Assembly over the electoral, human rights, or economic areas. This accommodation clearly manifested itself in the birth of the first Haiti mission (ONUVEH) in 1990. Because nearly 30 years had elapsed since the General Assembly had created a mission (the West Irian operation in 1962), the Secretary-General decided to consult the Security Council in advance of the Assembly vote. After discussion among its members, the Council agreed to the Assembly's establishment of the operation because ONUVEH involved electoral personnel and no military peacekeepers.[33] And the Council accepted the Assembly's creation of the Eritrea electoral verification mission and the Haiti and Guatemala human rights verification operations.

Indeed, as a legal matter, unless the Council were addressing a particular crisis through enforcement measures (and as a practical matter, even in such a case), there is nothing to stop the Assembly from placing these nonmilitary issues on its agenda and approving missions notwithstanding the views of the Council. The Assembly would defend its actions as furthering its roles under the Charter in economic, social, and human rights matters. The success of this type of arrangement will depend upon the Assembly's efficiency at creating such operations and its ability to work with the Secretary-General on their implementation.

2. The Assembly's Role

Based on the Assembly's legal, political, and administrative competence, for the bulk of new peacekeeping operations its participation will assume the following forms, some mirroring Council action and others unique to the Assembly.

First, like the Council, the Assembly may recommend the elements of a settlement that ultimately forms the basis for an agreement by the parties and a mandate of the mission. Its resolutions may address the same matters as those considered by the Council. While lacking the legal force of Security Council decisions, Assembly resolutions provide strong evidence of the opinions of governments.

Second, the Assembly may establish a peacekeeping operation, though sufficient practice has yet to emerge on the prevalence of this action in the future. The Assembly takes most of its decisions today without a vote, by consensus alone. This would seem the most likely form of decision for new peacekeeping operations. If a mission proved controversial, the Assembly would have to vote, and Article 18 of the Charter requires a two-thirds vote on "important questions," such as those concerning international peace. Yet if the Assembly supermajority did not include the major financial contributors to the operation, the UN could face an immediate political crisis reminiscent of the 1960s. Then, the Soviet Union, France, and others refused to pay their contributions to the expenses of ONUC, the Congo mission, and UNEF I, the first Sinai operation.

Third, as discussed earlier, the Assembly must approve the budget of a mission. Budget review will not follow a uniform pattern, but generally passes through four stages: (1) preparation of a proposed budget by the Secretary-General, in close consultation with key Security Council members; (2) consideration and revision of the proposed budget by the Advisory Committee on Administrative and Budgetary Questions (ACABQ), a standing committee of the Assembly composed of sixteen budgetary experts serving in a personal capacity (though traditionally from the five permanent members of the Council, other large donors, and some smaller states); (3) review of the proposed budget, as amended by the ACABQ report, by the General Assembly's Fifth Committee, composed of all Assembly members, in charge of administrative and budgetary issues; and (4) formal approval by the Assembly through a budget resolution or decision. The budget of the operation would receive separate treatment by the Assembly and these two committees, unless the Secretary-General included its expenses within the budget of another part of the Secretariat. This is possible, but unlikely if the mission involves sizable numbers of personnel.[34]

In addition, if the Secretary-General needs access to immediate funding, he may spend up to $5 million (formerly $3 million) per mission based on authority given him by the Assembly for "unforeseen and extraordinary expenses" related to the maintenance of peace. He may also spend up to $10 million to implement Security Council decisions with the prior concurrence of the ACABQ; and he may draw upon the peacekeeping "reserve fund" established in 1992, authorized at $150 million.[35] Between the time of the Assembly's appropriation of funds for a mission and the UN's receipt of amounts assessed against members, he may rearrange monies on hand through certain now-accepted forms of creative bookkeeping to permit immediate deployment of personnel.

Fourth, the Assembly oversees certain issues and other parts of the Organization involved in second-generation peacekeeping operations. It receives reports from the Secretary-General and other organs on human rights, elections, and economic development. It provides policy guidelines and directives to the Secretariat on issues addressed by the new missions. For example, the Assembly has approved reports of the Secretary-General on the UN's role in elections in member states and supported his efforts in this area.[36] It also exercises oversight through appointment powers and annual reports from other components of the Organization, such as UNDP and UNHCR, that increasingly participate in the new peacekeeping. Finally, the Assembly decides on administrative and management questions that concern the entire Organization, and, by implication, the efficiency of peacekeeping missions, such as its promulgation of staff regulations.

The Assembly thus remains in a secondary position in fulfilling the UN's three political functions. As administrator (in this case legislator as well), it approves the budget of the Organization, but does not carefully scrutinize the operation's mandate before its emplacement or the progress of the mission once established. As mediator, it can do little because its membership proves too large for serious deliberations to consider solutions to implementation problems. Rather than intervening actively as a third party, it confines itself to passing one resolution each session on the subject matter that engages a mission (under an agenda item typically entitled "The Situation in . . ."). The Assembly plays some role as guarantor, in that a resolution supporting the peacekeeping process indicates the opinions of governments about the political settlement. Yet the Assembly's follow-up resolutions lack the political and legal weight of the Council's decisions, which present a clearer, though by no means unblurred, picture of global policy toward a particular peace process.

THE SECRETARY-GENERAL

The heaviest workload within the UN system for the creation and execution of the new peacekeeping falls upon the Secretary-General. As the human symbol of the Organization, the Secretary-General will at times personally contribute to advancing a new peacekeeping operation. Beyond this, he delegates numerous duties to top aides, especially several Under Secretaries-General and a group of Special Representatives, while monitoring their progress and intervening as necessary. Finally, he stands at the apex of the UN Secretariat as, in the words of Article 97 of the Charter, "the chief administrative officer of the Organization," overseeing the work of thousands of employees in New York, Geneva, regional offices, and field operations.[37]

The pertinent target of scrutiny is thus the Secretary-General, wearing these three hats; reference to the Secretariat would overly emphasize managerial matters and neglect the full range of issues he and his closest assistants handle. Alone, through his top aides, and as principal for thousands more, he engages most directly in the administrator, mediator, and guarantor functions of second-generation peacekeeping.[38]

1. Implied Powers in the Extreme: The Secretary-General's Sources of Authority over the New Peacekeeping

However exiguous the Charter's guidance is for the Security Council and the General Assembly, it offers the most meager direction for the person and office actually managing the new operations. Four articles suggest constitutional starting points for his duties. Article 97 empowers him as the "chief administrative officer of the Organization." Article 98 instructs him to "perform such other functions as are entrusted to him by [the political] organs." Article 99 permits him to bring to the Security Council's attention "any matter which in his opinion may threaten the maintenance of international peace and security." And Article 101 allows him to pick the Secretariat's staff at his discretion, with prime consideration for their competence and "due regard" for geographic diversity. (See appendix I.) The Charter is a significant advance over the Covenant of the League of Nations in its designated responsibilities for the office, but on its face gives him little authority related to peacekeeping.[39]

As a legal matter, then, the Secretary-General possesses two sorts of powers: those conferred on him by the other organs of the UN (Article 98), and those inherent in the office. The first group are central for the new peacekeeping, for when the Council creates a mission, it assigns the Secretary-General numerous duties of the depth and breadth described in chapter 2—typically detailed in the mandate that the Secretary-General himself proposes. Much of his work as part of the UN's executor function thus originates in delegations from a political organ.

The Secretary-General does not, however, simply follow the instructions of a political organ. His responsibilities for fulfilling the three political functions flow additionally from his other source of power—his inherent authority under the Charter. Beyond the four citations to the Charter noted earlier, a search for constitutional underpinnings quickly yields results similar to those of earlier quests for the Charter bases for Council and Assembly competence over peacekeeping. As Paul Szasz, for many years a senior UN legal officer, has stated:

> [I]t has become pointless to try to locate the precise source of authority of each of the Secretary-General's political actions. The fact is that the Secretary-General can in the political field do what he can get away with, i.e. in a given situation what the competent representative organs will encourage or at least tolerate, and preferably what is acceptable to any specially concerned states or other entities.[40]

This frank recognition of the implied powers of the office corresponds to a long trend of decision by member states. What he "can get away with" has been the product of nearly 50 years of UN history, whereby the Secretary-General has, in the words of Thomas Franck, "invent[ed] himself."[41] It reveals a constant accretion of authority that he may channel into new peacekeeping operations.

This saga began with Hammarskjold, who expounded and acted upon a new vision for the office of the Secretary-General. Upon his reelection to the office in 1957, he spoke of the Secretary-General as responsible for advancing international peace by filling any "vacuum" resulting from the lack of guidance of the political organs.[42] He saw the Secretary-General as the most agile and able organ to fulfill his concept of an Organization that conducted itself proactively, through what he termed "executive actions," thereby distinguishing the Organization from the "conference pattern" of the League of Nations.[43]

The litany of actions indicative of this accumulation of responsibility since the 1950s would include the following:

• He has interpreted his authority under Article 99 to dispatch sizable, lengthy fact-finding missions, such as those to Laos and North Borneo in the 1960s;

• He has spoken out publicly and to member states regarding simmering crises and other world issues;

• Without seeking any formal permission from the Council or Assembly, he has used his good offices, conciliation skills, and active mediation abilities (individually or through surrogates) to try to prevent, defuse, or bring to a negotiated conclusion numerous state-to-state hostilities—from the Cuban Missile Crisis to eternal bickering over Cyprus to Cambodia;

• He has met state officials as a go-between even when the political organs had already taken sides on an issue (during the Iranian hostage crisis and elsewhere), relying upon the so-called Peking formula, first used by Hammarskjold when he visited Beijing in 1955 to negotiate the return of downed U.S. airmen notwithstanding the Council's and Assembly's view that only the Taiwan authorities could represent China;

• He has set up certain peacekeeping missions provisionally, before obtaining the formal authority of the Council—the Afghanistan monitoring mission (UNGOMAP) in 1988—and permanently, without seeking formal approval of the Council—the Nicaragua election mission (ONUVEN) in 1989.

The Secretary-General's legal footing in this regard is now so well-established that the UN's members rarely discuss it, and he no longer invokes a specific Charter basis for his action. This acceptance follows years of acrimony during the Cold War, when the Soviet Union argued for Security Council approval of all UN measures in the realm of international peace and security and the United States favored significant leeway for the Secretary-General. Since the late 1980s, their positions have converged, as they acknowledge the need for his peacemaking tasks but also seek to ensure that he ultimately remains a servant of the political organs. The risk today, in the words of Franck, is that the Secretary-General "has become the black box of the United Nations, into which . . . the members deposit their most pressing and intractable problems, in the hope that, through the operation of some ineffable but ineluctable process, a solution will emerge."[44]

The Secretary-General's authority does have a clear perimeter. He cannot act in disregard of the Charter, by, for instance, acting in areas reserved for or assumed by other organs or in contravention of their instructions. He thus could not negotiate with the target of Chapter VII sanctions over their removal without the approval of the Council. He could also not deploy a major military peacekeeping mission without the Council's assent (and the Assembly's for its budget). Short of these extreme cases and a few others more in the realm of speculation than reality, it remains futile to describe any *legal* contours for the Secretary-General's political functions: Szasz's aphorism prevails.

With his delegated and inherent powers, the Secretary-General can carry out his instructions and respond as necessary to a fluid settlement process. He must, of course, remain mindful of the instructions given him by the Security Council in their authorizing resolution. Yet that mandate, prepared by him and his staff, will give him substantial discretion over many aspects of the mission, either explicitly or simply by virtue of his role as administrator of the operation.

The result is a fluid relationship with, and authority vis-à-vis, the political organs, not different in essence from that between any chief executive officer and a legislature in a system of shared powers. He has the critical power to interpret the mandate, certainly in the first instance, and in many situations, definitively as well. When he and his agents need to fill in the interstices in the mandate for the countless situations where it is silent, they will have a number of options. These range from seeking formal, *ex ante* authority for his actions through a resolution or a statement of the Security Council president; to consulting the Council but not seeking advance authority; to obtaining *ex post* endorsement for his decisions; to not consulting the Council at all.

The Secretary-General's mode of interaction will be dictated by a confluence of considerations that will vary for each episode, including: the importance of the issue to the Council (countless small implementation decisions will not interest it); the impact upon the peace process of *ex ante* or *ex post* support of a political organ for his decisions; time pressures that may preclude formal Council endorsement; the views of the Security Council members regarding public support for his actions (they may wish to make an affirmative statement or choose not to be on the record with their views, even if they approve of his actions); and the degree of consensus on the Council (a divided Council would not be able to overrule controversial decisions). The Secretary-General and those under him must constantly judge the unfolding political scene in the host country and in New York in formulating their approaches. This dynamic has proved a constant theme in complex peacekeeping operations, beginning as early as the Congo mission in the 1960s and continuing through the 1990s.[45]

2. The Secretary-General's People and their Rounds

In carrying out the new peacekeeping, the Secretary-General relies on a sizable cadre at Headquarters and in the field. These officials act as his core agents.

a. The Under Secretaries-General

During the first thirty years of peacekeeping, missions fell within the bailiwick of the Under Secretary-General for Special Political Affairs, a position held by a series of outstanding senior international civil servants, such as Ralph Bunche and Brian Urquhart, and considered the most important position at the United Nations below the Secretary-General. This person also supervised UN peacemaking initiatives, resulting in a combination of enormous responsibilities possible only due to the limited number and scope of peacekeeping operations and the circumscribed activity of the UN in high-profile peacemaking during the Cold War.

After Urquhart's retirement in 1986, peacemaking work began to shift to the Executive Office of the Secretary-General, staffed by personal aides to the Secretary-General. In 1992, in response to the growing numbers and increased breadth and depth of peacekeeping, Boutros-Ghali created a separate Department of Peacekeeping Operations (DPKO), headed by an Under Secretary-General for Peacekeeping. He also established a Department of Political Affairs under two Under Secretaries-General for Political Affairs (later reduced to one) to lead peacemaking activities. The Under Secretary-General for Management assists with procurement and personnel matters. Other Under Secretaries-General will be involved as necessary, such as those heading the Department of Humanitarian Affairs (also created in 1992) and the Office of Legal Affairs.

b. The Special Representative of the Secretary-General

Since the 1960s, the Secretary-General has appointed civilian personal representatives to accompany certain peacekeeping operations. For the military missions typical of the first generation, the personal representative would attempt to engage in some type of parallel process of peacemaking. With the Congo operation (ONUC), the Secretary-General appointed his first "special" representative to oversee both the civilian and military components of the mission (Ralph Bunche), a precedent that continued with the second-generation operations.

Typically appointed at the level equivalent to an Under Secretary-General, the Special Representative has served as chief of the entire mission, reporting to and receiving instructions from the Secretary-General through the Under

Secretary-General for Special Political Affairs or for Peacekeeping. In some situations, the Secretary-General has appointed a Special Representative as his delegate to the negotiations leading up to a settlement; that person or a replacement could serve during the implementation phases. All of the recent second-generation operations have been led by a Special Representative.[46]

As the senior UN official in the territory, country, or region, the Special Representative assumes control of the operation on a day-to-day basis, both its internal administrative aspects and its external political functions vis-à-vis the parties. He or she serves as the focal point within the UN system for that mission and is the central figure in it. Although the Special Representative must act consistently with the mandate set by the Council, his scope of authority and discretion on political and administrative issues remains significant.

As a result, the Secretary-General's selection of a qualified and trusted person proves critical to the success of the mission. No clear pattern has emerged as to the criteria Secretaries-General have actually used for the selection of Special Representatives, but the following eight personal characteristics, in descending order of importance, should be considered.[47]

• *Political acceptability*: The major protagonists within the target country, on the Security Council, and elsewhere in the United Nations—including the Secretary-General—must accept the political outlook of the Special Representative. The Special Representative should have a personal and professional background that lacks any suggestion of unacceptable predispositions or conflicts of interest. The Secretary-General should thus avoid appointing someone from a state directly involved in the conflict or from a permanent member of the Security Council, a maxim ignored when an American was appointed to head UNOSOM II, the second Somalia mission. In some situations, the Secretary-General may need to appoint a Special Representative from a particular country, such as Japan or a newly emerging democracy, in order to promote its participation in peacekeeping matters or the UN system generally.

• *Diplomatic skills*: The Special Representative must have significant experience in the art of diplomacy. He or she must interact comfortably with persons of diverse cultures, possess a controlled temperament, listen carefully, choose written and spoken words with precision, understand the place of both quiet consultations and public diplomacy, and possess balanced judgment in responding to crises.

• *Political skills*: The Special Representative should also possess some of the skills of a politician, including the ability to persuade, cajole, bluff, pressure, or, in exceptional cases, dupe others to obtain his goals without alienating his interlocutors. The ability to find common ground between two rival positions by cleverly recasting their views and a Machiavellian knowledge of the levers of power can advance his roles as administrator and mediator. He or she must also be able to make careful judgments regarding the need for support from the UN's political organs for actions that may prove controversial with the immediate parties.

• *A generalist's outlook*: The Special Representative must not have a narrow professional expertise or world view. Thus, an economist, a human rights activist, or an active duty military officer will likely not meet the test. The Special Representative should have a sense of the complex interrelationships among the political, military, economic, legal, and other subjects he or she will address in running the operation.

• *Familiarity with the conflict*: The Special Representative should have an existing understanding of the political conflict that the settlement addresses. Learning the history of the dispute and the attitudes of the parties on the job increases the chances for political miscalculations and delays important decisions as the Special Representative masters his brief. If the Special Representative has personally participated in the peacemaking process prior to the settlement, he will have a special expertise. Nevertheless, it may prove extremely difficult to find a capable representative with such expertise (how many Somalia experts does the UN have?), and the current Secretary-General has minimized the importance of this criterion. Moreover, earlier involvement could present a disadvantage for an envoy. If one of the parties mistrusts the Special Representative because of stances he or she took or because of other unfriendly encounters during the pre-agreement negotiations, the Special Representative will be tainted and his political acceptability undercut.[48]

• *Stature*: The actors with whom the Special Representative must interact— notably the parties, the Organization, and member states—will accord a greater degree of attention, respect, and responsiveness to someone who has gained prominence in international affairs through prior public service. Such a person can use his reputation and personal connections to cut through political and administrative blockages more successfully than a less-established figure.

• *Knowledge of the UN*: Familiarity with the roles played by the Council and the Secretariat in peacekeeping, the UN budget process, and procurement and personnel rules will facilitate the Special Representative's job. In addition, an understanding of the decision-making process within the political organs will aid in judging how they can best provide political support for the operation. Thus, diplomats who have served in the Secretariat or in permanent missions may face a less steep learning curve. On the other hand, an effective deputy and staff can pass their wisdom on these matters to the Special Representative.

• *Management skills*: The new peacekeeping operations resemble in many ways large corporate entities, with a bureaucracy performing a multitude of tasks. The Special Representative should thus have some experience in managerial responsibilities. He need not possess extensive skills in this area if he delegates administrative duties to a competent deputy or other senior officials. But certain decisions will inevitably reach his level, for which this experience will be useful.

The Secretary-General will rarely find an individual with all these attributes; in all likelihood, nobody will fully meet them. In addition, the Secretary-General may be guided by less relevant criteria, such as friendship with the potential Special Representative, a desire to rearrange personnel within the Secretariat, or the need to curry favor with the Special Representative's home state. Although it seems unlikely that the Secretary-General would appoint someone truly unqualified, the appointment could prove far from optimal.

Yet, in the end, the difference for the outcome of the mission between the best person and another qualified person may be quite small. In any second-generation operation, the most able Special Representative will face numerous political and logistical challenges beyond his control. Ignoring this checklist will almost certainly harm the operation; but adherence to it offers no guarantee of success.

c. The UN Staff

Beneath these two senior layers of officials works the UN civil service at Headquarters, at the UN Offices in Geneva and other cities, and in the operation itself. Those in the field are recruited from within the Secretariat and the specialized and technical agencies (through posted notices) and report ultimately to the Special Representative for the duration of their service with the mission. Those at Headquarters and the UN Offices support the operation and report to an Under Secretary-General or official of equivalent rank, such as the High Commissioner for Refugees or the Director of UNDP. They typically form the bulk of civilian personnel in the mission, from senior-level officials working directly with the Special Representative to administrative support positions. Peacekeeping missions have become a career for some, as they dart from one part of the globe to the next; others seek assignment in one operation as a break or boost in their career path within the UN.

In addition, in an important innovation for staffing peacekeeping operations, the Secretariat has recently come to rely on United Nations Volunteers (UNVs) to serve in many nation-building positions. The UNV program, begun in 1970 and administered by UNDP, provides a low-cost, highly motivated corps of individuals to augment the international civil servants and seconded personnel. Paid only subsistence wages, they have served as election officials, health specialists, and refugee coordinators and have received high praise from mission leaders and outside observers.

The Secretary-General's responsibilities for the new peacekeeping, as carried out by him, the Special Representative, and the other players, can best be viewed as encompassing ten undertakings.

1. *Assistance in negotiation*: The Secretary-General can try to guide the parties toward a settlement through the classic techniques of good offices, conciliation, and mediation. Through a Special Representative, he can also offer expertise on issues such as military options, legal matters, and procedures for conduct of elections. The Secretary-General represents the UN at large diplomatic conferences and small meetings of the parties, and through shuttle diplomacy.

2. *Preparation of mandates*: With his staff, the Special Representative drafts lengthy reports that describe their proposed activities and are approved, as needed, by a political organ. They also prepare a budget for the General Assembly. Other than the settlement accords, no document becomes more central than these mandates to the organization of the mission. In drafting the mandate, the Special Representative must transform a peace accord or other invitation, often with imprecise or ambiguous descriptions of the UN's intended role, into a concrete list of tasks subject to budgetary and personnel constraints. He risks losing a sense of the fluidity of the settlement and the interrelationships among various articles and clauses when he turns it into a simple description of duties.[49]

3. *Selection of personnel*: In first-generation missions, most staff consists of organized military contingents from member states. For the new operations, the Secretary-General must recruit a wider array of talent. The Special Representative will select his senior staff, who will then enlist the services of personnel from: (a) the Organization, (b) member states (the source of all military and police personnel), (c) other international organizations, and (d) the private sector. Civil servants in particular member states will have expertise in certain issues, such as Commonwealth countries with elections, or Canada and India on military matters.

In trying to pick the best people, he will encounter a number of tough constraints: the Charter's policy favoring geographic diversity;[50] concerns of the host state(s) or others that nationals of countries predisposed to a particular outcome to the process not hold certain positions;[51] the need for a mix of people from the four mentioned categories that takes account of the strengths and weaknesses in their professional backgrounds; political pressures from member states seeking placement of their nationals in key positions; and demands from within the Secretariat (dictated, for instance, by personnel constraints or bureaucratic politics) for a staff member to be included in or excluded from a mission.[52] He may also have to haggle with the employees over job descriptions, titles, and pay.

4. *Harnessing of resources*: In first-generation missions, much, if not most, of the logistical support for the force has come from national military contingents. To start and maintain the new operations, the Special Representative must obtain material resources and deploy his selected staff in short order. Cooperation from the rest of the Organization is by no means assured, whether from the Secretariat bureaucracy in New York and Geneva or other entities within the UN system. He will lack line authority over other UN personnel to expedite procurement and hiring. His position as the senior official charged with implementing a Security Council resolution will give him some influence within the UN, but he will also have to rely upon his stature and acquaintances to galvanize the lumbering institution to support the mission. Frequent travel from the mission to Headquarters will be inevitable.

5. *Day-to-day management decisions*: With the aid of his chief assistants, the Special Representative will make the daily management decisions crucial to running an operation. He will have to establish lines of authority, set certain personnel policies, and make the administrative decisions that percolate up to his level. He may have to negotiate an agreement on the status of UN personnel or similar arrangements with the affected states. The rules and guidelines established by Headquarters for all UN operations on issues such as personnel and procurement will hinder his flexibility.

6. *Day-to-day political decisions*: As the senior UN diplomat on the ground, the Special Representative will occupy a great deal of time in meeting the belligerents, officials from local embassies, visiting dignitaries, and his own staff to assess the progress of the settlement and act accordingly. In interpreting the mandate of the mission, he will determine the extent of interaction with the UN's political organs, especially regarding questions not foreseen in the mandate. The most important of his duties, these proactive and reactive political functions promote the UN's roles as administrator, mediator, and guarantor of the settlement.

7. *Reporting to Headquarters*: The Special Representative must keep New York—specifically the Under Secretary-General for Peacekeeping and his staff—informed of the mission's progress. He will seek the approval of Headquarters for his most important decisions and statements, or at least give it advance warning. He will file detailed reports, some issued later in the name of the Secretary-General, and may be consulted on draft resolutions to be adopted by the political organs. He will certify to Headquarters that certain parts of the mission have been accomplished, such as a demobilization of guerrillas, a fair election, or the removal of human rights abusers from office. He may also request Headquarters to consult with diplomats from the permanent missions to obtain their support for an action he is contemplating.

8. *Executing instructions from Headquarters*: The Secretary-General could instruct the Special Representative to respond to a problem in the execution of the settlement, and the Special Representative will have to interpret and follow these commands. The Special Representative and Headquarters will have to establish a relationship appropriate to the mission, with authority delegated to the field for all but essential decisions.

9. *Public relations*: As a major political actor in the conflict where the operation has been inserted, the Special Representative will employ the media to advance the UN's goals. He will make public statements, grant interviews, and authorize leaks from unnamed officials. Creative, carefully timed use of the press can influence the immediate parties as well as policymakers in distant capitals.

10. *Issuance of legal opinions*: During the implementation phase, the Secretary-General or Special Representative or their legal advisers can issue opinions that many actors will regard as an authoritative, unbiased evaluation of the legal aspects of a situation. These opinions can offer interpretations of the settlement agreement itself, including the obligations of the parties and the responsibilities of the UN mission. The Special Representative can use these opinions to persuade other actors regarding a course of action he wishes to take.[53]

In the end, just as the UN acts as administrator, mediator, and guarantor on behalf of the international community, the Secretary-General and his staff most directly pursue these roles on behalf of the Organization. Within the constraints set by the Charter, the Council- or Assembly-approved mandate, the budget, the UN's internal operating rules, and the pressures placed on them by member states in matters political and administrative, they have an enormous well of discretion to respond to the developments of the moment.

ONE VOICE OR THREE?: COORDINATION AMONG THE UN'S ORGANS

The legal, political, and administrative competencies and duties of the three UN organs involved in peacekeeping form a somewhat disorganized quilt. At times clear lines separate their responsibilities. These lines may be drawn sequentially, as the General Assembly alone can approve the budget of a peacekeeping operation, and only after the Secretary-General has described its mandate. And they may appear by subject matter, as the Secretary-General will run the operations on a day-to-day basis, whereas the political organs exercise oversight. But the legal and political claims of the organs also overlap.

For the most part, the Organization did not encounter conflicting demands until recently. As holding actions, first-generation missions have required little of the Organization's active attention. Routinely renewed by the Council, with budget reauthorization by the Assembly, the operations have gone about their business of monitoring a cease-fire. As long as the truce held, the member states and the UN's senior officials have regarded them as a success, left implementation to lower-level UN bureaucrats, and refrained from high-level attention. The General Assembly did not seek active involvement, as it focused on decolonization, development, disarmament, and other parts of the North-South dialogue. The Council's responsibilities over peacekeeping represented no threat to the Assembly's interests because the Cold War ensured that those missions would remain limited in mandate. Despite the potential for serious clashes among the organs, a modus vivendi prevailed.

With the new peacekeeping, the Organization faces two threats to this accommodation. First, the organs can disagree over their legal and political competence and spheres of authority. As suggested earlier, the General Assembly may well assert a greater prerogative in the creation of operations than it has in the past. Relying upon the precedent of the Nicaragua mission (ONUVEN), the Secretary-General could try to push his authority to establish operations, or at least emplace them provisionally pending the approval of a political organ.

More likely and serious than any overt struggle over the lead responsibility for peacekeeping is the prospect that the organs will not speak with one voice once an operation is established. The Secretary-General's officials may not be able to assume that the member states in the political organs will always support them; or the Council and the Assembly may not adhere to the same line in their respective resolutions on a peacekeeping mission. The belligerents will have to interpret these inconsistent signals.

The problem is not new to second-generation peacekeeping. In inventing the "Peking formula" to obtain the release of the American airmen in China, Hammarskjold carefully distanced himself from a General Assembly resolution that condemned the mainland Chinese government.[54] The political organs have censured a particular country for aggression or other violations of international law, and then routinely dispatched the Secretary-General or his representative to negotiate a solution.[55] That negotiator knew that he could not advocate a position at odds with the policy of the political organ, but he could listen and adopt a less judgmental stance than the member states. During a peacemaking mission, the UN's members expect that the Secretary-General will not employ the hard line of their resolutions, acknowledging the utility of a "good cop, bad cop" method for the peaceful settlement of some disputes.

The question remains, however, as to whether this deliberate discordance can prevail in a *peacekeeping* operation. In the first instance, it cannot. The basis of the new peacekeeping must remain the consent and invitation of the parties and the peace accord describing the UN's role in the settlement. The Council, Assembly, and Secretary-General cannot disavow the will of the parties unless they are prepared to abandon the peacekeeping mission or transform it into peace enforcement.

Beyond this outer limitation, any uniform preference for one voice by the three organs seems ill-advised. As crystallized by Paul Szasz, "The UN is a many splendored thing,"[56] and subtle differences in their positions could actually advance the peace process. The Assembly could emphasize in its resolutions parts of the settlement that the Council deems less important, such as economic and human rights questions. Ambiguity among the overseeing organs might make clear to the parties that the world or its elites is watching them—that they must consider the views not only of the Secretary-General, but of the effective power sources on the Council and the well of world opinion in the Assembly. If, however, the Assembly and Council have sharply different views, as, for example, when the Assembly asked the Council in 1993 to lift its arms embargo on Bosnia-Herzegovina, they send a signal of interorgan and multilateral paralysis.[57]

Discordance could also represent a way for the UN to respond to the threats to impartiality inherent in the new peacekeeping. If one party undertakes outrageous or illegal actions, the political organs can adopt a strong, condemnatory position and signal to the parties the firmness of the international community's view. Far from the corridors of power in New York, the Special Representative could distance himself a bit and assume the role of mediator in a way that furthers the settlement process. (The parties may, however, ignore the political organs and the Special Representative entirely.)

The "good cop, bad cop" approach carries risks, however. If the political organs censure one of the belligerents, it may refuse to cooperate with or even retaliate against UN personnel on the scene. This scenario seems likely if the Security Council undertakes enforcement measures against a recalcitrant party simultaneously with a peacekeeping mission. For example, the Security Council adopted a tough position on Somalia in June 1993 by seeking the arrest and punishment of Mogadishu clan members who killed at least 25 Pakistani peacekeepers. But this compromised the mission's perception of impartiality, reduced its effectiveness, and contributed to a retaliatory attack on U.S. peacekeepers that led the Council to retreat from its position.[58] In a snowball-like effect, this mistrust can increase the need for reliance upon enforcement measures over consensual peacekeeping.[59]

As important as the content of the voices from the three organs is the process by which they assert their views. They should attempt to follow a coordinated approach, where each reviews the proposed statements or resolutions of the others before they are issued. This permits the three organs to offer suggestions to one another, prevents the action of one from undercutting another and embarrassing member states or the Secretary-General, and allows each to prepare for any reactions to the announcement. It also yields a useful by-product of building bridges among the organs. If they can coordinate their oversight, each will feel less threatened that the others are trying to usurp its authority.

SUPPORTING PARTICIPANTS

Beyond the mentioned principal participants, other actors are deeply engaged in sustaining the new peacekeeping.

1. Donors of Personnel

Although UN civil servants will staff much of the mission, member states contribute large numbers of personnel—all the military forces, as well as civilians seconded from government and the private sector. In the first instance, donors will be motivated by their national interest in the operation, pursuing agendas from regional stability to promotion of democracy.

Moreover, a broad array of states now participate. With the end of the Cold War and a consensus on the Security Council for the establishment of second-generation operations (thus far), the five permanent members, previously excluded from missions except in small numbers, now offer up personnel to demonstrate big power support. Immediate neighbors participate for similar reasons. This direct interest in a successful outcome can promote the guarantor function of peacekeeping, as evidenced by the sight of Chinese engineering battalions in Cambodia repairing bridges destroyed by their erstwhile Khmer Rouge allies. On the other hand, as a donor state's interest in the outcome of the peace process increases, so does the risk that the personnel it offers may not prove impartial.

Supervening the donors' foreign policy motivations for conferring their personnel, however, is another clear policy stance—avoidance of harm to their nationals. While some recent operations presented few dangers to personnel—such as the election missions in Haiti, Nicaragua, and Eritrea, and the Namibia operation—violence has erupted in others, such as Cambodia, Somalia, and Yugoslavia. When threats occur against mission personnel, donors can be counted on to pressure the UN to modify the mandate or to redeploy, protect, or withdraw the endangered staff. The participation of staff from the Permanent Five adds to that pressure, especially if they have donated many troops and civilians. If unsatisfied, donors may withdraw their military contingents (civilians being free to depart in any case), undercutting the UN's political functions throughout the operation. Based on Japan's constitutional restrictions on the use of force as well as popular sentiment, the Japanese government has passed legislation that, while finally allowing for participation in peacekeeping missions, severely curtails its troops' ability to act and react in hazardous situations.[60]

The Secretary-General must thus negotiate not only with the parties to maintain their consent, but with these donors as well. He can face a complete schism between the mandate of the Council to proceed with the mission and the hesitancy of donors to offer personnel or place them in harm's way. This institutional schizophrenia extends most pointedly to those very Council members that approved the mandate.

In the case of peace enforcement missions, these issues are especially vexing, as caustically summed up by the UN's commander in Bosnia in 1993, Lieutenant General Francis Briquemont: "I don't read the Security Council resolutions any more because they don't help me."[61] With UNOSOM II and UNPROFOR, major donor states, such as the United States, Britain, and France, have sought to avoid casualties by shying away from expansive and pro-active mandates for their forces.

2. The Rest of the UN System: Related Organs and Specialized and Technical Agencies

Outside the three primary organs, the remainder of the UN contributes to the new peacekeeping both through secondment of personnel and as independent actors. Among the entities that report directly to the political organs, the Office of United Nations High Commissioner for Refugees and the United Nations Development Program assume special significance. Under its organic documents and long UN practice, UNHCR has primary operational responsibility for the protection of refugees and displaced persons, a core function in most new peacekeeping missions. UNHCR's work represents much of the humanitarian dimension of recent operations. UNDP has taken an active role in organizing development assistance programs, usually in the form of specific projects. The UN Children's Fund, UNICEF, has also become involved in some missions.

The specialized agencies, with their menu of acronyms—WHO, ICAO, the ITU, and many more—do not belong to the Organization proper but are part of the UN's family or "system." They played an insignificant role in the earlier operations, with the exception of the Congo mission.[62] For the modern operations, they offer a wealth of technical expertise that the Special Representative may tap. Particularly for operations in countries shattered by civil conflict, these international civil servants can attempt to train local officials and assume control over certain apparati of government (for example, in the domains of transportation, public health, and revenue collection). Their integration into the mission will underline the place of nation-building in the new peacekeeping.

3. Regional Organizations

Regional organizations have become significant players in many second-generation missions and are often involved in the peacemaking process before the UN has devoted significant resources to the problem. The Organization of American States (OAS) for Central America and Haiti, the Association of Southeast Asian Nations (ASEAN) in the case of Cambodia, and the Economic Community of West African States (ECOWAS) for Liberia are prime examples. Once a settlement is reached, regional organizations can deploy personnel separately from the UN or combine their forces with the UN in joint peacekeeping duties.

For example, the Central American operations—ONUCA, ONUVEN, and ONUSAL—worked alongside OAS contingents in carrying out election monitoring, supervision of guerrilla demobilization, and other aspects of the regional peace accords. The mission in Liberia, UNOMIL, was deployed following military action by ECOWAS (with a suspiciously large Nigerian presence), and now shares responsibility for a nearly fruitless peacekeeping effort in that war-ravaged state.[63]

Regional organizations have not yet, however, assumed the lead responsibility for the creation or management of second-generation operations, with the possible exception of ECOWAS in Liberia.[64] (The Commonwealth of Independent States does, however, operate a first-generation mission, dominated by the Russian army, in the Abkhazia region of the former Soviet republic of Georgia.) Their limited experience in executive action and the dominance of larger members have caused their members as well as warring parties to turn to the UN as a more competent and impartial administrator, mediator, and guarantor of settlements. In the former Yugoslavia and Somalia, the European Community and the Organization of African Unity have been paralyzed by internal disputes. They have thus not acted as unified organizations in the operation of UNPROFOR or UNOSOM, although they have played active peacemaking roles. NATO has worked alongside UNPROFOR in surveillance, deterrence, and self-defense missions. The current Secretary-General has repeatedly urged such organizations to assume greater responsibilities as contemplated in Chapter VIII of the UN Charter.[65]

4. "Friends" of the Peace Process

Second-generation operations can receive the diplomatic assistance of small groups of states with a special interest in the settlement. Dubbed the "Friends of [the country's name]," these clusters typically include important regional powers as well as some or all of the Permanent Five. To a greater or lesser extent, they cooperate with UN officials at Headquarters and in the field during the peace process. Their historical and often personal ties to the competing parties may give them influence and leverage that the UN lacks, a critical trait in the event of actual or impending noncooperation of a party. The slow peace processes in Africa and elsewhere have benefited from such "friends." In Cambodia, a self-styled "Expanded Perm 5" group in Phnom Penh included the local mission chiefs from Indonesia, Australia, Japan, and Germany, and met frequently with the Special Representative.

5. International Financial Institutions

The economic health of a country forms an integral part of long-term nation-building. The state or region affected by a conflict will need assistance to stabilize a volatile economic situation, promote growth, and spur the confidence of residents, foreign traders, and investors. Yet, other than project financing done by UNDP, the United Nations lacks the financial resources and political support to make major, direct contributions toward restoring the economic health of a country.

The besieged country will need access to multilateral economic assistance through the Bretton Woods institutions (the World Bank and the International Monetary Fund, which are officially specialized agencies of the UN) and regional development banks. They can support the peace process by providing grants, loans, currency stabilization funds, and other economic support. Delegations of economists and lawyers will visit the country and meet with local and UN officials to determine the eligibility and readiness of the country for such assistance.[66]

6. Nongovernmental Organizations

Many international private voluntary organizations and other groups of a nongovernmental character will establish a presence in the beleaguered country or region to complement the UN. The International Committee of the Red Cross will undertake its responsibilities under the Geneva Conventions and Protocols regarding exchanges of prisoners and prison visits. Other groups may simply monitor the work of the United Nations; more likely, they will pursue projects approved by their home offices, running the gamut of non-military issues in the peace process. Local nongovernmental entities will create links with their foreign analogues.

Thus, humanitarian relief organizations (Care, Médecins Sans Frontières, Oxfam) will offer food and medical services and supplies; human rights organizations (Amnesty International, Human Rights Watch) will conduct education programs and follow human rights conditions; and election monitoring groups (the Carter Center, the National Democratic Institute for International Affairs) will deploy during elections as an additional presence to gauge the fairness of the polling. In addition, professional organizations will send missions to train local personnel in skills such as medicine, engineering, accounting, public administration, and law (including constitution-drafting); and educational and academic groups will assist in rebuilding public education, libraries, and research institutions.

7. The International Media

During most first-generation operations, the foreign press has limited its role to the occasional report of a cease-fire violation. Indeed, even the well-informed public in UN member states appeared to forget that the UN had operations in Kashmir, Cyprus, or the Golan Heights. Today, the major wire services and newspapers have employees or contractors providing reports on the progress of the settlement. These stories will greatly influence the public perceptions of the success of the operation, and create pressures upon the Secretary-General and the UN political organs to support, strengthen, modify, or abandon aspects of the mission. If, for instance, a reporter describes the human rights oversight of the operation as ineffective, the UN will respond more quickly than if the matter remained only under internal UN review.

Though the same three actors in the UN system take charge of the new peacekeeping as did for the old, the expansive mandates of the second generation demand changed roles for them and inject into the process participants who were mere bystanders before. Each organ has developed ample legal authority over time, assuming a willingness to read the Charter dynamically, to undertake its missions. The political and administrative competencies of the three vary significantly, leading to the current modus vivendi of shared responsibility. Under this accommodation, the Council creates and oversees most operations, the Secretary-General implements them, and the Assembly approves the budget. But though the allocation of authority has held, it remains a mutable situation and will likely adjust either for a particular mission or more generically. The one constant from past to present to future remains the leading role of the Secretary-General. Hammarskjold's concept of an executive arm of the Organization is now conventional wisdom and the duties of that organ immense. The question is whether they are too grand for its current resources.

TABLE 3.1

International Participants

SECURITY COUNCIL

1. Laying groundwork for settlement
2. Establishment of operations
3. Oversight of operations

GENERAL ASSEMBLY

1. Recommending elements of settlement
2. Establishment of operations
3. Approval of UN budget
4. Oversight of other aspects of the Organization

SECRETARY-GENERAL:
through Under Secretaries-General, Special Representatives, and UN staff

1. Assistance in negotiation
2. Preparation of mandates
3. Selection of personnel
4. Harnessing of resources
5. Day-to-day management decisions
6. Day-to-day political decisions
7. Reporting to Headquarters
8. Executing instructions from Headquarters
9. Public relations
10. Issuance of legal opinions

DONORS OF PERSONNEL

THE REST OF THE UN SYSTEM

REGIONAL ORGANIZATIONS

"FRIENDS" OF THE PEACE PROCESS

INTERNATIONAL FINANCIAL INSTITUTIONS

NONGOVERNMENTAL ORGANIZATIONS

THE INTERNATIONAL MEDIA

Part II
■
A Look Back

.4.

Fits and Starts: The League's and UN's Early Efforts at the New Peacekeeping

Although the new peacekeeping emerged as a major undertaking to settle disputes only in the late 1980s, it grew from two distinct sets of roots. First, it evolved from first-generation, military-centered operations beginning with UNTSO in the Middle East, UNMOGIP in Kashmir, and UNEF I in the Sinai, whose conceptual foundations, such as the consent of the parties and the impartiality of the force, Hammarskjold propounded. The international community's propensity to refer to the new operations as peacekeeping, despite their often nonmilitary emphasis, stems from the military origins of the missions.

The other, more critical amalgam of historical precedents concerned the early attempts by the international community to engage in the nonmilitary activities that define the current genre. A review of those undertakings demonstrates that the core of the new peacekeeping is comparatively old. The emplacement of an operation by an international organization into a conflict to assist the parties in implementing a political settlement originated with the League of Nations. Moreover, some of the UN's most ambitious recent endeavors, such as the attempt to control the civilian administration apparatus in Cambodia or to protect human rights in El Salvador, actually underwent important tests well before the 1990s. Most of these League and UN operations never earned the label "peacekeeping" because they included only small military components. Some plans for international oversight of territory never reached fruition; others are forgotten by contemporary policymakers. The more recent episodes pointed clearly toward the major missions since 1989.

This chapter addresses these significant precedents by the League of Nations and the United Nations. It begins with a discussion of the League's responsibilities over parts of the Treaty of Versailles and the new directions its endeavors meant for international organizations. It then turns to the United Nations, which continued a process toward nation-building through large and small missions as part of the decolonization agenda of its first thirty years. Rather than engaging in an exhaustive review of these League and UN efforts, for which there is already a vast literature, this chapter places them within the framework of, and thus analyzes them as precursors to, the new peacekeeping. With these important historical episodes in mind, chapter 5 then addresses the first of the second-generation UN missions—those from 1989 up to the Cambodia operation.

THE LEAGUE OF NATIONS: PEACEKEEPING BY OTHER NAMES

As the first modern experiment in a universal organization of states dedicated to international peace and security, the League of Nations, despite its many failings, established significant precedents for multilateral cooperation in settling interstate disputes. Its legal authority over these conflicts derived from two principal constitutive sources. First, the Covenant established a three-pronged scheme, under which members pledged to: (a) respect and preserve the territorial integrity and political independence of all members against external aggression; (b) submit all disputes to either arbitration, judicial settlement, or inquiry by the Council of the League (the League's analogue of the Security Council, with permanent and nonpermanent members), the latter of which would try to settle the matter; and (c) impose economic sanctions and recommend military measures against any member of the League that waged war in disregard of its Covenant obligations.[1] The Covenant, however, left open the option of lawful recourse to war if, for example, the League's mechanisms could not arrive at a solution or any time after three months following the tabling of a peace proposal.[2]

The League's members thus accepted a semblance of collective security through an international organization that would act as a mediator of disputes, but that lacked the authority to impose a solution upon its members. While the dismal history of the 1930s laid bare the unwillingness of the major European states to empower the League to preserve the peace when their vital interests were at issue, the League proved more effective in conflicts outside the core of disputes among the European powers. It created rapporteurs and commissions of inquiry to recommend settlements to disputes, paving the way for the preagreement peacemaking process attempted by the United Nations. In a few instances, the League even undertook executor functions not specified in the Covenant.

Besides the Covenant, the rest of the Treaty of Versailles, containing the substance of the peace ending the Great War, gave particular responsibilities to the League. The key victors—the United States, France, Britain, Italy, and Japan—tried to retain control of the execution of the most important parts of the treaty. Through the Supreme Council and its standing organ, the Conference of Ambassadors (in which the United States participated despite its absence from the League), they asserted the right to decide questions of, for example, German debt and rearmament.[3] But the signatories gave the League responsibilities over more minor parts of the treaty—what F. S. Northedge has called "the small change of diplomacy."[4]

1. Second-Generation Peacekeeping Before Its Time: The League's Governance of the Saar Basin

The League's most assertive effort in the direction of what became the new peacekeeping took place with its governance of the Saar Basin from 1922 to 1935, including the conduct of a plebiscite to determine the Saar's future status. The Saar case forms the classic prototype of second-generation peacekeeping, as the Versailles Treaty entrusted the League with a major part in administering the peace between the principal antagonists in the Saar region, Germany and France.

The Saar Basin, a small region of ethnic Germans in southwestern Germany on its border with France, had always held great significance for both states due to its rich coal mines. Under the Treaty of Versailles, Germany surrendered to France all the coal deposits within the Saar to compensate France for war damages.[5] The treaty did not, however, cede the territory to France, but instead offered a radical concept: the League itself, through a five-member commission chosen by the League Council, would administer the territory for fifteen years. Thereafter, the League would organize a referendum on the status of the territory, namely, incorporation into Germany or France or maintenance of the status quo. It would then decide on the area's sovereignty, "taking into account the wishes of the inhabitants as expressed by the voting."[6]

The treaty granted the Commission "all the powers of government hitherto belonging to [Germany], including the appointment and dismissal of officials, and the creation of such administrative and representative bodies as it may deem necessary."[7] Although German laws would remain in force, the Saar would join the customs territory of France, and the Commission could enact additional legislation as needed. Legally, the territory remained under German sovereignty, but the surrender of control rendered irrelevant any continuation of German authority pending the plebiscite. (The League, dominated by the victorious allies, felt none of the agony over sovereignty of the Saar that states would later experience with regard to the new peacekeeping.)[8]

The League went about its significant task with appropriate seriousness and diligence. At its first session in 1920, the Council selected five commissioners according to the treaty—one French, one non-French Saarlander, and one each from three countries other than France or Germany. In the Commission's early years, it set up civilian bodies to replace the French military administration; organized elections to reconstitute local assemblies; issued decrees on matters from police to revenue collection to public property to transportation; formulated a budget; and dealt with strikes by coal workers and public officials. The Commission, pro-French in outlook, tried to ensure that public servants would remain loyal to the League, but public sentiment was strongly pro-German. It administered the full range of political, economic, and other governmental functions for the territory. Its members did not consider themselves bound by the wishes of the local legislative bodies. The Commission consulted with Saar leaders from time to time, but rarely to their satisfaction.[9]

The Governing Commission reported frequently to the Council on its activities. In its first year, 1920, it issued five reports, and filed reports three or four times a year thereafter until its termination in 1935. With this sharing of information came the trust of the Council, which usually stayed out of the Commission's affairs.

An important early test of that confidence came in September 1920, after the Commission's Saarlander member, Alfred von Boch (of the Villeroy and Boch company), asked the Council for permission to resign. Von Boch sharply disagreed with his colleagues (especially the biased and autocratic French chairman, Victor Rault) over a Commission statute that he regarded as unfair to Germans. The Council accepted the resignation and appointed a replacement, but refused to address the merits of the dispute. In the words of the Council's report on the matter, "[I]t is important that the Council . . . should not intervene in the administration of the Saar Basin except for reasons of the highest importance."[10] Moreover, the Council rejected a request by von Boch that it send a delegation to the Saar to examine the Commission's work, noting that the Commission represented the appropriate channel for complaints by Saarlanders to the Council.[11]

Three years later, however, the Council did intervene, after the French chairman issued a decree restraining civil liberties and sought to increase the size of the local French garrison detested by the Saarlanders. At British insistence, the Council summoned the entire Commission to Geneva in July 1923 to review its decision. After long public meetings, the Council warned the chairman to consult his colleagues before acting on their behalf and to move toward creation of a local police to replace the French contingent.[12] This assertion of Council authority seems to have calmed the situation. After Germany joined the League in 1926, it did not bring any complaints about the Commission's activities to the Council.[13]

As the League administration entered its last several years, the Council turned to the question of the treaty-mandated plebiscite. In 1934, it created a plebiscite commission with three members, one expert, and fifty inspectors, as well as a tribunal to address disputes. All members of both bodies came from neutral countries. With the help of nearly a thousand election officials, the commission compiled a list of almost 540,000 voters. When the elections drew nearer, the League set up an international military force to ensure order in the territory. Its 3,300 members, from Britain, Italy, Sweden, and the Netherlands, constituted the first multinational military operation under the auspices of an international organization. In addition to acting as an administrator of the Versailles Treaty by governing the territory and organizing the election, the League also engaged in a mediation role, appointing a special rapporteur to negotiate with France and Germany over the terms of the plebiscite. The League obtained their written agreement not to pressure the voters or retaliate against anyone due to his position during the polling.[14]

Nevertheless, Hitler's policies propagated both intense German nationalism and fear among various sectors of the Saar's populace. The League refused, however, to intervene actively in the referendum. It thus did not, for instance, inform the Saarlanders of the precise future governing arrangements of the region in the event they opted for the status quo.[15] When the vote finally occurred on January 13, 1935, more than 90 percent of the inhabitants voted in orderly balloting for immediate reunification with Germany; France and other states quickly accepted the results of the voting. On March 1, the Council formally returned the governance of the Saar to Germany.

The experience of the Saar offered a glimmer of hope for international governance as a means of resolving territorial disputes. Although the administration had its setbacks, and surely grew out of a victors' treaty, the Commission nevertheless managed to carry it off reasonably successfully. The economy of the Saar grew, public services functioned, and civil institutions returned after the destruction of the war. The League organized the plebiscite fairly, although not in a neutral political environment, with active international participation, including the first multinational force.

At the same time, the Saarland mission offered the League a relatively easy task: its population was fairly unified, without internecine fighting; the territory had ample wealth and skilled labor; and the population did not rebel against League rule even if they hardly favored it. Finally, the major antagonists recognized a graceful way out of the conflict and eventually cooperated with the plan, even if Germany did not approve of it. The United Nations would not always prove as fortunate when its turn came.

2. A Variation on the Theme: The Free City of Danzig

The League also took significant responsibility for executing the Versailles Treaty's terms on Danzig (now Gdansk), a German enclave on Poland's Baltic coast that had been part of West Prussia before the war. The treaty tore Danzig away from both Germany and Poland, making it an independent country or "Free City." Poland received special rights, such as access to waterways and some control over Danzig's foreign policy.

At the same time, the treaty placed Danzig "under the protection of the League of Nations," another novel concept for an international organization.[16] While the League would not govern the territory as it had the Saar, the Versailles Treaty called for it to perform two key duties through the Council and a High Commissioner: (1) draw up Danzig's constitution and "guarantee" it; and (2) "deal[] . . . in the first instance" with all disputes between Danzig and Poland.[17] Under both the Danzig Constitution and the later Danzig-Poland treaty clarifying Poland's rights, the League had to approve amendments to the constitution, and the High Commissioner could veto any treaties he found incompatible with the city's status.[18] Once more, the League was to serve the three functions of the new peacekeeping. It would act as administrator, although only of tasks assigned it in the treaty, not of the territory itself; mediator of Danzig-Poland conflicts; and guarantor of the constitution and Danzig's territorial integrity and independence.

With the League's mandate in Danzig more manageable than that in the Saar and its power substantial, its work proved generally successful until the rise of the Nazis. Under his powers to mediate, the High Commissioner resolved numerous disputes between Poland and Danzig. Although many decisions were appealed to the Council or the Permanent Court of International Justice in the Hague, the parties complied with the final determinations in the early years. With the election of a Nazi-controlled government in Danzig in 1933, the political opposition faced official repression and sought to invoke the League's responsibilities as guarantor of the constitution. The Council examined a number of governmental decrees that violated the constitution, but failed to take any decisive action. It did refer one particularly obnoxious penal law to the Permanent Court, which struck it down.[19]

While League oversight slowed the Nazification of Danzig and offered some protection to minorities not available in Germany, by the mid-1930s the League's interest in and power over Danzig waned. The majority of the population looked forward to incorporation into Germany, and Poland preferred to handle its interests in Danzig bilaterally or with Germany. From 1937 onward, according to the League's foremost historian, the Council maintained only the "pretence" of guardianship over Danzig.[20] By 1938, Germany had effectively asserted its sphere of influence over Danzig, making its annexation by the Reich on the first day of World War II little more than a formality.

The Danzig experience began with great promise and ended as catastrophically as the League itself. For at least the first ten years, as the parties cooperated, the High Commissioner fulfilled his role as mediator and guarantor, allowing Danzig to emerge as perhaps "the purest example of an 'internationalized territory.'"[21] The High Commissioner intervened directly to protect the city, as required under the Versailles Treaty. Ultimately, however, when the members of the League found agendas more urgent than the League's obligation to protect Danzig, the constitutional regime foundered, and the city succumbed to the fate of German-speaking lands elsewhere in Europe.

3. Forgotten Forays Here and There

While the Saar and Danzig represented the two most prominent cases of League action previewing second-generation peacekeeping, other instances of League involvement to implement the terms of the World War I peace treaties deserve brief mention.[22] They show an important, but more low-key role for the League in executing, mediating disputes over, or guaranteeing parts of the postwar treaties.

• *Vilna*: Once the capital of the Lithuanian empire and later a leading commercial center in western Russia, Vilna (Vilnius) had long been a source of dispute between Poland and Russia. The status of the city and surrounding land was left unresolved in the Treaty of Versailles, leaving Poland with de facto control. In the Russian-Lithuanian peace treaty of July 1920, Moscow implicitly recognized Vilna as part of the new Lithuanian state,[23] and shortly thereafter the Lithuanian and Soviet Russian armies retook control of the territory from the Poles. Poland immediately appealed to the League for assistance. A League commission negotiated an armistice that autumn, but Poland quickly violated it, occupying the region anew.

The League persisted at finding a peaceful solution to the conflict. In October of that year, the Council recommended "[a] public expression of opinion [in the area] . . . under the auspices and supervision of the League of Nations."[24] Both Poland and Lithuania formally accepted the idea without conditions, seemingly providing the consent needed for a League-sponsored plebiscite. Yet despite detailed planning by the League, Poland and Lithuania refused to cooperate, the former refusing to withdraw its troops and the latter, backed by Russia, insisting that the city of Vilna be excluded from the plebiscite area. In March 1921, the League finally abandoned the idea, leaving the matter to direct negotiations.[25] The parties never reached any definitive settlement during the inter-war period, and the Soviet Union seized Vilna from Poland at the outbreak of World War II, eventually making it the capital of the annexed Lithuanian Soviet Socialist Republic.

• *Upper Silesia*: Article 88 of the Treaty of Versailles provided that an allied commission would conduct a plebiscite to determine the status of this densely populated, wealthy area between Germany and Poland. After the March 1921 plebiscite, the allies proved unable to agree upon a line to divide the territory between the two claimant states. The Council then recommended a boundary, as well as a transitional regime to promote the economic integration of the area.[26] The allies approved the plan, after which Germany, under protest, negotiated a new treaty with Poland on the status of the region.[27]

Under the 606-article convention, the League appointed presidents of a mixed commission to supervise the partition and of an arbitral panel to resolve private disputes. The League was also empowered to decide upon complaints regarding the treatment of minorities. The German minority in Polish Upper Silesia pressed numerous cases, resulting in Council decisions and judgments of the Permanent Court that both reduced tensions and advanced minority interests.[28]

• *Memel*: The League Council helped administer a 1924 treaty on the status of the small, formerly German territory in Western Lithuania that Lithuania seized in 1923 from French-occupying forces after three years of fruitless talks over its status. Under the treaty, the League appointed one of Memel's port commissioners and had to approve changes to the port regime and transit traffic scheme.[29] The regime functioned until Germany annexed Memel in March 1939, with barely a whiff of protest from the League.

• *Mosul*: Under the 1923 peace treaty between the allies and Turkey, Turkey and Britain were to negotiate a border in this oil-rich area between Turkey and Iraq (then under British mandate) or refer the matter to the League.[30] When negotiations foundered, the League dispatched a commission of inquiry to consider the feasibility of a plebiscite or some other method to draw a frontier. In July 1925, after six months of consultations in the region, the commission rejected a plebiscite as impossible given the absence of any neutral authority in Mosul and its concerns that residents would simply follow the views of powerful elements of society. The Council agreed and endorsed its 1924 provisional frontier, which the next year became codified in a new UK-Turkey treaty.[31]

• *Leticia*: In 1933, after Peru seized this sparsely populated trapezium along the Amazon from Colombia, the Council unanimously demanded the withdrawal of Peruvian troops and administration of the territory by a League commission pending a final settlement.[32] Although Peru originally rejected the proposal, a new government installed after the assassination of Peru's president accepted the general idea. Under a peace agreement concluded in May 1933, a commission of the League assumed control of the territory from Peru. Composed of three commissioners and aided by a 75-man military contingent, it governed Leticia for one year, after which it returned the region to Colombia.[33] Although the commission administered only a tiny populace, it did improve the area's health and educational facilities, and the experiment aided the transition from Peruvian to Colombian rule.[34]

• *Alexandretta*: Finally, the League developed elaborate plans for a role in the governance of this area of French-mandated Syria that Turkey wished to incorporate. Under a 1937 League-authored peace plan accepted by France and Turkey, Alexandretta would remain nominally part of Syria. The Council would also dispatch an envoy to ensure the governance of the territory under a special statute protecting non-Turks, mediate with Syria, and organize the election of a local assembly.[35] Before the League could undertake these duties, however, Turkey prevailed upon France to withhold cooperation from the League, and the two countries conducted their own, rigged elections. Turks won a majority in the assembly and shortly thereafter reunited the territory with Turkey.[36]

THE UNITED NATIONS: NEW PEACEKEEPING IN THE OLD ERA

As the League offered some assistance to its members in implementing postwar agreements, its successor took on corresponding mandates in the wake of the World War II. As with the League, the Allies did not entrust the UN with overseeing those postwar arrangements of vital strategic interest, such as the status of Germany or Poland. But the international community did foresee a place for the UN in executing settlements over disputes of less import. Some never evolved beyond plans on paper; others would send the UN on trails already blazed by the League as well as more dangerous, less-traveled paths.

1. The Aborted Cases

a. Trieste

The UN's first mission into this realm was supposed to occur in Trieste, a densely populated port city and territory on the Italian-Yugoslav (now Slovenian) border. The 1947 peace treaty between the Allies and Italy made Trieste a "Free Territory," whose "integrity and independence shall be assured by the Security Council of the United Nations."[37] The Security Council approved a provisional regime and Permanent Statute and was to appoint a governor of the territory.[38] Under the Permanent Statute, the governor would act on behalf of and report directly to the Council.

Trieste would follow the pattern of Danzig, as an independent state under the guardianship or guarantee of an international organization. Yet Trieste's governor would have greater explicit powers over the internal administration than did the League's High Commissioner for Danzig. Although a constituent assembly would prepare a constitution, the statute overrode it. As guarantor of the statute, the governor could effectively veto laws, regulations, or treaties he believed incompatible with it; appoint certain officials; and take emergency action. The local assembly could not override his decisions, although the Security Council could.[39] The governor would have inherent authority to mediate any disputes between Italy and Yugoslavia over the territory.

Had the plan for UN oversight of Trieste materialized, it would have engaged the United Nations in nonmilitary, second-generation peacekeeping early in its existence. Because of U.S.-Soviet rivalries, however, the Security Council never agreed on the appointment of a governor, and the UN did not establish any administration. The uncertainty over the territory's status ended only in 1954, when the United States, Britain, Italy, and Yugoslavia signed an accord dividing the territory between Italy and Yugoslavia, more or less along the lines of occupation of their armies.[40] The Cold War had thus delayed any enhanced UN role in administering peace agreements.[41]

b. Jerusalem

Jerusalem became the next candidate for UN governance. The Palestine partition plan approved by the General Assembly on November 29, 1947, sought to make Jerusalem "a *corpus separatum* under a special international regime . . . administered by the United Nations."[42] Under a detailed statute outlined in the Assembly's resolution, the UN Trusteeship Council would govern Jerusalem as an entity separate from both the proposed Jewish and Arab states in Palestine. The Trusteeship Council drafted the statute over the ensuing months, adopting it in April 1948.[43]

Under the statute, the Trusteeship Council would appoint a governor, who would, on behalf of the UN, "exercise executive authority in the City and . . . act as the chief administrator thereof."[44] His executive functions would include preservation of public order, operation of a government, conduct of foreign affairs, supervision over religious bodies, and special authority over the holy places. As a mediator, he would handle disputes among the religious groups as well as with neighboring states concerning the protection of the holy places. As with Trieste, a local legislature would maintain some autonomy, but the governor could veto any bills inconsistent with the statute. Also like the plan for Trieste, the UN would "assure," or guarantee, the territorial integrity of Jerusalem and the special regime in the statute.[45]

Envisaged as an attempt to circumvent the Arab-Israeli conflict, the proposed UN administration of Jerusalem ultimately fell victim to it. With the outbreak of the 1948 war, fighting waged in Jerusalem, and UN mediator Count Bernadotte could not prevail upon the sides to accept any solution (his efforts leading to his own murder by Israeli extremists). Although the General Assembly continued to endorse the idea of international governance of the city after the war and the Trusteeship Council drafted a revised statute, the Arabs and Israelis emphatically rejected the idea. Israel and Jordan refused to surrender control over their respective halves of Jerusalem between 1949 and 1967. Since the Six-Day War, Israel has ruled out any internationalization of Jerusalem involving an Israeli withdrawal.[46]

c. Korea

Finally, the UN made a modest effort to assume some type of oversight over Korea after World War II. With the peninsula divided into Soviet (North) and U.S. (South) zones of occupation, the United States and the Soviet Union were deadlocked over fulfilling a plan from their 1945 Moscow accord for a four-power trusteeship over Korea pending elections.[47] The United States brought the matter to the General Assembly, which, over Soviet objections, set up a series of commissions to foster Korea's transition to independence.

In November 1947, it established the UN Temporary Commission on Korea (UNTCOK), charged with observing elections and helping the elected delegates set up a government.[48] When the Soviets and North Koreans refused to cooperate, the Assembly ordered it to work in the southern half of Korea only. With its small staff, the multinational commission helped open up the electoral process a bit and superficially observed the elections held in the South in May 1948.

After those elections, the Assembly created the UN Commission on Korea (UNCOK) to assist in unifying the country.[49] But the North continued to refuse all cooperation and the South Korean authorities objected to its mandate as interfering in their domestic affairs. Blocked at every turn, it did little more than casually observe parliamentary elections in 1950 and provide information to the UN about the impending invasion later that year.[50] After the outbreak of hostilities, the General Assembly, in addition to approving the war against the North, created yet another commission, the Commission for the Unification and Rehabilitation of Korea (UNCURK).[51] It was equally overcome by the stalemate on the peninsula.

Had the reunification plans garnered the acceptance of the Soviet Union and North Korea, the UN's commissions might well have served as agents for uniting the peninsula and formed harbingers of a second-generation operation. The lack of their consent, however, rendered attainment of its goals impossible from the outset. Indeed, the political solution underlying the UN's plans consisted only of a series of General Assembly resolutions consistently opposed by the USSR. The UN thus performed none of the functions of the new peacekeeping.[52]

d. Kashmir

The division of British India in 1947 into the independent states of India and Pakistan gave rise to another UN initiative regarding disputed territory. In this case, the issue was the status of the Indian princely state of Jammu and Kashmir (commonly known by the latter name alone). Under British policy for the independence of India and Pakistan, the ruler of each princely state—those Indian territories not officially subject to direct rule by the Crown—could choose to join Hindu India or Muslim Pakistan. Jammu and Kashmir had (and has) an overwhelmingly Muslim population, but had a Hindu leader, the Maharajah.

In October 1947, government-supported Pakistani insurgents crossed into and occupied parts of the territory. Fearing loss of control over the state, the Maharajah desperately sought admission to India. Lord Mountbatten and the British government provisionally agreed, pending a referendum by the Kashmiris to resolve the matter definitively. India soon sent troops to occupy most of Kashmir, prompting the Security Council to create, in January 1948, the United Nations Commission for India and Pakistan (UNCIP). Composed of representatives of three, then five, UN member states, it was to help mediate the dispute.[53]

In April 1948, the Security Council recommended to the parties a definitive solution to the conflict—a plebiscite in the territory, to be executed by a UN plebiscite administrator (who would serve, as a formal matter, as an officer of the Jammu and Kashmir regional government). UNCIP would help lay the groundwork for the vote and then observe and certify it.[54] By early 1949,

India and Pakistan, which had also dispatched its regular troops to the area, had agreed to a cease-fire to be supervised by the UN Military Observer Group in India and Pakistan (UNMOGIP). This paved the way for Secretary-General Trygve Lie's nomination of U.S. Admiral Chester Nimitz as plebiscite administrator.[55]

There the matter lay and, indeed, has lain for over forty-five years. India opposed any plan that could lead to the loss of Jammu and Kashmir (especially the treasured central valley, or Vale); Pakistan ruled out any Indian control of the territory in the period before a plebiscite. Given the belligerents' irreconcilable views on troop withdrawals and the modalities of any plebiscite, UNCIP could not broker any arrangement to carry out the Security Council's plan, and the Council disbanded it in March 1950 in favor of a single UN representative. The parties never agreed on the appointment of the plebiscite administrator, especially after Pakistan's shift to the U.S. camp and India's tilt towards the Soviet Union in the 1950s scuttled the nomination of Nimitz. Despite wars in 1965 and 1971 and continuing tensions, the conflict remains unsolved, and UNMOGIP still monitors the cease-fire line as an extant first-generation peacekeeping operation.

Though far less expansive a UN role than that envisaged for Trieste or Jerusalem, the UN's plan for a plebiscite in Jammu and Kashmir continued the practice of the League and the World War I allies in addressing the final status of certain disputed areas through recourse to the will of the people. And whereas the post-World War I plebiscites were generally confined to Europe, the idea of a plebiscite in Kashmir as early as 1947 suggested that the same policy ought to apply in the decolonization process globally. (The Council's resolution did not, however, give the Kashmiris the option of independence.) In this case the Organization failed quite palpably to carry out such a policy, as it proved unable to bring India and Pakistan to peace or force India to accept the notion of Kashmiri self-determination. Elsewhere, however, the UN would oversee referenda to determine the future national affiliation of colonial peoples during the dismantling of Europe's empires.

e. Namibia

The General Assembly's establishment in 1967 of the United Nations Council for Namibia represented the last stillborn attempt at a direct UN civilian governance. The Assembly's action followed its decision the year before to terminate South Africa's League of Nations Mandate over the territory (the legal source of Pretoria's administrative authority since 1920), and place the territory under direct UN administration.[56] Under the 1967 resolution, later endorsed by the Security Council, the Assembly created the Council on

Namibia "[t]o administer South West Africa until independence, with the maximum possible participation of the people of the Territory."[57] From its planned headquarters in Namibia, it would promulgate any necessary laws or regulations, maintain law and order, ensure the removal of South African civilians, police, and military forces, and set up a constituent assembly to draft a constitution pending elections and independence. By 1973, the Assembly had named a Commissioner for Namibia as the territory's de jure administrator.

The widely hailed plan, however, lacked the assent of the South African government, which refused to cede any control to the Council on Namibia, thereby preventing any true administration. The Council observed and reported on Namibia for UN debates and had other modest achievements, such as establishing an institute to train cadre for post-independence positions and exercising consular functions on behalf of exiled Namibians.

2. State-building in the Congo

The UN's largest, bloodiest peacekeeping mission took place with the United Nations Operation in the Congo (ONUC). From 1960 to 1964, under a broad, vague mandate from the Security Council and under the control of the Secretary-General, ONUC conducted military missions unseen before or since in the annals of the League or United Nations. It forcibly restored order after the pullout of Belgian authorities, put down a secessionist movement, and helped the central government assert control over the country. In the process, the UN dragged itself into a multifaceted civil conflict, with the death of nearly 200 peacekeepers in hostile action and of Secretary-General Hammarskjold in a plane crash. It also led to a direct confrontation between the Secretary-General and two permanent members of the Security Council, the Soviet Union and France, creating a severe financial crisis with long-lasting effects.[58]

ONUC nevertheless left an important legacy for second-generation peacekeeping. The military aspects offer lessons with respect to the two core *conceptual premises* of peacekeeping—consent and impartiality. The civilian operation provides additional insights into the *operational capability* of the UN to engage in nation-building. An analysis of ONUC from these perspectives must, however, begin with a caveat: although it represented the most assertive example of UN involvement to solve a conflict and build a state, it rested upon neither the political settlement nor multifactional consent typical of the new peacekeeping. Rather, at Hammarskjold's urging, to avoid direct U.S. assistance, the Congo's government requested the assistance of the UN, and the Security Council responded with binding decisions. Instead of helping the parties to carry out a peace accord, the UN simultaneously sought to end the civil war and create a viable state, similar to its goals in Somalia beginning in 1992.

a. The Military Operation: Pushing the Bounds of Consent and Impartiality
The Security Council initially charged ONUC with a primarily military mission. This was to assist the government of the newly independent Congo in restoring order after a rebellion by parts of the national army against its Belgian officers had led to massive disorder, Belgian military intervention, and an attempted secession. After the Council, in its July 14, 1960, resolution, asked the Secretary-General to send such a force to the Congo, Hammarskjold clarified the principles under which ONUC would operate. It would act with the consent of the Congo government, but under the sole authority of the UN; the units would not intervene in any internal conflict, including by engaging in any joint operations with the government; and they would use force only in self-defense.[59] Hammarskjold thus reiterated the classic concepts of military peacekeeping, namely consent, not enforcement, and impartiality, not intervention. Both would face tough tests during ONUC's mandate.

The consensual nature of the operation collided with the views of the Congo's government. It often objected to the conduct of ONUC, demanding that it serve as an agent of the government or undermining its work to advance the government's own goals. Moreover, the Belgian-aided secessionist movement in the mineral-rich southeast region of Katanga did not willingly agree to allow the UN to enter Katanga to restore it to governmental control. The UN had not considered the latter's consent a legal prerequisite to the emplacement of ONUC, as long as the Congo government requested ONUC's presence; but the opposition to ONUC from an important party in the Congo's civil strife presented a grave challenge to ONUC's work compared with earlier peacekeeping operations.

To respond to these pressures, Hammarskjold (and, after his death in late 1961, U Thant) sought the backing of the Security Council for his actions. If he believed the Council resolution under which he operated did not provide ample legal and political support, he sought additional authority. If he felt he could interpret the resolution to achieve his ends, he did so. The Secretary-General's interpretations, however, led to sharp conflicts with the Soviet Union and Congolese Premier Patrice Lumumba, who found UN policy biased toward Western interests. Hammarskjold would respond to a challenging party that the Council could overrule him. But of course it never did because the Secretary-General's chief backer, the United States, could block any such idea.[60] His action maintained credibility in the eyes of most member states; but the disagreements with the USSR eventually paralyzed the Council.

Second, the Secretary-General, Under Secretary-General Ralph Bunche, and their subordinates engaged in nonstop mediation. Each military move followed talks with the rival parties to attempt to ensure that they would not prevent ONUC from carrying out its mission. When Katangese forces barred ONUC entry in August 1960, Hammarskjold sent Bunche to negotiate with local authorities to obtain it, rejecting Soviet demands for a forceful entry.

Third, if Hammarskjold or U Thant believed that the Council supported him, he would respond to instances of lack of cooperation by proceeding with his mission, even if it meant confronting, or even fighting, the factions. The UN deployed peacekeepers where the government or secessionists did not want them, rounded up foreign mercenaries, and even closed several airfields and a radio station. With explicit authority from the Council, ONUC defeated the Katangese secession through a series of battles and other armed encounters with the rebels from the summer of 1961 through early 1963.

These tactics made ONUC the most militarily proactive UN force in the Organization's history. When the parties balked at ONUC, the Secretary-General resorted to unprecedented means to permit the mission to continue. As a result, instead of merely interposing itself between two armies to observe a truce, ONUC took on functions akin to peace enforcement by trying to end the civil war in the Congo. This pulled the UN deeper into the war, with increasing casualties. In the end, however, the Congo emerged a unitary state, though weak and impoverished. Its existence, however troubled, stems in great part from the Secretary-General's and the member states' persistence in the face of obstinate domestic parties.

With respect to ONUC's oath of impartiality, Hammarskjold's promise that the UN would not take sides in the internal conflict or interfere in the domestic affairs of the Congo proved difficult, if not impossible, to reconcile with the international community's goal of ending the civil war in the Congo. He constructed careful arguments to prove the UN could act impartially. Hammarskjold asserted that the restoration of law and order would facilitate the departure of Belgian troops, thereby rendering any remaining differences between the government and the Katangese leadership over the status of Katanga purely an internal matter in which the UN would not interfere.[61] He sought Security Council resolutions that reaffirmed ONUC's impartiality and its law and order mandate; in his public statements and communications with the Congolese factions, he tried to avoid the perception or reality of any alliance with the Congo government.[62]

In time, however, Hammarskjold's subordinates in the field (especially Conor Cruise O'Brien and Sture Linner) and, eventually, U Thant, rejected these distinctions. They adopted a wholly different view of the facts, but one that they saw as consistent with impartiality. They saw the Katanga problem as per se part of an external intervention by Belgians, so that the UN could take measures against the Katangese as needed to end the intervention without choosing sides in an internal conflict. While not abandoning the position of impartiality and nonintervention, they saw more assertive UN actions as entirely consistent with those principles.[63]

The Council effectively endorsed this position in November 1961, when it ordered ONUC to use force to apprehend all foreign elements and mercenaries. The Council refrained from authorizing ONUC to use force for the avowed purpose of ending the secession, as that would have arguably compromised the UN's impartiality.[64] The Congo government's supporters in the UN, including the Soviet Union, favored this stronger power for ONUC, insisting that Belgian involvement justified jettisoning any pretense of impartiality and aiding the central government in quelling the Katangese secession.[65] The Congo mission demonstrated the diversity of possible responses to challenges to the peacekeepers' impartiality. Hammarskjold interpreted the situation to fit the doctrine; U Thant interpreted the doctrine to fit the situation; and the Soviet Union and others rejected the doctrine completely.

b. The Civilian Operation: The UN as Nation-builder

Beyond its unprecedented military operations to end the Congo's civil war, ONUC's mandate offered another new challenge for the Organization. It was to assist the Congo in constructing a functioning civilian administration to run the country after the hasty departure of Belgian colonial officials. This historically lesser known side of ONUC's work represented a seminal, though only partly successful, episode in UN nation-building and suggested the potential for a large civilian unit within a peacekeeping mission.[66]

The need for a civilian component within ONUC stemmed from the myopic colonial policies of Belgium, which concentrated nearly all administrative responsibilities for the territory within the Belgian community, offering scarcely any training or education to the Congolese in the skills needed to run the third-largest state in Africa. When Belgium granted the colony independence on June 30, 1960, most Belgian civilians fled, fearing chaos, leaving the new government without most of the officials who had run the colony.

The Security Council responded to the new nation's plight by giving ONUC a vast, but imprecise mandate in its initial resolution: ONUC would provide "technical assistance" to help the government restore order and thus permit the departure of Belgian military forces and the end of UN military assistance.[67] In a subsequent resolution, the Council "invite[d] the specialized agencies of the United Nations to render to the Secretary-General such assistance as he may require."[68]

Hammarskjold and Bunche responded to the crisis in the Congo and the mandate of the Council by organizing a large civilian section in ONUC. In his first report to the Council on the civilian operation, the Secretary-General stated:

> The United Nations must in the situation now facing the Congo go beyond the time-honoured forms for technical assistance in order to do what is necessary, but it has to do it in forms which do not in any way infringe upon the sovereignty of the country or hamper the speedy development of the national administration.[69]

In the case of ONUC, doing "what is necessary" entailed preventing the complete breakdown of the civil administration of the country. Hammarskjold appointed his friend and fellow Swede Sture Linner to head the civilian operation. The UN deployed hundreds of personnel from the Secretariat and the specialized agencies throughout the Congo administration for more than three years, until the military crisis abated. Although the UN could not recruit people as quickly as it wished, it emplaced 426 by the end of 1961 and 1,149 by the end of 1962.[70]

ONUC's civilian personnel first provided typical technical assistance and advice by training Congolese personnel in the business of governing a country. From the justice system to the airports, from the mines to social welfare programs and health, ONUC conducted a program of training and education. It tried to create the indigenous civil service that the Belgians never did. Second, UN officials themselves undertook technical tasks that the Congolese could not perform. Because the Congo faced so many dire crises, and training involved a long-term process, the UN provided direct operational assistance. UN personnel manned airports, worked in hospitals, operated the telecommunications system, distributed food, and opened up ports. They inevitably trained some Congolese by example, but the UN focused on filling the gaps left by the departing Belgian administrators.[71]

Third, and most novel, senior officials in the civilian side of ONUC performed what Hammarskjold called "activities on a level of higher administrative responsibility."[72] By this innocent phrase, Hammarskjold envisaged UN personnel assuming senior administrative duties to ensure the functioning of the government. The Secretary-General went to great pains to explain that officially these functionaries would perform this "senior responsibility" only at the specific request of the Congo government, even designating them as "consultants."[73]

In practice, they took charge of much of the policymaking within the Congo administration. ONUC set up a Monetary Council to act as a Central Bank, coordinated economic policy, channeled much foreign assistance to the Congo, provided teams to draft the constitution, and helped set up a new educational system. The Secretary-General's Special Representative, Rajeshwar Dayal, called the process one of "provid[ing] bone and sinew to the Administration in its different branches, denuded as it was of technical and administrative personnel."[74] Brian Urquhart, exaggerating slightly, stated that the UN "took over the whole administration of a country for a while."[75]

ONUC confronted challenges to the basic precepts of peacekeeping in its civilian work as well. First, the grave situation brought about by the near-collapse of government harshly tested the consensual basis of peacekeeping. Despite the Secretary-General's gestures to portray the civilians as advisers to the Congo government and to emphasize the consultations between ONUC and the government, the UN personnel often took the initiative to make or implement policy themselves, at times even against the wishes of Congolese authorities.

This practice infuriated the government, which complained of violations of the Congo's sovereignty and interference by the UN in its internal affairs. Hammarskjold admitted as much when he told the General Assembly in 1960: "You try to save a drowning man without prior authorization and even if he resists you; you do not let him go even when he tries to strangle you."[76] If a particular policy did not require the cooperation of Congolese officials (such as opening a road or disbursing foreign aid), ONUC could implement it comparatively easily. If the authorities actively opposed UN policies, ONUC's actions were often thwarted. One observer has argued that ONUC could have accomplished a great deal more if the Council had given it direct executive authority.[77] Inevitably, ONUC had to adopt some form of the contextual approach to the lack of consent discussed in chapter 2. This meant judging each episode of noncooperation on its merits to determine how to attempt the nation-building.

The principle of impartiality fared no better. The Soviet Union accused ONUC of lack of neutrality in the Cold War sense of the term. It complained that Westerners dominated ONUC's initial crop of senior civilians and blamed ONUC for pursuing a pro-American agenda to the detriment of the Congo.[78] It eventually stopped contributing to ONUC, and much of the civilian operation's budget came from the United States. The government of the Congo, for its part, feared that ONUC's activist policies often imposed an alien agenda upon them. Its opponents, including the Katangese, said the UN's assistance to the central government made it per se partial in the civil war.

Hammarskjold tried to remain above the fray in the East-West conflict by adjusting the composition of ONUC's civilian component, carrying out the operation in a very public manner, and avoiding the impression of trying to create a Western ally in the Congo. The UN never succeeded, however, in shaking off concerns by many participants and observers that its policy advanced Western, in particular American, interests only. The UN tried to address charges of partiality by factions within the Congo by agreeing to assist whatever officials had de facto control of a region. However, those occupying areas outside the central government's control usually declined to work with ONUC. In addition, ONUC's refusal to take sides during the 1960–61 constitutional crisis within the central government meant that certain factions would not cooperate with it.[79]

On the operational and administrative aspects important to the new peacekeeping, ONUC performed somewhat better, though the Congo remained in a state of great fragility during and after ONUC's term. Complemented by talent in the field, Hammarskjold and his staff in New York showed they could organize and operate a nonmilitary peacekeeping mission, at least in and around the country's capital and larger cities. Hammarskjold appointed a separate Chief of Civilian Operations, directly beneath his Special Representative, who presided over a group of the "consultants" on issues from agriculture to education to health, and a set of technical advisers. ONUC quickly recruited staff from the Secretariat, member states, and the specialized agencies, establishing policies on duration of employment, conditions of service, reimbursement, and lines of authority.[80] After the termination of ONUC's mandate in 1964, the UN engineered a phasedown of the civilian operation toward more traditionally organized and financed development assistance, led by UNDP and the U.S. Agency for International Development.

ONUC also provided frequent, detailed reports for consumption by the Council, the member states, and the public. These reports emanated from the Secretary-General, his Special Representative, and the Chief of Civilian Operations; during the first year of ONUC, the Secretary-General issued ten on the civilian operation alone. They dealt with more complex and varied subjects than reports by other first-generation missions.

c. The Legacy of ONUC

ONUC left a complex legacy for United Nations peacekeeping, as well as for the Congolese. Member states and Secretariat officials have recalled it principally from the perspective of the military aspects of peacekeeping. They have concluded that the morass in which ONUC found itself proved unarguably the necessity of a clear, feasible mandate; the support of the Security Council; and the cooperation of the local parties and donor states.[81] Many governments came to see the operation as confirming their misgivings about or opposition to UN involvement in the internal affairs of states. From the standpoint of second-generation operations, however, ONUC showed the unrealized possibilities for the UN to help build states through large civilian operations drawing on the expertise of the Secretariat and the specialized agencies. It nevertheless portended dangers for the new peacekeeping.

First, it demonstrated the constraints facing civilian operations if the military situation in a country has not stabilized. Nation-building should take place after a state achieves a modicum of domestic tranquillity, not during a civil war. Second, it illustrated the obstacles and dilemmas for military and civilian operations in the absence of full cooperation by the local parties. ONUC entered without support from some key belligerents and was mistrusted by the government. It undertook significant peacemaking (mediation) activities, while also testing the notion of consent and moving precariously close to peace enforcement.

Lastly, the Congo case showed the evanescence of neutrality, in the sense of an inability to affect the final outcome of the conflict, and the difficulty of maintaining a consistent perception of impartiality in intrusive peacekeeping operations. Unlike truce observation, each nation-building action would have some impact on the balance of power within the country, and the UN's responses to uncooperative parties would cause them to mistrust it.

The ever-expanding mandate, the high number of casualties, the death of Hammarskjold, and the continued miserable state of the Congolese economy left the international community greatly apprehensive about expansive peacekeeping after ONUC. As a result, it would not seriously contemplate the possibility of combat operations for many years. With one exception, it would avoid any nonmilitary peacekeeping missions for the next 25 years.

3. UN Direction, UN Debacle: The West Irian Case

The one exception to the UN's disdain for complex peacekeeping concerned another episode in the UN's decolonization saga. This was its decision in 1962 to create the United Nations Temporary Executive Authority (UNTEA) to end a long-running dispute between the Netherlands and Indonesia over the status of the western half of New Guinea.[82] This large, sparsely populated territory had proved a source of friction since Indonesia's independence from the Netherlands, as the Dutch sought assurances that the ethnically distinct Papuan inhabitants wished to become part of Indonesia. (The eastern half of the island remained a trust territory under Australian administration until independence in 1975 as Papua New Guinea.)

Following active mediation efforts and pressure principally by the United States through its special envoy, Ellsworth Bunker, the Netherlands reluctantly signed an agreement to hand over West Irian to the UN. Under the accord, the

UN would "administer the territory" for six months, after which it would turn governing authority over to Indonesia.[83] As for the will of the people, Indonesia would organize a nonelective consultation process "with the assistance and participation of" the UN, but only after the Indonesian takeover and as late as the end of 1969.[84] All too ready to rid itself of a messy conflict tied up with the decolonization process, the UN General Assembly created UNTEA by asking the Secretary-General to carry out the role spelled out for him in the agreement.[85]

UNTEA constituted the first true case of UN second-generation peacekeeping; only the Saar and Leticia operations compared with it. It thus opened a new chapter for the Organization. Coming in the wake of ONUC, the UN's decision to risk such a novel operation may seem surprising. Yet UNTEA evinced sharp differences from ONUC: a short duration; a clear, manageable mandate; unambiguous consent of the two state actors; a reasonably stable internal situation involving a thinly populated area; and a unified internal governing authority—the UN itself. On top of this, Indonesia and the Netherlands agreed to pay for the operation themselves.

U Thant dispatched his deputy chef de cabinet, José Rolz-Bennett, as his special representative, and the UN took over the territory on October 1, 1962, replacing 18 senior Dutch officials with UN personnel of neither Dutch nor Indonesian origin. UNTEA staffed lower-level positions with Indonesians, Dutch who agreed to stay on, and Papuans. The UN's formal administrator, Djalal Abdoh of Iran, arrived in November.

Within a few months, Indonesians had replaced nearly all the Dutch personnel; UN officials occupied the senior positions for the duration of the mandate. UNTEA transferred administrative and police responsibilities from Dutch incumbents to Indonesians sent from Jakarta and established a court system staffed by Indonesians. It also consulted with local assemblies, disseminated information to the inhabitants about the transfer of power, reactivated public works projects suspended upon the departure of Dutch personnel, and handled several health crises. UNTEA had a small military and police arm, the United Nations Security Force (UNSF), composed of 1,500 Pakistani infantrymen and 75 U.S. and Canadian air support staff. As scheduled, on May 1, 1963, the UN handed over the territory to Indonesia.

At first blush, UNTEA fulfilled its charge from the agreement. It seemingly showed the UN's capability for multifunctional peacekeeping, including administration of territory, in the tradition of the League's governance of the Saar. The UN functioned well as an administrator of both the agreement and the territory itself, and as a guarantor of a smooth transition and the rights of the local inhabitants during those six months.

In fact, however, UNTEA fell short of those perceptions. Although UN officials did occupy senior posts, most of the de facto transfer of power to Indonesia occurred well before May due to the influx of Indonesians. Moreover, the same considerations that made the operation appealing and feasible make it as unusual as the Saar: the transition had a predetermined outcome, with the more powerful state, Indonesia, having every incentive to cooperate. West Irian had only 90,000 people, a simple economic structure, no civil war, and a very rudimentary government to run. A small UN staff with a minimal military force could execute its limited mandate under these conditions.

Whatever the final verdict on UNTEA, the second stage of the process under the Dutch-Indonesian agreement proved a disaster that left the Organization with the diplomatic equivalent of egg on its face. In this phase, the UN was supposed to assist and participate with the government of Indonesia in determining the will of the Papuan people. When the UN conducted this process in 1968-69 (delayed in part by Indonesia's brief withdrawal from the UN), it met with the clear opposition of the Indonesian government, and its weak mandate from the 1962 agreement made the UN an impotent player.

Thus, for example, when the Secretary-General's Special Representative, Fernando Ortiz-Sanz, proposed a one-man, one-vote method, supplemented by consultation in remote areas where voting might prove impossible, the government vetoed the suggestion. Instead, it informed the UN that it would simply consult with representative councils around the territory. Despite UN requests, Indonesia did not constitute those councils democratically or under full UN observation, but through procedures that guaranteed selection only of Papuans supporting the government. Indonesia refused to issue an amnesty to jailed opponents of its rule. It rejected attempts by the Special Representative to permit exercise of political freedoms, such as advocacy of an independent Papuan state, brazenly claiming that Papuans should not have greater rights than other Indonesians. When government officials toured the territory in July and August 1969 to meet with the consultative assemblies, the sessions lasted only several hours, after which all endorsed incorporation.

In his final report to the Secretary-General in November 1969, Ortiz-Sanz expressed his "regret" that the Indonesian government did not fulfill its obligations to guarantee the rights of the Papuan inhabitants, noting that it "exercised at all times a tight political control over the population."[86] As for the will of the Papuans, he could write only that "it can be stated that . . . an act of free choice has taken place . . . in accordance with Indonesian practice."[87] The Assembly blessed the outcome by a vote of 84–0, but 30 African and Asian states abstained to express their disgust at the lack of any meaningful self-determination.[88]

The fiasco of the "act of self-determination" left a bad odor with the UN and its members. It brought home an important lesson for any future peacekeeping operations of this sort: that the UN's powers flow from the underlying political settlement, and when that settlement does not explicitly grant the UN the authority it needs (and sometimes even when it does), the most powerful actors in situ will control the success of the mission. In working with Indonesia to determine the people's preferences, the UN served as neither administrator, guarantor, nor mediator, because the 1962 agreement gave it no such power. At best, it served as a persistent pest and adviser, and one whose suggestions the Indonesians showed themselves perfectly prepared to ignore. Moreover, the second phase of the operation showed that the UN would have to adopt more intrusive methods of oversight if it wished to ensure that elections in disputed territories expressed the will of the people.

4. Related Activities During the Early Years

Beyond the major operations in the Congo and West Irian, the United Nations also conducted less elaborate missions that laid the groundwork for second-generation peacekeeping. In each case, the Secretary-General assisted the parties in dispute to implement some type of solution. The consensual basis for these operations often consisted of the acceptance, albeit grudgingly, by a Western colonial power of the right of self-determination of the inhabitants of its colony and a UN resolution on the procedures to effectuate this end. In some cases, the UN worked from an agreement between states over the future of disputed territory.

Like ONUC and UNTEA, these less formal efforts took place in the context of the decolonization process that defined much of the UN's first two decades, in which it assumed a special responsibility in helping to determine the will of colonial peoples. In this setting, where the UN faced no major challenges to its presence or impartiality, it developed important techniques that would benefit it later.

a. Decolonization Plebiscites

From the 1950s through the 1970s, the Organization oversaw elections in colonies and UN trust territories prior to independence. The UN was, in effect, aiding the colonial and local authorities with the modalities for transfer of power. It was also advancing its own objective, suggested in the Charter and affirmed in key General Assembly resolutions, to promote self-determination, self-government, and ultimately, independence of colonial peoples.[89] Beginning with British Togoland (now part of Ghana) in 1956 and ending with

Palau in 1990, the UN conducted 28 missions, mostly in Africa or the Trust Territories of the Pacific Islands.[90]

Typically, the General Assembly or Trusteeship Council would specify the mandate of the mission, while the administering or colonial power conducted the elections and agreed to allow UN participation. The depth of UN involvement varied; in some cases, such as Togoland and Rwanda-Urundi, it actively supervised the elections. This entailed appointing a commissioner or commission to advise the colonial power over the electoral procedures, including approval of the question on the ballot, and thereafter certify the election results.[91] In others, such as Papua New Guinea and several Pacific island territories, the UN limited its role to observation, a passive exercise that led to a report to the UN and the administering power on the fairness of the voting.

These missions all took place outside the scope of traditional peacekeeping activities. In size, they usually numbered fewer than 30 people. Yet they facilitated the decolonization process and presaged the more assertive electoral role the UN would assume later. They demonstrated a consensus in the international community that the UN could serve as the best guarantor of the fairness of the self-determination process in the decolonization context. The disinterestedness of the UN civil servants and their accountability to the political organs eased the way for the colonial powers to grant their territories independence. Moreover, the executive tasks of overseeing elections, plebiscites, and referenda resulted in the development of standards for free and fair polling that would guide the UN when electoral missions proliferated in the early 1990s.[92] Finally, the member states saw the UN as the best mediator to resolve implementation problems by working with colonial and local officials over the modalities of the polling.

b. Self-Determination through Fact-finding: North Borneo and Bahrain

In two significant cases during the decolonization process, the plans of the colonial power to grant independence collided with the interests of neighboring states asserting rights over the territory. The UN helped to resolve the matter, as the countries submitted the disputes to the UN under Chapter VI, seeking the assistance of the Secretary-General through fact-finding or good offices. With the parties' consent, the Secretary-General definitively determined the status of the territory.

The first episode occurred in 1963, when Britain was preparing to grant independence to the Federation of Malaysia, to be composed of territories on the Malay peninsula and North Borneo. As independence approached, two neighbors of the proposed state, the Philippines and Indonesia, questioned whether the inhabitants of parts of North Borneo truly wished to join Malaysia.

In fact, both states had historic territorial ambitions over the area. (The rest of Borneo belonged to Indonesia, with the tiny enclave of Brunei remaining a British protectorate until full independence in 1984.) After several years of harsh words by the competing claimants, the three states sought the UN's intervention. They signed an agreement in 1963 that accepted the territory's incorporation in Malaysia "provided the support of the people of the Borneo territories is ascertained by an independent and impartial authority, the Secretary-General of the United Nations or his representative."[93]

With no time for a referendum in Borneo before the scheduled independence date of Malaysia, the parties requested U Thant to conduct a complex fact-finding mission. U Thant would have to determine the views of the populace based on the results of prior elections held in the territory. He would review the procedures of those polls to see if the people had freely voted and if they had developed institutions of self-government to make their decision meaningful. U Thant accepted the request, with two caveats. He insisted that Britain assent to the arrangement, which it did, and that the parties accept in advance the finality of his decisions, which they did.[94]

Without any approval by a UN political organ, U Thant dispatched a ten-person team to Borneo. Headed by Secretariat official Lawrence Michelmore, it stayed there from August 16 to September 1. During the mission, however, Britain and Malay leaders announced that Malaysia would become independent on September 16, signaling clearly their readiness to ignore any negative determination by the mission. On September 14, the Secretary-General reported that the team had found that the vast majority of residents wished to join Malaysia and that the people had made an informed, considered choice. Indonesia and the Philippines complained that they had not been able to observe the team's work. While the Philippines eventually accepted the verdict, Indonesia continued to protest, fomenting violence in the territories and anti-British sentiment in Indonesia. It eventually used the issue as a basis for its temporary pullout from the UN in 1965.[95]

Six years later, the UN found itself in a similar situation. Britain had announced plans to grant full independence to its Persian Gulf protectorate of Bahrain in 1971, but Iran had long claimed sovereignty over the islands. As independence neared, however, the Shah of Iran, sensing his isolation on the issue, renounced recourse to force to regain Bahrain and said he would abide by the will of the Bahraini people.

U Thant offered to exercise his good offices in the matter, and Britain and Iran agreed on terms of reference for him: he would "send a personal representative to ascertain the wishes of the people of Bahrain," whose findings would bind the two states if endorsed by the Security Council.[96] Although called the United Nations Good Offices Mission, Bahrain, and composed of only six people, its mandate resembled the administrative functions of the new peacekeeping. U Thant announced his plans to the Security Council, but did not seek their authorization. Arguing that the matter required Security Council approval, the Soviet Union objected, but it did not block the mission.

Led by Vittorio Winspeare Guicciardi, the director of the UN's Geneva office, the mission visited Bahrain for three weeks in March and April 1970. It met with a full range of community organizations and invited individual views. In its report to the Secretary-General, it stated that the Bahrainis clearly favored an independent state. On May 11, 1970, less than two months after the parties and the Secretary-General had agreed on the mission, the Security Council unanimously endorsed the Secretary-General's finding.[97] Iran accepted the result, Bahrain obtained full independence the next year, and the UN congratulated itself.[98]

The Borneo and Bahrain episodes confirmed the international community's view of the UN's special legitimacy and institutional competence in gauging popular sentiment as part of the decolonization process. The methods for determining that will varied across operations, but member states saw the UN as fit to perform this executor role. Moreover, in these two cases, the depth of UN execution increased. Rather than determining if a referendum conducted by others met standards of procedural fairness, the UN itself had to ascertain directly the opinion of the population.

Finally, even more than the other decolonization missions, the Borneo and Bahrain cases showed the blurriness of the line between peacekeeping and peacemaking, which would become most apparent in the second-generation missions. The Secretary-General succeeded in defusing an interstate dispute through the peacemaking method of fact-finding; yet he also executed the tasks in the underlying interstate agreement, with binding results.

c. Transitional Roles in Libya and Eritrea

Finally, the UN participated in resolving the final status of two Italian colonies whose fate remained undetermined after World War II. The Allies had agreed in the 1947 Peace Treaty with Italy to determine the status of these territories (as well as Italian Somaliland, which later joined British Somaliland in forming Somalia) through negotiations.[99] When these foundered, they referred the matter to the Assembly.

In the case of Libya, after rejecting a proposal for collective trusteeship, the General Assembly decided in 1949 to appoint a UN Commissioner for Libya. He would work with France and Britain, the two administering powers, and elites from Libya's three provinces on a transition to independence. The

Commissioner would consult with a council of representatives of interested governments and Libyan leaders.[100] The Commissioner, Assistant Secretary-General Adrian Pelt of the Netherlands, encountered tremendous resistance from both Libyan officials and the administering states in creating a unified constitutional system.

In 1950, after protracted talks mediated by Pelt, the provincial government leaders agreed to form a National Assembly by nomination, rather than election, to protect the interests of the smaller provinces of Fezzan and Cyrenaica against the largest, Tripolitania. That assembly eventually drafted a federal constitution with Pelt's assistance and selected Sayid Idris, the Amir of Cyrenaica, as Libya's king. Pelt also attempted to bolster the power of the provisional central government as Britain and France surrendered more authority to the provincial leaders, and arranged for economic assistance to Libya. When Libya became independent on December 24, 1951, the Organization proclaimed it a successful case of UN assistance in self-determination.[101]

In Eritrea, the UN's results proved more fleeting. After a General Assembly commission visited the territory in 1947, the Assembly remained divided on the best solution. It ultimately adopted a Western-supported plan that rejected Eritrean demands for independence and endorsed mandatory integration with Ethiopia in a federal system. A UN Commissioner, Eduardo Matienzo of Bolivia, would assist the Eritreans and Ethiopians on devising an Eritrean constitution.[102] The General Assembly resolution and the constitution provided for substantial Eritrean governmental and cultural autonomy under overall Ethiopian sovereignty, and Matienzo persuaded both sides to accept the constitution. Hoping to end consideration of the issue despite legitimate fears about Ethiopia's intentions, the Assembly endorsed the plan in 1952.[103] Ethiopia almost immediately began to chip away at the accord, and by 1962 had annexed Eritrea, which would not see independence until 1993.

The Libya and Eritrea missions remain distant memories for the UN; indeed, both UN-prepared constitutions eventually became dead letters. Libya's fell fate to a 1969 coup and Eritrea's to the 1962 annexation. While isolated cases, they represent some evidence of the UN's willingness in special decolonization disputes to go beyond confirming or gauging the popular sentiment and try to forge a viable federal state. Yet, at least in Eritrea, the Organization's primary goal proved to be protecting the interests of existing member states, with the welfare of the populations concerned of secondary importance.

.5.

The Early Second-Generation Missions: 1989-1991

The late 1980s marked the formal beginning of the UN's new peacekeeping. After a generation-long hiatus following the Congo and West Irian operations, the UN's members allowed the Organization to assist states in executing long-term settlements to conflicts. In less than two and a half years, it would establish eight such missions—in Namibia (UNTAG), Central America (ONUVEN, ONUCA, ONUVEH, and ONUSAL), Western Sahara (MINURSO), and Angola (UNAVEM I and II). Some would be undertaken as part of the decolonization process; others were instituted to end regional conflicts left over from the Cold War; and one, in Haiti, responded to an attempt to establish democracy in a situation with few patently transnational repercussions.

This chapter analyzes these first of the new peacekeeping operations. In undertaking these missions, the Organization began to push the bounds of first-generation peacekeeping both operationally and conceptually. Significant, nonmilitary mandates would become well-accepted; and the UN's hesitancy to engage in peacekeeping that intersected with a state's domestic politics would greatly erode. Moreover, the challenges inherent in carrying out the three political functions of second-generation peacekeeping and maintaining impartiality when consent decays would reveal themselves. These operations would presage the even greater obstacles to the new peacekeeping faced in Cambodia.

THE KEY ADVANCE: UNTAG AND NAMIBIA

The major progression from the first generation of peacekeeping to the second occurred with the deployment of the United Nations Transition Assistance Group (UNTAG), the first UN peacekeeping mission, other than UNTEA, with a primarily nonmilitary mandate. UNTAG was to ensure the peaceful transfer of power in Namibia from the government of South Africa, which had been illegally administering the territory in defiance of the UN, to the people of Namibia. It would accomplish this goal by supervising the withdrawal of South African troops and, more important, overseeing, through the most assertive means up to that time, the election process to create a government of an independent state of Namibia.

Although UNTAG began its operations in 1989, the UN created it more than ten years earlier. In 1978, a five-state "Western Contact Group" (Britain, the United States, France, Germany, and Canada) issued a proposal to implement the 1976 Security Council resolution that had demanded "free elections in Namibia under the *supervision and control* of the United Nations." The proposal called for a large UN presence to scrutinize closely all South African activities related to the elections.[1]

Secretary-General Kurt Waldheim expanded upon the Contact Group's ideas in his own reports, envisaging an operation with a civilian component, consisting of civilian police and electoral workers, and a military component. As with all peacekeeping operations since UNEF I, it would operate with "complete impartiality" and the "full co-operation of all the parties concerned."[2] On September 29, 1978, the Security Council approved the Secretary-General's report, formally established UNTAG, and demanded that South Africa immediately cooperate with the UN.[3]

UNTAG could not deploy for more than ten years, however, because South Africa refused to accept it. As a result, the UN and its members, especially the United States, held protracted negotiations with South Africa over the terms for implementing the resolution. These centered on the linkage between South African troop withdrawal from Namibia and removal of Cuban troops from Angola.

This long delay in deploying UNTAG had two positive results, however. First, it gave the UN some lead time to organize the mission. The Special Representative of the Secretary-General, Martti Ahtisaari of Finland, made numerous visits to Namibia to determine the logistical requirements of UNTAG and began recruiting officials for the job long before its emplacement. UNTAG also developed training programs for its officials. In late 1988, South Africa, Angola, and Cuba agreed upon a date of April 1, 1989, for deploying UNTAG in Namibia, as well as UNAVEM I in Angola to monitor Cuban troop withdrawal.[4] Ahtisaari had a team in place by this time, although planners within the UN could not agree on the precise sizes of the components until the last moment, delaying much logistical preparation.[5]

Second, the hiatus permitted the UN to lay important parts of the political foundation for the mission. The Contact Group, for example, drafted constitutional principles for the new government. It also negotiated with South Africa over the respective roles of UNTAG, the UN Council for Namibia (created by the General Assembly in 1967 as the de jure administrator of the territory), and the General Assembly during the execution phase. These initiatives would have proved more difficult during the implementation.

1. The Breadth and Depth of UNTAG's Mission

The Namibia operation's composition reflected the multifarious agendas of the new peacekeeping.

• A military force of nearly 4,500 supervised an uneasy cease-fire and the confinement of South African forces to bases;

• A police component, eventually numbering 1,500, exercised close oversight over and later directly assisted the South West African police forces in an attempt to maintain law and order while respecting human rights and electoral fairness;

• An electoral division oversaw each stage of the election process, preparing a code of conduct for political parties, working with South African officials on an election law and procedures, and supervising voter registration and polling;

• UNHCR oversaw the repatriation of refugees; and

• Regional offices of UNTAG coordinated work in the provinces and engaged in a vast public information campaign regarding the elections.[6]

At UN Headquarters, the Secretary-General set up a high-level task force, chaired by his chef de cabinet and composed of three Under Secretaries-General (Special Political Affairs, African issues, and Legal Affairs), his senior military adviser, and a press spokesman. They tried to respond to the needs of the Special Representative, although the two centers of authority did not always agree on implementation questions.

From April 1, 1989, until the holding of elections November 7–11, UNTAG tried to perform its mandate, but the belligerents withheld complete cooperation. The first crisis nearly derailed the entire peace process. As UNTAG was arriving, more than 1,000 armed guerrillas of SWAPO (the South West Africa People's Organization, the primary force opposed to South African rule) infiltrated Namibia from Angola in violation of the cease-fire agreement. With only a small number of UN troops deployed, UNTAG could not deter the incursion.

It reluctantly bowed to South African demands to release its soldiers from their bases, and they soon repelled the SWAPO force in a bloody battle.

UNTAG exerted great, continuous pressure upon the South African authorities as well. It sought not just a technically fair election, but some approximation of a "level playing field" where voters would not feel intimidated. UNTAG negotiated with the government to revise its proposed electoral law to meet basic standards of fairness; to issue an amnesty and repeal discriminatory laws; to permit active UNTAG supervision of the polling; to eliminate the intimidation tactics of the South West African police force; and to open up the airwaves to UNTAG broadcasts. It had to mediate between the government and SWAPO constantly.

Despite these impediments, the elections themselves were conducted very smoothly, with a 97 percent turnout, no violence, and ballot secrecy preserved. Immediately after the vote tally, Ahtisaari could declare, in good faith, that a free and fair election had taken place, and he certified SWAPO as the winner. On March 21, 1990, the South African flag was lowered over the territory for the last time and Namibia became the world's newest state, ending a 70-year saga from League of Nations mandate to self-determination.

As the first of the modern new peacekeeping missions, UNTAG penetrated the Namibia political landscape with a significant depth of authority. It clearly surpassed the monitoring role—the most superficial depth of peacekeeping discussed in chapter 2—typical of most first-generation missions. It did not, however, involve itself at the level of direct conduct of the administration of Namibia, the deepest extent of authority, seen in the Saar or West Irian. Rather, South Africa continued to govern the area through its Administrator-General and to conduct the elections. But it exercised both supervision and control—the second and third levels of authority—in assisting in the transition to independence.

First, UNTAG's police functions included both monitoring and supervision. UN police followed South African police on missions and reported on their conduct, but also worked alongside them to induce respect for the integrity of the political process and the rights of Namibians. They could not order the police directly to take action. UNTAG's presence led to immediate improvements in police behavior, although the extent varied over time and across the territory with the cooperation of the individual police units. When UNTAG encountered especially uncooperative officers, it would investigate and refer the matter to political levels, whereupon South African authorities would eventually issue commands or replace personnel.

Nevertheless, the UN only belatedly managed to disband South Africa's counterinsurgency force known as Koevoet, and its former officers continued to intimidate SWAPO supporters. As polling neared and the South West African police force could not alone maintain a secure environment, UNTAG police performed these duties themselves.[7] UNTAG thus tried to serve as a guarantor of law and order in the territory. By acting proactively and reactively, it aimed to show the Namibian people that they could participate in the process to determine their future.

Second, with respect to the electoral process, UNTAG exercised a supervisory role, raising matters affecting the fairness of elections directly with South African officials and requesting changes in written codes or behavior by subordinates. The Security Council's 1978 authorizing resolution also gave UNTAG additional power, beyond supervision, that crossed the (admittedly blurry) line to control.[8] For example, the Administrator-General could make decisions regarding the modalities of the elections (as in the number of polling days, the locations of polling stations, actions barring individuals from voting or discounting their ballot) only with the consent of UNTAG.[9]

Furthermore, in order for each stage of the electoral process to advance, Ahtisaari had to certify that the previous stage had taken place to his satisfaction. Although the South African government officially conducted the elections, it needed UNTAG's approval for its actions during the entire process. During the polling, UNTAG personnel matched the South Africans almost one for one.[10] In the following months, UNTAG aided the elected constituent assembly in drafting the constitution. The UN thus moved beyond the observation role that crippled it in West Irian and more toward a guarantor of the fairness of elections.

2. The Legacy of UNTAG

Unlike ONUC, UNTAG's mission presented few basic challenges to the conceptual underpinnings of the new peacekeeping. Member states saw a clear role for the United Nations based on its historical oversight of the decolonization process. Within the Organization, beginning with Resolution 435 in 1978, the Security Council and the General Assembly had pursued separate paths in the peace process. During the final years, the Assembly and the UN Council for Namibia had to settle for a low profile on the issue, as the Security Council needed to create a perception of UN evenhandedness and allay South African fears about the impending UN mission.[11]

The South Africans and SWAPO consented to the presence of UNTAG, although both hindered its mission along the way, with the South Africans challenging various UNTAG actions as beyond its mandate. These necessitated additional Security Council resolutions and mediation by UNTAG, but never rose to the crisis level of ONUC. Moreover, both the South Africans and SWAPO accused UNTAG of showing favoritism toward the other. Unlike in the Congo, however, UNTAG did not find itself, at least after the April 1 incident, in the unenviable position of having to side with one party in a civil conflict in order to accomplish its mandate.

UNTAG's overall success underlined additional signposts for the new peacekeeping. First, by the time UNTAG deployed, the major antagonists had shown their clear readiness to end the dispute. This is essentially the obverse of the lesson of ONUC, namely, if the UN is to function effectively, a semblance of peace must prevail. A controlled military situation does not guarantee success, but it creates the prospect of one.

Encountering the full weight of international opinion, South Africa could not afford to oppose the UN too much; and SWAPO did not wish to risk an unfair election when it was certain to win a fair one. Though both tried to take advantage of the settlement, when pressured strongly by the United Nations, they ultimately cooperated and avoided recourse to arms. This greatly eased UNTAG's functions as executor and gave it considerable leverage as mediator. The Special Representative's power to certify each stage of the electoral process also gave him leverage, since he could block matters if he chose. On the other hand, at least one nongovernmental organization speculated that the time pressures upon Ahtisaari to complete the election may well have reduced his influence.[12]

Second, as an operational matter, UNTAG showed the importance of highly qualified personnel and detailed preparation. Ahtisaari, for example, had exceptional attributes and embodied the ideal Special Representative. He was an experienced and well-regarded diplomat; his prior position as the UN's Commissioner for Namibia made him a participant in the preparation of UNTAG's mandate and gave him unparalleled knowledge of the political situation and needs of the mission; and he served as the UN Under Secretary-General for Administration and Management during the formative years of UNTAG, providing it unique access to qualified staff and resources.

Along the way, numerous crises unfolded, and Headquarters sometimes saw Ahtisaari and his advisers as acting too favorably toward the South African authorities. But ultimately, they proved competent administrators and effective mediators. Achieving this degree of competence in future operations, whose underlying disputes would not tolerate the preparatory phase afforded UNTAG, would reveal the UN's lack of mechanisms to accelerate mobilization of sophisticated missions.

Finally, UNTAG followed a great investment of effort by the UN and individual states and faced few concurrent crises. Designed by powerful Western states, the plan also had the active support of the developing countries as furthering their decolonization and anti-apartheid agendas. Both groups saw this as a test case for the UN and supported it politically, although financial support came slowly. Equally important, UNTAG did not have to compete with other operations for the attention of the UN's senior leaders, the administrative bureaucracy, and the leading member states. The Cambodian conflict still lacked a solution; Yugoslavia remained one country; the Persian Gulf War seemed unimaginable; and the political instability in Somalia concerned few decision makers. Maintenance of the first-generation operations in the Middle East, Kashmir, Cyprus, and the Iran-Iraq border did not demand extensive oversight.

With a result that most states regarded as highly successful, UNTAG left the Organization elated with its accomplishment. As Secretary-General Perez de Cuellar stated in his 1990 Report:

> [T]he practicability of physically putting a solution in place through the management of the United Nations, given the requisite support of Member States, need no longer be in question. . . . The United Nations Transition Assistance Group in Namibia (UNTAG) turned out to be something far more than its somewhat pedestrian name implied. It . . . proved the executive ability of the United Nations in successfully managing a complex operation.[13]

UNTAG left its most important legacy for the new peacekeeping in the link it established between the operational aspects of earlier missions and the multifunctional mandates that define the second generation. The UN had to apply and combine its special legal, political, and technical competence over two distinct areas, military matters and decolonization. The tense security situation and need for a fair vote required the UN to deepen its involvement beyond that of its first-generation peacekeeping operations or its prior self-determination assistance efforts. This resulted in a mission whose operational complexity exceeded earlier cases by many orders of magnitude. It thus expanded the concept of peacekeeping to include electoral matters, police, human rights, and education functions.

MORE FOUNDATIONS LAID: THE LATIN AMERICAN OPERATIONS

With the winding down of the Cold War and the growing sense that the UN could engage in nontraditional tasks in the guise of peacekeeping operations, four new operations proliferated over a short period in the Western hemisphere. One, primarily electoral, attempted to monitor the establishment of democracy in Haiti. The other three, with mandates varying from military matters to electoral supervision to human rights oversight, emerged from agreements among the states of Central America to end ten years of internal and interstate conflict.

1. The UN Observer Mission to Verify the Electoral Process in Nicaragua (ONUVEN)

The dispatch in August 1989 of a team of officials under UN auspices to join the Organization of American States in overseeing elections in Nicaragua marked another sort of breakthrough in UN peacekeeping: for the first time, the UN participated in elections *within a member state*, not a non-self-governing territory. The idea for the mission originated in the 1987 peace accord among the five Central American states (Costa Rica, El Salvador, Guatemala, Honduras, and Nicaragua), commonly known as the Esquipulas II Agreement, in which they agreed:

> to invite the [OAS and] the United Nations . . . to send observers to verify that the electoral process has been governed by the strictest rules of equal access for all political parties to the communication media and by ample opportunities for organizing public demonstrations.[14]

Following Nicaragua's agreement in 1989 to hold elections and its request to the Secretary-General to send observers to "verify" that the process was "genuine during every stage,"[15] Javier Perez de Cuellar sent a study mission to Nicaragua and informed the General Assembly of his plans to set up a verification mission. Knowing the Assembly's members supported the peace plan and would not oppose his initiative, the Secretary-General informed them that he was setting up ONUVEN according to terms of reference that appeared in an exchange of letters with the Nicaraguan government.[16] Though he clearly had the backing of the UN's members, the Secretary-General legally relied upon his inherent authority under the Charter and the terms of an earlier General Assembly resolution that had requested him to support the Central American peace process.[17] Both the Assembly and Security Council supported the Secretary-General's decision in subsequent resolutions.[18]

ONUVEN, headed by American Elliot Richardson, worked in Nicaragua from late August 1989 through the February 1990 elections, along with an OAS counterpart mission. Although formally limited to verifying the fairness of the electoral process, ONUVEN contributed directly to that process. Through close oversight of Nicaraguan officials at each stage of the elections and throughout the country, it pointed out irregularities and prevailed upon the government to alter unacceptable behavior. It engaged in active mediation between the Sandinista government and the contras.

As a result, despite much resistance from the government, opposition parties were able to compete with the incumbents, and ONUVEN and the OAS monitors built some confidence among the Nicaraguan people about the reality of their choices and ballot secrecy.[19] During the polling, ONUVEN deployed 207 observers, who visited nearly half of all polling centers in Nicaragua. After the polling, it conducted a confidential "quick count" based on a sample of polling stations. This yielded an accurate prediction that would permit detection of any later tampering with the ballots or results.[20]

Although ONUVEN represented less of an operational challenge for the UN than UNTAG, it constituted a critical departure from the prior practice of the UN regarding elections. Seven years earlier, in a published opinion, the UN's Legal Counsel had strongly counseled against most UN involvement in elections within member states.[21] In 1990, the Secretary-General had to reconcile the Nicaragua case with earlier policy against such UN roles. He did so by emphasizing (a) its international dimension due to its link with the Central American peace process, as evidenced by the neighboring states' request to the UN; and (b) the General Assembly's prior endorsement of some form of UN verification during the peace process.[22]

But despite his promise to the Assembly that ONUVEN would have "no effect on established practice, nor would a precedent be set for possible further requests,"[23] ONUVEN had precisely that result. Deployed at the end of the Cold War, as more of the UN's members come to endorse free elections as the sole means to legitimate a government, it set a precedent for expanded UN roles in future elections. It reflected a shift in attitudes by states over the perennial questions of sovereignty and nonintervention as expressed in Article 2(7) and elsewhere. Member states could always follow Perez de Cuellar's lead and pigeonhole ONUVEN within traditional views of nonintervention, principally by pointing to Nicaragua's request for UN monitors as negating any worries. But, in the end, *res ipsa loquitur*—the thing speaks for itself. Previously, the UN would have avoided involvement in a country's domestic political campaign, because nobody would ask it and it had no interest in doing so, a conveniently self-reinforcing phenomenon.

ONUVEN's other distinguishing feature was its creation by the Secretary-General without the official, prior approval of a political organ. Perez de Cuellar, the Assembly, and the Council all wanted to act quickly and seemed ready to let the Assembly's vague endorsement in earlier resolutions of UN involvement stand as a sufficient legal and political basis for establishing ONUVEN. Their subsequent ratification of his actions gave him the political support he needed for his mission (vis-à-vis the parties in the region). It also satisfied member states' claims for an acknowledgment that he still served them and could not encumber the UN's resources without their concurrence.

2. The United Nations Observer Group in Central America (ONUCA)

During ONUVEN's tenure, the Security Council deployed a second, wholly military operation in the region: the United Nations Observer Group in Central America (ONUCA). Created in November 1989 to verify the military aspects of the Esquipulas II Agreement, the mission eventually had nearly 1,000 military observers in all five Central American states. Its military role began with supervision of a ban on outside assistance to the guerrilla movements in the countries concerned. Later, its mandate included oversight of a cease-fire and separation of forces in Nicaragua, and actual conduct of the cantonment, disarmament, and demobilization of the Nicaraguan contras.[24] Though ONUCA failed to detect many clandestine violations of the peace accords, it did facilitate national reconciliation within Nicaragua and the elections of 1990.

3. The United Nations Observer Group for the Verification of Elections in Haiti (ONUVEH)

The Haitian people's attempts to break the military's grasp on power and set up a democratic government also gave rise to new responsibilities for the UN. In the summer of 1990, the head of Haiti's then latest military-backed provisional government, Ertha Pascal-Trouillot, wrote Perez de Cuellar asking the UN to supervise the upcoming electoral process, including assisting in maintaining public order. The Latin American states in the General Assembly quickly prepared a draft resolution to accept the request.

Hesitant to send a mission into a situation with no clear international dimension (unlike the Nicaraguan elections), Perez de Cuellar decided to seek the views of the Security Council. The Council's members debated both the competence of the Organization under Article 2(7) of the Charter to dispatch a mission and the competence of the Assembly to authorize it, with Cuba and Mexico especially concerned. It ultimately acceded to the Assembly's desire to set up ONUVEH because it did not involve any military peacekeepers.[25] The General Assembly quickly approved the creation of ONUVEH on October 10, 1990, asking the Secretary-General "to provide the broadest possible support to the Government of Haiti" by observing and facilitating a secure environment for elections.[26]

The UN deployed a small mission to Haiti, which arrived in mid-October 1990, just nine weeks before the scheduled December elections. The observers included electoral experts funded by UNDP who advised the inexperienced government on the modalities of polling, electoral monitors, and public security advisers and observers. During the December elections, ONUVEH had 193 electoral observers and about 150 security personnel.

The observers viewed about 10 percent of the polling stations; the security personnel followed their Haitian counterparts in scattered areas of the country. The elections themselves occurred with virtually no disruptions, though ONUVEH found some irregularities due to poorly trained Haitian electoral staff. Building upon the Nicaraguan experience, it also utilized the quick count procedures to deter vote tampering. The Haitian people overwhelmingly elected Father Jean-Bertrand Aristide as President, and the UN certified the results as free and fair.[27]

In the months after the election, the General Assembly called for a series of emergency economic and civic education initiatives "in order to support the efforts by [Haiti's] people and Government in their struggle for democracy and economic survival."[28] The UN thus initiated a type of nation-building for a state that had never known democracy. In the end, that democracy proved short-lived: on September 30, 1991, a military coup ousted Aristide. He fled to the United States, and Haiti returned to its all-too-familiar autocracy.[29]

In the medium term, then, ONUVEH hardly yielded an outcome as satisfying as UNTAG or ONUVEN. It would appear that the operation was a success, but the patient died. The Assembly gave it a limited mandate, and it deployed, at a late time, few resources. It arrived in the midst of the registration process, with no power over the scheduling of the election; its small staff could not train Haitian officials properly and monitored only a small fraction of the polling sites on election day. The experience affirmed the importance of a monitoring presence covering the entire electoral process, which the UN would later underscore.[30]

Most important, ONUVEH's constrained mandate and short-term presence prevented it from initiating any process to preserve the electoral results over time. This the Haitian military may have predicted too well. For Haiti, a country with a history of military power grabs, the international community needed to begin actively supporting democracy before the elections, not afterward; but such an effort would have brought to light the intransigence of Haiti's military. Haiti's fate highlighted the link between nation-building and elections and the need for future missions to integrate them sooner.

Despite Haiti's return to oppressive rule, ONUVEH represented another turning point of sorts, for the UN crossed the line from deploying a second-generation mission (albeit a small one) only in situations with a clear interstate dimension to sending one into an essentially internal conflict. While the purely internal conflict is, in reality, a mythological beast—for instance, Haitian refugees greatly worried all her neighbors, especially the United States—the crisis in Haiti had minimal impact on regional security. By their actions, the member states and Perez de Cuellar signaled their acceptance of the notion of UN missions to oversee elections anywhere.[31] Beyond elections, ONUVEH suggested that the UN might deploy significant operations with nonmilitary mandates to respond to internal conflicts. Whatever ONUVEN had done to reflect and contribute to changed perceptions about sovereignty and nonintervention, ONUVEH appeared to go one step beyond.

Furthermore, the operation created an important precedent regarding the respective competence of the Council and the Assembly in creating new peacekeeping operations. Despite the Council's legalistic disclaimer that it might take up the Haiti matter again, its abnegation of authority meant that the Assembly could claim a right, based on precedent, to deploy peacekeeping missions as long as they lacked military forces, but even if they included public security components. It remains to be seen, however, whether the Council will prove so flexible in the future. It may well be that the small size of ONUVEH made the matter of secondary importance.

4. The United Nations Observer Mission in El Salvador (ONUSAL)

The next of the second-generation missions in Latin America took place in El Salvador as part of the regional peace process started by the Esquipulas II accords. In July 1990, the government of El Salvador and the opposition guerrillas of the Frente Farabundo Martí para la Liberacíon Nacional (FMLN) signed a landmark agreement on human rights as part of their political settlement ending ten years of civil war.[32] The accord contained a bill of rights for Salvadorans and a proposed mandate for a UN mission to verify the observance of those rights. It would monitor the human rights situation, investigate violations, and promote respect for human rights.

To help the Salvadoran parties carry out the agreement, the Security Council created ONUSAL in Resolution 693 of May 20, 1991. ONUSAL's mandate encompassed the monitoring of all existing and future agreements between the government and FMLN, but the Council limited its initial mission to the implementation of the human rights agreement already concluded. ONUSAL thus became the first UN peacekeeping mission with a primary mandate in the field of human rights. After the Salvadorans agreed in late December 1991 on a comprehensive peace accord, the Council expanded ONUSAL's mandate in January 1992 to cover military functions as well.[33] In May 1993, it was further enlarged to cover the monitoring of elections scheduled for 1994.[34]

ONUSAL deployed four divisions over time: the human rights, police, military, and electoral components. The human rights officials arrived in July 1991; the police and military units established the bulk of their presence with the expansion of ONUSAL's mandate in 1992; and the electoral officials came in large numbers in late 1993.[35] ONUSAL accomplished its military assignment only after many frustrating setbacks due to intransigence by the government and FMLN. Police monitoring proved less effective, as the armed forces, which had controlled the national police, were slow to surrender power to a newly trained outfit run by civilian authorities. ONUSAL's performance during the elections held in March and April 1994 was far from satisfactory. While the polling was generally fair and violence-free, many registered voters were unable to vote and illegal campaigning was not uncommon.

The human rights unit also achieved mixed results. ONUSAL helped improve the observance of human rights, especially through the close oversight of police, reporting of violations, and presentation of its findings to the government and the international community. Yet gross human rights abuses continued throughout the period of ONUSAL's mandate. ONUSAL also tried to conduct other nation-building activities, such as the transfer of land to ex-FMLN members; and reestablishment of governmental administration in former battle zones by aiding the return of local mayors who had fled earlier. In July 1992, the Secretary-General appointed a three-member Commission on Truth to investigate human rights violations during the 1980s. Its carefully researched report angered many within the military but may have facilitated the slow healing process of this fractured country.[36] The Salvadoran government has implemented only some of the Commission's recommendations for reform.

Though ONUSAL's work is not complete as of late 1994, some innovations in the new peacekeeping are already apparent. First, it demonstrated the applicability of the new paradigm to human rights missions, and indeed the possibility of deploying a human rights presence before or in lieu of a military force. In ONUSAL, the UN sent a mission to oversee a matter that cuts to the core of sovereignty and challenges a state's governance: the way it treats its citizens. It did not simply aim to ensure that the people could express their preferences freely among candidates, but that those in positions of power among the government and opposition respected citizens' rights.

Second, ONUSAL highlighted an evolution in the form of consent needed for the new peacekeeping. Unlike ONUVEN and ONUVEH, the invitation emanated not merely from a government, but also from a guerrilla force. Whereas the UN's pro-government approach had traditionally made it wary of working with guerrilla groups within states (except those recognized as liberation movements, such as SWAPO and the PLO), in El Salvador the UN needed to give equal treatment to a government and a well-organized opposition. The UN thus altered its view from that during the Congo episode. There, because member states wished to bolster the new government and marginalize the foreign-supported Katangese, it acted without a political settlement and with the consent of the government only.

Third, the integration of human rights into a peacekeeping operation introduced a special set of challenges to the UN's impartiality. ONUSAL had a mandate as executor to promote human rights and report on violations. Yet this often proved hard to reconcile with its role as mediator to move the parties along in the implementation of all the accords (not merely the human rights agreement). ONUSAL needed the government's cooperation, yet also had a responsibility to challenge ongoing serious violations of human rights.

The tensions within the operation represented a microcosm of a more fundamental dilemma for the UN: how to build peace in a shattered state when the Charter-mandated goals of advancing human rights and promoting the peaceful settlement of disputes seem to suggest opposite courses of action. Human rights observers would assert that the UN cannot act impartially toward human suffering, and that an emphasis upon human rights in the end advances the peacemaking process. Conciliators would argue precisely the reverse. The balance struck by ONUSAL did not satisfy all.[37]

Fourth, ONUSAL affirmed that the Security Council would interpret its responsibility for international peace to include human rights questions. Traditionally, the General Assembly had taken the lead in these issues, with the Council addressing them only secondarily in its deliberations on sanctions, international armed conflict, or humanitarian matters.[38] By emplacing ONUSAL to monitor human rights conditions even before the parties had concluded a final military settlement, the Council elevated human rights to at least an equal plane with the military elements of the settlement.

Finally, ONUSAL showed the possibility of a phased deployment of a new peacekeeping mission. If the parties to a conflict can only resolve their differences seriatim, rather than through a comprehensive accord, the UN can deploy a mission component by component. Each unit can try to push the peace process along as a confidence-builder (and thus guarantor), as well as administrator and on-site mediator. If the settlement looks toward future elections, the UN can lay the groundwork for them before dispatching a full electoral component.

UNRESOLVED OPERATIONS

Finally, in 1991 the Security Council authorized two additional second-generation operations that have thus far failed in their mandates and remained in a great state of flux as of late 1994. They are discussed here briefly with only the most tentative conclusions drawn at this date.

1. The UN Mission for the Referendum in the Western Sahara (MINURSO)

Western Sahara, the former Spanish colony in northwest Africa in which Morocco as occupier and the indigenous Frente Polisario have long competed for control, represents one of the last unresolved episodes in the UN's decolonization story. For many years, the Secretary-General had mediated between the two sides. When he at last had a settlement plan that the parties seemed to accept, the Council created MINURSO in April 1991 to implement it.[39] Under the plan, the UN was to deploy a large operation of civilian, security, and military units to oversee a demilitarization process and then organize and conduct a referendum.

Although several hundred military observers and a small number of police did deploy beginning in 1991, persistent disagreements between Morocco and the Polisario over the peace plan have halted its work. The dispute centers on voter eligibility, with the two sides at odds over Morocco's insistence on adding names of new residents sent by Morocco to a voter register based on a 1974 Spanish census. Intensive mediation by Boutros-Ghali and his Special Representative appeared to be yielding fruit by the middle of 1994, as the antagonists accepted a compromise plan on eligibility that would lead to a referendum in 1995.[40]

MINURSO is the latest, and likely last, peacekeeping mission undertaken as part of the UN's decolonization agenda. The UN proceeded with deployment in the absence of full consent to demonstrate its commitment to the principle of decolonization and to encourage the parties to compromise. Yet the issue languished because no state has backed up the Secretary-General's initiatives with sufficient pressure on the parties. In particular, Morocco's chief allies, the United States and France, have shown no taste for making Western Sahara an issue of importance in their relations with Morocco, and the UN has focused on more urgent matters.[41]

2. The UN Angola Verification Mission II (UNAVEM II)

The Security Council created UNAVEM II in May 1991 to supervise the peace agreement between Angola's government and the rebels of the National Union for the Total Independence of Angola (UNITA), an accord designed to end an especially bloody Cold War proxy conflict. Under its initial mandate, UNAVEM II was to verify a cease-fire and the demobilization of the warring armies. In March 1992, the Council enlarged the mandate to include observation of national elections and verification of their fairness.[42] UNAVEM II deployed a mere 350 military observers for the military-related duties, as well as a small police presence.

This modest contingent could not, however, verify the military arrangements, which both sides freely violated. For the electoral mission, UNAVEM II had 400 observers and 36 police monitors, a presence far too insubstantial for close oversight. The polling itself, held at the end of November 1992, nevertheless proceeded reasonably smoothly, with Special Representative Margaret Anstee declaring them "generally free and fair."[43] Yet within days of the elections, UNITA balked at the results, and Angola soon plunged back into civil war. Although most of UNAVEM II withdrew, the Council approved retention of a small contingent of observers to assist the UN in the peacemaking process and later imposed economic sanctions on UNITA.[44]

Although UNAVEM II remained a player in the peacemaking process, it proved unable to ensure any kind of transition to peace in Angola. The mission thus resembles ONUVEH, the first Haiti mission, in important respects: it operated in an atmosphere of the most tenuous consent, with UNITA especially willing to reject the peace process; and the parties and the Security Council give it a mandate and size too meager for the task at hand (although it was an improvement over the Haiti mission). Preoccupied with Yugoslavia, Cambodia, and then Somalia, the UN's members had little desire for a serious investment of time or resources in Angola. As a result, like Haiti, generally free elections took place, but the results collapsed. The UN was willing to continue UNAVEM II as a peacemaking mission, and the signature of a new peace accord by UNITA and the government in November 1994 increased the prospects that UNAVEM II may resume a second-generation peacekeeping role.

A LOOK BACK

While neither the League of Nations nor the United Nations affirmatively sought to establish foundations for second-generation peacekeeping, a review of their activities since 1920 provides ample evidence that the expansive missions since 1989 did not constitute completely sui generis undertakings. The League had governed the Saar territory for a respectably long period and organized an election for its future. Its mandate over Danzig, while less assertive, nevertheless involved constant oversight as required by the Treaty of Versailles. With the birth of the United Nations, peace agreements or proposals incorporated similar ideas—especially in Trieste and Jerusalem—but the Cold War and other rivalries prevented their effectuation.

During its first 40 years, member states generally kept the UN away from complex operations that might challenge their traditional presumptions that peacekeepers were truce observers and that intrusive missions would violate a state's sovereignty. The Congo left the UN fearful of sending the Organization into a volatile situation again; despite the modest successes of the civilian side in nation-saving, the UN concluded that it had best keep peacekeeping simple. Its one foray into international administration, in West Irian, represented a superficial triumph. But the brevity and relative simplicity of the mission, the predetermined outcome, and Indonesia's sabotage of the act of self-determination make it less appealing, if not offensive, in retrospect and less apposite to the current challenges.

The parallel operations outside the context of peacekeeping, however, showed more promise. From referendum-watching to innovative fact-finding, states called upon the UN as the sole legitimate actor to verify the will of colonial peoples.

By the late 1980s, the UN's ability to serve as administrator, mediator, and guarantor of political settlements faced a new set of scenarios. The UN started with an ambitious operation, UNTAG, but one comfortable from a doctrinal point of view and reasonably feasible operationally. From there, it moved to an internal situation, in Nicaragua, but again one that the international community could accept, as it seemed intertwined with peace and security in a regional context. In Haiti, this convenient rationalization disappeared, but the UN proceeded anyway, although belatedly. In El Salvador, the UN moved from the familiar ground of election oversight to the more sensitive area of human rights, asserting powers of investigation over local officials and intruding into previously forbidden sovereign areas.

The outcome of each operation, hardly uniform success, would depend upon the cooperation of the parties, the UN's political skills and operational capacity, and the willingness of outside states to support the mission and not just transfer the problem to the UN. But the pattern strongly suggested that one of Hammarskjold's core principles of peacekeeping during its first 30 years— the need to refrain from involvement in a country's internal politics—was proving increasingly anachronistic.

Among the UN's organs, the General Assembly's traditional oversight of decolonization and self-determination issues since the 1950s made it the logical body to set up the West Irian operation as well as the smaller missions in Libya and Eritrea. And the Security Council would acquiesce when the Assembly created the 1990 Haiti mission. But when full-fledged multifunctional operations were needed in the Congo, Namibia, El Salvador, Western Sahara, and Angola, the Council asserted its prerogatives inherited from the first-generation missions. By the 1990s, it was assuming the leading role in establishing second-generation missions. Both political organs gladly delegated operational control of the mission to the Secretary-General and his deputies, and in several cases (North Borneo, Bahrain, and Nicaragua) even allowed him to dispatch them on his own. The sharing of responsibilities seemed to be functioning without significant power clashes or disruptions.

As for the causal linkages between the earlier episodes and the second-generation operations, clearly one must reject any notion of a tide of history leading inexorably from the League of Nations to the new peacekeeping. The accumulation of case law works far more subtly. Instead, these efforts laid the groundwork for the newer missions by building among the UN's members a sense that the Organization could play a direct, operational role in facilitating difficult political transitions, such as transfers of territory or independence of colonies. Governments came to read the Charter more dynamically and, over time, to have fewer doubts about the UN's legal, political, and administrative competence to carry out these missions.

Thus, even if decision makers do not recall each case from 1920 until the late 1980s, these precedents have had a cumulative effect by demonstrating to both the Secretariat and the member states that the UN has not leaped into a conceptual or operational void with the new peacekeeping. Indeed, decision makers would remember and appraise the suitability of the major early missions (such as the Congo and West Irian) as models for the new ones. And some precedents also built actual expertise within the UN, as seems the case regarding elections, for instance. Most important, though, the older missions exerted a pull that reduced the resistance among member states to more expansive, and not simply military, variations of peacekeeping. This resistance weakened further with each of the second-generation missions.

By late 1991, the United Nations had to prepare for its biggest task yet in the realm of peacekeeping: a massive operation, the largest since ONUC, that would combine the functions of many prior missions and add mandates reminiscent of the Saar and West Irian—direct conduct of elections and control and supervision over governmental administration. That undertaking would not constitute an "operation," "observer mission," or even "force," but an "authority": the United Nations Transitional Authority in Cambodia.

Part III

■

The Cambodia
Experience

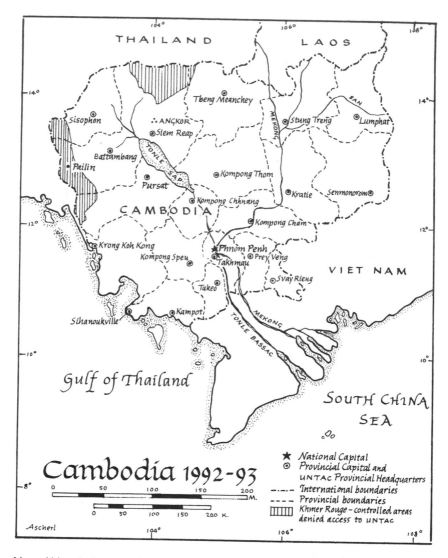

Cambodia 1992-93

	National Capital
	Provincial Capital and UNTAC Provincial Headquarters
—·—·—	International boundaries
– – –	Provincial boundaries
▥	Khmer Rouge–controlled areas denied access to UNTAC

Ascherl

Note: Although the map indicates only those areas under firm Khmer Rouge control and to which UNTAC was denied access, the Khmer Rouge conducted operations through-out Cambodia.

CHAPTER

.6.

Cambodia: Unending Conflict, Uncertain Solution

The long, sad history of the Cambodia conflict required any new peace-keeping mission to address numerous elements: a civil war among four factions, each of which had governed Cambodia since its indepen-dence; invasion by a neighbor seeking regional hegemony; external assistance to the factions, including from the major powers; a history of genocide and other gross violations of human rights; a vast refugee problem; thousands or millions of undetected mines; and a devastated economic infra-structure. To respond to this calamity, the UN created the most ambitious peacekeeping operation ever, combining all the tasks attempted in earlier missions with unprecedented duties. It pushed the administrative and political limits of the Organization beyond all earlier missions.

UNTAC represents an especially rich, as well as ripe, case study for detailed consideration and critical appraisal. It was a quintessential second-generation operation, charged by the Security Council with assisting the factions in Cambodia to execute a treaty purportedly settling comprehensively their con-flict. It had a multifaceted mandate—military and internal security matters, human rights, electoral conduct, governmental administration, economic reha-bilitation, and refugee repatriation. It taxed the UN logistically more than any operation to that time since ONUC. It engaged nearly the full panoply of actors involved in the new peacekeeping, within and outside the Organization.

Yet the consent necessary for carrying out its duties eroded almost from the beginning. As a result, the mission had to adjust its mandate over time as well as engage in a continuous process of decision making that pitted its need for impartiality against the demands for advancing the settlement plan. UNTAC was administrator of the Paris accords as well as mediator when the factions failed to cooperate.

Thus the following chapters not only recount UNTAC's place in the Cambodia peace process; more important for our purposes, they seek to review UNTAC from the perspective of the conceptual underpinnings of the new peacekeeping and the historical developments within the League and UN. UNTAC's performance is also, where feasible, compared with unfolding peacekeeping and peace enforcement operations in the former Yugoslavia and Somalia. As more data on UNTAC (and other missions) become available, its performance can be evaluated anew, and through different lenses.

An examination of UNTAC sheds light on a range of new questions that participants in second-generation operations must now begin to answer. This inquiry cuts across all missions, even though future operations will necessarily occur in different political settings and may have smaller or larger mandates than UNTAC. In particular, the ensuing chapters address these questions:

• Under what circumstances did the world community endorse the new peacekeeping as a means of settling this conflict? What weight was given to the international vs. the internal aspects of the conflict?

• What quality of consent did the UN's members demand before deploying UNTAC?

• How administratively prepared was the Organization to deploy UNTAC, especially its civilian divisions?

• What accounts for the differences in readiness and competence of the different parts of UNTAC?

• What courses of conduct were open to UNTAC when consent dissipated?

• How did the attitude of outside powers, especially those on the Security Council, toward Cambodia and other crises affect the decision-making process and the outcomes chosen?

• What approaches did UNTAC use or neglect in balancing its administrator, mediator, and guarantor roles?

• To what extent did the mission preserve the perception of impartiality critical to the new peacekeeping?

• How did UNTAC's leadership manage and coordinate the work of thousands of people in a large second-generation mission?

• How do UN civil servants exercise governmental administration and utilize other authority ostensibly given them by the Council and the parties?

• What aspects of the legacies of earlier missions did UN Headquarters and UNTAC overtly or implicitly incorporate in carrying out the mandate?
• How does one judge the success of a mission such as UNTAC?

The case study begins with an attempt to shed light on the circumstances behind this critical advance for the new peacekeeping. This chapter does so by describing the process by which the relevant actors in the international community arrived at UNTAC as an integral component of the solution to the Cambodian war, and the role for UNTAC foreseen in the peace accords that followed. The decision to deploy UNTAC was neither inevitable, orderly, nor uncontroversial. The actors involved did not begin from the standpoint of today, where parties to a conflict almost instinctively call for a UN presence in resolving their dispute. Instead, they arrived at UNTAC after frustration with other means, and haltingly constructed a creative structure for expansive and intrusive peacekeeping. This new operation was built upon earlier precedents of the League and UN, but transcended them in the breadth and depth of responsibility for the UN in a member state.

FAILED NATIONHOOD, CAMBODIA-STYLE

The conflict that gave rise to UNTAC recounts a story of a country at war with neighbors and itself for much of its modern history.[1] Once a great empire during the Angkor period (11th–13th centuries), for most of the last 700 years, Cambodia has lost territory, population, and regional power to its two larger neighbors, Vietnam and Thailand. France established a protectorate over the country in 1863, governing it along with Laos and the jewel in the Indochina crown, Vietnam. The French imported large numbers of Vietnamese as civil servants for their colonial administration. France also incorporated into Vietnam territory along the eastern Mekong River populated predominantly by ethnic Cambodians and once part of Cambodia (lower Cambodia or "Kampuchea Kraom").

In 1941, the Vichy French government elevated eighteen year-old Norodom Sihanouk to the throne of Cambodia. Sihanouk ruled the country for the next 29 years, under French, then Japanese control, and finally as sovereign when the French granted Cambodia independence in 1953. The nation developed slowly economically, as Sihanouk invested heavily in public infrastructure and education. He also acted ruthlessly to his opponents on the left and right and tolerated rampant corruption by his supporters and subordinates. Though he used his considerable skills to keep his country out of the main fronts of the

Vietnam War during the 1960s, he could not resist pressure from Vietnamese communists to allow transit of material to South Vietnam and to permit Vietcong sanctuaries in Cambodia. The Nixon Administration responded by organizing a massive bombing campaign against Cambodia beginning in 1969.

In March 1970, a group of conservative generals and civilians overthrew Sihanouk while he was out of the country. Led by General Lon Nol, the new government renamed the country the Khmer Republic and adopted a pro-American stance in the Vietnam War. The opposition Communist Party of Kampuchea, or Khmer Rouge, turned its energies on the weak Lon Nol regime. It garnered support in the countryside through often horrific methods and ultimately gained Sihanouk himself as an ally. After a five-year bloody war, the Khmer Rouge marched into Phnom Penh on April 17, 1975.

The next three and a half years constituted the era of "Democratic Kampuchea," the Khmer Rouge's appellation for the country.[2] The regime attempted a total restructuring of Khmer society, including a rejection of all foreign influences and heavy reliance on a communal agrarian economy. The central government engineered, encouraged, or tolerated massive human rights violations. It executed supporters of the old regime, educated citizens, ethnic minorities, monks, and their families; and its policies led to extensive loss of life in the countryside due to starvation, exhaustion, and disease. Although the exact number of deaths remains uncertain, estimates are that more than a million perished out of an April 1975 population of 7.3 million.[3] Democratic Kampuchea also turned aggressive against its former ally of Vietnam, conducting savage cross-border raids that left hundreds of Vietnamese civilians dead.

In response to these attacks, Vietnam invaded Cambodia on December 25, 1978, sweeping across the country. By January 9, 1979, it had occupied Phnom Penh and installed a puppet regime, the People's Republic of Kampuchea (PRK), led by ex-Khmer Rouge cadre who had fled to Vietnam during purges within the government. Democratic Kampuchea's army and leaders, along with hundreds of thousands of ordinary Cambodian citizens, fled to Thailand in the next year. The Khmer Rouge occupied small rural areas in Cambodia, primarily near the Thai border.

The UN's response to the crises in Cambodia had a certain predictability. During the Democratic Kampuchea years, the lack of information flowing out of the country hampered international involvement in the human rights nightmare, and Democratic Kampuchea's supporters insisted it was simply pursuing its path to social and economic development. In 1978, however, stories from refugees fleeing Cambodia prompted Canada, Norway, Britain, the United States, and Australia to raise the matter of Cambodian atrocities in the

UN Human Rights Commission. After Democratic Kampuchea refused to cooperate with any investigation, the chairman of the Commission's Sub-Commission on Prevention of Discrimination and Protection of Minorities prepared a detailed analysis based on information provided by the governments and nongovernmental organizations.[4] In an overabundance of caution, the report did not take a final position on the credibility of the reports, but urged the Commission to give Cambodia the "highest priority."[5] Before the Commission could act on that report, however, Vietnam had conquered Democratic Kampuchea.

The Vietnamese invasion, however, triggered an immediate response by friends of Democratic Kampuchea, adversaries of Vietnam and the Soviet Union, and the majority of non-aligned states that viewed the attack as a threat to small states everywhere. In the Security Council, the Soviet Union vetoed in early 1979 a resolution to condemn the invasion. That fall, the General Assembly voted overwhelmingly to denounce the invasion and demand the immediate withdrawal of "foreign forces."[6] When representatives of the PRK requested accreditation as Cambodia's legal representatives, the Assembly rejected their credentials and continued to seat delegates of Democratic Kampuchea, notwithstanding growing knowledge of its atrocities. At the urging of the Association of Southeast Asian Nations (ASEAN), the Assembly convened a special conference, the International Conference on Kampuchea (ICK).

Seventy-nine states attended the July 1981 conference, including Democratic Kampuchea, represented by its second-highest official, Ieng Sary, an architect of Khmer Rouge atrocities. The Soviet-bloc states boycotted it, seeing the conference as predisposed against Vietnam, and thereby preventing any chance for effective peacemaking. After five days, it adopted a declaration that emphasized the need to restore Cambodia's territorial integrity, but scarcely mentioned human rights.[7] It also set up an Ad Hoc Committee to undertake peacemaking efforts, and Secretary-General Kurt Waldheim appointed a Special Representative, Rafeeuddin Ahmed, to follow the issue.

The annual General Assembly resolutions on Cambodia during much of the 1980s reflected the opinion of most interested governments on the key elements of a future settlement: (a) withdrawal of Vietnamese forces; (b) creation of an interim administering authority; (c) national reconciliation under Prince Sihanouk; (d) restoration of Cambodia's independence and territorial integrity; (e) the right of Cambodians to determine their own destiny free of outside intervention; and (f) "effective guarantees" to achieve these ends. In a small gesture suggesting abhorrence of the Khmer Rouge, the Assembly did not call for the restoration of the government of Democratic Kampuchea, which still held Cambodia's UN seat.[8]

From 1981 to 1987, a military stalemate prevailed. The Vietnamese army dominated the country, except for small areas controlled by the Khmer Rouge and two smaller resistance groups—FUNCINPEC (Front Uni Nationale Pour Un Cambodge Indépendant, Neutre, Pacifique, et Coopératif), led by Sihanouk and his son Norodom Ranariddh; and the KPNLF (Khmer People's National Liberation Front), a pro-Western group led by Son Sann, a prime minister under Sihanouk, but with many sympathizers of the Lon Nol regime. Severe fighting often erupted, including a Vietnamese offensive in 1985 that spilled over into Thailand. The resistance received arms from China and ASEAN states, and other aid from Western states, including the United States. The resistance accused Vietnam of encouraging large numbers of Vietnamese to colonize Cambodia. Vietnam often spoke of "the genocidal crimes of the Pol Pot clique," asserting, with both justification as well as rationalization, that it had saved Cambodia. As for the PRK, it managed to offer Cambodians some chance to rebuild and recover after the horrors of Democratic Kampuchea, but the West, China, and ASEAN ostracized it diplomatically and cut it off economically.[9]

On the political front, in 1982, at the urging of China, ASEAN, and the United States, FUNCINPEC, the KPNLF, and the Khmer Rouge joined forces to create a Coalition Government of Democratic Kampuchea (CGDK). This semblance of a united opposition front was meant to muster international support for a resistance army still dominated by the Khmer Rouge. While the UN engaged in extensive humanitarian efforts on behalf of Cambodians in Thai camps through the United Nations Border Relief Operation and UNHCR, diplomatic efforts by the Ad Hoc Committee of the ICK and the Special Representative of the Secretary-General appeared to lead nowhere. The annual General Assembly resolution on Cambodia passed with increasing majorities, but no side had any interest in negotiation or compromise.[10]

A NEGOTIATING PROCESS BEGINS

The international community's acceptance of an expansive UN presence as the best possible solution to the Cambodia conflict emerged only after a long process in which interested states explored and exhausted other avenues. Beginning in 1987, many of the key antagonists grew frustrated with the war, opening up the possibility for diplomatic initiatives to create some prospect of a solution. The Indonesian Foreign Minister, Mochtar Kusuma-Atmadja, taking advantage of both his country's leadership position in ASEAN and its long-term ties with Vietnam, pushed his idea of an informal gathering, or "cocktail party," of the Khmer factions. The PRK issued its own peace plan, and the Soviet Union, under President Gorbachev, encouraged Vietnam to negotiate a settlement. Prince Sihanouk agreed to meet PRK Prime Minister Hun Sen for "cocktails for two," which occurred in the Paris suburb of Fère-en-Tardenois in December 1987 and January 1988.[11]

In July 1988, Indonesia, determined to broaden participation in the peace process to include Vietnam, convened the Jakarta Informal Meeting (JIM), inviting the four Cambodian factions, Vietnam and Laos, and the other members of ASEAN—Thailand, the Philippines, Malaysia, Singapore, and Brunei. The JIM's communiqué, the first consensus document in the peace process, stressed the need for a comprehensive settlement of the internal and external elements of the conflict, as well as Cambodian self-determination and national reconciliation. The JIM met again in February 1989.[12] Despite the agreed communiques, however, the Cambodia factions remained far apart on the means for such reconciliation.[13]

The negotiations took on increased urgency in April 1989, when Vietnam announced that it would withdraw all its troops from Cambodia by September 30. ASEAN and the United States feared that a withdrawal without a settlement would lead to a de facto acceptance of the PRK. At the same time, France, seeking to advance its national interests in a peaceful Indochina, expressed its desire to host an international conference on Cambodia. After another Sihanouk–Hun Sen meeting, the governments of France and Indonesia agreed to convene the Paris Conference on Cambodia, inviting all interested players to attend: the four factions, the six ASEAN states, Laos and Vietnam, the Security Council's five permanent members, Australia and Japan (as the other large interested states in East Asia) and several others—India (which had historic and cultural ties with Cambodia and had served on an international commission monitoring compliance with the 1954 Geneva Accords on Indochina); Canada (which had served with India); and Zimbabwe, invited as then-chairman of the Non-Aligned Movement. The Conference opened on July 30, 1989, at Paris' Kléber Center.

The 1989 Paris Conference became the turning point for the creation of UNTAC, for it highlighted the intractability of the Cambodian factions about sharing power. France and Indonesia attempted to forge such an agreement before the conference, but achieved only a superficial, and rather amusing, success — the four delegations would sit side-by-side behind a very long nameplate marked "Cambodge." As a result, the conference had to address the internal and external aspects of the conflict simultaneously.

It set up four committees for this purpose—on military aspects, international guarantees, economic rehabilitation and refugees, and a fourth, comprising the four factions and the two cochairs, to arrive at, in the words of the conference's mandate, "a quadripartite interim authority under the leadership of Prince Norodom Sihanouk with . . . responsibility of organizing . . . internationally supervised free elections."[14] The term "interim authority" reflected a compromise between the resistance's demand for a coalition government and the PRK's insistence on an advisory council subordinate to it. While the other three committees made substantial progress in preparing parts of the settlement on the international dimension of the settlement, the Ad Hoc Committee foundered on the core question of power-sharing. With no solution in sight, the conference adjourned after one month.

The Paris Conference left the international community frustrated. After a huge investment of time, diplomacy, and money, the Cambodian factions still seemed unready for peace. The West, moreover, which had supported Sihanouk since the early 1980s and still saw the non-communist resistance (FUNCINPEC and the KPNLF) as Cambodia's best option, saw further delays as harmful to their interests. Public support for the non-communists was eroding due to their alliance with the Khmer Rouge; the PRK, renaming itself the State of Cambodia (SOC), was moderating its behavior, for example, by restoring Buddhism as the state religion and permitting forms of capitalism; and the Vietnamese did indeed withdraw their combat forces from Cambodia. Yet the PRK feared the possibility of continued diplomatic isolation, the disengagement of the Soviet Union, and the guerrilla campaign of the Khmer Rouge.

Into this frustration the idea of UNTAC took hold. UNTAC's intellectual father was Congressman Stephen Solarz of New York, who, before and after the 1989 Paris Conference, proposed the idea of some type of UN management over Cambodia prior to elections. Although diplomats had casually mentioned the notion of a "trusteeship" over Cambodia earlier in the peace process, only Solarz persisted in advocating it to overcome the impasse on power-sharing.[15] He convinced the Australian Foreign Minister, Gareth Evans, of the idea's merits.

Evans endorsed it publicly in November 1989 and dispatched his diplomats to world capitals to sell the concept.[16] Simultaneously, the United States sought to salvage and influence the peace process by building on improved cooperation within the Security Council at the end of the Cold War, and advocated consultations among its five permanent members on a settlement. Thus the substance of a UN-dominated solution for Cambodia was married to a procedure making the Council the forum for peacemaking.

The concept of UNTAC thus originated from outside the Organization, from several diplomatic players seeking a way out of the ongoing impasse. Indeed, this had to be so: Ahmed and his team could not have proposed such a far-reaching plan, for the permanent members of the Security Council would have likely regarded it as irresponsible for international civil servants to make such an overture. Just as had occurred with the Namibia settlement plan, the powerful and interested states had to design and back the idea first, with UN officials providing intellectual legwork, but not leadership, along the way.

The Permanent Five met first in January 1990 in New York and took up the concepts in the Solarz-Evans plan, endorsing what they termed "an enhanced UN role."[17] In four subsequent meetings, they hammered out the details of their plan. By the summer of 1990, two competing visions of a UN role had emerged: one, backed by the Soviet Union, saw the UN monitoring the two competing governments—the SOC and the resistance's National Government of Cambodia (NGC)—to observe whether they were taking any action to undermine a fair election. The other, supported by China, advocated dismantling the SOC (and NGC) in favor of a direct UN administration of Cambodia.

At meetings in July and August 1990, the Five arrived at a compromise: the UN would exercise "direct . . . supervision or control" over five areas of civilian administration—foreign affairs, defense, security, information, and finance. These were viewed as critical to a "neutral political environment" for free and fair elections. The UN would also supervise the other functions of the two governments. The two governments, or "existing administrative structures" as they were called, would not disappear, but the UN would ensure that they acted consistent with a "neutral political environment" for elections.[18]

On other matters, the Permanent Five agreed early in their talks that, to ensure the fairness of the elections, the UN would organize and conduct them, a novel approach to holding elections in a country long dominated by one regime. They also laid out principles for other aspects of the settlement, including military arrangements, human rights, and international guarantees. On August 28, 1990, they issued their plan, the "Framework Document," that became the blueprint for the peace accord signed 14 months later.[19]

During this process, the Five consulted with those Khmer forces they were supporting politically, economically, or militarily. In particular, China and the USSR, as the chief arms suppliers to the resistance and the SOC, respectively, discussed the Five's work with their Cambodian allies, prodding them to accept elements of the emerging plan and representing their concerns in the Five's deliberations. The Cambodian factions also met and somewhat narrowed their differences, most significantly at a Tokyo round in June 1990 (although the Khmer Rouge boycotted that parley).

But other external factors underlay the new consensus. Most critically, Vietnam and China, the ancient adversaries in whose hands lay the key to a solution to the conflict, saw the need for a rapprochement due to their isolation at the end of the Cold War. That new relationship hinged on removing the chief obstacle to that goal, the Cambodian conflict. Their bargain, struck at Chengdu in September 1990, accepted the Permanent Five's plan as protecting each client's interests: the Vietnamese-installed SOC would remain in place, but the UN's powers would help bolster the resistance.[20] In addition, the change in Soviet foreign policy near the end of the Cold War led to Soviet endorsement of a plan that would ultimately result in the demise of the regime it supported in Phnom Penh for more than ten years. Finally, ASEAN, once a firm backer of the resistance, accepted the need for compromise. Its changed stance stemmed from both the election in 1988 of a more conciliatory Thai government, led by Chatichai Choonhavan, and the acceptance that the war had too long hampered ASEAN's goal of a peaceful and prosperous region.[21]

The four factions endorsed the Framework Document in its entirety on September 10, 1990. They also agreed to form the "Supreme National Council" (SNC) foreseen in the Framework Document as a body for national reconciliation and repository of Cambodian sovereignty in lieu of either competing regime, appointing six members from the SOC and two each from the three resistance factions. Assisted by Indonesia (as cochairman of the Paris Conference) and experts from the UN Secretariat, the Permanent Five transformed the Framework Document into a detailed draft settlement agreement by the end of November.[22] The resistance endorsed the draft in its entirety, but the SOC objected to provisions on military arrangements requiring full demobilization of its forces and suggesting UN control over the SOC before elections. Diplomatic momentum dissipated, however, by the end of 1990, as the major powers turned from peacemaking in Cambodia toward war-making in the Persian Gulf.

By the late spring of 1991, the SNC's members were prodded by the leading diplomatic actors to convene a series of meetings in Bangkok, Pattaya (Thailand), and Beijing, with France, Indonesia, and UN Secretariat officials. China and Vietnam, ready for compromise, continued to pressure the Khmer Rouge and the SOC, respectively. After intense negotiations, the Cambodian factional leaders elected Prince Sihanouk as president of the SNC and amended the draft peace accords to grant him special powers to break deadlocks in the SNC during the implementation of the accord (more on this later). They also compromised over demobilization of their military forces so that the weakening SOC would not lose its entire army. By October 1991, the factions seemed to have reached agreement, and the Paris Conference reconvened at the Kléber Center for a grand ceremony in which the 19 participating states signed the peace accords.[23]

THE PLAN: THE PARIS ACCORDS' VISION FOR UNTAC

The peace agreements signed on October 23, 1991, adopted a two-pronged approach to the settlement of the Cambodia conflict: a set of commitments aimed at resolving the international elements of the dispute, and another directed toward the struggle among the warring factions.[24] At the center of all these undertakings, as peacekeeper, civil administration overseer, human rights monitor and educator, election organizer, and more stood UNTAC. (See appendix II.)

1. Contrived Consent: The Supreme National Council and UNTAC

On one level, the Paris accords followed earlier models for consent, in that they constituted a written agreement, the legally firmest starting point for an operation. But the Permanent Five's plan for an enhanced UN role to overcome the impasse on power-sharing also gave birth to a radical new application of the concept of consent. The UN would need that consent for its operation because any suggestion of a UN trusteeship over Cambodia, however appealing, ran afoul of the UN Charter, which prohibits trusteeships over UN member states.[25] And although the Security Council could have conceivably approved a peace enforcement action under Chapter VII of the Charter, the Permanent Five had no desire to dispatch a large UN presence to impose a settlement upon unwilling factions. Thus, like all missions since UNEF I in the Sinai, UNTAC would require the consent of the host state. As with earlier second-generation missions involving conflicts with an internal dimension, such as ONUSAL, the consent of the host state equated with an invitation from both the government and the opposition.

This need for dual consent, however, confronted a difficult reality: both the PRK and the resistance (which still held Cambodia's UN seat) claimed to be Cambodia's government. UN member states held different positions on this question, from recognition of the SOC by the Soviet Union and its allies, to recognition of the NGC by China and others, to nonrecognition of either regime by the United States.[26] To circumvent the question of which entity constituted the government and which the opposition, the Five invented the idea of the Supreme National Council to include representatives from all four factions. It would serve as "the unique legitimate body and source of authority in which, throughout the transitional period, the sovereignty, independence and unity of Cambodia are enshrined,"[27] standing above the two "governments" until the formation of a government following elections.

The Paris accords envisaged the SNC's primary purpose as consenting to the operation by delegating to UNTAC the authority needed to implement the settlement. The drafters also hoped that the SNC could serve as a forum for reconciliation and even some governance, but the long acrimony among the factions left them dubious of that prospect. The UN thus obtained the consent of the relevant Cambodian parties through invention of a new, legally competent actor on the Cambodian stage, though one presumably politically impotent.

In granting its consent to UNTAC, the SNC would not, however, lack all legal authority. The agreements define specific relationships between UNTAC and the SNC. UNTAC would have to comply with the SNC's views, or, in the words of the accords, "advice," on any aspect of the settlement if (a) the SNC spoke unanimously or Prince Sihanouk, its president, provided the views on the Council's behalf; and (b) the advice was "consistent with the objectives of the present Agreement" *as determined by the chief of UNTAC,* the Special Representative of the Secretary-General. If the SNC did not provide views to UNTAC or the Special Representative found them incompatible with the goals of the agreement, the Special Representative would retain the prerogative to act as he wished.[28] Finally, UNTAC had complete plenary power over electoral matters, regardless of the SNC's "advice."

This formula reflected the political realities of the Cambodian conflict. If the twelve Cambodians representing the four factions could agree upon a course of action, or Prince Sihanouk relied upon his stature to speak on behalf of the SNC, the Special Representative could only reject its views if he found them inconsistent with the objectives of the accords. But it also created a potentially extraordinarily powerful UN mission, as the Special Representative could act whenever the SNC proved deadlocked (and Prince Sihanouk chose not to resolve the matter), and could overrule *all* the factions if he found their decision inconsistent with the settlement. While the settlement struck a careful balance between the need to respect Cambodian wishes and the urgency of implementing the settlement, it also empowered a peacekeeping mission with authority the UN had not asserted since the West Irian mission.

2. The Mandate: Breadth and Depth of UNTAC's Powers

Beyond UNTAC's authority vis-à-vis the SNC that served as the consensual basis for its mission, the Paris agreements also entrusted UNTAC with complicated assignments to implement the settlement. To undertake them, UNTAC would have to interact continuously with the entities that had actual control over Cambodia, namely the SOC (occupying 90 percent of the territory) and the three resistance groups.

Military Functions: Like the settlements in Namibia and El Salvador, the Paris accords included provisions to end the military conflict and create a peaceful environment for elections. Unlike the first-generation operations, UNTAC would not merely observe a cease-fire, but, like UNTAG and ONUSAL, oversee a wide array of activities aimed at ending permanently the military struggle. UNTAC would verify the withdrawal and non-return of Vietnamese troops; determine the timing of and monitor the cease-fire among the factions; establish a plan for, and then supervise, the regroupment, cantonment, and demobilization of the factional forces; receive and guard their weapons and equipment; monitor the ban on outside assistance along Cambodia's land and sea frontiers; locate and destroy caches of weapons; assist the International Committee of the Red Cross with prisoner exchanges; and contribute to mine-clearing operations. Like other peacekeeping missions, it had no mandate to force compliance with any of the factions' obligations.

To allow UNTAC to accomplish these missions, the agreements required the factions to provide the numbers and positions of, and weapons possessed by, their forces, and the location of arms caches, external resupply routes, and mines; Cambodia's neighbors were to inform UNTAC of the routes and means by which military aid was funneled to the factions; and UNTAC was to receive (the accords do not specify from whom) details regarding the withdrawal of foreign troops.[29]

Civil Administration: Prior to the Permanent Five's plan for an enhanced UN role, the UN had envisaged inserting its personnel into the Cambodian bureaucracy to work with functionaries to improve the administrative machinery, similar to the OPEX program (operational, executive, and administrative personnel) used by the UN in earlier days as a form of technical assistance.[30] Under the Paris accords, however, for the first time, the UN would be authorized to undertake key aspects of the civil administration of a member state. Although UNTAC would not itself administer the country, the Paris agreement called for it to control, oversee, and work through the existing regimes according to a three-tiered scheme.[31] UNTAC's power extended in theory over all governmental structures the four factions had created in the zones they controlled. As a practical matter, the accords would mainly concern the State of Cambodia.

 • First, "all administrative agencies, bodies and offices acting in the field of foreign affairs, national defence, finance, public security and information," the five areas most important to creating conditions for fair elections, would be placed "under the direct control of UNTAC."[32] The Special Representative could exercise whatever control he deemed necessary to ensure their strict neutrality, including by issuing binding directives.

 • Second, UNTAC would maintain "supervision or control" over any other governmental components that "could directly influence the outcome of elections,"[33] such as agencies responsible for education, agriculture, fisheries, and communications. The assumption was that these activities could impinge on electoral neutrality if administered in a partisan manner. Civilian police would operate under such supervision or control, and UNTAC would supervise other law enforcement and judicial processes to protect law and order and human rights. The Special Representative could issue "guidance" to these agencies, but legally this guidance would be as binding as the directives he issued to the bodies under direct control.[34]

• Third, UNTAC would intervene least in those agencies that the Special Representative judged "could continue to operate in order to ensure normal day-to-day life in Cambodia."[35] These organs, charged with less-politicized matters such as cultural affairs, would not be subject to supervision or control, but the Special Representative could conduct investigations to ascertain if they were subverting the settlement's objectives and take corrective steps.

The accords included two significant authorities for the Special Representative: first, with respect to all governmental entities, he could insert UN personnel with access to all operations and documents; second, he could require the removal or reassignment of any Cambodian personnel.[36] This last authority was also given to the Saar Governing Commission in the Treaty of Versailles more than 70 years earlier. It gave the Special Representative the legal ability to enforce his control over the regimes in place (again, mainly the State of Cambodia) by firing uncooperative functionaries. UNTAC officials would later note that this was the only "real power" that UNTAC had over the Cambodian administrations.[37]

The Paris accords thus took the UN down paths trodden only in the Saar and West Irian operations, though without their aspect of direct governmental administration. UNTAC's power penetrated depths of authority from monitoring to supervision to control, and it inevitably engaged in education functions in the civil administration arena as well. In prior missions, such as in Namibia and Nicaragua, the underlying peace accords lacked such a competence for the UN in civil administration because the incumbent regimes would not have accepted it, and those out of power settled for close UN oversight of the electoral process. The great mistrust among the Cambodian factions and their sponsors brought about a far more intrusive UN presence.

Elections: The Paris accords gave the UN the deepest level of authority possible with respect to elections by making UNTAC "responsible for the organization and conduct of these elections."[38] Although the League had undertaken such a mission in the Saar, the UN did not itself conduct elections in Namibia, Nicaragua, Haiti, and Angola, although, as we have seen, UNTAG virtually shared de facto responsibility over polling in Namibia with the South African government. The unique assignment given UNTAC in the electoral area originated in the same suspicions among the factions that brought about the mandate on civil administration. Close oversight, though enough for other conflicts, would not satisfy the resistance and its supporters.

The UN thus would employ its own personnel, who would follow instructions from the Special Representative only. UNTAC would not have to follow the SNC with respect to elections, even when it spoke unanimously or through Prince Sihanouk. Although the instances where the Special Representative would need to overrule the SNC in the electoral process might be rare, he retained the authority to do so. This could conceivably arise if the factional leaders agreed on electoral procedures that furthered their own ends but corrupted the process.

To carry out its responsibilities, UNTAC would establish electoral laws, procedures, and a code of conduct for parties; invalidate laws in contravention of the settlement; set the timetable; register voters and parties; organize and conduct the polling; ensure fair access to the media; educate voters; respond to complaints; arrange for foreign observation; and certify the elections as free and fair. UNTAC could promulgate laws and procedures for Cambodia in the electoral realm, a critical legislative function not given for other areas of civil administration.[39]

The elections themselves were to be based upon proportional representation within each province, with each political party offering lists of candidates. After lengthy negotiations on voter eligibility, stemming from the presence of ethnic Vietnamese and recent Vietnamese migrants in Cambodia, the agreement enfranchised all persons over the age of eighteen born in Cambodia or to a parent born in Cambodia, including refugees and displaced persons. Voting would be by secret ballot; the parties had to ensure freedom of speech, assembly, and movement; and each party would have fair access to the media.[40]

Human Rights: UNTAC also had a mandate to help implement the human rights provisions of the Paris accords, an important element of the settlement in view of the atrocities and genocide of the Khmer Rouge and the continued violation of human rights by the SOC. Under the accords, the factions had to respect human rights, permit activities by Cambodian human rights groups, avoid recurrence of past human rights abuses, and adhere to the key human rights conventions.[41] (Despite clear evidence of genocide by the Khmer Rouge, the drafters, recalling the acrimonious debates on the subject that had hampered much of the 1989 session of the Paris Conference, omitted specific mention of the word genocide or the 1948 Genocide Convention to obtain a consensus.)[42]

UNTAC had a broad mandate to "foster . . . an environment in which respect for human rights shall be ensured."[43] The goals here were both immediate and long range: to prevent a climate of fear from tarnishing the election, and to create a long-term consciousness among Cambodians about universally accepted human rights. The accords empowered it not only to monitor human rights conditions in Cambodia, but also to implement a human rights education program and, most significantly, to investigate complaints and take "corrective action."[44] UNTAC would thus have greater depth of authority than its Salvadoran counterpart.

Repatriation: The Special Representative of the Secretary-General had overall authority under the Paris accords for the repatriation of approximately 365,000 Cambodians who had fled the country during its years of war, the vast majority living in Thailand.[45] The accords gave UNHCR operational control due to its long-standing experience in these questions.[46]

Economic Rehabilitation: The UN's last major undertaking under the peace accords was to assist with the most immediate tasks of rehabilitating Cambodia after more than two decades of war. It would assess the country's needs and coordinate the receipt of foreign assistance. The UN would also work with the stand-alone consultative body responsible for longer-term reconstruction assistance, the International Committee on the Reconstruction of Cambodia.[47]

3. The Conceptual Conundrum in the Accords: Reconciling the Roles of UNTAC

The Paris accords pushed the conceptual underpinnings of the new peacekeeping to new limits. They relied upon a new form of consent by scrapping any notion of governments. They also gave the UN duties that upset all the traditional views of nonintervention and sovereignty.[48] Member states could assert that the UN had not deviated from its prior practice under Article 2(7), because UNTAC represented a response to an international situation, not a purely domestic conflict, and the Cambodian parties had consented to the operation. But the solution adopted looked toward a deeper level of UN involvement in internal governance and offered further evidence of the erosion of strict views of sovereignty. The consent, though legally valid, followed a great deal of pressure on the combatants by their sponsors.

More important, UNTAC had an exceptional mandate to exercise the three political functions of the UN. Its executor and guarantor responsibilities flowed from the Paris accords' clause delegating from the Supreme National Council to UNTAC "all powers necessary to *ensure* the implementation of this Agreement."[49] In executing the peace accord, it would have authority to administer in varying degrees Cambodia as a country. In principle, no ministry or official extended beyond UNTAC's control if its actions inhibited the "neutral political environment." As guarantor, UNTAC had to monitor tense situations and keep the settlement process on course. Although the accords emphasized that the Cambodians had primary responsibility for the success of the settlement, they gave UNTAC the legal authority to contribute as it saw fit, subject to the inherent limits in all peacekeeping. Lastly, the accords implicitly encouraged the Special Representative to become an active mediator, for UNTAC could more easily execute its mandate if the SNC reached decisions by consensus than if the Special Representative had to act in the vacuum created by SNC inaction.

UNTAC's mandate would test the UN's quest for impartiality in a manner reminiscent of ONUC, where the UN had a similarly assertive role as guarantor. It would also presage even more intractable situations in the former Yugoslavia and Somalia. Under ideal circumstances, the Special Representative could mediate among the members of the SNC, prod them toward consensus, implement the settlement with their unanimous support, and avoid any conflict among his various roles.

In fact, the signatories to the Paris accords suspected that the factions in the SNC would rarely speak with one voice, and assumed the Special Representative would act frequently in the absence of consensus. As executor and guarantor, he would necessarily have to act contrary to the views of at least some SNC members, thereby opening the door to accusations of bias. If he overruled different factions over different issues over time, he might avoid the perception of partiality. But this was by no means assured, and sustained discord with one party would increase the risk of a perception of favoritism.

THE PARIS ACCORDS AND THE CAMBODIA CONFLICT: PROLOGUE TO AN ANALYSIS OF UNTAC

The Paris accords represented the product of years of negotiation by both the Cambodian factions and their external supporters. They reflect compromises stemming from the strengths and weaknesses of those parties during the bargaining process, as well as coalitions of former adversaries (for example, China and Vietnam) and longtime friends (for example, Thailand and the United States). From this author's perspective, the Paris accords represented a realistic solution that advanced the interests of the Cambodian people and of regional stability as well.

Many policymakers, journalists, and human rights activists have condemned the Paris accords. Among the harshest critics were members of the U.S. Congress and scholars who attacked the notion of including the Khmer Rouge in both the negotiation and implementation of the settlement.[50] To these critics, the inclusion of the Khmer Rouge was tantamount to appeasement of a modern Nazi regime, which could only be put down through force. Some favored an embrace of the SOC as the solution; others pushed for an agreement that simply excluded the Khmer Rouge from the process. From their perspective, the Paris accords remained a fatally flawed agreement and UNTAC necessarily an apologist for the Khmer Rouge during its tenure.

The response to this view is not to suggest that the Paris accords represented the perfect agreement for the Cambodian people, for it did not. It is rather to point out the unalterable historical realities behind the Cambodia conflict. At least for the last 200 or so years, on through UNTAC's tenure, Cambodia has, to its detriment, been of interest to other states not because of the aspirations of its people, but because of its position in the power struggles over Indochina and Southeast Asia.

As David Chandler, among the foremost historians of Cambodia, has noted, one constant theme of Cambodia's modern history has been the effect of its location between Vietnam and Thailand, "two powerful, antagonistic neighbors" who have "forced the Cambodian elite to prefer one or the other or to attempt to neutralize them by appealing to an outside power."[51] Thus, China and Vietnam had every intention of continuing their struggle over Cambodia until they saw a reason to end it. The Khmer Rouge, not defeated like the Nazis, remained a powerful player due to support from China and ASEAN. For the most amoral or immoral reasons of realpolitik, those states saw it as the best counterweight to Vietnamese power.

The perfect solution might well have entailed large-scale political and military support of democratic forces in Cambodia against the Khmer Rouge, and prosecution of the Khmer Rouge leadership under the Genocide Convention. Alas, such a vision does not conform with the reality just described. Democratic forces were negligible to begin with, with none of the four factions having such a tradition. China was unwilling to give up support for the Khmer Rouge until it was ready, and in the manner it saw as amenable to its interests along its southern flank.[52] The United States was, for comprehensible if not readily acceptable reasons, not willing to place Cambodia above trade, human rights, and other regional security issues on its agenda with China.

Even were the Chinese to drop their support of the Khmer Rouge completely, the international community was not prepared to countenance a peace enforcement mission to defeat the well-stocked guerrillas. The difficulties in bolstering support for peacekeeping and peace enforcement in the former Yugoslavia—in the backyard of three of the five permanent members of the Security Council—should end any illusions about the possibility of peace enforcement in Cambodia.

So the Paris accords are what remained after all the other impossible, as well as possible but worse, alternatives were discarded. The powerful states negotiating over Cambodia's future may well have put the welfare of the Cambodians second to their own interests, although it is this author's belief that some participating states—Australia, in particular—had no such agenda. But more important, even if the peace agreement did not do everything imaginable to improve the situation of the people of Cambodia, it did lay a basis for a real possibility of change for the better. Most significantly, it gave Cambodians their first free choice of government in at least a generation, an option all human rights supporters should endorse.

As for the Khmer Rouge, as Elizabeth Becker, a harsh critic of U.S. policy in the 1980s has noted, the Paris accords marginalized them significantly, a far cry from earlier Chinese demands that the group share power equally with the State of Cambodia.[53] The accords laid the basis for China to separate itself from the Khmer Rouge without losing face. They also envisaged a postelectoral Cambodian government that all assumed would not be dominated by the Khmer Rouge. This new regime could then treat the movement as an illegal insurgency, rather than a rival government. This does not satisfy our sense of justice that the Khmer Rouge, or at least Pol Pot and his cadre, be punished now for their reign of terror, but it represents a critical step toward their long-term marginalization.

In reviewing and analyzing the work of UNTAC in the chapters that follow, the Paris accords will be regarded, then, as a fait accompli. Rather than examining what the international community might have done if Cambodia were Kuwait, or Yugoslavia, we will examine what it did given that it was Cambodia, a small, poor country in Southeast Asia with no real history of democratic institutions, watched over by more powerful states who never stopped pursuing their own interests as the peace process continued to unfold. Other conflicts that engage second-generation peacekeeping will likely produce similarly imperfect agreements; but these accords remain the most appropriate starting points for appraising the new UN operations.

.7.

UNTAC in Cambodia

T he signature of the Paris accords marked the end of the first stage of the Cambodian peace process, lasting more than four years from the first rumblings of a settlement in 1987, and the beginning of a new one, dominated by the anticipation, deployment, and operation of UNTAC. That phase would last from late 1991 until 1993, when UNTAC conducted elections, disengaged, and left the peacemaking process in the hands of Cambodians. This chapter recounts UNTAC's record during its 20 months in Cambodia, in the context of developments in the country and overseas that greatly influenced its ability to carry out its mandate. The following chapter looks inward at the mission itself, evaluating its performance, given the many exogenous constraints, as a second-generation operation.[1]

UNTAC'S HANDICAP: IDENTIFYING THE EXOGENOUS VARIABLES

In order to better place UNTAC within the conceptual and historical framework of second-generation operations, a prerequisite intellectual task must be undertaken: to isolate the exogenous constraints upon the functioning of UNTAC unique to the Cambodia context. This segregation does not suggest that future operations will not face similar limitations, or that such handicaps remain impervious to change by the missions. Indeed, the United Nations operation should, over time, alter the nature of these variables. But these influences define the opening position for UNTAC and thus account for many of its results.

1. Fragile Peace, Fragile Consent

Though the culmination of years of intensive negotiations, the signature of the Paris accords did not equate with a desire by the Cambodian factions, in particular the SOC and Khmer Rouge, for peace. Indeed, they ultimately accepted the Permanent Five's plan primarily because of external pressure upon them. The SOC did fear for its future in the absence of Vietnamese combat troops and Soviet aid; and the resistance did worry that an end to Chinese support and the international consensus against the Khmer Rouge would lead to legitimation of the SOC. But other considerations proved more powerful motivators of behavior. The SOC saw itself in control of 90 percent of the country, and the Khmer Rouge thought it could continue to mount a guerrilla war with its own means of support.[2] The factions only unwillingly succumbed to the pressure of their outside supporters, who had tired of the Cambodia conflict.

This opposition to peace did not necessarily mean that the factions signed the accords with the deliberate, but hidden, intent of violating them, although this is clearly a possibility. But it did signify that they had competing conceptions of how the accords would affect them and undermined the consent critical to peacekeeping. With such tenuous consent, the smallest action by the UN against the interests of a party would be met with entrenched resistance, accusations of bias or violations of the accord, and impasse. UNPROFOR in the former Yugoslavia and UNOSOM II in Somalia would later face these consequences, too.

The most important manifestation of this often illusory consent concerned the active resistance of the Khmer Rouge and the State of Cambodia to UNTAC whenever it sought to execute its mandate contrary to their fundamental interests. The Khmer Rouge feared the loss of control over territory and people that would result from UN entry into its zones and demobilization of its forces. For this reason, in June 1992, early in UNTAC's deployment, it refused to join in Phase II of the cease-fire—the regroupment, cantonment, disarmament, and partial demobilization of the factional armies.

The SOC opposed most levels of UNTAC control, and seized upon the Khmer Rouge's refusal to disarm as a justification for resisting UNTAC control (an argument with which some in UNTAC sympathized but that others regarded as an excuse to maintain its grip on Cambodian society).[3] It emphasized that it was cooperating with UNTAC and that UNTAC would not be able to undertake its mission if the SOC withheld support as the Khmer Rouge had done.[4] But the SOC's cooperation proved limited at best, and superficial at worst.

By late 1992 and early 1993, the resistance of the two key belligerents to the settlement had turned lethal. The Khmer Rouge massacred scores of ethnic Vietnamese, and SOC elements began killing opposition party officials. As the election neared, the Khmer Rouge aimed its sights at UNTAC itself, ultimately leading to the deaths of some two dozen UNTAC personnel in hostilities. These irreparable setbacks for UNTAC would necessitate an eventual transformation in UNTAC's priorities as the election neared.

This poor quality of the consent had deleterious side-effects. First, the desire by the main factions to continue armed conflict left UNTAC undertaking its duties in a war scenario. This starting point was precisely opposite to that preferred for new peacekeeping operations, as shown earlier by ONUC and later with UNOSOM. Although the fighting never returned to its pre-1991 levels and the cease-fire prevailed more often than not, all UNTAC's civilian functions proved far more burdensome to conduct. Members of UNTAC and Cambodians suggested that all of UNTAC's mandate hinged upon demobilization of the armies and effective police control to create an atmosphere of peace and domestic order.[5] Battles, gunfire, troop movements, roadblocks, new mines, and the tension of war all worked against UNTAC.

Second, the actors in the process had inconsistent perspectives toward the relationship among the SNC, UNTAC, and the SOC. The drafters of the Paris accords saw the SNC as a shell, designed to delegate functions to UNTAC, although they hoped it might become a body for national reconciliation as well. UNTAC would have the power, with the SOC following its instructions. The SOC emphasized its own authority recognized under the accords, noting that it still controlled the governmental apparatus, even if the SNC embodied Cambodian sovereignty. It believed UNTAC had to take account of its control and work with it.

The Khmer Rouge, and the rest of the resistance to a lesser extent, saw the SNC as the only national entity with their participation and thus the only legitimate source of power. The SNC stood for the quadripartite interim government they had sought during ten years of negotiation. UNTAC would act as the agent of the SNC; the SOC would be powerless. And UNTAC saw the SNC as an important reconciliation body where it hoped many decisions would be made. When the SNC did not so act, UNTAC had to assume more responsibility itself. As a result, the SNC, UNTAC, and the SOC—those theoretically giving the consent, those receiving it, and those through whom the UN would have to work—never reached common ground on a process for interaction to advance the settlement.

Aggravating this situation was the behavior of Prince Sihanouk. Regarded by the global and regional powers since the early 1980s as the person best able to bring the country together, and to whom the Paris agreements accorded a unique position, he personally embodied the fragility of support for UNTAC among powerful Cambodians. In giving Sihanouk special authority under the accords, the drafters had assumed he would cooperate with UNTAC. Such support would have greatly strengthened UNTAC's hand, as Sihanouk could have stood behind UNTAC as an authority figure capable of pushing the factions toward compliance with UNTAC control.[6]

Instead, the prince proved weak at best, and detrimental at worst. In the SNC, he hesitated to break deadlocks, preferring that the UN's Special Representative make the tough decisions. Sihanouk feared that action on his part would compromise his neutrality and passed the blame to UNTAC for unpopular measures. At the same time, he demanded that the UN consult with him and defer to his preferences.[7] By late 1992, the prince opted out as an active player in the process. His long, purportedly medical visits to Beijing and Pyongyang kept him away from Cambodia, where he might have used his political skills to try to calm the situation and promote elections. He issued frequent statements from these cities in which he attacked UNTAC or posited his own plan, in defiance of the Paris accords, for reconciliation after the elections.[8] He offered his support for the elections only after UNTAC made clear that it would not postpone or cancel them, and returned to Cambodia for the polling only after entreaties by Secretary-General Boutros-Ghali and the "friends" of the peace process.[9]

2. A Shattered Country

The fragility of the settlement was matched by the devastation of the country after more than 20 years of war and economic sanctions. Cambodia's physical infrastructure of roads, electrical capacity, airstrips, running water, and telecommunications operated at levels found in the rest of Southeast Asia decades earlier. Into this shattered land the signatories to the Paris accords asked the UN to insert tens of thousands of troops and civilians. As a result, the UN needed to devote significant resources and time to setting up the most basic administrative backbone of UNTAC, including housing, telephones, and transportation. This included importation of nearly all UNTAC's equipment and construction of a telephone network. The abject state of the country also placed a cap on the amount of foreign assistance Cambodia could absorb and led to severe inflationary effects when large numbers of foreigners arrived with money to spend. Undetected mines made some roads impassable and land designated for returning refugees uninhabitable. Banditry and low-level skirmishes rendered travel at night virtually impossible.

More important than infrastructure, the conflict had nearly exhausted Cambodia's human capital and talent. Most educated members of the population had fled to Thailand, France, or the United States, or been killed during the Khmer Rouge years. The workforce lacked the basic abilities to perform even many unskilled jobs. Years of conflict had traumatized the population. Every family had experienced some loss over the years; Cambodia had the highest proportion of amputees in the world due to mine injuries; and unemployment was rampant.

This human devastation taxed UNTAC. For its own needs, it had trouble locating qualified local staff. When UNTAC sought to execute control over the SOC administration, it found bureaucrats so untrained they could not respond to requests for documents and in need of extensive education to carry out UNTAC's directives. When components investigated human rights abuses and corruption, both witnesses and perpetrators practiced deceit and concealment, inhibiting collection of credible evidence and execution of corrective measures.[10]

3. Limited Interests, Competing Crises

After the signature of the Paris accords, most states viewed Cambodia as "the UN's problem," which essentially meant the Secretary-General's problem. Always a "sideshow" on the world political stage, Cambodia did not receive the sustained attention of the international community, which was focusing on more pressing crises in Somalia, the former Yugoslavia, and the former Soviet Union.[11] The most engaged players did assist UNTAC in mediatory efforts through a so-called Expanded Perm 5 in Phnom Penh. It was usually composed of the ambassadors of the Permanent Five, Australia, Indonesia, Japan, and Germany. But these states saw a limit in the amount of political capital to expend in pushing the factions toward cooperation.

Thus, according to these actors, Cambodia did not merit worsening U.S. relations with Thailand or China, or French or Singaporean relations with Vietnam; or endangering Japanese economic interests in the region. The Thai government feared its own military too much to force them to break their longstanding commercial and military ties with the Khmer Rouge. While the Security Council's votes suggested an ironclad international consensus in favor of the Paris accords, the Council's members did not match it with a highlevel commitment that might have put additional weight behind UNTAC's actions. Ironically, the accords themselves eliminated a major source of influence over the factions, namely provision of arms and other support, since the settlement banned external military aid to Cambodia.

Furthermore, the troop donor states constrained UNTAC. For example, the government of Australia, a key author of the Paris plan, had made clear its unwillingness to see any of its troops involved in hostile operations. When several

Indonesian soldiers were wounded, even members of the rubber-stamp Indonesian parliament called for the recall of the Indonesian battalion.[12] The attitude of troop donors affected the limits to which UNTAC could push the idea of self-defense, which is always allowed under consensual peacekeeping. As for the possibility of peace enforcement, as in Somalia and the former Yugoslavia, troop donors did not want their soldiers waging war and rightly questioned the utility of peace enforcement to secure compliance with the Paris accords.

Beyond the member states themselves, the UN Secretariat, in particular the Department of Peacekeeping Operations, dealt with a multitude of other crises during UNTAC's time in Cambodia. The immediate and far worse humanitarian disasters in Bosnia and Somalia required sustained high-level attention, especially due to the danger posed to peacekeeping and peace-enforcing troops. DPKO also had responsibility for elections in Angola, the fighting that followed it, a new operation in Mozambique, ONUSAL's complex work, and the older first-generation missions. Had any of these operations been under the control of a single government, dozens or even hundreds of people in a national capital would have overseen them. DPKO could devote only two people to work predominantly on Cambodia; the Under Secretary-General spent only a fraction of his time on UNTAC.

The international community thus decided to deploy UNTAC despite, as well as because of, the Cambodians' refusal to lay aside their differences and cooperate fully with it. Once UNTAC arrived, the Council kept it there notwithstanding serious opposition to its work by the two armed elites in Cambodia. The member states had scrupulously avoided this type of situation in earlier operations, in light of the morass that became of the Congo mission. Yet the leading diplomatic players could see no other realistic option, convinced that withdrawal would mean disaster for the UN and Cambodia. They were unwilling to sanction any peace enforcement, yet seemingly hoping that UNTAC could perform its mission alone.

WAITING FOR UNTAC: THE PREPARATION

During the negotiation of the Paris accords, as the idea of an enhanced UN role developed, officials from the UN Secretariat stressed to the Permanent Five that the establishment of UNTAC would require significant preparation. Planning, recruitment, and deployment would, they noted, take many months, not days or weeks.[13] During the months before the signature, Secretariat personnel following Cambodia focused on achieving the settlement. As for its implementation, only the military aspects received significant attention, in light of the importance of maintaining a cease-fire.

A survey mission visited Cambodia in August and September 1991, after which the Secretary-General recommended to the Security Council the deployment of a small United Nations Advance Mission in Cambodia (UNAMIC) immediately upon signature of the agreements. On October 16, 1991, the Council created UNAMIC, with a primary mission to work with the factional military leaders to maintain, before UNTAC's arrival, the cease-fire required under the accords.[14] Headed by Bangladeshi diplomat Ataul Karim and with 200 international staff, UNAMIC arrived on November 9, 1991, and set up several monitoring points in the country.[15]

On October 31, the Security Council endorsed the Paris agreements in Resolution 718 and authorized the Secretary-General to appoint a Special Representative for Cambodia. Perez de Cuellar did not, however, appoint a Special Representative immediately. The leading contender, Rafeeuddin Ahmed, the UN's senior diplomat on Cambodia since 1981, had the greatest familiarity with the actors and the peace process, although several states desired someone of greater international stature to head UNTAC. But Perez, near the end of his term, refused to commit his successor to a Special Representative whom Perez had picked. Secretariat officials continued planning the organization of UNTAC during the rest of 1991, including dispatching an Advance Electoral Planning Unit to begin the enormously complex work of organizing and conducting an election in a country of seven million people.

In January 1992, Boutros Boutros-Ghali surprised most participants in and observers of the Cambodia peace process by appointing Yasushi Akashi, the Under Secretary-General for Disarmament, his Special Representative for Cambodia. A career UN diplomat who had once served as his nation's permanent UN representative, Akashi had had no recent involvement in Southeast Asian issues. He had served on a UN good offices mission attempting to resolve Thai-Cambodian border disputes in the early 1960s. Boutros-Ghali's precise motives may never be known, but were likely influenced by the prospect that a Japanese national in charge of the UN's largest peacekeeping operation would lead to financial support for UNTAC and other missions. Additional factors included the need to remove an official at the Under Secretary-General level from Headquarters as part of his plan to reduce the number of officials reporting directly to him; and, apparently, requests by Ahmed for guarantees regarding his future employment that Boutros-Ghali would not accept.[16]

On February 19, 1992, four months after the conclusion of the Paris accords, Boutros-Ghali submitted to the Security Council his lengthy plan of implementation. The report recommended that UNTAC consist of seven components: human rights, elections, military issues, civil administration, police, repatriation, and rehabilitation. It also described UNTAC's basic organization and personnel requirements and contained a timetable, with the election scheduled for late April to early May 1993.[17]

During the report's preparation, Akashi began to enlist his senior staff, with key diplomatic players lobbying him heavily to include their nationals. Those included came from diverse, though mostly Western, backgrounds: Behrooz Sadry, an Iranian national and chief of the UN's Field Operations Division, as the Deputy Special Representative; Australian Lieutenant General John Sanderson as the force commander; Reginald Austin, a Zimbabwean law professor and alumnus of the Zimbabwe peace process, to oversee the elections; Gérard Porcell, a French judge, to run the civil administration component; Dennis McNamara, a New Zealander career UNHCR official, to oversee human rights; Klaas Roos, a Dutch police chief and alumnus of the Namibia operation, to head the civilian police; Sergio Vieira de Mello, a Brazilian senior UNHCR official with experience on Indochinese refugee issues, to head repatriation; and Berndt Bernander, a Swedish senior UNDP official, to lead rehabilitation.

In addition, Karim became political adviser; Vishakan Krishnadasan, a Sri Lankan lawyer, the legal adviser; and Roger Lawrence, an American with the UN Conference on Trade and Development, the economic adviser. Timothy Carney, an American foreign service officer, headed an information division and Eric Falt, of France's UN mission in New York, was tapped as the press spokesman.[18] Discussions with member states that would donate military contingents or policemen also began. The Council adopted the Secretary-General's report and created UNTAC on February 28, 1992.[19]

Secretariat officials also devoted considerable attention to UNTAC's budget. The UN and the Cambodian and other parties wished to deploy UNTAC quickly, but preparation and approval of the budget of such an enormous undertaking would require several more months. The Secretary-General could legally spend only a small amount without Assembly approval ($3 million on his own and $10 million with the approval of the Advisory Committee on Administrative and Budgetary Questions). He thus requested a $200 million advance appropriation in January 1992, which the Assembly approved on February 14, noting that "the unusual approach . . . is prompted by the extraordinary circumstances of the tasks to be performed by [UNTAC]."[20]

Boutros-Ghali submitted his proposed budget after the creation of UNTAC, on May 7, requesting $764 million through October 1992. After the ACABQ found ways to cut costs, the Assembly appropriated $606 million through October 1992.[21] At its fall 1992 session, it appropriated another $484 million, followed by appropriations of $85 million in September 1993 and $369 million in May 1994.[22] The total costs of UNAMIC and UNTAC thus approximated $1.7 billion.

Table 7.1

UNITED NATIONS TRANSITIONAL AUTHORITY IN CAMBODIA
Organizational Chart

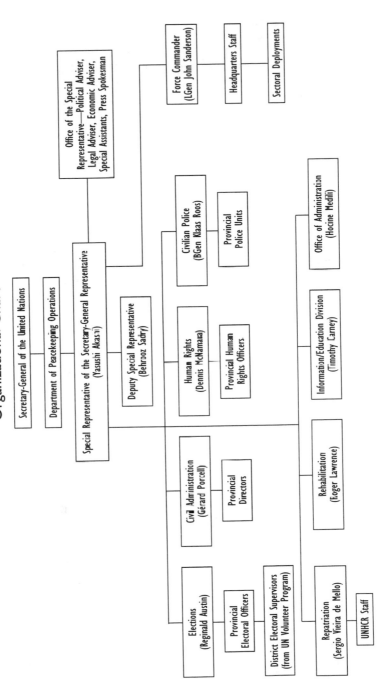

Secretary-General of the United Nations

Department of Peacekeeping Operations

Special Representative of the Secretary-General Representative
(Yasushi Akashi)

Office of the Special
Representative—Political Adviser,
Legal Adviser, Economic Adviser,
Special Assistants, Press Spokesman

Force Commander
(LGen John Sanderson)

Headquarters Staff

Sectoral Deployments

Deputy Special Representative
(Behrooz Sadry)

Civilian Police
(BGen Klaas Roos)

Provincial
Police Units

Office of Administration
(Hocine Medili)

Human Rights
(Dennis McNamara)

Provincial Human
Rights Officers

Information/Education Division
(Timothy Carney)

Civil Administration
(Gérard Porcell)

Provincial
Directors

Rehabilitation
(Roger Lawrence)

Elections
(Reginald Austin)

Provincial
Electoral Officers

District Electoral Supervisors
(from UN Volunteer Program)

Repatriation
(Sergio Vieira de Mello)

UNHCR Staff

THE DEPLOYMENT

When Akashi's aircraft arrived in Phnom Penh on March 15, 1992, it contained only the most skeletal staff. Deployment of the entire operation of some 22,000 international personnel dragged on for many months. Both Headquarters and UNTAC had to recruit large numbers of civilians and military personnel and procure and transport substantial quantities of materiel. Despite much outstanding staff work, logistical shortcomings hindered the operation throughout its tenure.

The military, sent by member states, deployed most rapidly, with 10,000 troops by early June 1992, 14,000 by July, and nearly the entire 15,900 by September. It set up bases throughout Cambodia, with battalions from 11 countries (Bangladesh, Bulgaria, France, Ghana, India, Indonesia, Malaysia, Netherlands, Pakistan, Tunisia, and Uruguay). Smaller contingents from 32 nations served as military observers; construction engineers; demining instructors; communications, logistics and transportation contingents; and other support personnel. The repatriation unit also arrived quickly, relying on its personnel already in Cambodia and Thailand.

Other components deployed slowly. Of the 3,600 civilian police (CIVPOL) needed, only 193 arrived by the end of April 1992; 1,780 by July; and 2,500 by September, with full levels only at the end of 1992. They came from some 32 countries, with India the largest contributor. The electoral component also took until the fall of 1992 to reach its full complement in the capital and provinces. This included roughly 70 in Phnom Penh, a provincial electoral officer and small staff in each provincial capital, and 465 district electoral supervisors recruited entirely from the United Nations Volunteer program.

The civil administration component established offices in every province only in July and did not have a fully functioning complement of several hundred in Phnom Penh and the provinces until the fall. According to the Secretary-General's proposed structure, the human rights component would have a small presence in Phnom Penh only. When human rights officials pressed for human rights officers in the field, UNTAC managed to deploy one in each province by October 1992. Finally, UNTAC hired more than 8,000 Cambodians as support staff, including drivers, interpreters, messengers, clerks, and cleaners. During the elections, it would employ 50,000 as polling officials.

1. Causes of Delay

The Paris accords caught the UN unorganized for the task at hand. First, the late choice of the Special Representative delayed important decisions. Perez de Cuellar's reluctance to make an appointment, and the decision by Boutros-Ghali not to select Rafeeuddin Ahmed, meant that UNTAC received a new-comer to the peace process several months after the signature of the accords. This postponed the appointment of top personnel, with ripple effects in the areas of procurement and recruitment of subordinate officials. Moreover, other than a few short missions to survey the military and electoral situation, the Secretariat lacked a detailed picture of the logistical demands until after UNTAC arrived.

Second, the Secretariat had no complete plan for staffing the most unusual and, for the Khmer Rouge, the most important, part of UNTAC, the civil administration component. The UN lacked a pool of persons trained in civil administration who could be readily identified and sent to Cambodia.[23] Instead, two streams of applications arrived at Headquarters and UNTAC. One came from career UN civil servants, responding to notices placed within UN offices throughout the world; and a second, ad hoc set was promoted by governments or sent in by individuals in the private sector. The former had the advantage of understanding the UN's bureaucracy and modus operandi. However, having spent their careers in agencies such as UNDP or the UN's Department of Public Information, they often lacked expertise in the subject matters of the operation. The outside applicants included many with relevant experience, but without any knowledge of the UN's workings.[24]

Ahmed has stated that, because of the time required for planning, UNTAC should have delayed its deployment for three months and arrived fully staffed in June 1992, blaming the Council for dispatching UNTAC too early.[25] This explanation, however, ignores the political realities of the period. Cambodians desperately wanted UNTAC to arrive. The presence of UNAMIC, the advance mission, did nothing to curb frequent violations of the cease-fire, including a large Khmer Rouge operation in January 1992. Low-level civil disorder had erupted in Phnom Penh, with deadly riots against SOC corruption and a SOC-inspired attack on Khmer Rouge leader Khieu Samphan upon his return to Cambodia. Further wait risked the unraveling of the Paris accords. UNTAC had little choice but to proceed with phased deployment.

The consequences of the few cases of good planning highlight the short-comings of most of the civilian side. Because Vieira de Mello and the refugee component organized the UNHCR staff quickly, repatriation could start in March 1992, while the rest of UNTAC remained effectively nonfunctional. Electoral preparation also began well before UNTAC's arrival. Building on the UN's experience in Namibia, Central America, and elsewhere, a small group of officials drafted the election law, wrote detailed timetables, and planned the logistics. The UN Volunteer Program also attracted qualified district electoral supervisors quickly, creating a presence in the provinces by the summer of 1992.

In addition to its inability to obtain good personnel on an expedited basis, UNTAC's demands for quick emplacement of equipment sorely tested Headquarters. While the military contingents came with most of their own equipment, UNTAC had to work within the UN's complex procurement rules for its other needs. Designed to control the UN's expenses, they require competitive bidding on a global scale and centralize many procurement decisions at Headquarters. They contain waiver provisions allowing field operations to make certain decisions on their own and exempt some procurement from competitive bidding. Akashi hoped that the two senior officials from New York he installed as Deputy Special Representative (Sadry) and director of administration (Hocine Medili) could prevail upon their colleagues in New York on procurement and personnel matters.

Instead, they could usually not obtain waivers of procurement rules and expedited treatment. The Department of Peacekeeping Operations' proliferating responsibilities meant that UNTAC had to vie for the attention of UN Headquarters on administrative matters. Through frequent visits to New York, Akashi and Sadry tried to galvanize the UN's administrative bureaucracy because DPKO could not alone move it to address UNTAC's pressing needs. Desks, computers, telephones, prefabricated offices, and other necessary equipment arrived late, hampering the initiation of UNTAC's important civilian activities until the fall of 1992.[26]

2. Costs of Delay

The delay in deployment, especially of the civil administration component, proved costly. By arriving without significant staff, UNTAC raised expectations early among Cambodians regarding its power that it could not meet. Moreover, during the early months, in what has been called UNTAC's "honeymoon period," the SOC seemed more amenable to UNTAC civil administrative control. Yet UNTAC lacked the resources to implement this part of its mandate.[27] UNTAC's inability to exercise control fueled Khmer Rouge suspicions that UNTAC would not neutralize the SOC but let it rule Cambodia. This gave the Khmer Rouge a convenient excuse for withdrawing from the peace process, one that even their opponents abroad found somewhat justifiable. But once the Khmer Rouge had withdrawn and UNTAC would not force it to comply, the SOC saw UNTAC's actions as one-sided.[28] When UNTAC finally had the staff for more effective supervision, the SOC had turned especially recalcitrant.

EXECUTING THE SETTLEMENT AND THE EROSION OF CONSENT

The Paris accords' stated purpose was to permit the Cambodian people to exercise their right of self-determination through free and fair elections. To support that right, they charged UNTAC with three broad tasks: supervising the military arrangements to create a peaceful backdrop for elections; overseeing the creation of a neutral political environment for the elections, without the dominance of one faction; and organizing and conducting the polling. UNTAC's other duties, such as promoting respect for human rights and repatriating refugees from Thailand, were to support these goals.

1. The Quest for a Peaceful Country

a. The Khmer Rouge Withdraw from the Peace Plan

The settlement plan entrusted UNTAC's military component with monitoring the cease-fire required under the accords and then supervising Phase II of that cease-fire. That phase required the regroupment, cantonment, disarmament, and partial demobilization of the 200,000 soldiers in the four factional armies (at least three-quarters belonging to the SOC), as well as 250,000 SOC militia. Despite violations of the truce by both sides, UNTAC did impressive preparatory work for Phase II, which officially began on June 13, 1992. Military forces from the SOC, KPNLF, and FUNCINPEC began to comply with the agreement, with 55,000 eventually appearing at cantonment sites.

The Khmer Rouge, however, after giving hints of their intention following UNTAC's arrival, refused to join Phase II or to allow UNTAC into its zones of control. The guerrillas claimed that the Paris accords were not being implemented properly insofar, they stated, as Vietnamese troops remained in Cambodia and the State of Cambodia had not surrendered power to the SNC.[29] The group cited the continued dominance of the SOC as its justification. This represented a somewhat clever legal strategy, as the Paris accords did not specifically state that demobilization had to proceed before the creation of a neutral political environment. (Nothing in the accords, however, suggested that the neutralization of the SOC was a legal prerequisite for Phase II, and a better interpretation would reject such a linkage.)[30]

Diplomatic efforts started in order to return the Khmer Rouge to the fold. With support from the Permanent Five and Indonesia, Thailand and Japan led intensive negotiations with the Khmer Rouge throughout the summer and fall of 1992, with no success. The Khmer Rouge called for the establishment of "consultative committees" of the SNC within each SOC ministry in addition to UNTAC control, but the other players in the peace process found this unacceptable.[31] These states also prepared new Security Council resolutions, and their diplomatic missions in Phnom Penh actively aided UNTAC through mediation and consultations with the factions.

At the end of November 1992, the Security Council was frustrated with the Khmer Rouge's intransigence and asked Cambodia's neighbors to honor an SNC-passed moratorium on the export of Cambodian logs that would deprive the Khmer Rouge of some of their outside income.[32] Yet, as noted earlier, despite demands from human rights groups, journalists, and others for stiffer action against the Khmer Rouge, the Security Council and troop donor states did not favor escalation through peace enforcement.

One particular episode demonstrated UNTAC's conundrum in the face of this decaying consent to its presence. On May 30, 1992, just before the Khmer Rouge announced their formal refusal to comply with Phase II, a handful of lightly armed, youthful Khmer Rouge guerrillas blocked an armed UN convoy, accompanied by Akashi and General Sanderson, from entering a Khmer Rouge zone near Pailin, in western Cambodia. Wary of moving beyond a bamboo pole erected by the band, the UN retreated.[33]

In this episode, later referred to as the "bamboo pole incident," Akashi interpreted the consent of the factions quite restrictively. He implicitly determined that moving past the token presence of guerrillas would push UNTAC too close to peace enforcement. Sanderson defended the decision, arguing that only the military forces on the ground can correctly gauge the risk in a situation and determine whether to act notwithstanding a "no" from one faction. In the May 30 incident, he explained that ignoring the roadblock would have caused the Khmer Rouge to stop them farther down the path with heavier weapons and mines. This would, he maintained, have led to bloodshed and sabotaged diplomatic efforts to gain Khmer Rouge compliance.[34]

Sanderson was undoubtedly aware that neither the big powers nor the troop contributors (including his own government) were willing to countenance any intensification of the conflict. UNTAC thus refrained in its execution mission in favor of mediation. It also believed it could best preserve its impartiality by negotiating in response to Khmer Rouge intransigence.

Others in UNTAC, notably its deputy force commander at the time, General Michel Loridon of France, and the media disputed the decision. They argued that UNTAC had clear authority under the Paris accords and Security Council resolutions to move past the guerrillas. Any fighting that ensued would thus constitute self-defense of a peacekeeping operation, rather than peace enforcement. They believed that the only way to convince the factions of UNTAC's seriousness was to execute its mandate in the face of resistance, not retreat and compromise. To them, the incident represented a turning point toward

UNTAC's loss of credibility.[35] Loridon was replaced because of his arguments with Akashi and Sanderson over these matters.

b. UNTAC Adjusts

As a result of Khmer Rouge violations of the accords, UNTAC could not carry out Phase II of the cease-fire. The cantonment areas emptied out as the troops returned to the field or went on so-called agricultural leave in their villages. The bulk of the military component, the infantry battalions, was left without its main task and became more of a presence than any type of supervisor. Some battalions found other work to perform, such as significant civic project assistance by the Indonesian battalion.

By the end of 1992, Akashi and the UN had abandoned any pretense of Phase II. Recognizing that UNTAC's ultimate purpose was the conduct of the elections, UNTAC reorganized the zones in which the military were deployed to correspond better to the electoral provinces and districts. This would permit deployment of military units near population centers and UN electoral officials. As violence by the Khmer Rouge and SOC increased, the component provided armed escorts to electoral workers. During the elections, the military guarded most polling sites.

As for the other units, the approximately 500 military observers (UNMOs) remained well occupied. They traveled to remote areas to report on the movement of the armed forces and the military clashes throughout the mandate period, manned border checkpoints, and conducted liaison with neighboring governments. Some UNMOs served with a Strategic Investigation Team created in May 1992 to investigate Khmer Rouge accusations of a remaining Vietnamese troop presence. Hampered by a dearth of reliable information, the unit did not find any Vietnamese until March 1993, when it conclusively identified a handful of demobilized Vietnamese. That discovery itself may well have led to a Khmer Rouge massacre of at least 34 ethnic Vietnamese a few days later.[36] UNTAC had no difficulty in finding Thai forces routinely crossing into Khmer Rouge zones.[37]

The Mine Clearance Training Unit, staffed by experts from eight countries, began the process of training and supervising Cambodians in the agonizingly slow process of clearing mines. Its priorities included roads and resettlement areas for returning refugees. Logistics, communications, transportation, and medical units provided critical support functions. And the two thousand soldiers in the engineering battalions from five countries (the largest from Thailand, Japan, and China) began to restore bridges, roads, and other parts of the physical infrastructure devastated by the war. Although officially supporting the military component, the engineering battalions initiated a public service for Cambodians through what amounted to civic assistance programs.

c. Civilian Police (CIVPOL)

CIVPOL had a mandate to supervise the police of the four existing administrative structures; like the other components, it focused primarily on the SOC. Its 3,600-man contingent corresponded to one CIVPOL for every 15 local Cambodian policemen. CIVPOL would not respond directly to criminal incidents, seeing its mandate as limited to alerting and following SOC police officers. The component investigated many crimes, although with inconsistent success in identifying culprits.

CIVPOL was plagued from the beginning by more internal problems than any other component. Many donor states lacked any tradition of police respect for citizens or accused criminals, and did not send their best officers in any case. Some, including an entire group from Bulgaria, were corrupt and even criminal in their behavior. Most complaints by local Cambodians against UNTAC stemmed from inappropriate behavior by CIVPOL members, including sexual harassment and rudeness. This badly tarnished UNTAC's image with the populace. Moreover, some spoke no French or English, preventing communication with the rest of UNTAC.

Members of other components routinely criticized CIVPOL officers for neglect and incompetence. Provincial human rights officers eventually sought out from among the local CIVPOL contingent those officers qualified to undertake investigations, as others had failed to gather facts properly or revealed the names of witnesses or victims to the SOC. Electoral officials voiced similar concerns, fearing that CIVPOL behavior put district electoral supervisors in danger.[38]

Thus, despite the existence of a clear precedent in the Namibia operation's police force, the UN failed to attract an efficient, knowledgeable cadre. Beyond the force's uneven level, the UN also organized no real preparation for it. Other than the briefest of human rights awareness classes once members arrived in Cambodia, the officers received no training.[39]

2. Attempts at Creating a Neutral Political Environment: The Civil Administration Component

The civil administration component had the most unprecedented challenge in UNTAC. It was to exercise control, supervision, and oversight over the factional governments in the zones they controlled, according to the three-tiered scheme in the Paris accords. For most of Cambodia, this meant asserting authority over the incumbent State of Cambodia, both because it controlled 80 to 90 percent of the territory and because the Khmer Rouge refused to allow UNTAC into its zones. During the summer and fall of 1992, UNTAC established seven branches within the component's headquarters as well as sent representatives to each of Cambodia's provinces. Five of the branches oversaw the areas intended for "direct control," namely foreign affairs, defense, information, security, and finance. A "specialized control" branch followed other parts of the SOC's apparatus that could affect electoral neutrality. An investigations section considered complaints from Cambodians regarding conduct undermining a neutral political environment.

Translating the component's mandate into daily oversight proved far more complex. Although UNTAC designated July 1, 1992, as the day upon which it would assume full control over the five areas, the component lacked the manpower and planning to begin any oversight on time. As its staff trickled in during the first six months, component director Porcell and his aides defined three types of control to exercise in the pertinent ministries: a priori, involving a prior knowledge of, and the ability to change, proposed governmental decisions; a posteriori, permitting UNTAC to receive documents and require alterations in governmental action; and appraisal, in which UNTAC would propose improvements in the workings of ministries. By the fall of 1992, six months after UNTAC arrived, it had developed operational guidelines for the ministries describing UNTAC's role.[40]

The control to be exercised turned directly upon the limited size of the component. Porcell and other senior UNTAC officials recognized that full "direct control" would have required dozens of persons in the SOC's ministries examining papers and attending meetings. UNTAC thus decided to concentrate on those aspects of the civil administration that had the greatest impact upon elections.[41] This approach differed from the Paris accords, which gave UNTAC "direct control" over the five areas on the assumption that all business conducted in those ministries per se affected the elections.[42]

Despite these policies, the nature of the State of Cambodia apparatus ensured that the SOC leadership's intransigence would stymie UNTAC's work on all fronts. As a typical socialist government, party and state were united; key government officials served as functionaries of the SOC's Cambodian People's Party (CPP). When UNTAC tried to control, supervise, or oversee a state agency to create a neutral political environment, decisions would simply move to party channels. Beyond this, like many Asian bureaucracies, neither the SOC nor the CPP undertook decisions through formal processes such as meetings accompanied by pre- and post-decisional memoranda. Rather, key individuals made decisions on their own and conveyed them directly to subordinates, usually without any record.

In theory, this should not have hampered UNTAC's mandate, since a neutral political environment turned more on results than process. Thus, in theory,

UNTAC would know if a SOC agency had favored the CPP regardless of how it reached its decision. In practice, however, UNTAC was ill-matched for the SOC and could not identify the source of many decisions or know the means to remedy a situation. If UNTAC utilized its power to issue a directive or remove a bureaucrat, it could have no confidence that such action would correct the problem.[43] Indeed, Soviet participants in the drafting of the accords admitted that they accepted control of the SOC precisely because of the ease with which the SOC could resist it; the SOC may well have accepted the accords from the same cynical perspective.[44]

Moreover, the SOC was an inherently corrupt institution. Many civil servants had no loyalty to anything but money, family, or party. The bureaucracy lacked the mentality of an entity dedicated to public service, and UNTAC had little hope of inculcating one. Thus, if UNTAC fired one corrupt person, it knew with virtual certainty that the official replacing him would prove just as likely to use the powers of his office to advance his own, his family's, or the party's agenda.[45]

The offices within the component made a start on UNTAC's duties under the Paris accords, but suffered due to the SOC's limited willingness to cooperate:

• The *foreign affairs service* concentrated on issuance of passports and visas to ensure that all Cambodians could travel and return to Cambodia. A border control unit supervised immigration and customs at frontier checkpoints. It helped train SOC agents in collecting duties and monitoring border traffic, but could do little about the movement of persons and goods at the numerous unmonitored crossing points or in Khmer Rouge-controlled areas. The service did not address the foreign policy of the SOC, regarding it (incorrectly, it would seem) as irrelevant to a neutral political environment.[46]

• The *defense service,* with its small staff, could not control the State of Cambodia's defense establishment. Although UNTAC officials could read daily correspondence and examine files, ministry officials responded uncooperatively to requests for documents or for investigations of complaints of intimidation by SOC soldiers. The service spent much time addressing the sale of ministry property by officials for their own profit. It succeeded only in obtaining, after many months, an inventory of questionable accuracy of governmental properties. The service wrote a code of conduct for political activity by the military, which the SOC and non-communist resistance armies adopted, but which all ignored freely.[47]

• The *public security service* spent much of its early months trying to defuse a tense situation in Phnom Penh in which the SOC wanted to evict forcibly a group of squatters; it achieved some success in taming the actions of the SOC police. The component prepared a penal law for the transitional period, which the SNC approved in September 1992. It also drafted directives on matters such as the political activity of police, possession of arms, detention, road traffic, and rights of association. The SOC sometimes enforced the directives applying to the general public, such as traffic rules, but circumvented those applying to its own officials.

The service also trained police, judges, and prosecutors about the penal law, which was a complicated statute modeled on its French counterpart. Yet it made little dent in the corruption, inefficiency, and lack of independence of the judiciary. UNTAC inspected prisons, but conditions remained deplorable. Control over the SOC's ministries of national security and justice proved of marginal utility as decisions shifted to party organs.[48]

• The *finance service* faced a nearly impossible task, as ruling party money mingled freely with government funds. Abandoning any hopes of eliminating corruption, it concentrated on controlling practices that could directly affect the elections. The service established elaborate procedures and deployed about 30 people in the SOC finance ministry and central bank to track revenues and expenditures, requiring UNTAC approval before disbursement of funds.[49] A more rudimentary process took place at the provincial level, although with few tangible results.

Although UNTAC could compare official revenues with official expenses, it could not prevent flows of money off the books. UNTAC protested the more blatant corruption practices, sometimes with good results. It had greater successes in training SOC bureaucrats in basic public finance, such as accounting practices, customs processing, and taxation. SOC revenues increased due to better collection and increases in hotel and gasoline taxes. UNTAC also monitored the major civilian expenditures of the KPNLF and FUNCINPEC.[50]

• The *information* service monitored Cambodian media and issued guidelines for the press. It also convened groups where journalists could state their complaints about lack of press freedoms. The service managed to convince the SOC to require its TV station (the only national station) to carry messages of UNTAC and all the political parties.[51]

• The *specialized control service* exercised the second level of responsibility under the Paris accords, control or supervision, over a range of areas assigned to it by Akashi in May 1992: public health, education, culture and monuments, tourism, transport, telecommunications, civil aviation, ports and inland waters, agriculture, forestry, fisheries, mining and petroleum, energy, and the civil service.

Among its small achievements, it prepared a code of conduct for civil servants of the factions and reviewed national distribution of fertilizer in response to concerns of political bias. It also established a National Heritage Protection

Authority in a near-futile attempt to prevent looting of national architectural treasures, ended some corruption by SOC port officials, and eliminated some practices in higher education that linked student advancement to party loyalty. UNTAC proved impotent in trying to control the SOC's civil aviation authority due to the entrenched corruption of its chief, Prince Norodom Chakrapong, a son of Prince Sihanouk. UNTAC was thus unable to nullify aviation agreements that the SOC signed with other countries in disregard of the Paris accords (which gave this power to the SNC alone). The service's small staff and lack of information-gathering resources prevented any systematic supervision of the SOC administration.[52]

• Finally, the *investigative service* tried to examine any SOC behavior affecting the political environment. It did not address other human rights violations or breaches of the electoral law, which those components handled. Given the impossibility of achieving this broad task with the service's small staff, it focused on harassment by government officials and land disputes, especially evictions to sell land to foreigners, because these episodes entailed a high risk of resultant public unrest.[53] UNTAC looked into the merits of thousands of complaints, creating some pressure upon the SOC to avoid intimidation, but leaving Cambodians dissatisfied.[54]

Beyond the ministries implementing governmental policy, UNTAC also sought control over the SOC Council of Ministers, the senior executive governmental policymaking body. The council made all key governmental decisions, and SOC officials, especially those in the provinces, would usually delay responding to UNTAC complaints until authorized by the council.[55] Yet UNTAC sought that control too late. Its request came only in the fall of 1992, after UNTAC realized the limitations of overseeing the ministries, and the SOC refused to allow it.

The component relied heavily upon codes of conduct over entire ministries, but rarely used its stronger powers under the Paris accords. Akashi and Porcell removed a handful of corrupt officials. These included the governor of Kompong Chhnang province, the director of the port of Sihanoukville, and a foreign ministry official responsible for issuance of passports. UNTAC did so, however, through a quiet request to the SOC leadership, not any public firings.[56] Similarly, its directives for corrective action took the form of requests, not orders. In many cases, the SOC ignored them, asserting lack of conclusive evidence. In a showdown with UNTAC in January 1993, Akashi attempted to remove the governor of the important province of Battambang (a nephew of Chea Sim, the chairman of the CPP), based on his complicity in political intimidation. The SOC refused, daring UNTAC to remove SOC Premier Hun Sen first.[57]

The civil administration component thus achieved mixed short-term results: it eliminated some blatant corruption, dissuaded others through monitoring, improved the functioning of some ministries through oversight and technical assistance, and may have helped start a process of creating a working governmental bureaucracy. But as for its main goal under the Paris accords of ensuring a neutral political environment, the component could not overcome the opposition from the SOC. And any prospects for control over the Khmer Rouge zones had long since been scuttled by the faction's defiance of UNTAC. One provincial official analogized his role to that of merely a political officer writing situation reports.[58]

By early 1993, as the elections neared, UNTAC saw the failures of the civil administration efforts. Abandoning hope of neutralizing the SOC bureaucracy, Porcell decided to focus on the most egregious cases and challenge the SOC much more directly. He deployed "Control Teams" from headquarters that would arrive without warning at a provincial government office and search it. As a result, UNTAC uncovered written proof of "widespread and persistent use" of the state apparatus to support the Cambodian People's Party. UNTAC also uncovered SOC culpability for attacks on opposition leaders and intimidation of the population.[59] UNTAC publicized this evidence, but the SOC did not desist. Before the elections occurred, Akashi and Boutros-Ghali conceded that the requisite neutral political environment had not materialized, and instead spoke of "basic minimum acceptable conditions."[60]

3. The Electoral Mandate

The electoral component's imposing mandate of organizing and conducting the elections necessitated detailed planning and execution. The component assumed a rather low-key and professional role during the first nine months of UNTAC's operation, laying the groundwork for the elections. By early 1993, as the failure of the military and civilian control mandates sunk in, UNTAC focused nearly all its energies on the elections.

a. The Early Months: Laying the Foundations

The only seriously controversial election issue during 1992 was the proposed electoral law, over which UNTAC consulted with the Supreme National Council and which Akashi promulgated in August 1992.[61] The law included a code of conduct for political parties, nearly identical to that drafted by UNTAG for Namibia in 1989. The drafting of the electoral law gave rise to another important test of UNTAC's response to decaying consent, one in which it would take a very different course of action from the "bamboo pole incident."

During the law's drafting, the resistance demanded that ethnic Khmer living in southern Vietnam (an area once part of the Khmer empire and long a source of irredentist claims by Cambodian leaders), as well as Cambodians overseas, be allowed to vote. They also insisted that many ethnic Vietnamese in Cambodia be barred from voting.[62] To bolster its nationalist credentials, the SOC accepted these conditions, as did Prince Sihanouk. Akashi, however, with his plenary authority under the accords in the area of elections, rejected most of their requests. He did not give any special rights to ethnic Khmer in Vietnam; he agreed to let Cambodians overseas vote, but only at three polling stations and only if they registered in Cambodia; and he refused to bar ethnic Vietnamese in Cambodia from voting, although he did narrow the definition of eligible voters from that in the Paris accords.[63]

In this instance, UNTAC clearly leaned away from mediating, in the direction of execution and guaranteeing the integrity of the elections. Akashi even overruled and angered Prince Sihanouk and a unanimous SNC. His decision reflected the importance of avoiding the historical, intractable questions of the status of Vietnamese in Cambodia and Cambodians in Vietnam. Despite repeated protests from the resistance factions and Prince Sihanouk, and the Khmer Rouge's announcement that it would boycott the election unless UNTAC amended the criteria, Akashi refused to change the law.

Yet to some in UNTAC, Akashi compromised too much. They found his modification of the registration criteria incompatible with the Paris accords and a sign of retreat in the face of unreasonable demands from the factions. They believed it sent a message to the factions that they could successfully renegotiate unambiguous sections of the Paris accords and push UNTAC away from administering the settlement.[64]

Austin and the rest of the electoral component continued their organizational efforts despite the overall atmosphere of decaying consent. Although the Khmer Rouge would not allow UNTAC into its zones of control, the SOC did not impede UNTAC's efforts to set up the elections (which the SOC assumed it would win). The component thus spent the early months preparing for the registration of voters, which took place between October 1992 and February 1993. About 800 five-person teams of UN officials and Cambodians panned out throughout Cambodia (except in the Khmer Rouge areas). This resulted in a significant success for UNTAC: more than 4.6 million people, nearly all those eligible to vote, registered. UNTAC also registered 20 political parties, but could not persuade the Khmer Rouge's Party of Democratic Kampuchea to participate.

b. Organizing Amidst Violence

By late 1992, UNTAC was planning the mechanics of the polling and forming various links with the populace about the elections. It ultimately recruited 50,000 Cambodians and 1,000 foreigners to man some 1,600 polling stations. Beginning in 1993, with the assistance of the Information and Education division, the electoral component undertook a nationwide campaign through radio, television, videos, comic books, and stickers to convince the population of the secrecy of their vote. This effort responded to voter intimidation, primarily by the SOC, and of temporary seizure of voter identification cards by the Khmer Rouge and the SOC. Indeed, it became the linchpin of a fair election in light of the absence of a neutral environment due to SOC and Khmer Rouge misdeeds.[65] Akashi also arranged for CIVPOL to guard opposition party offices after attacks on them in December, and helped convince the opposition not to withdraw from the process. UNTAC also banned opinion polls, as they could be a cover for intimidation tactics.

During the two to three months before the elections, the mission had to respond to increased levels of violence. In March, the Khmer Rouge committed the first of a series of new massacres against ethnic Vietnamese. Along with other attacks on Cambodians, the group would kill some 131 Cambodians by the time of the election.[66] UNTAC also arranged for transportation for party officials when the SOC would not allow the opposition's aircraft to land at main airports. UNTAC began to impose penalties for violations of the electoral law. Some SOC officials lost their right to vote and others paid a fine for holding an illegal rally. Despite the deaths of 200 Cambodians during the campaign attributable to the Khmer Rouge and the SOC, more than 1,500 campaign rallies took place with little violence.[67]

After a Japanese electoral volunteer was killed in early April 1993, apparently by a local resident angered that he had not been chosen as a poll worker, more than 60 UN Volunteers left the country, and UNTAC provided security for those assigned to dangerous areas.[68] The Khmer Rouge attacked UNTAC outposts from late March through mid-May; of the 13 deaths of UNTAC civilian and military personnel in hostile action during this period, all but a handful could be attributed to Khmer Rouge elements. This necessitated evacuating UNTAC from several tense areas, redeploying other officials, and eliminating polling sites in some Khmer Rouge-threatened zones. The Khmer Rouge also issued vitriolic public statements against the elections.[69]

c. The Polling

Although threats and actions against UNTAC increased during the weeks before the elections, UNTAC proceeded with the polling, which took place from May 23–28. To the great surprise of many UNTAC officials and foreign observers, no significant violence marred the elections. As a result, nearly 90 percent of registered Cambodians turned out at 1,400 fixed and 200 mobile polling stations, voting peacefully and with full preservation of ballot secrecy. Cambodians even emerged from the Khmer Rouge's zones to vote.

After completion of the polling, Akashi announced on May 29 that, in light of the peaceful atmosphere and lack of significant technical irregularities, the conduct of the elections had been free and fair.[70] As it counted the ballots, UNTAC released the results twice a day, over SOC objections, in order to preserve the transparency of the process. By June 10, all counting was complete and Akashi announced the results to the SNC. The royalist opposition, FUNCINPEC, received 45.5 percent of the vote and 58 of the 120 seats in the constituent assembly; the State of Cambodia's Cambodian People's Party received 38.2 percent and 51 seats. The remaining 16 percent went to smaller parties, the largest to the Buddhist Liberal Democratic Party, affiliated with the pro-U.S. KPNLF, which won 10 seats.

Akashi then issued a careful statement in which he discussed the fairness of the election as a whole. While acknowledging the absence of a neutral political environment and the many threats to the process, he proclaimed "this latest phase of the election process has been performed in a free and fair manner . . . fairly and accurately reflect[ing] the will of the Cambodian people" and called on the winners and losers to "bury the hatchet of yesterday" and cooperate.[71] Austin and the electoral component also prepared a meticulous rebuttal of the SOC's accusations of procedural improprieties that instead blamed the incumbents for numerous acts of intimidation before the polling.[72]

The Khmer Rouge's decision not to disrupt the polling, like much of the secretive organization, cannot be easily explained. Diplomats and UN officials suggested a number of motivating factors. Thailand and China, the Khmer Rouge's erstwhile allies, had strongly urged the group not to disrupt the elections; the Khmer Rouge may have suspected that the opposition parties would fare well in the polling; the group lacked the manpower systematically to disrupt the polling; and the Khmer Rouge leadership and lower levels may have been unwilling in 1993 to countenance or participate in large-scale violence against ordinary Cambodians.

Whatever the reason, the violence-free polling handed UNTAC a needed victory. Despite UNTAC's inability to accomplish much of the core of its mandate, namely restoration of peace and political neutrality, Cambodians turned out in large numbers to vote on their future, and rejected the government that had run their country for 14 years. It appeared that UNTAC's campaign for the

hearts and minds of ordinary Cambodians had succeeded where its more her-
culean assignments had missed their mark.

4. Promotion and Protection of Human Rights

The human rights component had a twofold mission: to foster a tolerable
human rights situation for free and fair elections, and to create a long-term consciousness of human rights in order to prevent a return to Cambodia's atrocious
past. With its staff of about 40 in the capital and provinces (except for areas
controlled by the Khmer Rouge), the unit tried to monitor conditions and
responded to hundreds of complaints by Cambodian citizens. The absence of
any kind of neutral political environment due to the lack of effective civil
administration control gave the component a larger-than-expected responsibility for fostering a climate of confidence for the elections.[73]

The component eliminated numerous abuses, but remained powerless
against systematic, orchestrated violations, such as Khmer Rouge massacres
of scores of ethnic Vietnamese and SOC murders of at least a dozen opposition leaders and intimidation of many more. The lack of an effective judicial
system also meant that UNTAC had an important role in trying to promote civil
and political rights in a country with no tradition of such freedoms.[74] UNTAC
obtained the release of hundreds of political detainees and visited prisons to
check compliance with UN standards on the treatment of the remaining prisoners.[75] Conditions improved slightly, but hundreds remained in miserable jails
without the prospect of a trial.

UNTAC also reformed the penal and judicial codes, but depended upon the
SOC to implement those laws, which it did not. Human rights nongovernmental
organizations severely criticized UNTAC for its lack of success in improving
the human rights situation to a greater degree, pointing out that UNTAC sacrificed human rights protection in order to advance the implementation process
toward the elections. They especially lamented UNTAC's reluctance to take the
strong "corrective action" allowed under the Paris accords.[76]

Under McNamara's leadership, the unit also embarked on an extensive
mass media campaign to explain the Universal Declaration of Human Rights.
In conjunction with CIVPOL and the civil administration component, it ran
education and training seminars for judges, defenders, police, and others in
positions of responsibility. Members of all factions, even a small number
from the Khmer Rouge, attended these presentations. UNTAC helped local
Cambodian human rights organizations set up and convinced the SNC to ratify major international human rights conventions.[77]

In January 1993, after numerous attacks on resistance politicians, Akashi
issued a directive on prosecuting human rights violators.[78] He appointed an

Australian lawyer, Mark Plunkett, as UNTAC Special Prosecutor, with authority to arrest and try people within the courts of Cambodia. The prosecutor
arrested a handful of Khmer Rouge and SOC cadre on murder charges and
issued arrest warrants for others. His work, however, was stymied by
UNTAC's lack of manpower to apprehend fleeing suspects and the refusal of
the politicized and nearly moribund SOC courts to cooperate. Akashi authorized UNTAC to detain suspects beyond 48 hours, but a prison built for this
purpose remained empty. The special prosecutor did have a certain deterrent
effect, but he did not prosecute any rights violators.[79]

Finally, aware of the short shelflife of its limited successes, the group
pressed the UN Commission on Human Rights for a post-UNTAC UN role in
Cambodia. At its February 1993 meeting, the Commission asked the UN
Centre for Human Rights to establish an operational presence in Cambodia.
It also appointed a Special Representative to assist the elected government and
guide a future UN presence, but, in response to pressure from ASEAN and
China, rejected Akashi's request for a Special Rapporteur who would have had
a stronger mandate to investigate and report on human rights abuses.[80]

5. The Repatriation Process

Though UNTAC had formal responsibility for the repatriation of the 365,000
Cambodian refugees and displaced persons, UNHCR had control over the
mission, and Vieira de Mello served as the senior UNHCR representative in
Cambodia. Despite dire prognostications from many refugee experts, the repa-
triation operation occurred smoothly. It began on March 30, 1992, with 526
Cambodians returning from Thailand. By September, more than 115,000 had
returned to Cambodia, and more than 240,000 by the end of December 1992.
The operation ended by March 1993, when the last camp in Thailand closed.

UNTAC originally planned to send most returnees to designated farmland.
However, the shortage of mine-free, arable land caused UNTAC to offer
returnees cash instead. While this led a disproportionate number to settle in
the cities and towns, and delayed resettlement for large numbers of returnees,
the process took place with few casualties. Outside agencies such as the World
Food Program (a joint operation of the UN and the Food and Agriculture
Organization) delivered food to internally displaced persons. The UN's work
ended a 13-year crisis that had brought hardship for the Cambodians, financial strain on the UN, and political difficulties for Thailand.

Repatriation proceeded smoothly for several reasons. First, as noted earlier,
UNHCR had a significant leadtime to prepare the process and a large presence
in the region to carry it out. Second, most Cambodians in Thailand genuinely
wished to return, preventing the prospect of large-scale forcible or involuntary

repatriations.[81] Most important, the lack of cooperation of the Khmer Rouge and the SOC that crippled much of UNTAC did not carry over to the repatriation process, as all four factions cooperated continually with UNTAC and UNHCR. For the factions, repatriation proved the easiest part of the Paris accords to implement. It not only did not threaten their vital interests, but the new arrivals represented potential sources of support.[82]

6. Economic Rehabilitation

UNTAC's rehabilitation component coordinated foreign assistance for the reconstruction of the country; it had no budget for its own projects.[83] The component assessed Cambodia's immediate economic needs and developed a strategy for restoring the most pressing inadequacies in the country's infrastructure. It oversaw a donor's conference in Tokyo in June 1992, at which more than $800 million was pledged, and then worked with donors to identify and facilitate funding of specific projects.

Donors approached UNTAC with proposals, which then obtained the approval of a "Technical Advisory Committee" of the SNC to assure the factions that the funds would benefit the Cambodian people and not the SOC apparatus alone. (The Khmer Rouge refused to participate in the committee.) The SNC approved many projects, but little of the money pledged at Tokyo was disbursed during UNTAC's tenure, as most donors designated funds for long-term projects.

The component also chaired an SNC Technical Advisory Committee on natural resource exploitation, which prepared the directive issued by the SNC in September 1992 banning the exportation of logs. Originally meant to protect Cambodia's forests, this measure received the endorsement of the Security Council in November 1992 to pressure the Khmer Rouge to comply with the Paris accords by limiting their income from Thai logging interests. The component also prepared a ban on exports of gems, which the SNC approved in February 1993. The SOC and the Khmer Rouge both violated the bans with impunity, as Thai, Japanese, and other companies continued to make gem and timber exploitation profitable.[84] Log exports significantly decreased in the months preceding the elections, although the long-term prospects for the ban remain grim.[85]

Despite the component's talented staff under Lawrence (about a dozen in all), the realities of Cambodian politics sometimes overwhelmed it. Most notably, the traditional practice of states and multilateral development banks of providing economic assistance to a country's government proved incompatible with Cambodian politics. In Cambodia, the SOC constituted only one faction, the other three had a legally equal role, and the SNC served as Cambodia's external representative.

Early in the implementation, UNTAC prepared Boutros-Ghali's April 19, 1992, appeal for international aid for Cambodia. It included a proposal to use these funds to finance the SOC's budget deficit (previously financed through printing of money).[86] While perhaps prudent economics, the plan infuriated the resistance. They saw it as propping up the flailing SOC before elections, and UNTAC abandoned the idea.[87] Furthermore, when representatives of the IMF and World Bank visited Cambodia, they followed their practice of meeting finance ministry officials who would oversee the use of multilateral assistance. But they initially met only with the SOC, viewing the other factions as nongovernmental and the SNC as legally unable to guarantee appropriate use of the money.[88] Most multilateral loans were never finalized because at least one of the resistance factions opposed the targets of funding. Finally, the component could not prevent some donors, notably Japan, from giving money directly to the SOC by bypassing the SNC's committee.[89] UNTAC tried to facilitate rehabilitation while preserving electoral neutrality, in the process encountering the characteristic challenges to impartiality of the new peacekeepers.

Supporting players outside UNTAC did contribute somewhat to the rehabilitation process. Nongovernmental organizations funded modest projects with more immediate results than those funded by donors. UNDP, which opened an office even before the signature of the Paris accords, worked closely with UNTAC on much of the detailed assessment of the country's development needs. It also directly funded projects, including assistance to returnees in rural development, job training in fields from health care to agriculture to air traffic control, repair of roads and bridges, and AIDS awareness. UNESCO ran a program to map out the Angkor site as well as smaller projects related to education; WHO and UNICEF addressed sanitation and other public health needs. Despite these efforts, Cambodia remained a desperately poor country during the UN's tenure, with most of its ills impervious to short-term fixes.

7. The Education Function

UNTAC's Information and Education Division (not a component, although part of it performed the information control function for the civil administration component) provided critical assistance in the production and dissemination of information to Cambodians. It ran Radio UNTAC (which broadcast messages from all political parties as well as UNTAC), developed video presentations, and printed and distributed posters, leaflets, T-shirts, and other trinkets on the elections and human rights. Carney's and the division's efforts constituted one of UNTAC's major successes, as UNTAC sought to convince

Cambodians of the secrecy of their vote despite the violence and omnipresent SOC. While the extent to which it eliminated these fears will never be fully known, the high voter turnout can be traced, in part, to the division's work. It also contained a small "analysis/assessment unit," a thinktank of Khmer-speaking Cambodia experts who traveled widely to gather intelligence on the plans of the factions, especially the Khmer Rouge, and the Cambodian people's opinions about UNTAC.

8. UNTAC and the Supreme National Council

Under the Paris accords, UNTAC had to consult with the SNC and comply with its "advice" if it furthered the settlement. Although the drafters of the agreement assumed an impotent SNC, Akashi took this obligation seriously. He attempted to convene the SNC as a forum for the factions to argue their positions and reach a consensus. He hoped that the SNC or Sihanouk would initiate or endorse policy that he could then implement with their support.[90] While Akashi saw many aspects of the mandate as clear from the Paris accords, such as UNTAC's three levels of control and supervision, he sought SNC guidance on issues not addressed by the agreements. These included the content of codes of conduct and the electoral law, receipt of foreign aid, and the definition of "foreign forces" whose presence was banned under the agreement.

Akashi adopted a number of strategies with the SNC, sometimes trying to mediate among its members' positions, other times leaving the issue to the Cambodians to tackle, and still others seeking Prince Sihanouk's decision. Akashi did not view disagreements among members or their failure to attend meetings as a signal for taking immediate independent action. He knew of the difficulty of imposing a policy on an unwilling faction and also wished to place the political burden on the SNC and Sihanouk to make policy.[91]

For some issues, this tactic worked, as the SNC considered an issue through a Technical Advisory Committee and then took decisions, unanimously or through Sihanouk. Among its more notable accomplishments, the SNC accepted some foreign assistance, promulgated a penal law, issued moratoria on export of timber and gems, and adopted a definition of foreign forces. On several occasions, Akashi successfully pressured Sihanouk to overrule Khmer Rouge objections to proposed decisions after Sihanouk had stated his preference that Akashi make the decision.[92]

Over time, the feebleness of the SNC lived up to the expectations of the drafters of the Paris accords. Akashi adjusted his approach accordingly, sensing the importance of free and fair elections regardless of the views of the factions. During the preparation of the electoral law, he overruled the opposition factions after the prince refused to do so. As Prince Sihanouk recoiled from overruling the Khmer Rouge and then left the country for long periods, and the Khmer Rouge boycotted SNC meetings, Akashi had to act more on his own, often against Khmer Rouge wishes. As the election neared, he issued directives notwithstanding SOC opposition voiced in the SNC. The most notable decisions were to set up the special prosecutor's office and the control teams. As a result, SNC meetings became increasingly irrelevant as decision-making fora, and Akashi focused on implementing UNTAC policy regardless of SNC endorsement.

UNTAC'S POST-ELECTORAL FUNCTIONS AND WITHDRAWAL

Although the successful election represented the culmination of most of UNTAC's work, the operation remained in the country for several more months, its numbers dwindling as military and civilian officials withdrew. UNTAC had three primary goals during this period: to assist the Cambodian political leadership between the elections and the installation of a new government; to prepare for a small UN presence after the termination of UNTAC's mandate; and to ensure the orderly departure of UNTAC's 22,000 international personnel.

1. Aiding the Establishment of the New Government

The May 1993 elections left a divided, unstable Cambodian polity, with the opposition the largest vote-getter, but the incumbents firmly in control of the state machinery. The Khmer Rouge maintained a confusing stance, condemning the elections but accepting their results. It resumed earlier violence by attacking several trains and murdering groups of ethnic Vietnamese. During the weeks following the elections, UNTAC closely watched the political dealings between the two main political leaders, Hun Sen and Prince Ranariddh (with his father lurking in the background). With the strong backing of the Security Council, Akashi defended the electoral results and prevailed upon recalcitrant SOC leaders to accept them as the voice of the Cambodian people.[93]

Akashi did not, however, play any role of power broker, and UNTAC accepted a government military offensive against the Khmer Rouge after the elections. Instead, UNTAC attempted to build confidence among the winners and losers in the elections. One example was its effort to secure international funding to pay the SOC's civil servants, who had received virtually no salary in recent years and were a potential source of instability for any new government. The civil administration, human rights, and rehabilitation components also kept functioning as a measure of support for the transition. Members of the military and CIVPOL ran training programs for Cambodia's newly unified armed forces and police.

Senior UNTAC officials, such as the legal adviser, helped counsel the con-stituent assembly formed after the elections in drafting the new constitution. This advice served to educate the drafters about important principles of con-stitutional law. More important, UNTAC aimed to strengthen the human rights provisions of the constitution to conform with the Paris accords (which required a liberal democracy and the inclusion of a bill of rights).

After weeks of uncertainty over the status of the head of state and the pre-cise formula for power sharing between FUNCINPEC and SOC, the con-stituent assembly approved Cambodia's new constitution on September 21, 1993. It made Cambodia a kingdom again with Sihanouk as king. According to the Constitution, the king "shall not hold power," but he is also assigned the roles of guarantor of Cambodia's independence, sovereignty, and territorial integrity, and the rights of its people, as well as referee in power struggles.[94] On September 24, the new government was installed, with Ranariddh as First Prime Minister, Hun Sen as Second Prime Minister, and cabinet portfolios divided primarily between FUNCINPEC and SOC officials. In its first year, it had great difficulty in gaining control of the SOC bureaucracy and still faced a Khmer Rouge insurgency.

2. The UN's Post-UNTAC Presence

In preparing for a post-UNTAC UN role in Cambodia, UNTAC consulted extensively with the new government. Akashi and Boutros-Ghali agreed upon the idea of a UN office in Phnom Penh, headed by a UN representative, to coordinate the work of UN agencies in Cambodia. The Secretary-General also appointed a Special Representative for Human Rights in Cambodia, as required by the Commission on Human Rights in its February 1993 resolution—Justice Michael Kirby of the Court of Appeal of New South Wales, Australia. The Cambodian office of the UN Centre for Human Rights opened on October 1, 1993. The first regional office of the Centre, it was meant provide a minimal degree of human rights oversight in Cambodia.[95]

The new government also asked the UN to deploy a small group of unarmed military observers for six months after UNTAC'S departure to help build confidence in the provinces. Though Boutros-Ghali doubted the utility of such a small presence, the Security Council unanimously approved the send-ing of 20 "military liaison" officers for six months, with a rather unclear man-date.[96] The team worked until May 1994, reporting on continued fighting between the Khmer Rouge and the new national army and meeting with gov-ernmental officials. It had no power or funds, however, to improve the army, which remained plagued by low morale. Finally, UNTAC and Boutros-Ghali emphasized the need for continued funding of humanitarian relief to Cambodia, especially in the realm of demining, and committed the UN to a continued financial and managerial role in the UNTAC-created Cambodian Mine Action Centre.

3. UNTAC Departs

UNTAC's military and civilian officials departed Cambodia during the summer and fall of 1993. The military component withdrew by national battalion, with those deployed in stable areas leaving first and those in the more tense northwest leaving last. Some troop movements had to be rearranged due to attacks by Khmer Rouge elements. By the middle of November, the military component had departed. Other components left much faster than they had arrived, with nearly all of CIVPOL and the electoral component out by the middle of August.

The civil administration, human rights, and rehabilitation groups departed more gradually to help the transition to the new government, but left by late September. A small number of CIVPOL and civilians remained behind with the military liaison officers and mine clearance specialists. The continued tension in the country was highlighted when a German UNTAC medic was killed by an unknown assailant in Phnom Penh on October 14, 1993. This brought to at least 22 the total number of UNTAC personnel killed in hostilities.[97]

Withdrawal of equipment proceeded with difficulty as well. Theft of UNTAC equipment had always affected the operation, but its scope increased vastly after the elections, as organized gangs specialized in stealing UNTAC vehicles with the complicity of SOC officials. UNTAC extracted most of its movable equipment, but also arranged for some to be purchased by nongovernmental organizations, and then donated to the new government.

.8.

Tackling UNTAC: A Model Operation?

The foregoing review of UNTAC's tenure shows a UN operation attempting to carry out a complex mandate amidst constant resistance to its authority. While UNTAC never had to administer directly a piece of land as did the UN in West Irian, it suffered from operational shortcomings and faced the political dilemmas inherent in maintaining impartiality in an atmosphere of decaying consent. Indeed, UNTAC is paralleled in these respects only by the troubles of ONUC in the Congo, UNPROFOR in the former Yugoslavia, and UNOSOM II in Somalia.

This chapter looks beyond UNTAC's immediate accomplishments and defeats to evaluate, in light of the exogenous constraints on the operation, UNTAC's performance as a second-generation mission. It begins by addressing the need by decision makers for an overall, final verdict on peacekeeping missions, proposing several perspectives for such determinations and applying them to UNTAC. But only a more detailed critique of UNTAC can lead to a better comprehension of, and improved performance by, second-generation missions. The chapter thus offers a detailed appraisal of UNTAC's operational and political competence. It concludes with consideration of the roles played by the other major actors within the UN system.

DETERMINING THE "SUCCESS" OF UNTAC?

Decision makers in world capitals and at United Nations Headquarters, mired in numerous foreign policy crises, often find themselves seeking a verdict on peacekeeping operations. Searching for an unequivocal outcome, they ask, "Was UNTAC a success?," presuming that "lessons" and "prerequisites" automatically flow from this seemingly authoritative determination. In fact, UNTAC had both significant triumphs and important failures, and the ultimate success of UNTAC cannot be appraised absolutely. Although first-generation operations might have had clear benchmarks, notably maintenance of a cease-fire to enhance the prospect of peacemaking, second-generation peacekeeping's manifold agendas suggest the need for inquiry from a number of perspectives.[1]

1. Comparison with the Paris Accords and the Secretary General's Plan of Implementation

Compared with its original written mandate, UNTAC counts as a partial success. It organized and conducted all aspects of an impressive election involving millions of voters, helped build some human rights awareness, and repatriated hundreds of thousands of refugees, the most significant areas of concordance with the Paris accords. UNTAC, however, failed in two critical areas. It did not supervise the cantonment, disarmament, and demobilization of the factions, and thereby ensure a peaceful country for elections. Nor did it exercise the degree of control and supervision over the competing regimes, in particular the State of Cambodia, envisaged under the agreement to create a neutral political environment.

Yet placing UNTAC's performance alongside its mandate to determine the extent to which UNTAC undertook all the duties given it by the Security Council fails to account for the many aspects of the Cambodia situation beyond UNTAC's control. These were, most critically, the Khmer Rouge's near-total defiance of UNTAC and the SOC's intransigence on civil administration. Unless the UN is assumed to possess unlimited influence over all aspects of the political situation—if only it had enough money, personnel, and the political backing of the international community, hardly a realistic set of hypotheses—this instrument alone proves too blunt for a useful scrutiny of UNTAC or any other operation. A mission can and should change the opening exogenous constraints; but it cannot ignore or eliminate them. Moreover, the approach fails to consider activities by UNTAC not foreseen in the settlement plan but which nevertheless contributed to the peace process. These would include mine clearance, public works projects, technical assistance programs, and intangible accomplishments like confidence-building.

2. Comparison with Other Peacekeeping Operations

Relating UNTAC to other missions suffers from a number of analytical deficiencies. First, it would judge a complex operation such as UNTAC successful simply because it performed some duties, like conduct of elections, beyond the simpler mandates of truce-monitoring operations like UNDOF in the Golan Heights. Contrariwise, it could regard UNTAC as a failure compared to UNDOF because the latter has kept the peace, or compared to UNTAG because Namibia emerged as a peaceful democratic polity. This comparison, however, neglects the most critical difference between these missions and UNTAC—the cooperation of the parties during their tenure (Israel and Syria for UNDOF, and South Africa and SWAPO for UNTAG).

3. Impact upon Cambodia

From this perspective, UNTAC has the markings of a significant, short-term success, but its long-term impact remains uncertain. Most important, the holding of Cambodia's first free election despite a climate where the two main antagonists disrupted the process has resulted in a new beginning for Cambodian politics, one where the people have been at least somewhat empowered and voiced their views. Cambodia has a government with both internal and international legitimacy. The repatriation of refugees has brought in new talent and ended an unpleasant chapter in the lives of the returnees and the countries that harbored them. The human rights awareness programs has created what one UNTAC official called a "preconsciousness" among Cambodians and a pool of advocates for democratic principles.[2] The new foreign assistance will help start rebuilding Cambodia's wrecked economy.

This perspective would also regard UNTAC as a success by recognizing the differences it made to Cambodians outside its formal responsibilities under the Paris accords. UNTAC officials and resistance politicians alike, discouraged by the SOC's resistance to UNTAC control, nevertheless found much to credit in UNTAC's role as guarantor. As stated by one provincial director and echoed by a resistance official, UNTAC helped "shake Cambodians out of the apathy and fatalism" that had dominated the country, and became a small symbol of hope.[3] The technical assistance programs, not mentioned in the Paris accords but undertaken to aid civil administration control, began a process of return to normalcy and may have laid a few seeds for a future middle class.

Yet the persistence of antagonism between the Khmer Rouge and the new government and the superficiality of the reconciliation between the winners and losers after the elections leaves considerable doubt as to whether UNTAC will have enabled Cambodia truly to turn the corner. One fair election offers no guarantee of a long-term commitment to multiparty democracy. While Cambodia did not turn to full-scale civil war after the elections as did Angola, it is still a militarized country plagued by lawlessness and violence. The

Khmer Rouge remains in control of portions of western Cambodia, and the new government, crippled by internal bickering, seems incapable of defeating it. UNTAC's departure seems to have heralded a return to internecine conflict and a business-as-usual attitude by corrupt governmental officials of whatever factional stripe.[4]

This third approach seems the most analytically useful for appraising the success of UNTAC and other new peacekeeping operations. It focuses on the purpose of the new peacekeeping, namely assisting a country at implementing a solution to a conflict. It also takes account of the context of the new peacekeeping, as bound into the processes of peacemaking and peace-building. It seeks to determine the effects of the new peacekeeping operation upon the country's situation, with the UN as executor, mediator, and guarantor, not only the extent to which it performed a list of assignments. Such an approach will not likely result in an unqualified verdict of success or failure, but it locks the observer on the right target.[5] At the same time, a comparison of the situation in a country with the mission to that without it could lead to overly positive evaluations. No matter what UNTAC or any other operation does or does not accomplish, it is likely to have some positive influence on the state.

4. Impact upon the United Nations

A final, more systemic perspective would address the effect of an enormous operation such as UNTAC upon the ability of the United Nations to address other crises. In effect, the issue here concerns the opportunity costs of UNTAC to the Organization. Such an appraisal seems pertinent in light of the finite political, financial, and human resources of member states and the UN. An operation successful under the three earlier perspectives may represent a failure for the UN if it prevents the Organization from undertaking equally or more important assignments.

Thus, on the one hand, if UNTAC had not occupied some part of the UN's attention for the two years beginning with the signature of the Paris accords, the Organization would have had some additional resources to devote to other crises. In responding to the disasters in Somalia and Bosnia, member states took into account the UN's recent creation of UNTAC, an operation that states assumed would cost between one and two billion dollars. Similar amounts could not be dispensed so readily elsewhere. This may well have contributed to the small size and limited mandate that the Security Council originally gave UNOSOM in mid-1992, despite widespread starvation and anarchy in Somalia.

Yet this approach suffers from two flaws. First, assuming member states and the UN have a quantifiable amount of resources to devote to these crises, the calculus of relative priority is hardly facile. While some international conflicts, notably those involving massive loss of life and the risk of spreading, are more grave than others, the choices facing the international community are rarely clear-cut. Thus the starvation in Somalia, or anarchy in Rwanda, may be more serious than the conflict in the Western Sahara, but how does it compare with Angola, which has bled profusely from civil war for many years? Was Cambodia more or less urgent than El Salvador?

Second, the amount of resources the international community can devote to these situations is not fixed (even if it is finite). Thus opportunity costs appear impossible to gauge meaningfully. Other than the unexceptionable proposition that UNTAC did somewhat constrain the UN's actions elsewhere, it is difficult to determine the extent. Did it significantly hinder the deployment of UNOSOM? Would its absence have resulted in even more forceful action in Yugoslavia? While the critical member states clearly take account of ongoing commitments, they rarely view global politics as a zero sum game. Instead, if new emergencies arise, states try to muddle through, rearranging old resources and finding new ones as necessary.

Thus, while the deployment of UNTAC may have contributed to the delay in action in Somalia in 1992, more important influences were also at work. Among these were a preoccupation with Yugoslavia, a general lack of interest in Somalia until television news dramatized the horrific situation, and a reluctance to countenance peace enforcement action in a predominantly internal conflict. When the international community, especially the United States, agreed on the need to intervene forcibly, the United States deployed it troops, and the United Nations followed with an enlarged and reauthorized UNOSOM.[6]

Indeed, during the two years from the signature of the Paris accords to UNTAC's withdrawal, the organs of the UN authorized ten other missions— UNOSOM I and II, UNOMSA (South Africa), ONUMOZ (Mozambique), MICIVIH (Haiti), UNOMUR (Rwanda-Uganda), UNOMIG (Georgia), UNOMIL (Liberia), UNMIH (Haiti), and UNAMIR (Rwanda)—while expanding UNPROFOR and ONUSAL and maintaining the existing first-generation missions. While the willingness of members to donate troops, pay for them, and follow the missions actively remains far from satisfactory, they have nonetheless been deployed, member states have donated troops and other personnel, and the UN has somehow found money to maintain them, albeit often through tin-cup diplomacy. In the future, this trend may well reverse, but it will remain somewhat fruitless to calculate the effect of one operation upon the resources devoted to others.

From a more cynical perspective, UNTAC's most demonstrable impact on the UN was its mere existence. By creating UNTAC, the affected global and regional powers succeeded in removing the Cambodia conflict from active consideration by the political organs and placed it in the lap of the Secretariat. Whatever repercussions this may have had on the UN's performance elsewhere, UNTAC provided the political cover members needed to say they had solved the Cambodia problem and to move on to other issues.

INSIDE UNTAC: EXAMINING THE ENDOGENOUS VARIABLES

UNTAC's mission was, as noted, hampered from the outset by important exogenous variables: the fragile consent and inadequate cooperation of the Cambodian elites; the shattered country in which it operated; an often disengaged attitude among outside powers preoccupied with other crises; and an unprepared, overstretched Secretariat, neither ready to dispatch such an unprecedented, multifunctional mission nor able adequately to oversee it. While no mission will operate in an ideal environment, this opening position immediately distinguishes UNTAC from operations such as UNTAG in Namibia, or the smaller electoral mission in Nicaragua, which operated under far more favorable circumstances. Any appraisal of the other operations will require a similar isolation of the exogenous variables.

Yet, from Akashi down to the United Nations Volunteers in tiny hamlets across the country, UNTAC was an independent actor during its 20 months in Cambodia. Thus, as with earlier second-generation missions and their predecessors, the mission's operational competence and performance of its political functions merits independent assessment.

1. Operational Competence

a. UNTAC's Understanding of Cambodia

While first-generation operations could suffice with only military expertise, the new peacekeeping requires an integration of knowledge of the history, culture, and current politics of the country into the daily functioning of the mission. This need for basic knowledge will affect all future missions; in this UNTAC proved only partly competent.

First, UNTAC did not adequately teach its personnel about the historical struggle between Cambodia and its neighbors, the Khmer Rouge years, or the invasion by Vietnam. Most knew only what they had read in newspapers, a knowledge gap that proved especially dangerous as it affected UNTAC's treatment of the SOC and Khmer Rouge.[7] Many in UNTAC saw the SOC only as saviors of Cambodia from genocide and the tremendous anti-Vietnamese bias among the population as simply irrational racism.

In particular, the eagerness of many within the civil administration component (with a large contingent of French officials) to blame the Khmer Rouge for all of the difficulties of Cambodia or every violent episode during the implementation period created a perception and reality of some bias by parts of UNTAC. These officials would, however, point out that the Khmer Rouge's noncompliance was of a fundamentally different nature than the SOC's and the root cause of UNTAC's difficulties. Journalists and many nongovernmental organizations shared this predisposition, inviting a stream of media commentary urging UNTAC to take firmer actions against the Khmer Rouge, especially after the bamboo pole incident.

Compounding this trend, UNTAC did not effectively utilize the small reservoir of international expertise on Cambodia. Two categories of people had such expertise: expatriate Cambodians, living primarily in the United States and France, many of whom had strong loyalties to the factions; and a small number of scholars from academia, journalism, think tanks, and governments. UNTAC had a policy of refusing to give expatriate Khmer positions of responsibility for fear that political or family concerns would tilt their decisions. This general rule is reasonable, but UNTAC could have profited from some of these people through exceptions or at least an open invitation to them to offer their assessments of events.[8]

With respect to non-Khmer specialists, UNTAC retained a small, impressive group (including Stephen Heder and Christophe Peschoux), mostly within the Information and Education Division. But UNTAC lacked a true political section, and the political adviser to Akashi lacked expertise on Cambodia other than his service with UNAMIC.[9] Senior levels of UNTAC did not consistently take account of or defer to the views of experts.

Some of UNTAC's missteps would appear to have stemmed from this problem, notably the UN's economic rehabilitation proposal for funding the budget deficit of the SOC, with its perceived bias toward the incumbents. The perception of sympathy to the SOC increased the suspicions of the Khmer Rouge, who saw UNTAC as simply propping up the SOC. In a sense, UNTAC necessarily was doing this, as the SOC had administrative control of most of the country.

Second, although UNTAC could not expect its staff or senior officials to speak fluent Khmer, an extraordinarily difficult language, it did not amply educate all personnel about basic aspects of Cambodian culture and customs. On the seemingly mundane matters of politeness, treatment of women, and ways to respond to disputes, most behaved well, but some, especially the Bulgarian military contingent and many in CIVPOL, were ignorant of or flouted Cambodian mores. (One particularly egregious example occurred when a policeman in his car killed a bicyclist and fled the scene after depositing a small amount of money on the corpse.) While during the early months of the deployment, Cambodians had great respect for UNTAC, many came to have mixed emotions about the mission in light of such inconsiderate and rude behavior.[10] This attitude compromised UNTAC's role as guarantors of the Paris accords, as Cambodians saw it as contributing to Cambodia's woes.

b. Internal Management

As a multifaceted operation, UNTAC needed an effective internal management. Akashi did not devote much attention to this question. He may well have seen management as less important than his political dealings with the Cambodians or the quest for personnel and supplies for the operation. His deputy, Sadry, did spend some time on these issues. UNTAC was an appropriately flexible organism, shifting its priorities over time from military and civilian control to conduct of the elections. But the lack of institutionalized management procedures, even if inevitable given the demands on their time, compromised the efficiency of the operation.

Most decision making was organized only on a component-by-component basis, without sufficient procedures for sharing of information and coordination of responses. Aside from thrice-weekly staff meetings and the later "action cell" (composed of Sadry and the heads of the components) to make recommendations on measures against the SOC, UNTAC lacked a transparent intercomponent coordination process, and component heads acted very independently.[11] The lack of clear procedures led to disgruntlement that components were pursuing different agendas, that UNTAC had no clear set of priorities, and that Akashi was not considering all views. This exacerbated more fundamental differences among the components over UNTAC's political approach to intransigence by the Khmer Rouge and SOC.

One manifestation of the lack of cooperation among components occurred in UNTAC's procedures for investigating and responding to unacceptable behavior by the factions. Three separate mechanisms developed. The civil administration component had an investigation division and, under the Paris accords, an administrative sanction—the power to demand the removal of an official. The electoral component had its own investigations branch and, under the UNTAC-drafted electoral law, an electoral sanction—the power to de-register and fine parties or candidates. The human rights component had its own investigators and a criminal sanction—indictment by the special prosecutor. But these investigations required coordination, as many cases would concern two or three components. Use of sanctions would also affect the SOC's attitude toward UNTAC as a whole. Only in 1993 did UNTAC create the "action cell" to coordinate sanctions against violators of the accords.[12]

The relationship among the components at the provincial level remained equally confusing. The provincial representative of the civil administration component had the title "provincial director," yet the heads of the other components insisted that he lacked line authority over the local human rights or electoral officers. This arrangement meant that officials had to refer any disagreements between units at the provincial level to UNTAC Headquarters. Although provincial offices had regular meetings of staff from all the components present, and most provincial officials worked well together, UNTAC never outlined a clear mechanism to resolve any differences.[13]

UNTAC's relations also became strained with the international media that flocked to Cambodia for the mission. While the press acted on its hunting instinct for negative stories, particularly those involving casualties, Akashi and his staff did not use the press effectively. The press spokesman's short temper often antagonized journalists, and UNTAC only belatedly undertook an active effort to court the media to emphasize its accomplishments.[14] In one almost farcical episode in March 1993, a Russian-made UNTAC helicopter carrying journalists on an official trip designed to highlight UNTAC's accomplishments crashed, injuring the occupants, and generating yet another negative story. While UNTAC officials repeatedly used the media to fight internal battles, UNTAC itself rarely used it to push the factions along or galvanize international support. Fortunately for UNTAC, the successful outcome of the elections became the media's final verdict on UNTAC, one the UN gladly endorsed.

The consequences of such poor management were exacerbated by the lack of personnel in the Department of Peacekeeping Operations, which left Akashi with the authority to make most political decisions in the field. Unlike an embassy following instructions from a foreign ministry, UNTAC had great discretion in political matters because DPKO had little time for backstopping.[15] (New York did micromanage in some respects, including its control over procurement and a decision just before the elections to evacuate dependents of UNTAC personnel, notwithstanding UNTAC's advice to the contrary.) This laissez-faire attitude was welcomed by UNTAC's senior leadership and may, in the end, have enhanced UNTAC's effectiveness. Member states surely showed little interest in following the Cambodia operation very closely. On the other hand, closer oversight by DPKO might have led Secretariat officials and interested states to review UNTAC's work from a more distant, objective standpoint. They could then prepare appropriate instructions, as the Secretary-General's task force had provided key guidance to UNTAG in Namibia.

2. Political Performance: Reconciling the Three Functions

The inherent tensions among the functions of the new peacekeepers proved especially unwieldy for UNTAC. The Paris accords themselves contained the germ of the conflict; the unfolding events of the settlement period brought it to full fruition. UNTAC had to implement its mandate in an atmosphere where the two main protagonists blocked its actions, and where both accused it of bias toward the other. The dilemmas in advancing the settlement while mediating among the factions exceeded those in nearly all earlier missions. They would prove harbingers of severe tensions in the former Yugoslavia, Somalia, and El Salvador.

a. The Special Representative of the Secretary-General

The greatest responsibility for carrying out these functions fell on Yasushi Akashi. Akashi met some of the key criteria for an effective Special Representatives as discussed in chapter 3: he was politically acceptable, possessed good diplomatic skills, had lengthy experience with and knowledge of the UN, and had a generalist's outlook. At the same time, despite his earlier assignment in Cambodia, he lacked extensive familiarity with the recent politics of the conflict as well as significant international stature. Some participants in the peace negotiations saw these shortcomings as the source of UNTAC's difficulties.[16] These problems likely cost UNTAC time and influence with the factions, although even someone who met all the conditions for an ideal Special Representative, such as Indonesian Foreign Minister Ali Alatas, a key broker of the Paris accords, might well have achieved the same results.

The most relevant trait of the Special Representative for evaluating UNTAC's political performance is his political skill. On this score, Akashi came under intense criticism by many inside and outside UNTAC as politically unsophisticated for UNTAC's mandate. They claimed that his reliance upon the traditional Japanese search for consensus to overcome impasses hampered UNTAC's effectiveness. These arguments appealed to journalists, who could blame one person for the problems of the operation. This view also enabled some UNTAC staff, discouraged by its mixed results, to blame Akashi if he failed to heed their advice.

In fact, Akashi well understood the enormous job before him, and saw his separate roles as administrator, mediator, and guarantor.[17] He did adopt an approach that reflected his own background, a generally quiet, consensual-based manner to resolving disputes. Akashi's strategy was thus quickly distinguishable from his counterpart in UNOSOM II, Admiral Jonathan Howe of the United States, who favored strong action against Mogadishu's defiant warlord, Mohammed Aideed.

Akashi thus very reluctantly asserted the full range of his authority under the Paris accords, especially the powers to make binding directives and to remove or reassign personnel. As noted, he never ordered the removal of any official, preferring a quiet request to SOC Prime Minister Hun Sen to replace someone. If the request was ignored, Akashi would not press the issue publicly. Where he might have used the foreign media to put pressure on the Khmer Rouge and the SOC to comply with the accords, he chose to act behind the scenes.

Akashi saw himself as having only a finite reservoir of political goodwill with the SOC leadership, which he had to utilize sparingly to overcome the differences between UNTAC and the SOC.[18] Only in the five months before the electoral campaign did he deviate from this approach. As he reoriented the mission toward the election, he belatedly took more assertive steps, such as the appointment of the special prosecutor, the dispatch of the control teams, and the use of sanctions under the electoral law.

Akashi thus sought his own balance between confrontation and conciliation—between executing and guaranteeing the accords, on the one hand, and mediating disputes, on the other. He clearly took his mediation roles very seriously. Indeed, one of his advisers stated that UNTAC was really "bilateral diplomacy with four parties."[19] He and his top aides negotiated indefatigably with the SOC (and with the Khmer Rouge, when they chose to speak with him) over the settlement.

At the same time, he maintained a clear vision on what he regarded as the one central goal of UNTAC, namely the conduct of free and fair elections in May 1993. He overruled the Supreme National Council's proposed changes to the electoral law and insisted on standing by the electoral timetable from the beginning. Akashi maintained this stance even when it became clear that a neutral political environment did not prevail and when Khmer Rouge–caused violence marred the months before the elections. He rejected the advice of many in UNTAC who favored a delay. Akashi's persistence could have stemmed from a personal desire to ensure that UNTAC would perform its primary mission and that his stewardship would not be regarded as a failure.[20] But it also created a goal and momentum in furtherance of the new peacekeeping's executor and guarantor roles, with UNTAC, in Akashi's words, as "custodians of the Paris accords."[21]

Many in UNTAC and other circles in Phnom Penh found, with good reason, Akashi's allocation of mediation and execution skewed toward conciliation and compromise. They encouraged him to use his powers more freely. The "Expanded Perm 5" urged him to exercise his powers early, when the factions seemed more likely to take heed of UNTAC's instructions.[22] Some senior officials in UNTAC lamented that he did not use the removal power, UNTAC's key lever, more frequently and decisively. They suggested that this would have created the required fear in the minds of the SOC to pressure them into compliance with the civil administration control. Instead, they claimed that UNTAC suffered a type of psychological defeat by "looking big and acting small."[23]

These complaints, and the responses to them, highlight the possibility for numerous interpretations of the appropriate balance among the roles of the new peacekeepers, especially when consent disintegrates. For example, for UNTAC to have taken decisive action against the SOC early, before effective deployment of the civil administration component, would have required utilization of great political skills, whether through bluffing or in the use of the media. It might not have worked, and could have caused the SOC to walk out of the peace process. Similarly, stronger action against the Khmer Rouge might have caused them to resist even more than they did. One UNTAC official said Akashi needed to avoid intense confrontation with the Cambodians lest they regard him as a type of Japanese proconsul, a historical figure Akashi would not wish to emulate.[24]

Heavy-handedness to obtain the removal of SOC personnel thus could have led to a short-term gain and long-term loss: some officials would be removed, but the SOC would prove even more uncooperative toward UNTAC. And the Security Council's unwillingness to countenance enforcement action might well have made UNTAC the loser in a head-to-head standoff with a faction threatening armed resistance.

On the other hand, even if not always successful, tough action against the SOC might have led the Khmer Rouge to think that UNTAC was creating the neutral environment required under the Paris accords. That carrot, plus the stick of UN entry into Khmer Rouge zones notwithstanding bamboo poles and other indicia of Khmer Rouge defiance, might have kept the Khmer Rouge in the peace process. The second-guessing game has no end.

b. The World View of the UN Civil Servant

Akashi's preference for mediation over assertive executive action resonated clearly with the career UN officials serving in UNTAC. They came from a tradition that places a premium on diplomatic discourse and proper relations with host authorities; in conference settings, UN officials, like many diplomats from member states, prefer to avoid confrontation through compromise, delay, or obfuscation (such as use of ambiguous phrasing in UN documents). This behavior reflects the need to interact with states with sharply contrasting political views and interests. The UN civil servant thus starts any relationship with foreign officials by trying to establish a smooth rapport.[25] Within UNTAC, midlevel UN civil servants in the civil administration group took great pride in establishing friendly working ties with SOC officials. They were pleased that they could see the provincial governor when they wished and raise any matter with him in a cordial setting.[26]

This attitude, however, entails significant costs in new peacekeeping operations, where executing and guaranteeing a settlement assume primary importance. Defiance or hesitancy by one party does not always, or even often, merit utilization of the traditional tools of the UN civil servant. If civilian peacekeepers grant the violating side reprieves or seek a compromise over every refusal to act, they signal to the uncooperative party that its behavior is costless. UN officials need to challenge nefarious activities and employ the resources at their disposal to eliminate the problem, even at the price of losing amicable working relationships.

For UNTAC, the discord between this background and the demands of the new peacekeeping left the UN bureaucrat unprepared for the control and direction required in the civil administration component. The lack of personal experience in governmental administration by most of these people compounded the effects of this predisposition.[27] Instructions turned into requests, which evolved into favors, until the UN official interacted well with his SOC counterpart, who ignored him.

This pattern also affected perceptions of the operation's impartiality. Some opposition party officials, as well as the Khmer Rouge, feared UNTAC was too friendly toward the State of Cambodia because it regarded the SOC as the de facto government to be salvaged in some way. They regarded this as contrary to a settlement that entitled the resistance to respect even if its officials did not sit in the ministries.[28]

The human rights function also suffered on account of this UN tradition within the rest of UNTAC. By its very nature, human rights monitoring requires a challenge to accused violators and persistence until the practice ceases. The UN's preference to avoid publicly offending human rights violators except in egregious cases has led to decreased sensitivity by many UN officials about the importance of the human rights agenda.[29] For instance, although the Paris accords gave UNTAC important responsibilities regarding human rights, the Secretary-General's original report assumed UNTAC would not have provincial human right officers because the other components would monitor human rights.[30] This failed to take account of the particularized expertise required for human rights work and the need for an independent monitor of conditions. Such specialization is required even if the ultimate decision to respond to a particular practice factors in other considerations.

A more subtle by-product of the UN system concerns its great reverence for texts and tasks. Texts form the consensual basis for an operation; tasks represent its operationalization. Thus, the Secretary-General's original design for UNTAC represented a translation of one into the other. The numerous memoranda from senior UNTAC officials to subordinates offered more detailed lists of tasks. While a large operation must rely upon some compilation of duties to guide lower functionaries, the process can lose sight of the dynamism, interconnections, and underlying purposes of the original accords.[31] Faced with a list of tasks, the UN official may assume that he or she lacks the authority to go beyond them.

In UNTAC's case, the various services and provincial directors within the civil administration component often did not seem to interpret their legal authority under the accords creatively enough. "Control" came to mean accomplishing a series of duties, or preparing a written directive, not imagining and taking whatever measures seemed necessary to effect the neutral political environment. Only late in the mandate period, when UNTAC established the control teams, did it take full advantage of the accords as empowering instruments.

c. Contention in the Components

Not all members of UNTAC shared the perspectives of Akashi or the UN civil servants on the proper balance of mediation and execution. The disagreements that arose reflect systemic tensions in the new peacekeeping. The absence of adequate management, coordination, and decision-making processes exacerbated these differences within UNTAC. First, international civil servants and foreign officials seconded to UNTAC mistrusted each other's talents and motives in some ways. Career officials complained that outsiders lacked diplomatic skills and knowledge of the UN system, or tended to advance national goals.[32] Those seconded to UNTAC noted the UN civil servants' penchant for avoiding confrontation, claimed they had a greater interest in career advancement than in the success of the operation, and found them lacking in the necessary skills.[33]

Second, the different perspectives were often divided along lines of nationality. The "Anglo" group of British, American, Canadian, Australian, New Zealander, and southern African officials dominated the human rights and electoral components due to their interest in and experience with these matters. Some viewed the "Franco" group, which ran much of the civil administration component, as too timid to challenge the SOC on its egregious practices. They accused the French of hoping that the SOC would win the election, thereby permitting the least disruption in Cambodia and advancing French economic and cultural interests in the region.[34] The French group, in turn, defended their approach to the SOC as faithfully implementing the accords.

They noted that quiet mediation would move the peace process along better than vocal objection. However, they believed UNTAC should have emphasized its executor role more with the Khmer Rouge.[35]

Each bloc thus argued that it favored confrontation (execution) over conciliation (mediation). However, the Anglo group seemed to direct their policy more at the SOC, and the French at the Khmer Rouge. In an early showdown, Akashi fired the French deputy commander of UNTAC's military component, General Michel Loridon, in July 1992 due to his strong, and at times, public advocacy of force to secure compliance by the Khmer Rouge.[36] In the end, though, Akashi satisfied neither bloc, leaning toward mediation over execution vis-à-vis both factions. His late appointment of a special prosecutor for human rights abuses (an Australian national) represented a victory of sorts for the Anglos.

These divisions translated into acrimonious debate among components over UNTAC's strategy and priorities. With its plenary authority to organize an election notwithstanding the views of the factions, the electoral component saw little need for compromise over the implementation of the Paris accords. The human rights component also emphasized strong measures against the SOC. Both units recognized that tough action might cause the SOC to withhold cooperation from UNTAC on civil administration, but favored a principled approach despite the costs.[37] If their efforts failed, they still held the moral high ground, with a clear conscience that they took all necessary steps against the violator of the accords. Some human rights officials, including the special prosecutor himself, appeared to lose sight of the component's place within UNTAC's overall mission. They argued that the special prosecutor should have an independent authority to arrest and prosecute human rights violators without high-level approval.[38]

The civil administration component could not, however, afford to neglect the costs of punitive action, for the SOC still controlled the governmental apparatus. Harsh language, threats, or more would not only not always accomplish UNTAC's ends, but might well complicate or undermine them. This lesson was brought home in Somalia 1993 when UNOSOM II tried such tactics against clan leader Aideed and suffered deadly reprisals from him. The component could not accept the absolutist views of the electoral and human rights units, who saw a clear goal and a direct way to achieve it. The civil administration group had to incorporate mediation into their execution, and the political nature of their work struck some in UNTAC as a sign of weakness.

During the mandate, each worked against the other through leaks to an always eager foreign press. The human rights component proved especially adept at this technique as a way of putting pressure on the civil administration component to act. Akashi tried to, but ultimately could not, control these leaks, which invariably reflected poorly on UNTAC.

The contentions within the components echo the controversies over Akashi's balancing of his three political roles. Both should serve as cautionary notices to those planning or assessing future second-generation operations. Different actors, and the same actors in various situations, can endorse contrasting, bona fide responses to perceptions of bias and eroding consent, and paths to reconciliation of the various political roles. Moreover, simple chains of causation have little utility for evaluating the results of new peacekeeping operations. For each observer convinced that Akashi's consensual approach caused the Cambodians to lose respect for UNTAC, another can properly point out the consequences of alternative tactics. Each will draw contrary lessons of the best political strategy for new operations.

THE REST OF THE UN: ONE VOICE OR MANY?

1. The Security Council

The Council played an important background role during UNTAC's tenure. After creating UNTAC in February 1992, it passed five resolutions before the commencement of polling. It then endorsed the elections in June 1993 and approved UNTAC's withdrawal in August 1993. In November 1993, it welcomed the formation of the new government, urged compliance with human rights, and approved various measures regarding the UN's future presence in Cambodia.[39]

Passed primarily in response to the Khmer Rouge's violations of the Paris accords, and to a lesser extent, SOC actions as well, the pre-election resolutions incorporated three different messages. First, the Council repeatedly called upon the parties to comply with their commitments. The resolutions initially focused upon the Khmer Rouge's refusal to disarm; later, they addressed acts of violence by the SOC too. The Council used strong language against the parties' violations and in November endorsed limited economic sanctions against the Khmer Rouge.

These resolutions attempted to assist UNTAC's administrator role by demonstrating to the factions, and the Khmer Rouge in particular, the united sentiment of the international community behind the Paris accords. China, the Khmer Rouge's former ally, abstained on one early resolution, but voted in favor of all others, which were passed unanimously. Yet the precise effect of these resolutions on SOC and Khmer Rouge behavior remains unknown, and the Council was unwilling to back its words with forcible measures. This reflected its skepticism over both the usefulness and the human costs of peace enforcement in Cambodia. In addition, despite clear evidence from UNTAC of Thai complicity in aiding the Khmer Rouge, the Council adopted only watered-down language to encourage Thai compliance with the settlement.[40]

Second, and more significant for the new peacekeeping, the Council generally supported UNTAC in its work. It expressed appreciation to UNTAC and Akashi and condemned attacks on UNTAC, warning the factions that UNTAC acted with the backing of key UN member states. It also repeatedly endorsed UNTAC's and the Secretary-General's views that the elections should proceed as planned. This gave a boost to UNTAC's executive functions. It attempted to eliminate doubts by the factions that UNTAC would retreat from the electoral timetable and provided UNTAC with what Akashi called "ammunition" to push the factions forward.[41]

Third, the Council asked UNTAC and the Secretary-General to take particular measures, such as accelerated deployment, set-up of border checkpoints, actions toward a neutral political environment, and an examination of UNTAC's post-electoral role. UNTAC, of course, initiated or approved of most of these requests in advance through its review of draft resolutions. The Council, then, was targeting these messages at the Cambodians; its requests to UNTAC gave the mission some additional leverage with the parties. (The request to accelerate deployment was, however, likely directed at UNTAC and Secretariat officials and at troop and police-contributing countries.)

The Council's resolutions after the elections provided a speedy and unequivocal message to the SOC and the Khmer Rouge that the UN's members would recognize the duly elected government of Cambodia. They signaled to the SOC especially that it must accept the results of the voting. The Security Council's last two resolutions, in August and November 1993, sent two additional signals. First, the Council confirmed that UNTAC would depart on time, leaving Cambodia and its future to the new government. The Organization and its members were glad to see UNTAC finally terminate its mission and had no interest in a major post-UNTAC presence. Nevertheless, the Council also affirmed that second-generation peacekeeping would not entirely end with the departure of a mission. The UN and its agencies would try to help the new regime and perpetuate the peace-building process, though on a much smaller scale.

2. The General Assembly

The Assembly's only major part during the mandate period was its review and approval of UNTAC's budget. It appropriated money in four- to six-month intervals after the ACABQ and the Fifth Committee reviewed the Secretary-General's requests and reduced the requested amounts somewhat.

3. UN Agencies

While many specialized agencies contributed personnel to UNTAC, the largest agencies present were UNDP and UNHCR. UNDP worked reasonably well with UNTAC, acknowledging the latter's preeminent position in coordinating assistance. UNHCR staffed the repatriation component. The agencies also, however, recognized the advantages of an identity distinct from UNTAC. Through separate staff, license plates, offices, and stationery, each could distance itself if needed from UNTAC. For example, UNHCR emphasized its independence in discussions with the Khmer Rouge over the repatriation process at a time when the faction was breaking with UNTAC on the rest of the peace plan.[42]

UNTAC's successes and failures flowed from an interrelationship among the exogenous and endogenous variables affecting its performance, one not amenable to categorical causal relationships. Although UNTAC's management left much to be desired, it is impossible to know the extent to which it harmed the mission's final outcome, although the poor media coverage was one evident side effect. The political work of Akashi and his staff showed both great skill as well as some significant mistakes. Despite impressive talent at UNTAC's senior levels, the unwillingness of Akashi and many UN functionaries in UNTAC's middle ranks to utilize their authority under the Paris accords more assertively compromised UNTAC's effectiveness.

Criticism of UNTAC must be placed in perspective. As the largest peacekeeping operation since ONUC and the first with such a broad mandate, its modus operandi could not be expected to have satisfied all who worked in it, interacted with it, or observed it. It clearly could have done better operationally and politically. Yet it does not seem magnanimous to conclude that, on the whole, given the exogenous constraints, it capably carried out important parts of the UN's administrator, mediator, and guarantor functions under the Paris accords. It was neither an unequivocal success nor failure, but it did demonstrably contribute to a new beginning in Cambodia's political saga. With UNTAC now departed from the scene, the Organization and its members will need to ponder courses of action for improving the performance of UNTAC's successors elsewhere.

Part IV

■

Toward the Future

.9.

The New Imperatives for the New Peacekeeping

The years immediately preceding the UN's 50th anniversary have seen the Organization and its members attempting to accommodate the old institution of peacekeeping to the contemporary challenge of nation-building. Nation-building began decades ago, when the UN participated in nation-*birthing* through assistance in colonial self-determination and one endeavor to help a nascent government, in the Congo, gain control of its territory. But the frequency of operations since 1989 suggests that, notwithstanding some grimaces in American political circles with the term nation-building, the new peacekeeping is beginning to form a core function of the United Nations in the fields of international peace and security, self-determination, human rights, and economic development.

If this trend is to continue, and the operations to achieve more consistently favorable outcomes over time, decision makers in the Organization and in member states must recognize the challenges at hand and engage in a more coherent and imaginative approach to them. The most obvious question in these days of an overstretched Organization concerns the circumstances under which the UN should deploy second-generation peacekeeping (a different question from the deployment of peace enforcement missions). This chapter thus begins by offering a series of issues for participants to consider in dispatching new missions, a model that rejects any pat formulas for successful peacekeeping as irrelevant to the tasks at hand. The chapter then offers recommendations regarding the five most critical issues for the future of the new peacekeeping: improvements to the UN Secretariat, oversight of missions by member states, prevalent concerns about the legitimacy of Security Council decisions, appropriate responses to decaying consent, and funding of peacekeeping.

CREATING AND OVERSEEING SECOND-GENERATION OPERATIONS: SIGNPOSTS FOR DECISION MAKERS

If the new peacekeeping endures as a major UN commitment, the Organization and its members can expect to engage in a continuous process of decision making on whether to establish operations and how to carry them out. The decision to establish a new operation assumes primary importance because the mission alters the political landscape in the affected state or states and forces the UN to reallocate its limited resources in yet another direction. Implementation of the operation demands political, personal, and economic resources of member states as well as an institutionalized expertise from within the Organization.

Given the recent emergence of the new phenomenon of second-generation missions, any recipe for successful peacekeeping seems beyond reach, and, more important, largely irrelevant to the decision maker.[1] In a sense, the recipe has limited pertinence when one knows in advance that the necessary amounts of the "ingredients" will prove lacking. Each conflict involves different, often unpredictable obstacles, some more political, others more administrative or logistical. Few conflicts, and no serious ones, will invite effortless UN involvement, and the UN will never have the luxury to deploy a mission under ideal circumstances. Officials in New York and world capitals cannot rigidly adhere to some formulaic list of factors to determine their course of action.

Rather, they should identify the immediate, germane issues for the Organization's attention. Recognition of these in turn forms a prerequisite for determining the goals to be set for the UN over time. As the results of more operations trickle in, both the issues themselves and the goals will be transformed. In a halting start to this process, the Security Council has begun to clarify the elements for decision.[2] In addition, the United States government issued in May 1994 a comprehensive policy on peacekeeping through a classified Presidential Decision Directive.[3] More a distillation of long-standing United States government views than any bold departure from them, the policy outlines the factors of concern to the United States. It also downplays peace enforcement in favor of consent-based missions.[4]

The record of UN operations suggests that decision makers must focus on two core issues in determining whether and how to conduct the new peacekeeping: the amenability of the underlying conflict to UN participation in its solution; and the capability of the Organization and its member states to effect useful involvement.

1. Appraisal of the Conflict and Its Settlement

The critical question in examining the underlying dispute is deceptively simple: Are the parties demonstrating a basic readiness to end the conflict and cooperate with the UN in implementing a solution? Although the parties to a settlement cannot be expected to have resolved all their differences, the UN's members must ask if they have accepted a mechanism, such as a peace plan or treaty, for settling them and agreed to the UN's place in that process. This readiness was apparent before the UN dispatched UNTAG to Namibia in 1989, ONUVEN to Nicaragua in 1989, and UNTEA to West Irian in 1962. It was only suspected, or simply hoped for, before the UN deployed ONUSAL to El Salvador in 1991, UNAVEM II to Angola in 1992, and UNTAC to Cambodia in 1992.

The question of choosing conflicts and settlements in which to involve the UN can be broken down into two subsidiary inquiries. First, is the plan adopted by the parties a viable solution to the conflict? An evaluation of the suitability of conflicts to solution proves, however, quite daunting. Are domestic conflicts more or less soluble through political settlements than interstate disputes? The former at least involve only one principal state actor, but internecine conflict, with private armies abounding, may prove far more resistant to solution than an interstate war in which combatants act as mere agents for governments.

Are ethnic conflicts, such as those in the former Yugoslavia, more immune to solution than the Cold War mop-ups in El Salvador or Cambodia, without significant ethnic dimensions?[5] Moreover, are peace accords in which both sides make significant concessions less long-lived than those in which one side has triumphed over the other? Before partaking in second-generation peacekeeping, decision makers must form a consensus on the legitimacy of and compliance mechanisms behind the settlement or, in the words of the New Haven School of international law, its authority and control.[6]

Second, assuming the parties are ready to end the conflict, we must inquire whether and to what extent the UN should play a part in implementing an agreement. During the peacemaking process, decision makers will scrutinize the conflict and the demands of the parties and other relevant states for a UN deployment. In some situations, the parties may refrain from seeking a significant UN role. For example, the long-term Israeli mistrust of the United Nations resulting from years of anti-Israel rhetoric and practices has meant the lack of a substantial UN place in the implementation of the 1993–94 Israel-PLO accords, with their non-UN international "presence."[7]

If member states see the UN as a beneficial participant, officials in member states and the Secretariat should ascertain the proper mandate. This requires consideration of the appropriate depth of involvement, from superficial monitoring to intrusive conduct, and breadth of participation in the solution. Can a simple election monitoring mission, such as UNOVER in Eritrea, meet the parties' needs, or do they and outside actors demand the more assertive operations seen in Cambodia or El Salvador? If they cannot concur on the scope of the mission, the UN will almost assuredly err on the side of modesty, and face the consequences later. Such shortsightedness could reproduce the weak mandates, small sizes, and disastrous outcomes of the 1969 West Irian and 1990 Haiti election missions.

If the answer to the fundamental question of readiness for peace is demonstrably negative, and the member states nevertheless decide to deploy a mission, they face an immediate and substantial risk of devoting huge resources to the conflict and inviting consideration of peace enforcement, or abandoning it as the costs soar. The community may nevertheless wish to dispatch such operations and should do so to alleviate and contain humanitarian disasters. But, as the former Yugoslavia and Somalia have shown, the absence of a solution and a commitment to one grossly undermines the work of peacekeepers. It also diverts the Organization from other conflicts where it can play a more constructive role.

Thus, barring compelling humanitarian justifications for deploying a mission in the absence of a commitment to cooperation, the UN ought to reconcile itself in these situations to a role as peacemaker or facilitator of others' mediation efforts. While this may amount to a triage effect, forcing peace on unwilling belligerents has not proved particularly effective.[8]

2. Appraisal of the UN's Capabilities

The second set of issues concerns the capabilities of the UN and individual states to undertake the responsibilities of a new peacekeeping operation. These touch on matters both political and administrative, and must be addressed when deciding to establish a mission and continually during it.

• *The readiness of the international community to devote sufficient resources to accomplishing the mandate.* Regardless of the depth or breadth of UN involvement and the clarity of the mandate, decision makers must gauge their own and other states' determination to contribute political, monetary, human, and physical resources to accomplish the UN's goals. For some operations, whether modest like the election mission in Nicaragua or expansive like UNTAG in Namibia, the answer may be a simple yes. UNTAC received significant resources, but also competed with other crises for the world's attention.

If states riven by war continue to need UN assistance in building peace, the UN may well have to constrict the mandates of some missions to accommodate many simultaneous operations. The UN and member states must also properly convey this calculation to the interested parties. Candor about the extent of international commitment to a peace process lays to rest expectations that exceed the Organization's capabilities or neglect the realities of the conflict.

Should consent eventually decay, member states must explicitly evaluate their commitment to the peace plan. This will be the most critical determinant of the UN's response if domestic parties or outside states ask the Organization to respond to breaches of an accord with economic sanctions or peace enforcement. In those cases, the lives of UN personnel on the scene may have to be balanced against the lives of the populace lost through inaction.

• *The Organization's lead time in preparing the operation.* The UN is characterized by perpetual kinesis. Most interstate and domestic conflicts reach its attention only after they have deteriorated to a crisis involving loss of life. Thus, on the one hand, many situations do not permit months of advance work. Yet the UN cannot simultaneously devise and deploy an operation, a fate that encumbered UNTAC. In deciding whether to dispatch a mission and of what scope, decision makers must thus ask how much time they have to prepare it. First-generation missions are clearly easier to plan. Yet the UN cannot adopt any arbitrary cutoff, and will respond to some crises in relatively short order.

• *The talents of mission leaders and staff.* In planning a mission, the Secretary-General and interested member states must address the competence of those employed for the job. In identifying a Special Representative, they should consider the attributes addressed in chapter 3, but be ready to accept a less than ideal package. Questions will arise whether the Special Representative's immediate staff has the political and managerial skills to run a large operation with a politically sensitive mandate, including the ability to improvise and work together as a team. While no missions have seemed plagued with incompetence, UNTAC demonstrated the possibilities for improvement.

In addition, member states will need to consider the extent to which lower-level officials are prepared for an operation. They must gauge the extent to which mission staff needs to know about the country and the requirements for other areas of expertise. For UNTAC, those seemed quite germane; for other mandates, they may be less so. Finally, decision makers should evaluate whether the mission needs personnel from UN specialized agencies, especially if the mandate includes training of local officials in aspects of governance.

• *The Secretariat's ability to recruit and procure personnel and material.* Establishment of a mission of any size requires speedy dispatch and transportation of staff and equipment. Slow deployment of peacekeepers and materiel can have irreversible effects. The UN's success in obtaining resources for ONUC in 1960 contrasts with the difficulties of UNTAC in 1992. Yet member states are unlikely ever to respond with personnel and money as quickly as the crisis demands, and the Organization will always have competing commitments in the areas of recruitment and procurement.

• *The appropriate roles for execution and mediation.* The new peacekeepers must always keep in sight the settlement they are to help the parties implement. Pursuit of that agenda, accepted by the parties themselves, is their primary task. Yet decision makers will have to consider the place of mediation in supporting that process, and the extent to which the operation may have to modify its execution functions to place a settlement back on track. As amply demonstrated by UNTAC, this pie can be cut in many ways. While the mission leaders should not waste time planning responses to each scenario, they should formulate a general strategy for the operation that indicates how mediation will support execution.

• *The proper degree of oversight and support from New York.* Mission planners will also need to consider the role of the Secretary-General and the political organs during the operation's duration. The former may need to galvanize the Secretariat to provide administrative support or convene interested countries for diplomatic discussions. The latter may have to adjust the mandate of the mission and stand behind it, including through mandatory sanctions against uncooperative parties. Yet each will have its own priorities, which may well not include the mission in question. (How interested was China in the El Salvador operation, or Indonesia in the Nicaragua mission?)

MAKING THE TRANSITION:
PRIORITIES FOR THE UN AND ITS MEMBERS

While a checklist for successful operations seems premature if not useless, enough has been learned from the recent past to suggest some priorities to make the new peacekeeping more effective, and to recommend policies toward that end. Suggestions for the improvement of peacekeeping capabilities have casually circulated through the corridors of the UN buildings for years, and the Organization has mechanisms of some utility for considering them. The Secretariat has conducted internal reviews of operations and will likely continue to do so in the future.

Member states endlessly debate proposals in several General Assembly committees. These include the Special Committee on Peacekeeping Operations (created in 1965 as part of the deal to end the peacekeeping financing crisis of the early 1960s) and the Special Committee on the Charter of the United Nations and on the Strengthening of the Role of the Organization. With *An Agenda for Peace,* Boutros-Ghali has begun to take an assertive posture in these questions through public statements and detailed reports.[9] Discussion within member states is now widespread, especially in the European Community and the United States in the wake of the casualties suffered by UNPROFOR and UNOSOM II.

Unfortunately, most of this debate continues to emphasize the military side of the house, whether improvement of first-generation operations or nonconsensual peace enforcement. The public agenda reflects this bias, including attention upon Boutros-Ghali's call in *An Agenda for Peace* for a rapid deployment force and proposals for a UN volunteer army.[10] But, as Cambodia, Central America, and Somalia demonstrate, peace-building and nation-building depend as much on the nonmilitary aspects of peacekeeping. The stark words of a senior military officer in UNOSOM II, caught amidst fighting in Mogadishu, highlight the new demands:

> [T]he U.N. has stayed behind these walls too long . . . [and] has waited too long to give something to the people of this city—roofs over their heads, schools for the kids, a judicial system in place. I mean real resources going to the city.[11]

1. Improvements to the Secretariat

It is by now apparent that some systemic, structural changes in the Secretariat are required. These would supplement broader reforms to improve the entire Organization, such as a major restructuring of the Secretariat and revamping the UN's financing.[12]

a. Integration of Peacemaking and Peacekeeping

The inextricable link between peacekeeping and peacemaking must manifest itself in the UN's institutional readiness for the endeavor. During the era of first-generation operations, peacekeeping and peacemaking fell under the responsibility of the Under Secretary-General for Special Political Affairs, a position held by a series of impressive senior international civil servants and the most important below the Secretary-General. The limited number and mandate of peacekeeping operations and the circumscribed activity of the UN in high-profile peacemaking during the Cold War permitted one person and office to supervise both activities. The same actors at Headquarters could judge the effect of the progress of one upon the other. Thus, for the Congo, the Middle East, or Kashmir, one small office (indeed, often one man, Ralph Bunche) became the UN's action cell for monitoring and defusing crises.

This quaint arrangement worked only as long as the most powerful member states excluded the UN from the resolution of many serious interstate conflicts. As Cold War tensions eased and the Security Council assumed new responsibilities, improvement of the Secretariat's capabilities became necessary, inviting outside proposals for major restructuring.[13] Boutros-Ghali ordered a significant change early in his term by creating a separate Department of Peacekeeping Operations (DPKO) and Department of Humanitarian Affairs (DHA), placing peacemaking functions within a Department of Political Affairs (DPA).[14] Although this move responded to the growing number and complexity of peacekeeping operations, it sacrificed the unity of peacemaking and peacekeeping within the Secretariat that prevailed for most of the UN's first 40 years.

Some have suggested recombining the two departments into a revived Office of Special Political Affairs.[15] Such an office could be divided along regional lines, with each subdivision undertaking new and old peacekeeping, as well as peacemaking for the region. This approach, however, would likely inhibit effective oversight of the new peacekeeping. The civilian and military missions across the new operations share many problems. On questions of recruitment, training, procurement, relations with Headquarters, or political matters such as the limits of consent, a regional approach risks duplication of efforts, inconsistency, and loss of institutional memory. Moreover, while all new peacekeeping operations include peacemaking, most UN peacemaking does not involve a peacekeeping operation. The separate Department of Peacekeeping Operations reflects that these missions are important on their own, even though they include peacemaking functions.

If the basic office structure remains as at present, the two departments must nevertheless coordinate their activities more convincingly. First, joint work by DPA and DPKO must begin early. DPA, which assumes the lead in UN efforts to bring the parties toward a settlement, should bring in experts from DPKO as soon as the outlines of the settlement show the prospect of a significant UN presence. This will likely require convincing the antagonists that UN fact-finding missions and contingency planning will not prejudice the final outcome of the negotiations.

Second, the Secretariat should expand its nascent practice of creating task forces across departments.[16] Before a settlement, DPA would convene and chair these meetings; during the preparation for and implementation of the operation, DPKO would take charge. In 1993, Boutros-Ghali directed that DPA lead the political aspects of peacekeeping operations, while DPKO focus on more military and organization areas. This could help integrate peace-making into peacekeeping by providing for continuity in oversight by DPA. It could also increase the barriers between the two by denying DPKO lead responsibility over the core political questions.[17]

Third, peacekeeping missions should include staff who participated in the peacemaking process. This may be difficult, as a Secretariat official may choose the conclusion of the settlement as a logical time for transfer within the UN. It could even prove undesirable in the case of UN officials who may have so antagonized the parties during the peacemaking stage that they are no longer regarded as impartial. As a general matter, however, the UN should try to assimilate their expertise not merely at Headquarters, but in the field.

At no level is this more important than that of the Special Representative of the Secretary-General. Although Yasushi Akashi did an admirable job, the disadvantages of starting without a detailed background on the subject cannot be discounted. The UN should work from the premise that a Special Representative who serves the Secretary-General before the signature of a peace accord will also represent him after it. Exceptions may need to be made if another outstanding candidate emerges or if the Special Representative has become tainted during the negotiations (as happened with Alvaro de Soto, the key UN peacemaker for El Salvador who was properly passed over to lead ONUSAL), but the presumption noted would significantly help.[18]

Finally, the Secretary-General and member states should give renewed con-sideration to recent proposals for the creation of Deputy Secretaries-General.[19] Three or four such positions would serve the management objective of reduc-ing the number of people reporting directly to the Secretary-General. They would also allow for decision making below the Secretary-General but at a suf-ficiently high level. For the new peacekeeping, it would mean that one person could supervise the Undersecretaries-General for Peacekeeping and Political Affairs and harmonize their efforts. The burgeoning number of peacekeeping and peacemaking missions would prevent this person from participating in many operational matters, but he or she could serve as a high-level represen-tative of the Secretary-General in especially delicate cases.

b. Supervision of Nonmilitary Functions

Since the establishment of UNEF I in 1956, the UN has accumulated sub-stantial expertise in the military aspects of traditional peacekeeping. The Secretary-General employs a senior general as his military adviser, and together they have assembled the forces that dominate the first-generation missions and represent a significant element in the new peacekeeping. (They have much less success, however, in assembling and commanding UN forces in peace enforcement missions.) This institutional capacity and memory must, however, be matched for the nonmilitary aspects of new operations. In the case of UNTAC, for instance, only the electoral and repatriation components (in addition to the military force) had conducted detailed studies well in advance of UNTAC's arrival. The civil administration, civilian police, human rights, and rehabilitation components did not, and engaged in on-the-job preparation that cost the mission valuable time.

Boutros-Ghali took a welcome step toward engendering competence in nonmilitary matters when he created the Electoral Assistance Unit within the Department of Political Affairs in 1992. This unit, headed by a senior UN civil servant (its first chief was Horacio Boneo) serves as a self-described "focal point" within the United Nations for all electoral assistance activities. These range from technical advice at the request of a state conducting elections to supervision of polling during a peacekeeping operation. With the General Assembly's endorsement, Boutros-Ghali also created special trust funds to finance UN electoral assistance. The UN has also begun to institutionalize expertise within the unit, for example, through debriefing of UNTAC's electoral component.[20] Building on the UN's tradition in the electoral field, the unit seeks to regularize the UN's response to electoral mandates in future peacekeeping operations. Although established too late to assist in Cambodia or Angola, it aided operations in El Salvador, Mozambique, and Eritrea.

Moreover, the unit has provided significant assistance in the electoral field outside of peacekeeping operations. Its involvement in elections with few international repercussions confirms that the UN has moved beyond its tentative approach in the 1990 Haiti mission and regards its electoral responsibilities as no longer limited to exceptional cases with a "clear international dimension."[21] As most member states begin to accept the right to free and fair multiparty elections, the UN has effectively abandoned any international/ domestic distinction. Instead it has focused on how it might best contribute to the democratization process, regardless of the underlying circumstances behind the elections.[22]

The UN needs corresponding offices for civilian police, civil administration, human rights, economic rehabilitation, mine clearance, and possibly other subjects. Presently, specialized personnel are scattered in the United Nations Development Programme, the Centre for Human Rights, and elsewhere. Some part of the Secretariat should address these areas as they relate to the new peacekeeping. DPKO represents the logical situs for such offices as long as it continues to direct peacekeeping operations. Composed of a small number of experts seconded from the UN system, these units would participate in the planning of operations, help train UN and foreign personnel, and form liaisons with member states and other parts of the UN system. Boutros-Ghali's 1993 appointment of a police adviser and a demining official suggests recognition of the need for improvement in this area.

c. A Training Program in Nonmilitary Peacekeeping

Beyond establishing a formal planning mechanism at Headquarters, the UN must ensure that officials engaged in the new peacekeeping are competent for their new responsibilities. UNTAC, for instance, demonstrated particular shortcomings in the areas of civilian police, civil administration, and human rights. Training for both international civil servants and individuals seconded from member states thus becomes imperative. The UN must end its habit of, in the words of Martti Ahtisaari, "always creating a new team,"[23] and form a pool of available civilian personnel ready for deployment in weeks, not months. While the Secretariat's creation of a roster of interested civilians outside the UN is constructive, it does not address their preparation for duty.[24] The need for training is more urgent than in the military sphere, where troops are trained by their governments.[25]

The subjects for which preparation is required are numerous. International civil servants need education in areas such as public administration, human rights, and basic economics. Acquisition of intelligence-gathering skills and politico-military expertise is critical if they will be monitoring compliance with a political settlement.[26] They should also learn strategies and tactics for handling the political aspects of their work, especially responding to violations of settlements. Some awareness of press relations will also prove useful. Those seconded from governments, who may have some of these talents already, should learn to apply them in the context of a UN mission.

One far-reaching method to accomplish this goal would entail the establishment of a full-fledged training institute within the United Nations, akin to the United States Foreign Service Institute.[27] The United Nations Institute for Training and Research (UNITAR) is not organized for this purpose. Rather, it currently trains a modest number of governmental officials, generally from developing countries, primarily in diplomatic work. A revamped, reconstituted UNITAR or a new organization would train UN functionaries and civilians from member states in the substantive work required for the new peacekeeping. It would graduate a new corps of UN civilian reservists, each with a general background in peacekeeping and individual spheres of expertise. As missions neared, the institute could offer language classes to civilians, depending upon time constraints.

The Organization could adopt a less ambitious agenda. The new functional offices within DPKO or elsewhere in the Secretariat could organize training sessions for the designated civilian peacekeepers of the future.[28] The Electoral Assistance Unit has already begun training programs. If this proved too expensive, the Secretariat could prepare courses to be taught by governments. It could also contract out the services to private organizations, such as management consultants, human rights groups, or sophisticated financial institutions. The Organization must assume some initiative and not simply leave training to member states.[29]

Regardless of which training scheme is adopted, the Secretariat should also devise a short (one- to two-week) course for each peacekeeping operation, that all civilian, and perhaps military, members would be required to attend. It would focus on the country's history, culture, customs, and politics, and include a basic language instruction, such as understanding the alphabet.

Finally, future leaders need to know how to manage an operation. When peacekeeping had predominantly military personnel, the military chain of command, coupled with several flow charts to explain the place of the few civilians, sufficed as an internal management tool. For more sophisticated operations, the dangers in lack of priority-setting, ineffective intercomponent coordination and decision making, mistrust across nationalities, and press leaks call for leaders who understand the workings of large-scale bureaucracies.

The UN appears to have assumed that all its senior officials in New York or elsewhere are so equipped, although they typically supervise much smaller staffs. Senior officials who will form the pool of likely future Special Representatives need management training, with the benefit of outside experts. Again, the model of the U.S. Foreign Service Institute, which cultivates American foreign service officers at various stages in their career for managerial responsibilities, is worth emulating.

d. Integration of Human Rights Awareness in Peacekeeping

If new peacekeeping operations continue to include human rights activities, the United Nations will need to adjust its vision of the place of those rights in its agenda for peace. For example, although ONUSAL began as a human rights operation and kept those issues in the spotlight (if not always to the satisfaction of human rights advocates), much of UNTAC fell victim to the more habitual UN attitude. This problem calls for more than teaching future peacekeepers the texts of human rights conventions. It turns on an institutional awareness about the centrality of human rights to the new peacekeeping.[30]

The UN already has an organizational basis for this greater consciousness: the Centre for Human Rights, the large office within the Secretariat that acts as both a repository of expertise and the staff for the UN's human rights institutions, such as the Commission on Human Rights. The Centre cannot, however, ensure that key decision makers in the planning and execution of peacekeeping operations incorporate human rights concerns, for its Geneva location puts it outside the mindset of those in New York working with the political organs on peacekeeping.[31]

Whereas military matters are considered by the Secretary-General's military adviser, electoral concerns receive high-profile attention through the Electoral Assistance Unit, and economic development is folded into planning due to UNDP's New York venue, human rights issues elude integration into the design of missions. Unless senior Centre officials persist and those in New York listen, or if member states, usually Western ones, repeatedly raise the matter, the human rights elements become neglected. Centre officials have continually lamented their distance from the political decision making in the Organization. The Centre had virtually no involvement in the planning of UNTAC and played only a small role in assisting ONUSAL.[32]

Several solutions are possible. The UN could transfer the entire Centre to New York, although this would disrupt the UN's relations with its genial Swiss hosts as well as the lives of the Centre's staff. A more realistic alternative would entail relocating that part of the Centre that does not directly serve the committees, commissions, and conferences in Geneva to New York. There it would form a new office along the lines of the Electoral Assistance Unit. (The Centre already has a small office in New York.) The personnel currently working in the Centre's Advisory Services, Technical Assistance and Information Branch should be transferred to New York, and a senior official within the Secretariat should supervise them and ensure the inclusion of their views in planning operations.

The 1993 World Conference on Human Rights endorsed a diluted version of this concept, and both the conference and the General Assembly have urged devotion of greater resources to the Centre and incorporation of its expertise into the UN's political work.[33] The creation of a UN High Commissioner for Human Rights by the Assembly in 1993 may ameliorate the situation as well.[34] Increased involvement of the Centre should lead to deployment of more human rights experts in the field (although if they served as political officers, the parties to a conflict might discount their views in light of their background). More important, it would sensitize the political officers of a mission to the importance of human rights.

e. Review of Procurement and Recruitment Practices

With the new peacekeeping, the days have passed when the UN can assemble an operation primarily with self-sufficient national contingents composed of soldiers and their own equipment, logistical unit, and other support. The demand for civilians caught the UN unprepared in the case of Cambodia. Other operations have avoided this fate only because they had more lead time (UNTAG) or fewer personnel (the electoral missions).

The Secretariat thus needs to reexamine its ability to deploy people and supplies quickly for time-sensitive assignments. It should adopt procedures to facilitate waivers of competitive bidding, decentralized procurement, and expedited recruitment, although some changes in these areas will require the approval of member states through the General Assembly.[35] Again, the UN should consider the services of a management consultant in this regard.

f. Coordination with Specialized and Technical Agencies

To engage in even elementary nation-building, the UN must draw upon people with technical skills to train and work with local personnel. ONUC broke new ground in this area in 1960; UNTAC practiced it to a smaller extent, training officials in accounting, tax collection, and air traffic control, and employing its military component to train the post-election Cambodian army. This technical assistance will assume a larger profile in operations to rescue other states devastated by civil conflict. Although UNDP supervises longer-term projects, the mission itself must have specialists for the most pressing needs.

The most available source of talent lies within the specialized and technical agencies of the UN system, although member states may also be able to second personnel quickly. The International Telecommunication Union, International Civil Aviation Organization, World Meteorological Organization, International Maritime Organization, Food and Agriculture Organization, and World Health Organization represent obvious candidates for participation in peacekeeping. At a practical level, DPKO should establish a coordination mechanism to involve them in new operations, including through secondments. These agencies will also have the best access to government and private experts in the relevant fields.

g. Learning from the Past

Lastly, the officials and staff of new peacekeeping operations form a font of knowledge for improving the functioning of the Secretariat. Thus, the Secretary-General should create and formalize a process whereby the leaders of each mission complete evaluations and those in positions of responsibility actually read them. A detailed report on the managerial and administrative problems of the mission will aid those UN components that provide support; the Secretariat would then convene meetings to consider the recommendations in these reports. Equally, if not more important, the Special Representative would prepare a much shorter study, more reflective and personal in nature, for the benefit of future mission leaders.[36]

2. The Political Organs and UN Members: The Burdens of Leadership

Beyond improvements in the Secretariat, the political organs and, thus, the member states must assume the onus of responsibility for these missions. The new peacekeeping provides a tremendous temptation to states both strong and weak to applaud or assume credit for the triumph of the pre-agreement peacemaking phase and then pass the burden onto UN officials. In a world where the priorities of governments shift virtually incessantly, foci of attention turn to the next crisis, on the assumption that a peace treaty and the dispatch of peacekeepers marks the end of the settlement process. The new peacekeeping becomes "the UN's problem," with members hoping to avoid active intercession except in the face of an imminent collapse of the peace. The Secretary-General can easily encourage this attitude in his desire for free rein over the mission.

While a certain disengagement by outside states from the settlement process seems inevitable once a plan is adopted and the Secretary-General begins running an operation, a major abnegation of accountability would be unwise. Oversight by the political organs serves a number of purposes. First, it indicates to the relevant elites in the target country that the international community retains interest in their problem. This creates the potential for dissuading violations and promoting the UN's guarantor function. Second, it provides a measure of support to the officials and staff of the missions that their work is not ignored by member states.

Third, it affords member states a measure of control over the mission. While the political organs have little choice but to entrust the Secretary-General and his staff with substantial responsibility and discretion (like any executive organ), the checks of the political organs ensure that the Secretariat's actions do not deviate from the views of the most interested states. Moreover, as the UN sends peacekeepers into more dangerous situations, domestic constituencies in donor states will demand greater control over their fate. The debate in the United States concerning its troops in Somalia is only one obvious example of this problem; similar issues arose concerning Japanese participants in UNTAC.

Fourth, even if the member states have faith in the Secretary-General, oversight of the Special Representative and the military and civilian leaders in an operation helps counteract the possibility that these officials may be following not only the UN's orders, but those of their home state. This dual loyalty seems more likely as the UN exhausts its traditional sources of troops for first-generation missions (such as Fiji, India, Pakistan, the Scandinavian countries, and Canada) and relies on other states, especially the Permanent Five, for senior officials, civilians, and soldiers. Officials from these states with major global interests may show less deference to the Secretary-General's control and threaten the impartiality of peacekeeping.

Oversight must reflect a balance between the needs of the member states to follow the settlement and the effects of supervision on the efficiency of the operation. States will not seek, and the Secretary-General would resist, intrusive supervision. This would include daily or weekly public reports on the operation or convocation of the Security Council each time one party appears to be reneging on a peace accord. More practical alternatives, however, remain for increased participation by member states.

a. Accurate Intelligence, Efficiently Shared

First, as a prerequisite to greater involvement, the Secretariat should provide a more candid account of the progress of operations than is often printed in the periodic reports of the Secretary-General. These documents represent the product of weeks of careful effort by officials in the peacekeeping mission and the Secretariat and contain significant factual details. Nevertheless, they can remain laden with "UN-speak," such as use of the passive voice to avoid assessing blame for behavior, and accentuate the positive aspects of the peace process. (UNTAC's reports improved over time, candidly admitting the derailment of parts of the settlement and the hurdles to fair elections.) For the UN to maintain the perception of impartiality, it probably must follow a cautious approach. Nevertheless, the Secretariat should supplement its reports with frequent oral briefings. This would prove particularly important for states without diplomatic missions inside the countries that host operations.

Second, the Security Council could create formal subgroups, to meet on a weekly or biweekly basis, to monitor each mission. While the Secretariat and interested members of the Council (the Permanent Five and those "friends" of the peace process on the Council) currently share information and consult at the working level, a more formal mechanism would have special benefits. It would encourage the nonpermanent members of the Council to view the missions as central to the UN's purposes in the area of peace and security and to offer their views. The subgroups would also parallel the work of the "friends'" diplomats in the affected country, as the subgroups could help push the Secretariat and the Council to act on issues requiring immediate attention. And for those states not on the Council and without the resources to monitor operations, representatives of the regional and other groupings to which they belong can serve as conduits of information to and from the Council subgroup deliberations.[37]

b. Principles for Oversight

Beyond access to information and the modalities of deliberation lies the more substantial matter of the degree of authority and flexibility to be afforded to the Special Representative. The need for a standard for judging which issues merit the attention of Headquarters became apparent as early as the Saar administration, with the League of Nations Council's decision to refrain from interference "except for reasons of the highest importance."[38]

Yet this dictum offers no operational guidance for Headquarters or a Special Representative. It also represents an overly passive stance, reflecting the desires of the League's members to avoid making the Saar a topic of continuous Council debate. At the other extreme, Secretary-General Waldheim suggested a policy of extremely close oversight of first-generation operations in his 1973 guidelines for UNEF II, the Sinai mission deployed after the Yom Kippur War. In his words, "All matters which may affect the nature or the continued effective functioning of the Force will be referred to the Council for its decision."[39] This too is not reasonable for the new peacekeeping.

For second-generation missions, the appropriate relationship between Headquarters, comprising the political organs and the Secretary-General, and the field became a contentious subject as early as the Namibia mission. There New York saw the operation as too pro-South African, and the issue remains an important one. Three power clusters in the UN have legitimate expectations that their views deserve deference, if not more, in the implementation of the mandate: the member states, the Secretary-General and his top aides, and the Special Representative. The immediate parties to the conflict will, of course, have their own demands as well.

To date, a modus vivendi has prevailed, with most authority exercised in the field. This outcome appears to be the product as much of lack of resources and interest by member states and the Secretary-General as a deliberate policy to afford discretion to the field. It is thus necessary to propose some basic guidelines for oversight in consent-based peacekeeping.

As a first principle, the political organs and Secretary-General should grant the Special Representative a wide berth in the internal management of the operation. This would encompass selection of personnel, bureaucratic structure and decision making, and requisition of equipment. New York should accept the inevitability of infrequent reporting from the field on these questions. Moreover, short of a compelling basis to believe that the Special Representative's policies on these matters are undermining the mission, New York should defer to him.

As for the political responsibilities inherent in advancing the settlement process, the Special Representative should, at a minimum, be required to file daily reports of several pages with the Department of Peacekeeping Operations. Akin to cables from an embassy to its foreign ministry, these memoranda would summarize the day's activities, offer a brief political assessment of developments, and propose courses of action. With respect to decision making, the Special Representative should maintain significant discretion. In the first instance, he should be free to discuss implementation questions with representatives of political factions or "friends," or authorize components of the mission to undertake initiatives to advance the peace process, subject only to an after-the-fact notification to Headquarters.

This discretion, however, has its limits. New York-based actors should oversee the Special Representative more assertively regarding important decisions. With the extreme positions of the Saar Commission and UNEF II described earlier discarded, Headquarters should base its degree of supervision primarily on two criteria: (1) the risk of any decision by the Special Representative fundamentally derailing the completion of the mandate; and (2) the risk of any decision imperiling the safety of mission personnel or the inhabitants of the affected country.

The first factor reflects the Organization's and member states' Charter-based duty to promote international peace, the UN's role as guarantor of the underlying peace accords, and their corresponding interest in ensuring that the Special Representative does not act contrary to these goals. The second incorporates the legitimate concerns of states that UN personnel not face undue danger, and the concern of all states that a peacekeeping operation lessen, or at least not increase, the dangers to which the affected populace is exposed. Both elements also derive from the core peacekeeping principles of consent and impartiality. Any action by the Special Representative weakening either of these pillars would impede the execution of the mandate and potentially increase the physical peril for UN and local participants.

As the aggregate of these two risks increase (or, correspondingly, the conceptual foundations underneath the operation weaken), the degree of oversight by New York should intensify. In some cases, the Special Representative need only notify Headquarters that he will execute a certain decision unless it objects. An officer in DPKO, after brief consultations with others, can then decide to defer to him. More precarious moves, such as imposition of sanctions on a violating party, would require a formal request for permission. DPKO would then consult with the political organs, such as the Security Council subgroups or other aggregations of interested states, and approve or deny the request.

In order for this approach to work, both the Secretary-General and the member states must trust the Special Representative's judgment to ascertain those proposed decisions to be sent to Headquarters for review. Furthermore, UN Headquarters must be able to dispose of issues quickly. Exceptional emergency situations may preclude consultation, underlining the centrality for confidence by New York in the Special Representative.

3. Confronting the Legitimacy Question

For the new peacekeeping to assume a place as a core undertaking of the United Nations, member states must accept the appropriateness of the enterprise and the means for carrying it out. At one level, the practice of states over the past five years suggests that the requisite expectation of lawfulness and legitimacy is now present—that the creation of new operations, primarily under the auspices of the Security Council, speaks for itself. Yet resistance still looms to both the concept and the procedure.

a. The Nonintervention Bias

First, the developing world still has qualms that expansive UN operations could constitute intervention by the Organization in their internal affairs. Many states in the General Assembly remain enamored of a strict view of nonintervention. This is witnessed by the Assembly's insistence on passing a resolution embodying these principles to accompany any resolution on the UN's role in elections.[40] The predisposition of the former colonies of Africa and Asia against international supervision over member states, notwithstanding their preference for UN involvement in non-self-governing areas, cannot be expected to change imminently.

Yet the new peacekeeping has garnered the support of the members of the Non-Aligned Movement (and its de facto alter ego in the UN, the anachronistically designated Group of 77). They have voted for, participated in, and supported the recent missions in Latin America and Cambodia. They appear to accept the operation in Somalia as an appropriate UN role not merely due to its humanitarian urgency, but in order to reconstruct a shattered polity. The final statement of the 1992 summit of the Non-Aligned Movement applauded the new forms of UN peacekeeping without any qualification concerning the need to respect the principle of nonintervention.[41]

The NAM appears willing to accept the UN involvement inherent in second-generation operations because the first principle of these missions is the consent of the affected state(s) through invitation or signature by elites of a peace settlement. This resonates with the NAM's view of sovereignty and nonintervention. The NAM also acknowledges that the desire of formerly warring states or factions for UN oversight of peace accords has placed new demands on the Organization that it cannot simply ignore.[42] Finally, larger members of the NAM have likely recognized their own political interest in the success of the new peacekeeping. It increases their profile in areas far from their own territories, especially through deployment of personnel.

b. A Broader Base of State Participants

Of greater consequence to the future of the new peacekeeping are the claims by the majority of the UN's members for increased participation in the decisions of the Organization in the field of international peace and security. These demands have multiplied as the Security Council, open to at most seven developing states (three nonpermanent seats being reserved for developed states), has come to operate much as the Charter's drafters intended. On all but the most controversial matters, it works quite collegially, with the United States, Britain, and France determining its agenda on most issues and often quickly achieving the support of Russia and a majority of the nonpermanent members. As a result, a type of "groupthink" has emerged, with only a few states, led by China, offering traditional developing world perspectives.[43] While the developing world states accept second-generation peacekeeping, they seek assurances that a few powerful states not dominate the process.[44] These demands now form a primary item on the NAM's agenda.[45]

The seriousness with which these calls for greater involvement should be treated is not self-evident. The practice to date of second-generation peacekeeping could well suggest that most states have neither the time nor interest to follow new UN operations far from home. Some, indeed many, in the developing world majority likely prefer sharing the accolades for the recent successes of the UN and accept the creation, oversight, and payment of these missions by a small group of developed states on the Security Council.

On the other hand, if these claims are not considered, the Council risks establishing new operations without the active support of the General Assembly. Even though most states make only a negligible contribution to the peacekeeping budget, a pattern of apathy or opposition by a large number not on the Council could undermine future operations. Their opposition would cripple new missions if reflected in the consensus-based budgetary process. Apathy would prove just as harmful if states that have traditionally donated personnel stopped doing so or if other actors failed to use their diplomatic resources to resolve disputes over implementation.

The alternative least disruptive to the Organization would entail acceptance by the Council of greater participation by the General Assembly. This role would go beyond the increased Assembly activities in budgetary and nonmilitary matters discussed in chapter 3 that seem inevitable in any case.

Frequent consultations regarding new operations before and after their establishment would help allay the fears of the NAM that the Permanent Five bypass most states in the supervision of peacekeeping. Construction of a formal informational loop would contribute to greater democratization as well.[46] The Council should try harder for a genuine partnership with the Assembly.

The Non-Aligned majority may not accept such a junior partner role. Their claims for participation may be satisfied only through adjustment of the membership of the Council. At its 1992 session, the Assembly officially deemed this matter ripe for discussion by the political organs, and in 1993, it set up a working group on the issue.[47] The West seems ready to accept some form of permanent membership for Japan and Germany, although Britain and France reject any suggestion of combining their seats into one assumed by the European Union.[48]

The NAM, for its part, focuses upon greater representation of its members. Indonesian President Soeharto called in 1992 for increasing the Council by six members—Japan, Germany, Indonesia, India (the two most populated nonpermanent members), and one state each from Africa and Latin America.[49] A Council of 17 or 21 members would still prove a manageable deliberative and decision-making body. New seats for permanent members would recognize the effective power of individual large, developing states in Asia, Latin America, and Africa. It would appear, however, to address only marginally the underlying challenge of fostering broad participation by the majority of the Assembly's members. This might be accomplished if the new members create a formal consultative mechanism with fellow developing world states. However, the new permanent members may well find their elevated status and the increased demands on their time quickly distancing them from their non-aligned brethren.

The possibilities for adjusted membership remain numerous, with combinations of new permanent members and new rotating members. The UN's deliberations in this regard will not simply be dictated by the issue of peacekeeping. States will also appraise the effects of reform in Council membership on the Council's responsibility for nonconsensual enforcement through diplomatic, economic, and military sanctions. Whether any adjusted membership satisfies the majority of UN members will become apparent only after some years. Regardless of the scheme adopted, the Council will still need to collaborate with the General Assembly, as it remains the sole organ of the UN with universal membership.[50]

4. Needed: A Review of Responses to Decaying Consent

The brief history of second-generation peacekeeping suggests that UN operations to implement settlements will continue to operate in situations of decaying consent, as one or more parties hesitate to carry out their obligations. This seems especially so in those exceptional cases of involvement without a settlement. Eroding consent can exhibit itself across a spectrum of activities, from refusal to meet with UN officials through military action against them.

The transformation from a framework for decision that considers the context of the violations (as set out in chapter 2) to practical policy guidance must be undertaken with due caution. The history of the new phenomenon is still quite short; the full aggregate of data from UNTAC and other missions will take more time to analyze; and the ongoing operations are in too great a state of uncertainty to permit clear lessons in this regard. Indeed, the questions raised may simply be immune to any authoritative, comprehensive guidance. Thus, rather than offering any rules for responses in these circumstances, prudence dictates a more modest set of recommendations.

a. Preventing the Worst Resistance

All missions since the Congo operation have confirmed that the ideal insurance against the most damaging manifestations of decaying consent is a demilitarized atmosphere. Where the protagonists have forsaken recourse to arms, the UN need not remain preoccupied with the possibility of violent resistance to its actions. Yet while some new peacekeeping operations are deployed in countries where the military struggle has ended, or where the conflict never resulted in an extensive militarization of the land, many will occur in states with armed factions. The UN will and should refrain from dispatching second-generation missions in the absence of a reasonably effective cease-fire. But the mere risk of hostilities, inevitable in the settlement process, has not and should not prevent deployment of a mission. Indeed, the "lesson" of the Angola operation to the effect that fair elections cannot take place in the presence of armed factions was completely undercut by the results in Cambodia.

Once emplaced in a country with armed parties, the mission should attempt a demilitarization program as soon as possible, presumably in fulfillment of a peace plan. Thus, despite the primarily nonmilitary mandate of the new peacekeeping, missions may have to devote substantial resources to military components, and the performance of UN military units remains worthy of attention.[51] Nevertheless, because peacekeeping is based on consent, the war-fighting capability of UN military units is less relevant than many insist and should not be at the top of the peacekeeping agenda.

b. Consideration of a New Starting Point

Should resistance to a peacekeeping operation occur, participants will disagree regarding the proper response. Thus, for example, when the UN had to decide whether UNTAC would conduct the elections in Cambodia notwithstanding the failure of Phase II of the cease-fire, some suggested the entire process should have been suspended until the disarmament and demobilization could proceed.[52] The successful outcome of the elections calls this position into question, but, at the time, it would have seemed as reasonable as the action ultimately taken. Despite its decision to proceed with the elections in the face of potential (and later, actual) violence, UNTAC generally adopted a strict view of consent. It sought to persuade the factions to comply rather than test its authority under the Paris accords.

As the number of missions proliferates, however, member states and Secretariat officials need to ponder the value of a more liberal view of consent. This would entail encouraging future Special Representatives to make firm decisions about the implementation process and use diplomatic tools to convince the parties to comply with UN directives. These decisions would arise in two circumstances: carrying out unambiguous provisions in peace accords (such as a requirement to disarm beginning on day x); or interpreting ambiguous clauses and filling lacunae in the accords.

Under this new strategy, if the parties do not comply with UN decisions within a reasonable period (meaning a matter of days, rather than weeks), officials in the operation should, as a general rule, begin to attempt to correct the situation themselves and take the parties at their word when they consented to the operation initially. In very exceptional circumstances, threats, or even uses, of coercion may prove necessary, although nonforcible means must be exhausted first. New York would oversee these actions according to the approach outlined earlier.

The greater the extent to which the UN can perform its executor role without the need for active, affirmative cooperation of the parties, the less it will need to rely on such remedial measures. Thus, for instance, the UN can conduct refugee repatriation and electoral administration more independently of factional behavior than it can oversee disarmament.[53] And specific language in a peace accord empowering the Special Representative to act on his own may make it harder for the sides to reject his decisions, although Cambodia shows they may well ignore him.

Such a new policy would lead to a proper balance among the UN's administrator, mediator, and guarantor roles. Where a settlement contains a clear obligation upon the parties, the UN's primary mission must be to assist them in fulfilling it. When legitimate interpretive disputes arrive, the UN can mediate, but should be prepared to make the final, authoritative determination. A philosophy that accepts violations of clear commitments or of interpretive decisions made by the UN as merely new issues for mediation entails few costs to the violator. The UN serves neither to execute the accord nor guarantee an outcome, but to avoid confrontation at all costs. Over time, this position erodes the accord and pushes the parties back toward their positions prior to its signature.

This new opening position would not entail the end of the UN's role as mediator. As noted, it would play an active mediation role in the event of interpretive disputes. Moreover, even when a party has violated the accord, the UN can engage in discussions to elicit compliance that do not compromise its position or suggest a willingness to tolerate impunity. Finally, and most significantly, the operation may lack the human and physical resources to rectify a violation and thus have no alternative but discussions.

This new vantage point would pose risks: (a) the possible transformation of the mission from peacekeeping to peace enforcement; (b) the potential for physical danger to UN civilian and military peacekeepers; and (c) the damage to the credibility of the operation if a recalcitrant party continues to resist a more assertive UN posture.

With regard to the first risk, the use of firm measures within a consensual peacekeeping mission does not constitute, ipso facto, a step across the thin line to enforcement action. The earlier settlement agreed to by the parties does afford the UN some leeway in responding to violations. The memories of Hammarskjold's broad interpretation of the right of an operation to engage in self-defense during the Congo crisis and the ensuing battles with Katangese rebels should no longer paralyze officials from taking the many steps short of such massive uses of force.[54]

The Security Council will have to monitor the actions of the Special Representative. In Cambodia, the Council supported UNTAC's actions, including its surprise raids on State of Cambodia offices to seize documents, despite significant resistance by the two largest factions. This stands as evidence that the Council is accepting a broader or less revocable notion of consent. The Council is thus allowing an operation to engage in assertive, if not somewhat coercive, action as peacekeeping without seeing a need to invoke peace enforcement authority for these measures. If, however, the Council determines that the prior consent no longer provides acceptable legal and political grounds for the Special Representative's actions, it will order him to stand down. In exceptional circumstances, it will authorize peace enforcement.

The hesitancy of the Secretary-General and member states to place peacekeeping personnel in harm's way is rational and inevitable, although improvements in the UN's military capacities might allay member states' concerns that UN forces are ill-prepared to employ force when needed. Yet the dangers from a more liberal view of consent may not be as great as feared. The party opposing the UN's interpretation is likely to manifest its resistance through non-military means, as elevating opposition to the level of retaliation against UN personnel would invite universal condemnation and withdrawl of the mission. (The Khmer Rouge's attacks on UNTAC personnel drew a stern rebuke from its diplomatic allies and likely contributed to its decision not to disrupt the elections.[55]) If the UN's determination to carry out a decision did endanger UN personnel, it would clearly have to reassess the situation. This would occur, for instance, if a recalcitrant party had so abandoned the peace process that it systematically attacked peacekeepers.

Finally, with respect to the credibility of the mission, a failed attempt to overcome an uncooperative faction will doubtless give rise to perceptions that the UN is a paper tiger. Yet inaction in the face of such opposition can lead to the same conclusion more quickly. If the mission simply lacks the means to execute a decision, it should not attempt to do so. But its aim should be to make and implement as many decisions as necessary and feasible.

The principle proposed for consideration here will not apply to all peace-keeping. In first-generation operations, where the UN has the consent of the parties to deploy in the contested territory, but no overall peace accord is in place, the UN operates from a different type of consent. If the parties violate a cease-fire, the mission lacks the legal or political foundation of a preexisting settlement that it can claim to be implementing. It operates with less initial consent and concomitant flexibility. The only possible outcome may be retreat, as taken by U Thant in withdrawing UNEF I from Egypt in 1967.

Where consent has evaporated, as with peace enforcement missions, the proposal would appear inapplicable unless the international community were prepared to escalate its involvement and defeat a recalcitrant party. UNPROFOR and UNOSOM II, which both have peace enforcement assignments, bear witness to the impossible situations facing peacekeepers when the parties refuse to cooperate and the political commitment of key member states, in particular the United States as the leading military power, is uncertain.

In the former Yugoslavia, the UN has refused to send relief convoys into isolated areas when cease-fires broke down, opting instead for days of renewed negotiations to convince the combatants to suspend hostilities. In Somalia, the UN used force in 1993 against the militia of clan leader Mohammed Aideed in response to attacks that killed at least 25 Pakistani peacekeepers, only to suffer reprisals that killed 18 U.S. soldiers. Since those episodes, the UN has abandoned confrontation for mediation and brought Aideed into negotiations over the country's future.

5. Funding: Amount and Timing

The UN's long-running financial woes cast a shadow over its future. In the early 1960s, the UN nearly ground to a halt over the issue of whether peace-keeping costs were official UN expenses. Although all member states now accept their legal duty to pay their assessments, the UN today faces a crisis due to the failure of many states to follow through on that obligation. Since 1992, both Boutros-Ghali and a Ford Foundation panel headed by former Federal Reserve Board Chairman Paul Volcker and former Bank of Japan senior official Shijuro Ogata have issued thoughtful recommendations on this subject.[56] The financial difficulties affect the new peacekeeping in two ways: amount and flow of money.

First, the arrearages of several large donors, notably the United States and Russia, has meant that troop donors are not compensated for many years. The UN has managed to obtain military personnel for its peacekeeping (vice peace enforcement) operations, though not always in sufficient numbers. Moreover, donors are angry over payment delays. As the number of missions grows, a guaranteed supply of troops is less assured, and quite unlikely for peace enforcement missions.[57] The UN will also lack the funds to hire sufficient qualified civilian personnel for second-generation operations. And training of civilian peacekeepers and other proposals to improve the Secretariat will necessitate increased assessments on member states, voluntary contributions, and restructuring to save costs.

Flow of funds constitutes an equal threat. The thin and irregular stream of contributions from member states has left the UN with low cash reserves.[58] This small margin inhibits the Secretary-General's ability to spend money on new operations on a priority basis. It impedes conclusion of long-term supply contracts and delays payments to civilians in peacekeeping operations. (Military personnel donated by member states can receive a salary from their governments even if the UN is slow to pay them.)

In the case of UNTAC, delayed approval and disbursement of funds hurt the operation during the critical early months. Paychecks came late, civilians resorted to personal savings for urgent expenses, and funds for purchases of supplies arrived long after the goods were required.[59] Under pressure from the largest donor states, the General Assembly has compounded the financial difficulties by precluding expenditure of significant amounts of money until it has approved the budget of the mission in plenary session. While any large-scale bureaucracy has necessary procedures for disbursing funds, most develop methods for expediting payments during times of crisis.

The creation in 1992 of the $150 million peacekeeping reserve fund represents a positive step, but the money must be provided and the fund is too small in any event.[60] Boutros-Ghali and the Ford Foundation study have also proposed expedited obligation procedures. The former calls for the Assembly to appropriate one-third of an operation's cost immediately upon its creation by the Security Council, and the latter favors authority for the Secretary-General to spend 20 percent of the cost immediately upon Council action without Assembly approval.

Borrowing authority remains quite controversial. Long sought by the Secretary-General, but opposed by the Ford Foundation study, it might rectify some shortages in amounts, but would not likely address cash flow problems. Moreover, the UN would have difficulty obtaining credit as its income depends solely upon the willingness of member states to pay.[61] An experimental program for a finite duration should nonetheless be undertaken.

Boutros-Ghali has made UN finance a top priority of his administration. Yet the funding question primarily involves the responsibility of the UN's members, particularly the larger donors. Until they observe their Charter obligation to pay assessments on time and in full, the crisis will remain severe, with corresponding effects on the new peacekeeping. The Clinton administration's plan to reduce the U.S. percentage of peacekeeping assessments from the current 31.7 percent to 25 percent will do little to improve the overall picture except shift a small amount of funding to states more likely to pay on time.[62] Even if shortfalls are eliminated, the Assembly will need procedures to expedite approval of the budget and the disbursement of funds.

Lastly, the UN must focus on financial control. Boutros-Ghali's appointment in August 1993 of an Assistant Secretary-General for Inspections and Investigations was followed by the General Assembly's creation in July 1994 of an Office of Internal Oversight Services headed by a new Under Secretary-General.[63] This has begun to address perceptions within the United States of irresponsible UN spending and contribute to the somewhat greater political acceptability within the United States of payment of assessments.[64] Yet member states must give the UN leeway in this sphere. Overly strict and centralized financial controls will prevent missions from procuring the materials and hiring the people they need quickly. The possibility remains that the delinquent states will be convinced to pay their arrearages only if the Secretary-General is unable to deploy or maintain an important mission, or is forced to terminate one, due to lack of funds.[65]

.10.

Conclusions

The second generation of peacekeeping remains an experiment in progress. Through the dispatch of operations with significant, non-military roles, the UN's members have employed a novel and versatile instrument to end conflict in states riven by civil and interstate war. This latest effort has grown from earlier peacekeeping missions as well as other historical precedents, but has its own conceptual foundations. The data trickling in has offered evidence of the competence of the United Nations in overseeing settlements and nation-building, as well as its evident deficiencies. Systemic change in the UN to enable it to meet today's demands is needed, and member states and Secretariat officials must turn their attention to proposals for improvement. But in the final analysis, the UN will only build up the capability to conduct these operations over time, and if its members give it the resources it requires.

THE LEGACY OF HAMMARSKJOLD

This study thus comes full circle by returning to the vision of Hammarskjold. In the words of his biographer and protégé Brian Urquhart:

> Hammarskjold's basic view of international peace and security was that a reliable and just world order could only be built pragmatically by making precedents and by case law. By this process he hoped that

the United Nations would be gradually transformed from an institutional mechanism into a constitutional instrument recognized and
respected by all nations.[1]

For the United Nations, the case law of second-generation peacekeeping is
comparatively small and recent. Member states seem prepared to assign new
military and civilian duties to the Organization in overseeing political settlements. In that sense, the UN has achieved the recognition that Hammarskjold
sought as the best institution for these uniquely international responsibilities,
albeit as much through default as through its own accomplishments.

It is only gradually beginning, however, to receive the respect of nations for
this new role. Early missions in Namibia and Nicaragua, considered successes, showed the UN's potential and prompted member states to entrust it
with more extensive assignments. More recent episodes have highlighted the
risks of employing a peacekeeping mission in a country still divided upon
itself. These include Cambodia, with UNTAC's mixed results, and the setbacks, if not failures, in the Western Sahara, Angola, Rwanda, and Liberia. The
former Yugoslavia and Somalia have vividly revealed a totally new dimension
of danger in the transformation from peacekeeping to peace enforcement.

Reforms of the Charter and of the United Nations will shape the development of the common law of second-generation peacekeeping, just as constitutions and statutes dot the legal landscape on which the common law grows.
They can facilitate as well as constrain the development of that common law.
If the UN continues to engage in the new peacekeeping, the Organization and
its members will have to modify existing structures and erect new ones.
Otherwise, it will simply confirm the suspicion of one UNTAC official who
opined that "the lesson of all this is that the UN does not learn lessons."[2]

Beyond these considerations, however, formal doctrine and detailed rules
of engagement seem unnecessary, whether they address the limits of consent,
neutrality, and impartiality, or the administration of an operation. They will
take months, if not years, to develop, and risk both rigidity and irrelevance. The
conceptual groundwork for the new peacekeeping does not demand elaborate
studies or long-term projects by commissions. *An Agenda for Peace* is a
worthwhile start in this direction. Leaders within the UN should continue the
intellectual and operational endeavor. Those in national capitals and the academy should emulate their example.

As the Organization develops the basic conceptual and bureaucratic tools
for these operations, it must remain adaptable to new situations. Somalia is not
like Cambodia; and that which follows in Haiti, the former Yugoslavia, or elsewhere will differ in critical ways from all that came before. Missions will offer

contrasting, if not apparently contradictory, lessons. The common law will build in time in its own way. Future decision makers should ask whether the distinctions among the factual situations of various operations should make a difference in formulating principles to guide them. Doctrine will follow the process but not lead it.

Invocation of Hammarskjold is also appropriate because the new peacekeeping represents an extension of his major contribution to the United Nations. This was the transformation of the UN from a generally deliberative body in the areas of peace and war into an operational organization. He achieved this metamorphosis by activating two institutions under his personal guidance—peacekeeping and peacemaking. Second-generation peacekeeping integrates his two most significant progeny into a consolidated enterprise that attempts to fulfill the Charter's main purposes. This integrative effort has shown halting promise, but it clearly constitutes a turning point in the realm of international peace and security.

THE NEW LEGITIMACY CRISIS AND THE PROSPECTS FOR THE NEW PEACEKEEPING

As appropriate as is recognition of Hammarskjold, today's conflicts are of a fundamentally different order than those facing the Cold War-constrained United Nations of his time. The international community might leap into the breach and empower the UN in novel ways, with the recent operations a prelude to more ambitious plans. Perhaps the first five years of the new peacekeeping will lead to endeavors that further transcend traditional peacekeeping and advance toward nation-saving. These missions might respond to the needs of failed states racked by anarchy and economic collapse, and amount to a de facto, consent-based UN conservatorship to restore them to health. The operations in Cambodia, El Salvador, and Somalia have many hallmarks of an attempt at conservatorship, even if the term rings alarm bells among most developing world states.[3]

But the UN's most powerful members, and the United States in particular, are far from endorsing such a UN posture. First, the second generation must stand on its own, a hardly inevitable course of events. One cannot afford undue optimism, and few of the proposals offered here represent quick or cheap fixes.

Indeed, even if second-generation peacekeeping continues to be undertaken in an ad hoc manner without systemic change, the most basic challenge confronting it is an issue of legitimacy beyond the matter of Security Council reform. This question is, quite simply, whether the member states will themselves carry out and permit the Organization to carry out the decisions of the political organs. For an adjustment in the Council's membership to reflect the planet's population offers no guarantee that those on and off it will actually commit the political, financial, and human resources necessary to missions.[4]

This emergent legitimacy crisis permeates all the issues discussed in this book and all the suggestions for improved second-generation peacekeeping, whether oversight of missions, responses to decaying consent, Secretariat restructuring, or funding. All depend on the willingness of states to make the new peacekeeping effective. It is premature to gauge the long-term attitudes of member states toward the new peacekeeping or the course they will chart through the crisis.

After five years, it does appear, however, that because first- and second-generation peacekeeping remain consent-based and generally without significant casualties, a consensus is forming on the need to support the missions. This consensus will erode, however, if more missions fail in their fundamental objectives. Over time, expansive forms of peacekeeping may prove beyond the capacity of the UN and the political will of its members. And an equally disturbing prospect, one beyond this book, is the crisis facing nonconsensual action, characterized by the dismally large gap between the words of Security Council resolutions and the actions of member states.[5]

Enhanced UN involvement may also represent unsound policy for solving conflicts. Multifaceted operations like UNTAC and UNOSOM II deflect accountability off of the immediate antagonists and onto the United Nations. This ultimately inhibits the long-term prospects of nation-building. Moreover, opponents of international intervention in domestic crises will assert that it merely prolongs civil conflict that is best resolved through the decisive victory of one side.[6] These concerns suggest that, whatever the future of the new peacekeeping, those carrying it out must facilitate the peace-building process, rather than try to take sole charge of it. They do not, however, demand the conclusion that, when a people is exhausted due to long-term conflict and cannot reconstruct a civil order on its own, the international community should abstain from assisting it.[7]

Lighter UN structures short of extensive administrative oversight may represent the optimal UN presence. This level of commitment would both encourage domestic elites to assume their obligations to their people and offer a degree of international guarantee. Even in an area like elections, where UNTAC scored a significant triumph through plenary control of the process, the UN may be able to ensure a fair election equally well through methods short of full administration.[8] The UN must seek a balance that takes advantage of its talents but does not remove the burdens of responsibility and incentives from the immediate parties. And perhaps some day, regional organizations will assume a larger role in peacekeeping.

The international community appears to have decided, grudgingly and tentatively, to initiate a new process of peacekeeping on the assumption that the latest experiment offers tangible contributions to world order and the advancement of human rights. This community decision of the immediate post–Cold War era, however, marks only one point in a dialectic among the UN's members. In the end it is those states, more than the civilian and military footsoldiers at UN Headquarters and in the field, who will determine the fate of the new peacekeeping.

A·P·P·E·N·D·I·X 1

EXCERPTS FROM THE CHARTER OF THE UNITED NATIONS

CHAPTER I
PURPOSES AND PRINCIPLES

ARTICLE 1

The Purposes of the United Nations are:

1. To maintain international peace and security, and to that end: to take effective collective measures for the prevention and removal of threats to the peace, and for the suppression of acts of aggression or other breaches of the peace, and to bring about by peaceful means, and in conformity with the principles of justice and international law, adjustment or settlement of international disputes or situations which might lead to a breach of the peace;

2. To develop friendly relations among nations based on respect for the principle of equal rights and self-determination of peoples, and to take other appropriate measures to strengthen universal peace;

3. To achieve international co-operation in solving international problems of an economic, social, cultural, or humanitarian character, and in promoting and encouraging respect for human rights and for fundamental freedoms for all without distinction as to race, sex, language, or religion; and

4. To be a centre for harmonizing the actions of nations in the attainment of these common ends.

ARTICLE 2

The Organization and its Members, in pursuit of the Purposes stated in Article 1, shall act in accordance with the following Principles.

3. All Members shall settle their international disputes by peaceful means in such a manner that international peace and security, and justice, are not endangered.

4. All Members shall refrain in their international relations from the threat or use of force against the territorial integrity or political independence of any state, or in any other manner inconsistent with the Purposes of the United Nations.

7. Nothing contained in the present Charter shall authorize the United Nations to intervene in matters which are essentially within the domestic jurisdiction of any state or shall require the Members to submit such matters to settlement under the present Charter; but this principle shall not prejudice the application of enforcement measures under Chapter VII.

CHAPTER IV
THE GENERAL ASSEMBLY

ARTICLE 9
Composition

1. The General Assembly shall consist of all the Members of the United Nations.

ARTICLE 10
Functions and powers

The General Assembly may discuss any questions or any matters within the scope of the present Charter or relating to the powers and functions of any organs provided for in the present Charter, and, except as provided in Article 12, may make recommendations to the Members of the United Nations or to the Security Council or to both on any such questions or matters.

ARTICLE 11

2. The General Assembly may discuss any questions relating to the maintenance of international peace and security brought before it by any Member of the United Nations, or by the Security Council, or by a state which is not a Member of the United Nations in accordance with Article 35, paragraph 2, and, except as provided in Article 12, may make recommendations with regard to any such questions to the state or states concerned or to the Security Council or to both. Any such question on which action is necessary shall be referred to the Security Council by the General Assembly either before or after discussion.

3. The General Assembly may call the attention of the Security Council to situations which are likely to endanger international peace and security.

ARTICLE 12

1. While the Security Council is exercising in respect of any dispute or situation the functions assigned to it in the present Charter, the General Assembly shall not make any recommendation with regard to that dispute or situation unless the Security Council so requests.

2. The Secretary-General, with the consent of the Security Council, shall notify the General Assembly at each session of any matters relative to the maintenance of international peace and security which are being dealt with by the Security Council and shall similarly notify the General Assembly, or the Members of the United Nations if the General Assembly is not in session, immediately the Security Council ceases to deal with such matters.

ARTICLE 13

1. The General Assembly shall initiate studies and make recommendations for the purpose of:

a. promoting international co-operation in the political field and encouraging the progressive development of international law and its codification;

b. promoting international co-operation in the economic, social, cultural, educational, and health fields, and assisting in the realization of human rights and fundamental freedoms for all without distinction as to race, sex, language, or religion.

ARTICLE 14

Subject to the provisions of Article 12, the General Assembly may recommend measures for the peaceful adjustment of any situation, regardless of origin, which it deems likely to impair the general welfare or friendly relations among nations, including situations resulting from a violation of the provisions of the present Charter setting forth the Purposes and Principles of the United Nations.

ARTICLE 17

1. The General Assembly shall consider and approve the budget of the Organization.

2. The expenses of the Organization shall be borne by the Members as apportioned by the General Assembly.

ARTICLE 18
Voting

1. Each member of the General Assembly shall have one vote.

2. Decisions of the General Assembly on important questions shall be made by a two-thirds majority of the members present and voting. These questions shall include: recommendations with respect to the maintenance of international peace and security, the election of the non-permanent members of the Security Council, the election of the members of the Economic and Social Council, the election of members of the Trusteeship Council in accordance with paragraph 1(c) of Article 86, the admission of new Members to the United Nations, the suspension of the rights and privileges of membership, the expulsion of Members, questions relating to the operation of the trusteeship system, and budgetary questions.

3. Decisions on other questions, including the determination of additional categories of questions to be decided by a two-thirds majority, shall be made by a majority of the members present and voting.

ARTICLE 22

The General Assembly may establish such subsidiary organs as it deems necessary for the performance of its functions.

CHAPTER V
THE SECURITY COUNCIL

ARTICLE 23
Composition

1. The Security Council shall consist of fifteen Members of the United Nations. The Republic of China, France, the Union of Soviet Socialist Republics, the United Kingdom of Great Britain and Northern Ireland, and the United States of America shall be permanent members of the Security Council. The General Assembly shall elect ten other Members of the United Nations to be non-permanent members of the Security Council, due regard being specially paid, in the first instance to the contribution of Members of the United Nations to the maintenance of international peace and security and to the other purposes of the Organization, and also to equitable geographical distribution.

ARTICLE 24
Functions and powers

1. In order to ensure prompt and effective action by the United Nations, its Members confer on the Security Council primary responsibility for the maintenance of international peace and security, and agree that in carrying out its duties under this responsibility the Security Council acts on their behalf.

ARTICLE 25

The Members of the United Nations agree to accept and carry out the decisions of the Security Council in accordance with the present Charter.

ARTICLE 27
Voting

1. Each member of the Security Council shall have one vote.

2. Decisions of the Security Council on procedural matters shall be made by an affirmative vote of nine members.

3. Decisions of the Security Council on all other matters shall be made by an affirmative vote of nine members including the concurring votes of the permanent members; provided that, in decisions under Chapter VI, and under paragraph 3 of Article 52, a party to a dispute shall abstain from voting.

CHAPTER VI
PACIFIC SETTLEMENT OF DISPUTES

ARTICLE 33

1. The parties to any dispute, the continuance of which is likely to endanger the maintenance of international peace and security, shall, first of all, seek a solution by negotiation, enquiry, mediation, conciliation, arbitration, judicial settlement, resort to regional agencies or arrangements, or other peaceful means of their own choice.
2. The Security Council shall, when it deems necessary, call upon the parties to settle their disputes by such means.

ARTICLE 34

The Security Council may investigate any dispute, or any situation which might lead to international friction or give rise to a dispute, in order to determine whether the continuance of the dispute or situation is likely to endanger the maintenance of international peace and security.

ARTICLE 36

1. The Security Council may, at any stage of a dispute of the nature referred to in Article 33 or of a situation of like nature, recommend appropriate procedures or methods of adjustment.
2. The Security Council should take into consideration any procedures for the settlement of the dispute which have already been adopted by the parties.

ARTICLE 37

1. Should the parties to a dispute of the nature referred to in Article 33 fail to settle it by the means indicated in that Article, they shall refer it to the Security Council.
2. If the Security Council deems that the continuance of the dispute is in fact likely to endanger the maintenance of international peace and security, it shall decide whether to take action under Article 36 or to recommend such terms of settlement as it may consider appropriate.

ARTICLE 38

Without prejudice to the provisions of Articles 33 to 37, the Security Council may, if all the parties to any dispute so request, make recommendations to the parties with a view to a pacific settlement of the dispute.

CHAPTER VII
ACTION WITH RESPECT TO THREATS TO THE PEACE, BREACHES OF THE PEACE, AND ACTS OF AGGRESSION

ARTICLE 39

The Security Council shall determine the existence of any threat to the peace, breach of the peace, or act of aggression and shall make recommendations, or decide what measures shall be taken in accordance with Articles 41 and 42, to maintain or restore international peace and security.

ARTICLE 40

In order to prevent an aggravation of the situation, the Security Council may, before making the recommendations or deciding upon the measures provided for in Article 39, call upon the parties concerned to comply with such provisional measures as it deems necessary or desirable. Such provisional measures shall be without prejudice to the rights, claims, or position of the parties concerned. The Security Council shall duly take account of failure to comply with such provisional measures.

ARTICLE 41

The Security Council may decide what measures not involving the use of armed force are to be employed to give effect to its decisions, and it may call upon the Members of the United Nations to apply such measures. These may include complete or partial interruption of economic relations and of rail, sea, air, postal, telegraphic, radio, and other means of communication, and the severance of diplomatic relations.

ARTICLE 42

Should the Security Council consider that measures provided for in Article 41 would be inadequate or have proved to be inadequate, it may take such action by air, sea, or land forces as may be necessary to maintain or restore international peace and security. Such action may include demonstrations, blockade, and other operations by air, sea, or land forces of Members of the United Nations.

CHAPTER VIII
REGIONAL ARRANGEMENTS

ARTICLE 52

1. Nothing in the present Charter precludes the existence of regional arrangements or agencies for dealing with such matters relating to the maintenance of international peace and security as are appropriate for regional action, provided that such arrangements or agencies and their activities are consistent with the Purposes and Principles of the United Nations.

2. The Members of the United Nations entering into such arrangements or constituting such agencies shall make every effort to achieve pacific settlement of local disputes through such regional arrangements or by such regional agencies before referring them to the Security Council.

3. The Security Council shall encourage the development of pacific settlement of local disputes through such regional arrangements or by such regional agencies either on the initiative of the states concerned or by reference from the Security Council.

CHAPTER IX
INTERNATIONAL ECONOMIC AND
SOCIAL CO-OPERATION

ARTICLE 55

With a view to the creation of conditions of stability and well-being which are necessary for peaceful and friendly relations among nations based on respect for the principle of equal rights and self-determination of peoples, the United Nations shall promote:

a. higher standards of living, full employment, and conditions of economic and social progress and development;

b. solutions of international economic, social, health, and related problems; and international cultural and educational co-operation; and

c. universal respect for, and observance of, human rights and fundamental freedoms for all without distinction as to race, sex, language, or religion.

ARTICLE 56

All Members pledge themselves to take joint and separate action in co-operation with the Organization for the achievement of the purposes set forth in Article 55.

CHAPTER XV
THE SECRETARIAT

ARTICLE 97

The Secretariat shall comprise a Secretary-General and such staff as the Organization may require. The Secretary-General shall be appointed by the General Assembly upon the recommendation of the Security Council. He shall be the chief administrative officer of the Organization.

ARTICLE 98

The Secretary-General shall act in that capacity in all meetings of the General Assembly, of the Security Council, of the Economic and Social Council, and of the Trusteeship Council, and shall perform such other functions as are entrusted to him by these organs. The Secretary-General shall make an annual report to the General Assembly on the work of the Organization.

ARTICLE 99

The Secretary-General may bring to the attention of the Security Council any matter which in his opinion may threaten the maintenance of international peace and security.

ARTICLE 100

1. In the performance of their duties the Secretary-General and the staff shall not seek or receive instructions from any government or from any other authority external to the Organization. They shall refrain from any action which might reflect on their position as international officials responsible only to the Organization.

2. Each Member of the United Nations undertakes to respect the exclusively international character of the responsibilities of the Secretary-General and the staff and not to seek to influence them in the discharge of their responsibilities.

ARTICLE 101

1. The staff shall be appointed by the Secretary-General under regulations established by the General Assembly.

3. The paramount consideration in the employment of the staff and in the determination of the conditions of service shall be the necessity of securing the highest standards of efficiency, competence, and integrity. Due regard shall be paid to the importance of recruiting the staff on as wide a geographical basis as possible.

CHAPTER XVI
MISCELLANEOUS PROVISIONS

ARTICLE 103

In the event of a conflict between the obligations of the Members of the United Nations under the present Charter and their obligations under any other international agreement, their obligations under the present Charter shall prevail.

A·P·P·E·N·D·I·X 2

EXCERPTS FROM THE
AGREEMENT ON A COMPREHENSIVE POLITICAL
SETTLEMENT OF THE CAMBODIA CONFLICT
(PARIS, 23 OCTOBER 1991)

The States participating in the Paris Conference on Cambodia, namely Australia, Brunei Darussalam, Cambodia, Canada, the People's Republic of China, the French Republic, the Republic of India, the Republic of Indonesia, Japan, the Lao People's Democratic Republic, Malaysia, the Republic of the Philippines, the Republic of Singapore, the Kingdom of Thailand, the Union of Soviet Socialist Republics, the United Kingdom of Great Britain and Northern Ireland, the United States of America, the Socialist Republic of Viet Nam and the Socialist Federal Republic of Yugoslavia,

In the presence of the Secretary-General of the United Nations,

Have agreed as follows:

PART I
ARRANGEMENTS DURING THE TRANSITIONAL PERIOD

Section I. Transitional Period

Article 1. For the purposes of this Agreement, the transitional period shall commence with the entry into force of this Agreement and terminate when the constituent assembly elected through free and fair elections, organized and certified by the United Nations, has approved the constitution and transformed itself into a legislative assembly, and thereafter a new government has been created.

Section II. United Nations Transitional Authority in Cambodia

Article 2(1). The Signatories invite the United Nations Security Council to establish a United Nations Transitional Authority in Cambodia (hereinafter referred to as "UNTAC") with civilian and military components under the direct responsibility of the Secretary-General of the United Nations. For this purpose the Secretary-General will designate a Special Representative to act on his behalf.

(2). The Signatories further invite the United Nations Security Council to provide UNTAC with the mandate set forth in this Agreement and to keep its implementation under continuing review through periodic reports submitted by the Secretary-General.

Section III. Supreme National Council

Article 3. The Supreme National Council (hereinafter referred to as "the SNC") is the unique legitimate body and source of authority in which, throughout the transitional period, the sovereignty, independence and unity of Cambodia are enshrined.

Article 4. The members of the SNC shall be committed to the holding of free and fair elections organized and conducted by the United Nations as the basis for forming a new and legitimate Government.

Article 5. The SNC shall, throughout the transitional period, represent Cambodia externally and occupy the seat of Cambodia at the United Nations, in the United Nations specialized agencies, and in other international institutions and international conferences.

Article 6. The SNC hereby delegates to the United Nations all powers necessary to ensure the implementation of this Agreement, as described in annex 1.

In order to ensure a neutral political environment conducive to free and fair general elections, administrative agencies, bodies and offices which could directly influence the outcome of elections will be placed under direct United Nations supervision or control. In that context, special attention will be given to foreign affairs, national defence, finance, public security and information. To reflect the importance of these subjects, UNTAC needs to exercise such control as is necessary to ensure the strict neutrality of the bodies responsible for them. The United Nations, in consultation with the SNC, will identify which agencies, bodies and offices could continue to operate in order to ensure normal day-to-day life in the country.

Article 7. The relationship between the SNC, UNTAC and existing administrative structures is set forth in annex 1.

Section IV. Withdrawal of Foreign Forces and its Verification

Article 8. Immediately upon entry into force of this Agreement, any foreign forces, advisers, and military personnel remaining in Cambodia, together with their weapons, ammunition, and equipment, shall be withdrawn from Cambodia and not be returned. Such withdrawal and non-return will be subject to UNTAC verification in accordance with annex 2.

Section V. Cease-Fire and Cessation of Outside Military Assistance

Article 9. The cease-fire shall take effect at the time this Agreement enters into force. All forces shall immediately disengage and refrain from all hostilities and from any deployment, movement or action which would extend the territory they control or which might lead to renewed fighting.

The Signatories hereby invite the Security Council of the United Nations to request the Secretary-General to provide good offices to assist in this process until such time as the military component of UNTAC is in position to supervise, monitor and verify it.

Article 10. Upon entry into force of this Agreement, there shall be an immediate cessation of all outside military assistance to all Cambodian Parties.

Article 11. The objectives of military arrangements during the transitional period shall be to stabilize the security situation and build confidence among the parties to the conflict, so as to reinforce the purposes of this Agreement and to prevent the risks of a return to warfare.

Detailed provisions regarding UNTAC's supervision, monitoring, and verification of the cease-fire and related measures, including verification of the withdrawal of foreign forces and the regrouping, cantonment and ultimate disposition of all Cambodian forces and their weapons during the transitional period are set forth in annex 1, section C, and annex 2.

PART II
ELECTIONS

Article 12. The Cambodian people shall have the right to determine their own political future through the free and fair election of a constituent assembly, which will draft and approve a new Cambodian Constitution in accordance with Article 23 and transform itself into a legislative assembly, which will create the new Cambodian Government. This election will be held under United Nations auspices in a neutral political environment with full respect for the national sovereignty of Cambodia.

Article 13. UNTAC shall be responsible for the organization and conduct of these elections based on the provisions of annex 1, section D, and annex 3.

Article 14. All Signatories commit themselves to respect the results of these elections once certified as free and fair by the United Nations.

PART III
HUMAN RIGHTS

Article 15(1). All persons in Cambodia and all Cambodian refugees and displaced persons shall enjoy the rights and freedoms embodied in the Universal Declaration of Human Rights and other relevant international human rights instruments.

(2). To this end,

a. Cambodia undertakes:

• to ensure respect for and observance of human rights and fundamental freedoms in Cambodia;

• to support the right of all Cambodian citizens to undertake activities which would promote and protect human rights and fundamental freedoms;

• to take effective measures to ensure that the policies and practices of the past shall never be allowed to return;

• to adhere to relevant international human rights instruments;

b. the other Signatories to this Agreement undertake to promote and encourage respect for and observance of human rights and fundamental freedoms in Cambodia as embodied in the relevant international instruments and the relevant resolutions of the United Nations General Assembly, in order, in particular, to prevent the recurrence of human rights abuses.

Article 16. UNTAC shall be responsible during the transitional period for fostering an environment in which respect for human rights shall be ensured, based on the provisions of annex 1, section E.

Article 17. After the end of the transitional period, the United Nations Commission on Human Rights should continue to monitor closely the human rights situation in Cambodia, including, if necessary, by the appointment of a Special Rapporteur who would report his findings annually to the Commission and to the General Assembly

PART IV
INTERNATIONAL GUARANTEES

Article 18. Cambodia undertakes to maintain, preserve and defend, and the other Signatories undertake to recognize and respect, the sovereignty, independence, territorial integrity and inviolability, neutrality and national unity of Cambodia, as set forth in a separate Agreement.

PART V
REFUGEES AND DISPLACED PERSONS

Article 19. Upon entry into force of this Agreement, every effort will be made to create in Cambodia political, economic and social conditions conducive to the voluntary return and harmonious integration of Cambodian refugees and displaced persons.

Article 20(1). Cambodian refugees and displaced persons, located outside Cambodia, shall have the right to return to Cambodia and to live in safety, security and dignity, free from intimidation or coercion of any kind.

(2). The Signatories request the Secretary-General of the United Nations to facilitate the repatriation in safety and dignity of Cambodian refugees and displaced persons, as an integral part of the comprehensive political settlement and under the overall authority of the Special Representative of the Secretary-General, in accordance with the guidelines and principles on the repatriation of refugees and displaced persons as set forth in annex 4.

PART VI
RELEASE OF PRISONERS OF WAR AND CIVILIAN INTERNEES

Article 21. The release of all prisoners of war and civilian internees shall be accomplished at the earliest possible date under the direction of the International Committee of the Red Cross (ICRC) in coordination with the Special Representative of the Secretary-General, with the assistance, as necessary, of other appropriate international humanitarian organizations and the Signatories.

Article 22. The expression "civilian internees" refers to all persons who are not prisoners of war and who, having contributed in any way whatsoever to the armed or political struggle, have been arrested or detained by any of the parties by virtue of their contribution thereto.

PART VII
PRINCIPLES FOR A NEW CONSTITUTION FOR CAMBODIA

Article 23. Basic principles, including those regarding human rights and fundamental freedoms as well as regarding Cambodia's status of neutrality, which the new Cambodian Constitution will incorporate, are set forth in annex 5.

PART VIII
REHABILITATION AND RECONSTRUCTION

Article 24. The Signatories urge the international community to provide economic and financial support for the rehabilitation and reconstruction of Cambodia, as provided in a separate declaration.

PART IX
FINAL PROVISIONS

Article 28(2). The signature on behalf of Cambodia by the members of the SNC shall commit all Cambodian parties and armed forces to the provisions of this Agreement.

Article 29. Without prejudice to the prerogatives of the Security Council of the United Nations, and upon the request of the Secretary-General, the two co-Chairmen of the Paris Conference on Cambodia, in the event of a violation or threat of violation of this Agreement, will immediately undertake appropriate consultations, including with members of the Paris Conference on Cambodia, with a view to taking appropriate steps to ensure respect for these commitments.

Article 30. This Agreement shall enter into force upon signature.

ANNEX I
UNTAC MANDATE

Section A: General Procedures

1. In accordance with Article 6 of the Agreement, UNTAC will exercise the powers necessary to ensure the implementation of this Agreement, including those relating to the organization and conduct of free and fair elections and the relevant aspects of the administration of Cambodia.

2. The following mechanism will be used to resolve all issues relating to the implementation of this Agreement which may arise between the Secretary-General's Special Representative and the Supreme National Council (SNC):

(a) The SNC offers advice to UNTAC, which will comply with this advice provided there is a consensus among the members of the SNC and provided this advice is consistent with the objectives of the present Agreement;

(b) If there is no consensus among the members of the SNC despite every endeavor of its President, H.R.H. Samdech Norodom Sihanouk, the President will be entitled to make the decision on what advice to offer to UNTAC, taking fully into account the views expressed in the SNC. UNTAC will comply with the advice provided it is consistent with the objectives of the present Agreement;

(c) If H.R.H. Samdech Norodom Sihanouk, President of the SNC, the legitimate representative of Cambodian sovereignty, is not, for whatever reason, in a position to make such a decision, his power of decision will transfer to the Secretary-General's Special Representative. The Special Representative will make the final decision, taking fully into account the views expressed in the SNC;

(d) Any power to act regarding the implementation of this Agreement conferred upon the SNC by the Agreement will be exercised by consensus or, failing such consensus, by its President in accordance with the procedure set out above. In the event that H.R.H. Samdech Norodom Sihanouk, President of the SNC, the legitimate representative of Cambodian sovereignty, is not, for whatever reason, in a position to act, his power to act will transfer to the Secretary-General's Special Representative, who may take the necessary action;

(e) In all cases, the Secretary-General's Special Representative will determine whether advice or action of the SNC is consistent with the present Agreement.

3. The Secretary-General's Special Representative or his delegate will attend the meetings of the SNC and of any subsidiary body which might be established by it and give its members all necessary information on the decisions taken by UNTAC.

Section B: Civil Administration

1. In accordance with Article 6 of the Agreement, all administrative agencies, bodies and offices acting in the field of foreign affairs, national defence, finance, public security and information will be placed under the direct control of UNTAC, which will exercise it as necessary to ensure strict neutrality. In this respect, the Secretary-General's Special Representative will determine what is necessary and may issue directives to the above-mentioned administrative agencies, bodies and offices. Such directives may be issued to and will bind all Cambodian Parties.

2. In accordance with Article 6 of the Agreement, the Secretary-General's Special Representative, in consultation with the SNC, will determine which other administrative agencies, bodies and offices could directly influence the outcome of elections. These administrative agencies, bodies and offices will be placed under direct supervision or control of UNTAC and will comply with any guidance provided by it.

3. In accordance with Article 6 of the Agreement, the Secretary-General's Special Representative, in consultation with the SNC, will identify which administrative agencies, bodies and offices could continue to operate in order to ensure normal day-to-day life in Cambodia, if necessary, under such supervision by UNTAC as it considers necessary.

4. In accordance with Article 6 of the Agreement, the authority of the Secretary-General's Special Representative will include the power to:

(a) Install in administrative agencies, bodies and offices of all the Cambodian Parties United Nations personnel, who will have unrestricted access to all administrative operations and information;

(b) Require the reassignment or removal of any personnel of such administrative agencies, bodies and offices.

5. (a) On the basis of the information provided in Article I, paragraph 3, of annex 2, the Special Representative of the Secretary-General, will determine, after consultation with the Cambodian Parties, those civil police necessary to perform law enforcement in Cambodia. All Cambodian Parties hereby undertake to comply with the determination made by the Special Representative in this regard;

(b) All civil police will operate under UNTAC supervision or control, in order to ensure that law and order are maintained effectively and impartially, and that human rights and fundamental freedoms are fully protected. In consultation with the SNC, UNTAC will supervise other law enforcement and judicial processes throughout Cambodia to the extent necessary to ensure the attainment of these objectives.

6. If the Secretary-General's Special Representative deems it necessary, UNTAC, in consultation with the SNC, will undertake investigations of complaints and allegations regarding actions by the existing administrative structures in Cambodia that are inconsistent with or work against the objectives of this comprehensive political settlement. UNTAC will also be empowered to undertake such investigation on its own initiative. UNTAC will take, when necessary, appropriate corrective steps.

Section C: Military Functions

I. UNTAC will supervise, monitor and verify the withdrawal of foreign forces, the cease-fire and related measures in accordance with annex 2, including:

(a) Verification of the withdrawal from Cambodia of all categories of foreign forces, advisers and military personnel and their weapons, ammunition and equipment, and their non-return to Cambodia;

(b) Liaison with neighbouring Governments over any developments in or near their territory that could endanger the implementation of this Agreement;

(c) Monitoring the cessation of outside military assistance to all Cambodian Parties;

(d) Locating and confiscating caches of weapons and military supplies throughout the country;

(e) Assisting with clearing mines and undertaking training programmes in mine clearance and a mine awareness programme among the Cambodian people.

2. UNTAC will supervise the regrouping and relocating of all forces to specifically designated cantonment areas on the basis of an operational timetable to be agreed upon, in accordance with annex 2.

3. As the forces enter the cantonments, UNTAC will initiate the process of arms control and reduction specified in annex 2.

4. UNTAC will take necessary steps regarding the phased process of demobilization of the military forces of the parties, in accordance with annex 2.

5. UNTAC will assist, as necessary, the International Committee of the Red Cross in the release of all prisoners of war and civilian internees.

Section D: Elections

I. UNTAC will organize and conduct the election referred to in Part II of this Agreement in accordance with this section and annex 3.

2. UNTAC may consult with the SNC regarding the organization and conduct of the electoral process.

3. In the exercise of its responsibilities in relation to the electoral process, the specific authority of UNTAC will include the following:

(a) The establishment, in consultation with the SNC, of a system of laws, procedures and administrative measures necessary for the holding of a free and fair election in Cambodia, including the adoption of an electoral law and of a code of conduct regulating participation in the election in a manner consistent with respect for human rights and prohibiting coercion or financial inducement in order to influence voter preference;

(b) The suspension or abrogation, in consultation with the SNC, of provisions of existing laws which could defeat the objects and purposes of this Agreement;

(c) The design and implementation of a voter education programme, covering all aspects of the election, to support the election process;

(d) The design and implementation of a system of voter registration, as a first phase of the electoral process, to ensure that eligible voters have the opportunity to register, and the subsequent preparation of verified voter registration lists;

(e) The design and implementation of a system of registration of political parties and lists of candidates;

(f) Ensuring fair access to the media, including press, television and radio, for all political parties contesting in the election;

(g) The adoption and implementation of measures to monitor and facilitate the participation of Cambodians in the elections, the political campaign and the balloting procedures;

(h) The design and implementation of a system of balloting and polling, to ensure that registered voters have the opportunity to vote;

(i) The establishment, in consultation with the SNC, of coordinated arrangements to facilitate the presence of foreign observers wishing to observe the campaign and voting;

(j) Overall direction of polling and the vote count;

(k) The identification and investigation of complaints of electoral irregularities, and the taking of appropriate corrective action;

(l) Determining whether or not the election was free and fair and, if so, certification of the list of persons duly elected.

4. In carrying out its responsibilities under the present section, UNTAC will establish a system of safeguards to assist it in ensuring the absence of fraud during the electoral process, including arrangements for Cambodian representatives to observe the registration and polling procedures and the provision of an UNTAC mechanism for hearing and deciding complaints.

5. The timetable for the various phases of the electoral process will be determined by UNTAC, in consultation with the SNC as provided in paragraph 2 of this section. The duration of the electoral process will not exceed nine months from the commencement of voter registration.

6. In organizing and conducting the electoral process, UNTAC will make every effort to ensure that the system and procedures adopted are absolutely impartial, while the operational arrangements are as administratively simple and efficient as possible.

Section E: Human Rights
In accordance with Article 16, UNTAC will make provisions for:

(a) The development and implementation of a programme of human rights education to promote respect for and understanding of human rights;

(b) General human rights oversight during the transitional period;

(c) The investigation of human rights complaints, and, where appropriate, corrective action.

L·I·S·T O·F A·B·B·R·E·V·I·A·T·I·O·N·S
U·S·E·D I·N T·H·E N·O·T·E·S

Add.	Addendum
Art.	Article
Consol. T.S.	Consolidated Treaty Series
Corr.	Corrigendum
ESC	United Nations Economic and Social Council
ESCOR	United Nations Economic and Social Council Official Records
FBIS	United States Foreign Broadcast Information Service
GA	United Nations General Assembly
GAOR	United Nations General Assembly Official Records
ICJ	International Court of Justice Reports
ILM	International Legal Materials
LNOJ	League of Nations Official Journal
LNTS	League of Nations Treaty Series
Para.	Paragraph
PCIJ	Permanent Court of International Justice Reports
Res.	Resolution
Res. and Dec.	Resolutions and Decisions
SC	United Nations Security Council
SCOR	United Nations Security Council Official Records
Sec.	Section
Ser.	Series
Sess.	Session
Supp.	Supplement
TCOR	United Nations Trusteeship Council Official Records
UN Doc.	United Nations Document Number
UNTS	United Nations Treaty Series
UST	United States Treaties Series

N · O · T · E · S

Introduction

1. Report of the Secretary-General on the Work of the Organization, UN GAOR, 46th Sess., Supp. No. 1, p. 4, UN Doc. A/46/1, 1991.

Chapter One

1. GA Res. 998, UN GAOR, 1st Emergency Special Sess., Supp. No. 1, p. 2, UN Doc. A/3354, 1956.

2. Moreover, the United Nations had previously deployed various commissions and committees, composed of representatives of member states acting in that capacity, to observe cease-fires and facilitate settlements. Among these were missions sent to the Balkans (notably the UN Special Committee on the Balkans), Indonesia (the UN Commission for Indonesia and related bodies), and Kashmir (the UN Commission for India and Pakistan). For details, see David W. Wainhouse, *International Peace Observation: A History and Forecast* (Baltimore: Johns Hopkins University Press, 1966), pp. 221–41, 293–323, 357–73.

3. The UN also sent a four-person mission to the Dominican Republic to monitor the cease-fire after the 1965 bloodshed. Though DOMREP, as it was called, is typically listed by the UN Secretariat as a peacekeeping operation, it is not listed here due to its minuscule size.

4. Charles William Maynes, "Containing Ethnic Conflict," *Foreign Policy* 90 (Spring 1993): 3, 8–9.

5. Paul F. Diehl, "When Peacekeeping Does Not Lead to Peace: Some Notes on Conflict Resolution," *Bulletin of Peace Proposals* 18 (1987): 47, 50–51.

6. George L. Sherry, "The United Nations, International Conflict, and American Security," *Political Science Quarterly* 101 (1986): 753, 762.

7. Accords on the Peaceful Resolution of the Situation in Afghanistan, 14 April 1988, 27 ILM 577.

8. Among the rapidly growing literature on this subject, see especially Ted Robert Gurr, *Minorities at Risk: A Global View of Ethnopolitical Conflicts* (Washington, DC: United States Institute of Peace Press, 1993); Gidon Gottlieb, *Nation Against State: A New Approach to Ethnic Conflicts and the Decline of Sovereignty* (New York: Council on Foreign Relations Press, 1993); Morton H. Halperin and David J. Scheffer, *Self-Determination in the New World Order* (Washington, DC: Carnegie Endowment for International Peace, 1992); and Maynes, supra note 4, pp. 3–21.

9. Charter of Paris for a New Europe, 21 November 1990, 30 ILM 190.

10. See, for instance, Thomas G. Weiss and Meryl A. Kessler, "Resurrecting peacekeeping: the superpowers and conflict management," *Third World Quarterly* 12 (1990): 124–46. These began with Soviet President Gorbachev's 1988 speech to the General Assembly and continued with more detailed initiatives. See Letter dated 22 September 1988 from [the] Deputy Head of the Delegation of the Union of Soviet Socialist Republics to the forty-third session of the General Assembly addressed to the Secretary-General, 22 September 1988, UN Doc. A/43/629 (aide-memoire describing Soviet proposals).

11. 17 June 1992, UN Doc. A/47/277–S/24111.

12. Id. pp. 6, 16.

13. Report of the Secretary-General on the Work of the Organization, UN GAOR, 48th Sess., Supp. No. 1, p. 59, UN Doc. A/48/1, 1993. The Secretary-General also introduced a new term in this report, *peace operations*, that includes the full gamut of UN efforts to promote international peace. Id. p. 61.

14. See Victor-Yves Ghébali, "Le développement des opérations de maintien de la paix de l'ONU depuis la fin de la guerre froide," *Le Trimestre du Monde* 1992/4 (November 1992): 67–85; Georges Abi-Saab, "La deuxième génération des opérations de maintien de la paix," *Le Trimestre du Monde* 1992/4 (November 1992): 87–97.

15. For other ways of slicing the pie, see John Mackinlay and Jarat Chopra, "Second Generation Multinational Operations," *The Washington Quarterly* 15 (Summer 1992): 113–31 (categorizing all new peacekeeping and peace enforcement operations as "second generation"); Marrack Goulding, "The evolution of United Nations peacekeeping," *International Affairs* 69 (1993): 451, 456–60 (six types of peacekeeping).

16. Second and final report of the Secretary-General on the plan for an emergency international United Nations Force requested in resolution 998 (ES-I), adopted by the General Assembly on 4 November 1956, 6 November 1956, UN GAOR, 1st Emergency Special Sess., Annex, Agenda Item 5, p. 19, UN Doc. A/3302 [hereinafter Second UNEF I Report].

17. See Wainhouse, supra note 2, p. 542 (in describing first-generation operations, "the main objective in peace observation is not to *impose* but rather to *interpose*.")

18. Although Boutros-Ghali opened the door in *An Agenda For Peace* to eliminating this core distinction between peacekeeping and peace enforcement by defining peacekeeping as taking place "hitherto" with the consent of the parties, he eliminated the word "hitherto" in definitions proffered in 1994. Improving the capacity of the United Nations for peace-keeping: Report of the Secretary-General, 14 March 1994, UN Doc. A/48/403–S/26450, p. 2 [hereinafter 1994 Secretary-General Peacekeeping Report].

19. SC Res. 687, 3 April 1991, UN SCOR, 46th Year, Res. and Dec., p. 11, UN Doc. S/INF/47.

20. SC Res. 836, 4 June 1993.

21. SC Res. 814, 26 March 1993, see also SC Res. 897, 4 February 1994.

22. Introduction to the Annual Report of the Secretary-General on the Work of the Organization, 16 June 1959–15 June 1960, UN GAOR, 15th Sess., Supp. No. 1A, UN Doc. A/4390/Add.1, 1960. See also Oran R. Young, *The Intermediaries: Third Parties in International Crises* (Princeton, NJ: Princeton University Press, 1967), pp. 135–51 (describing Hammarskjold's image of peacekeeping). For an excellent analysis of the promises and problems of peacekeeping as seen from the perspective of first-generation operations only, see Paul F. Diehl, "Peacekeeping Operations and the Quest for Peace," *Political Science Quarterly* 103 (1988): 485–87.

23. The deployment of UNPROFOR in Macedonia takes preventive diplomacy a step further, as the UN seeks to dissuade initiation of hostilities along a hitherto peaceful front.

24. See, for instance, Derek W. Bowett, *United Nations Forces: A Legal Study* (New York: Frederick A. Praeger, Publishers, 1964), pp. 268–73 (focusing on military purposes, although recognizing that peacekeeping might include supervision of plebiscites). More recent studies have begun to recognize other functions, although they again are largely devoted to military operations. See Mackinlay and Chopra, supra note 15; Paul F. Diehl and Chetan Kumar, "Mutual Benefits from International Intervention: New Roles for United Nations Peace-keeping Forces," *Bulletin of Peace Proposals* 22 (1991): 369–75.

25. Abi-Saab (1992), supra note 14, pp. 92–93; Ghébali, supra note 14, pp. 76–78; see also the Statement by the President of the Security Council, 30 April 1993, UN Doc. S/25696.

26. Abi-Saab (1992), supra note 14, p. 93.

Chapter 2

1. Second UNEF I Report, supra chapter 1 note 16. The Secretary-General also noted that the Assembly had asked that the force consist of military units recruited from states other than the five permanent members of the Security Council. See also Summary study of the experience derived from the establishment and operation of the Force:

report of the Secretary-General, 9 October 1958, UN GAOR, 13th Sess., Annex, Agenda Item 65, pp. 8, 27–32, UN Doc. A/3943; and the "UNEF II Rules," Report of the Secretary-General on the implementation of Security Council resolution 340 (1973), 27 October 1973, UN SCOR, 28th Year, Supplement for October, November, and December 1973, p. 91, UN Doc. S/11052/Rev.1. These two important reports note two additional tenets: that peacekeepers may act only in self-defense and that interested regional states be excluded from donating troops.

2. The Security Council has begun to reconsider these precepts as well. See Note by the President of the Security Council, 28 May 1993, UN Doc. S/25859 (listing seven "operational principles").

3. Vienna Convention on the Law of Treaties, 23 May 1969, art. 26, 1155 UNTS 331, 339.

4. See, for example, Robert O. Keohane and Joseph S. Nye, *Power and Interdependence: World Politics in Transition* (Boston: Little, Brown, 1977), pp. 30–35; W. Michael Reisman, "Private Armies in a Global War System: Prologue to Decision," *Virginia Journal of International Law* 14 (1973): 1–55.

5. The view that nonstate actors operate outside the constraints of international law and do not consent to peacekeeping operations, for example, Henry Wiseman, "Peacekeeping in the International Political Context: Historical Analysis and Future Directions," in *The United Nations and Peacekeeping: Results, Limitations and Prospects: The Lessons of 40 Years of Experience,* edited by Indar Jit Rikhye and Kjell Skjelsbaek (New York: St. Martin's Press, 1991), pp. 39–41, has been rebutted in theory and practice. See "Law of Treaties," [1958] 2 *Yearbook of the International Law Commission* 20, 24, UN Doc. A/CN.4/SER.A/1958/Add.1. Most second-generation operations have involved commitments by nonstate actors.

6. Final Declaration of the Geneva Conference on the problem of restoring peace in Indo-China, 21 July 1954, 935 UNTS 95.

7. Ruling Pertaining to the Differences between France and New Zealand Arising from the Rainbow Warrior Affair, 6 July 1986, reprinted in *American Journal of International Law* 81 (1987): 325–28.

8. For further thoughts on the sources of UN involvement, see William J. Durch, "Getting Involved: The Political-Military Context," in *The Evolution of UN Peacekeeping: Case Studies and Comparative Analysis,* edited by William J. Durch (New York: St. Martin's Press, 1993), pp. 16–22.

9. See generally Myres S. McDougal, Harold D. Lasswell, and James C. Miller, *The Interpretation of Agreements and World Public Order: Principles of Content and Procedure* (New Haven, CT: Yale University Press, 1967), pp. 21–34.

10. Oscar Schachter, "The Twilight Existence of Nonbinding International Agreements," *American Journal of International Law* 71 (1977): 296–304.

11. Procedure for the establishment of a firm and lasting peace in Central America, 7 August 1987, reprinted in Letter dated 27 August 1987 from the Permanent Representatives of Costa Rica, El Salvador, Guatemala and Nicaragua to the United Nations addressed to the Secretary-General, 31 August 1987, UN Doc. A/42/521–S/19085.

12. See The Situation Concerning Western Sahara, Reports of the Secretary-General, 18 June 1990 and 19 April 1991, UN Docs. S/21360 and S/22464.

13. See Model status-of-forces agreement for peace-keeping operations: Report of the Secretary-General, 9 October 1990, UN Doc. A/45/594.

14. Case Concerning the Territorial Dispute (Libya/Chad), 1994 ICJ 6 (Feb. 3).

15. The relevant provision in the Vienna Convention on the Law of Treaties is Article 46, which precludes a state from invoking a violation of its internal law as a basis for invalidating its consent to the treaty, unless the violation of internal law was "manifest" and it concerned a rule of internal law "of fundamental importance." 1155 UNTS p. 343. In the world of civil conflicts, with competing factions and regimes, such "internal law" often does not exist or is itself a subject of the civil dispute.

16. See Durch, supra note 8, pp. 32–36 (describing risks in settlements).
17. See Steven R. Ratner, "The United Nations in Cambodia: A Model for Resolution of Internal Conflicts?" in *Enforcing Restraint: Collective Intervention in Internal Conflicts*, edited by Lori Fisler Damrosch (New York: Council on Foreign Relations Press, 1993), pp. 264–67.
18. Peacekeeping operations that do not involve the UN can be created directly out of settlement agreements. This was the case, for example, with the international control commissions created under the Agreement on the Cessation of Hostilities in Viet-Nam, 20 July 1954, 935 UNTS 149; the Protocol to the Declaration on the Neutrality of Laos, 23 July 1962, 456 UNTS 324; and the Agreement on Ending the War and Restoring Peace in Viet-Nam, 27 January 1973, 935 UNTS 52.
19. See Bowett, supra chapter 1 note 24, pp. 180, 311 (explaining that consent is indicative of the type of operation undertaken, but is not an independent basis of authority).
20. Id. pp. 307–08.
21. Reparation for Injuries Suffered in the Service of the United Nations, 1949 ICJ 174, 182–83 (Apr. 11); and reaffirmed in Certain Expenses of the United Nations (Article 17, paragraph 2, of the Charter), 1962 ICJ 151, 167–68 (July 20).
22. UN Charter, art. 1(1).
23. Id. art. 2(3).
24. See, for example, the Manila Declaration on the Peaceful Settlement of International Disputes, GA Res. 37/10, UN GAOR, 37th Sess., Supp. No. 51, p. 261, UN Doc. A/37/51, 1982. The Secretary-General, upon the request of the Assembly, recently compiled a useful, if sterile, study on peaceful settlement of disputes. See United Nations Office of Legal Affairs, *Handbook on the Peaceful Settlement of Disputes between States* (New York: United Nations, 1992), UN Sales No. E.92.V.7, UN Doc. OLA/COD/2394.
25. UN Charter, art. 55.
26. See the discussion in the following chapter regarding recent cases before the World Court challenging certain Security Council acts as ultra vires.
27. Leland M. Goodrich, Edvard Hambro, and Anne P. Simons, *Charter of the United Nations: Commentary and Documents*, 3rd rev. ed. (New York: Columbia University Press, 1969), pp. 60–63; Rosalyn Higgins, *The Development of International Law Through the Political Organs of the United Nations* (London: Oxford University Press, 1963), p. 71.
28. Bowett, supra chapter 1 note 24, pp. 425–26: "[N]o consent by the territorial State . . . can authorise functions which do not stem from the necessity to maintain or restore *international* peace and security. Hence the problems of *internal* peace are not, as such, problems for which a United Nations Force should assume any functional responsibility." (emphasis in original) At the same time, Bowett did recognize that UN operations to suppress genocide and gross violations of human rights would be permissible, as those conditions can endanger international security by encouraging intervention, and that rectifying such conditions advances the goals of the Charter. Id. pp. 426–27.
29. 1923 PCIJ (Ser. B) No. 4, p. 24 (Feb. 7). The corresponding article of the Covenant, art. 15(8), spoke of "a matter which by international law is solely within the domestic jurisdiction" of a member state. Although the Charter's use of the word *essentially* rather than *solely* could suggest that the drafters intended for a larger sphere of issues to be off-limits to the United Nations than were to the League of Nations, the practice of the United Nations indicates little support for this position. See Higgins (1963), supra note 27, pp. 74–76.
30. Higgins (1963), supra note 27, pp. 63–81; Gilbert Guillaume, "Article 2, Paragraphe 7," in *La Charte des Nations Unies*, 2nd ed., edited by Jean-Pierre Cot and Alain Pellet (Paris: Economica, 1991), pp. 141, 152–55. See also Menno T. Kamminga, *Inter-State Accountability for Violations of Human Rights* (Philadelphia: University of Pennsylvania Press, 1992), pp. 87–126; Goodrich, Hambro, and Simons, supra note 27, pp. 70–71.

31. Thomas M. Franck, "The Emerging Right to Democratic Governance," *American Journal of International Law* 86 (1992): 46–91; David Stoelting, "The Challenge of UN-Monitored Elections in Independent Nations," *Stanford Journal of International Law* 28 (1992): 371–424; Morton H. Halperin, "Guaranteeing Democracy," *Foreign Policy* 91 (Summer 1993): 105–22.

32. Vienna Convention on the Law of Treaties, art. 31(3)(b), 1155 UNTS p. 340.

33. See, for example, James B. Steinberg, "International Involvement in the Yugoslavia Conflict," in *Enforcing Restraint*, supra note 17, pp. 27–75.

34. See, for example, Declaration on the Inadmissibility of Intervention In the Domestic Affairs of States and the Protection of Their Independence and Sovereignty, GA Res. 2131, UN GAOR, 20th Sess., Supp. No. 14, p. 11, UN Doc. A/6014, 1965. See also Lori F. Damrosch, "Politics Across Borders: Nonintervention and Nonforcible Influence over Domestic Affairs," *American Journal of International Law* 83 (1989): 1–50.

35. Higgins, in commenting upon the Congo operation, seems to go a bit further. While acknowledging that the United Nations sought to avoid taking sides in the internal conflict, she suggests that the touchstone for whether a UN action violated Article 2(7) was the central government's consent—actual or implied—to the activity. See Higgins (1963), supra note 27, pp. 106–110. An alternative view would regard the UN's siding even with the government in a civil war as a violation of Article 2(7). The new peacekeeping, however, does not need to address this question, because it is predicated upon the consent of all the relevant parties to an internal conflict.

36. GA Res. 48/131 and 48/124, UN GAOR, 48th Sess., Supp. No. 49, pp. 250, 243, UN Doc. A/48/49, 1993.

37. See Louis Henkin, "International Law: Politics, Values and Functions," *Recueil des Cours* 216 (1989 IV): 13, 24–26; W. Michael Reisman, "Sovereignty and Human Rights in Contemporary International Law," *American Journal of International Law* 84 (1990): 866–76; see also Steven R. Ratner, "The Cambodia Settlement Agreements," *American Journal of International Law* 87 (1993): 1, 22–25.

38. J. L. Brierly, *The Law of Nations: An Introduction to the International Law of Peace*, 6th ed., edited by Sir Humphrey Waldock (Oxford: Clarendon Press, 1963), p. 47; see also Inis L. Claude, Jr., *Swords into Plowshares: The Problems and Progress of International Organization*, 4th ed. (New York: Random House, 1971), p. 22 ("a principle of irresponsibility").

39. (Nicar. v. U.S.), 1986 ICJ 14, 108 (June 27).

40. For further discussion, see Gerald B. Helman and Steven R. Ratner, "Saving Failed States," *Foreign Policy* 89 (Winter 1992–93): 3, 9–11.

41. GA Res. 217, UN Doc. A/810, pp. 71, 75, 1948.

42. 16 December 1966, 999 UNTS 171, 179.

43. GA Res. 46/182, Annex, para. 3, UN GAOR, 46th Sess., Supp. No. 49, at 49, 50, UN Doc. A/46/49, 1991 ("humanitarian assistance *should* [not "shall"] be provided with the consent of the affected *country* [not "state"] and *in principle* on the basis of an appeal by the affected *country*") (emphasis added).

44. Report of the Secretary-General on the Work of the Organization, UN GAOR, 46th Sess., Supp. No. 1, p. 5, UN Doc. A/46/1, 1991.

45. *An Agenda for Peace*, supra chapter 1 note 11, p. 5.

46. Margaret A. Novicki, "A New Agenda for the OAU: Salim Ahmed Salim," *Africa Report* (May/June 1992): 36, 37.

47. Vienna Convention on the Law of Treaties, art. 53, 1155 UNTS p. 344.

48. For a full discussion of this controversial episode in the history of the United Nations, see Arthur W. Rovine, *The First Fifty Years: The Secretary-General in World Politics 1920–1970* (Leyden: A. W. Sythoff, 1970), pp. 393–400; Thomas M. Franck, *Nation Against Nation: What Happened to the U.N. Dream and What the U.S. Can Do About It* (New York: Oxford University Press, 1985), pp. 87–93. The documentation is set out

chronologically in Rosalyn Higgins, *United Nations Peacekeeping 1946–1967: Documents and Commentary*, vol. 1 (London: Oxford University Press, 1969), pp. 335–67.

49. The "smoking gun" used to support this view is a private memorandum that Dag Hammarskjold wrote interpreting the November 20, 1956, aide-memoire between the United Nations and the government of Egypt on the stationing of UNEF. In it, Hammarskjold says the government of Egypt understood and accepted his view that a unilateral withdrawal of consent would constitute bad faith and that such a demand should be negotiated with the United Nations. See Aide-Memoire of 5 August 1957, reprinted in Higgins (1969), supra note 48, pp. 363–66.

50. Professor Bowett provided five useful principles that retain their pertinence to the new peacekeeping: (1) the original consent by a state to an operation does not itself imply an unfettered right to withdraw consent and unilaterally terminate a mission; (2) if the operation does not require consent (and is thus peace enforcement for our purposes), withdrawal of consent cannot terminate a mission; (3) where consent is a legal requirement for the presence, then prima facie the force must withdraw in a reasonable time if consent is terminated; (4) the host state can waive the right to request withdrawal; (5) the UN generally has the right to terminate an operation if it would not violate an agreement with the host state. Bowett, supra chapter 1 note 24, p. 422.

51. See Myres S. McDougal, Harold D. Lasswell, and W. Michael Reisman, "The World Constitutive Process of Authoritative Decision," in *International Law Essays: A Supplement to International Law in Contemporary Perspective*, edited by Myres S. McDougal and W. Michael Reisman (Mineola, NY: The Foundation Press, 1981), pp. 191, 192. For an early effort to evaluate the possibility of peacekeeping with less than full cooperation of the parties, see Wainhouse, supra chapter 1 note 2, pp. 553–58.

52. I appreciate insights from Gustave Feissel of the UN Department of Political Affairs and Anthony Banbury of UNTAC on the concepts of witness and authority.

53. For a corresponding categorization of depth of involvement in the electoral context only, see Enhancing the effectiveness of the principle of periodic and genuine elections: Report of the Secretary-General, 18 November 1992, UN Doc A/47/688, p. 18 [hereinafter 1992 UN Election Report].

54. The contrasting visions of the United Nations between the "conference" model and the "activist" model were best stated in Hammarskjold's Introduction to the Annual Report of the Secretary-General on the Work of the Organization, 16 June 1960–15 June 1961, UN GAOR, 16th Sess., Supp. No. 1A, UN Doc. A/4800/Add.1. See also Raimo Väyrynen, "The United Nations and the Resolution of International Conflicts," *Cooperation and Conflict* 20 (1985): 141–142.

55. Conor Cruise O'Brien and Feliks Topolski, *The United Nations: Sacred Drama* (New York: Simon & Schuster, 1968), p. 11.

56. Diehl (1988), supra chapter 1 note 22, pp. 505–06; Diehl (1987), supra chapter 1 note 5, pp. 48–49.

57. Abi-Saab (1992), supra chapter 1 note 14, p. 91.

58. Saadia Touval, *The Peace Brokers: Mediators in the Arab-Israeli Conflict, 1948–1979* (Princeton, NJ: Princeton University Press, 1982), p. 4. Some studies, for instance, *International Mediation in Theory and Practice*, edited by Saadia Touval and I. William Zartman (Boulder, CO: Westview Press, 1985), equate mediation with third-party intervention, while most studies use the term in the more limited sense in the text. See also *Handbook*, supra note 24, p. 40. Two other exceptional conceptual studies of third-party intervention are Young (1967), supra chapter 1 note 22, and *Dynamics of Third Party Intervention: Kissinger in the Middle East*, edited by Jeffrey Z. Rubin (New York: Praeger, 1981).

59. Examples can be found in *Handbook*, supra note 24, pp. 42–43, 102–3, 128–33; Young (1967), supra chapter 1 note 22, p. 60; and the periodic Repertory of Practice of Organs of the United Nations published by the Organization.

60. Georges Abi-Saab, *The United Nations Operation in the Congo 1960–1964* (Oxford: Oxford University Press, 1978), pp. 195–200. One UNTAC official called this practice "la structure onusienne." Interview with UNTAC Civil Administration Service Chief, 5 March 1993.

61. Interview with UNTAC senior adviser, 5 March 1993.

62. These terms appear among the options available to states for the peaceful settlement of disputes listed in Article 33 of the Charter.

63. Arthur Lall, *Modern International Negotiation: Principles and Practice* (New York: Columbia University Press, 1966), pp. 84–100; see also Wainhouse, supra chapter 1 note 2, p. 601 (noting how peacekeepers can be the best mediators during implementation of political settlements).

64. Touval (1982), supra note 58, pp. 326–27; Young (1967), supra chapter 1 note 22, pp. 36–37. See also Saadia Touval, "Why the U.N. Fails," *Foreign Affairs* 73 (September/October 1994): 44–57 (criticizing UN's capabilities as mediator).

65. See Touval (1994), supra note 64, pp. 51–54.

66. For more on escape routes, see Anthony Parsons, "The United Nations and the National Interests of States," in *United Nations, Divided World*, edited by Adam Roberts and Benedict Kingsbury (Oxford: Clarendon Press, 1988), pp. 47, 51–57; Alan M. James, "Unit Veto Dominance in United Nations Peace-Keeping," in *Politics in the United Nations System*, edited by Lawrence S. Finkelstein (Durham, NC: Duke University Press, 1988), pp. 75, 83–94.

67. I. William Zartman and Saadia Touval, "Mediation in Theory and Practice," in *International Mediation in Theory and Practice*, supra note 58, pp. 260–68.

68. Id. at 267.

69. Id. at 268.

70. See *Oppenheim's International Law*, 9th ed., vol. 1, edited by Sir Robert Jennings and Arthur Watts (Harlow: Longman, 1992), pp. 1322–25; Ratner (1993), supra note 37, pp. 30 and nn. 178–180 (describing legal guarantees and giving examples). Although the Charter does not specifically permit the UN to assume a guarantor role, the Secretary-General concluded during consideration of the Trieste question in 1947 that the Security Council's powers under Article 24 ("primary responsibility for the maintenance of international peace and security") were not limited to those enumerated elsewhere in the Charter—a harbinger of the later ICJ rulings in the *Reparation for Injuries* and *Certain Expenses* cases. See UN SCOR, 2nd Year, No. 3 (10 January 1947), p. 44 (opinion of the Secretary-General).

71. SC Res. 687, supra chapter 1 note 19, para. 4.

72. Declaration on International Guarantees, 14 April 1988, 27 ILM 584.

73. Memorandum of Agreement between the Governments of the United States of America and the State of Israel, 26 March 1979, 32 UST 2141; Letters from President Carter to Prime Minister Begin and President Sadat, 26 March 1979, 32 UST 2146, 2148.

74. Agreement Concerning the Sovereignty, Independence, Territorial Integrity and Inviolability, Neutrality and National Unity of Cambodia, 23 October 1991, 31 ILM 200.

75. Interview with Rafeeudin Ahmed, 26 February 1993.

76. Interview with Stephen Heder, 6 March 1993.

77. Interview with Kusnadi Pudjiwinarto, 25 February 1993.

78. This last point is made by Touval (1982), supra note 58, pp. 321–26.

79. First report of the Secretary-General on the plan for an emergency international United Nations Force requested in resolution 998 (ES-I) adopted by the General Assembly on 4 November 1956, 4 November 1956, UN GAOR, 1st Emergency Special Sess., Annex, Agenda Item 5, p. 14, UN Doc. A/3289. See also GA Res. 1000, para. 3, UN GAOR, 1st Emergency Special Sess., Supp. No. 1, pp. 2, 3, UN Doc. A/3354, 1956.

80. See, for example, First progress report to the Secretary-General from his Special Representative in the Congo, Mr. Rajeshwar Dayal, 21 September 1960, UN SCOR,

15th Year, Supplement for July, August and September 1960, pp. 176, 184, UN Doc. S/4531 [hereinafter 21 September 1960 ONUC Report]; Memorandum on implementation of the Security Council resolution of 9 August 1960, operative paragraph 4, 12 August 1960, UN SCOR, 15th Year, Supplement for July, August, and September 1960, p. 64, UN Doc. S/4417/Add.6 [hereinafter 12 August 1960 ONUC Memorandum].

81. See UNEF II Rules, supra note 1; Diehl (1988), supra chapter 1 note 22, pp. 498–99; Bowett, supra chapter 1 note 24, pp. 196–200; Wiseman, supra note 5, pp. 41–45.

82. Benjamin Rivlin, "Regional Arrangements and the UN System for Collective Security and Conflict Resolution: A New Road Ahead?" *International Relations* 11 (1992): 95, 101. I am grateful to Gustave Feissel for the quoted phrase. Sui generis forces include the Multinational Force and Observers monitoring the 1979 Egypt-Israel Peace Treaty and the commissions created to oversee various unsuccessful peace accords in Indochina in the 1950s to 1970s.

83. Young (1967), supra chapter 1 note 22, p. 81; Oran R. Young, "Intermediaries: Additional Thoughts on Third Parties," *Journal of Conflict Resolution* 16 (1972): 51, 56.

84. UN Charter, art. 1(1).

85. Young (1967), supra chapter 1 note 22, p. 81 (citing Ann Douglas, "What Can Research Tell Us About Mediation?" *Labor Law Journal* 6 (1955): 545, 550–51).

86. Dag Hammarskjold, "The International Civil Servant in Law and in Fact" (30 May 1961), reprinted in *Servant of Peace: A Selection of the Speeches and Statements of Dag Hammarskjold, Secretary-General of the United Nations, 1953–61,* edited by Wilder Foote (New York: Harper & Row, 1962), pp. 329, 338.

87. See Diehl (1988), supra chapter 1 note 22, p. 486. As discussed further in the Cambodia chapters, the UN may itself have to adjust its positions over time. For example, during the negotiations for a settlement, the political organs of the Organization could have condemned one party as responsible for the conflict; yet during the implementation of the settlement, the UN must exercise equal scrutiny of both sides.

88. See Theo van Boven, "The Role of the United Nations Secretariat in the Area of Human Rights," *New York University Journal of International Law and Politics* 24 (1991): 69, 75–79.

89. Hammarskjold, supra note 86, p. 348.

90. See, for example, Serge Lalande, "Somalia: Major Issues for Future UN Peace-keeping," paper prepared for the International Colloquium on New Dimensions of Peace-keeping, Graduate Institute of International Studies, Geneva, 10–11 March 1994; Charles Dobbie, "A Concept for Post-Cold War Peacekeeping," *Survival* 36 (Autumn 1994): 121, 135–46 (examining consequences of the use of force for consent and impartiality). For a prescient insight into the consequences of loss of impartiality, see Tom Farer, "From Warlord to Peacelord? Like It or Not, the West Needs to Enlist Aideed—or Face Disaster," *The Washington Post,* 12 September 1993, p. C2.

91. See Saadia Touval and I. William Zartman, "Mediation in Theory," in *International Mediation in Theory and Practice,* supra note 58, pp. 8–9.

92. Yves Beigbeder, *International Monitoring of Plebiscites, Referenda and National Elections: Self determination and Transition to Democracy* (Dordrecht: Martinus Nijhoff, 1994), p. 145.

93. Article 100 states in pertinent part: In the performance of their duties the Secretary-General and the staff shall not seek or receive instructions from any government or from any other authority external to the Organization. . . . Each Member of the United Nations undertakes to respect the exclusively international character of the responsibilities of the Secretary-General and the staff and not to seek to influence them in the discharge of their responsibilities.

94. Touval (1982), supra note 58, pp. 12–16.

95. See Wiseman, supra note 5, p. 43.

Chapter 3

1. UN Charter, art. 24(1).

2. See, for example, Goodrich, Hambro, and Simons, supra chapter 2 note 27, pp. 278–79; Bowett, supra chapter 1 note 24, pp. 65–68, points to Article 34, allowing the Council to "investigate any dispute," as a basis for some missions under Chapter VI, although he also found a strong basis within Article 40.

3. See Higgins (1963), supra chapter 2 note 27, pp. 235–36; Denys Simon, "Article 40," in La Charte des Nations Unies, supra chapter 2 note 30, pp. 667, 680–85; Bowett, supra chapter 1 note 24, pp. 280–84.

4. See Goodrich, Hambro, and Simons, supra chapter 2 note 27, pp. 306–08; Simon, supra note 3, pp. 686–89.

5. The Council may, however, make binding decisions under Chapter VI or any other part of the Charter. Legal Consequences for States of the Continued Presence of South Africa in Namibia (South West Africa) Notwithstanding Security Council Resolution 276 (1970), 1971 ICJ 16, 52–53 (June 21).

6. The genealogy of this expression is difficult to determine. It appears that Hammarskjold first referred publicly to a Chapter "VIa" of the Charter in a 1959 press conference. Transcript of Press Conference in Copenhagen (4 May 1959), in Public Papers of the Secretaries-General of the United Nations: Dag Hammarskjold 1958–1960, edited by Andrew W. Cordier and Wilder Foote (New York: Columbia University Press, 1974), p. 377.

7. Some, for example, Abi-Saab (1978), supra chapter 2 note 60, pp. 103–06, have suggested that certain aspects of the Congo operation amounted to peace enforcement. The UN's official view was that the Congo action was taken under Article 40 to supervise compliance with provisional measures proposed by the Security Council. See E. M. Miller [pseudonym for UN Legal Counsel Oscar Schachter], "Legal Aspects of the United Nations Action in the Congo," American Journal of International Law 55 (1961): 1, 2–9. See also Bowett, supra chapter 1 note 24, p. 180 (endorsing UN view).

8. See, for example, Bowett, supra chapter 1 note 24, p. 179; Dan Ciobanu, "The Power of the Security Council to Organize Peace-Keeping Operations," in United Nations Peace-Keeping: Legal Essays, edited by A. Cassese (Alphen aan den Rijn: Sijthoff & Noordhoff, 1978), pp. 15, 23–41; see also the Reparation for Injuries and Certain Expenses cases cited supra chapter 2 note 21.

9. Goodrich, Hambro, and Simons, supra chapter 2 note 27, pp. 277–78, 287–89.

10. Id. pp. 302–03.

11. SC Res. 807, 19 February 1993.

12. Provisional Verbatim Record of the Three Thousand One Hundred and Seventy-Fourth Meeting, 19 February 1993, UN Doc. S/PV.3174, pp. 13–15 (remarks of Ambassador Merimée of France).

13. SC Res. 836, supra chapter 1 note 20. See also SC Res. 847, 30 June 1993 (invoking Chapter VII for renewal of entire mandate).

14. Thus, for those who prefer to locate peacekeeping within Chapters VI and VII, as things stand today, peacekeeping can occur under Chapters VI or VII; peace enforcement can only be based upon Chapter VII. The distinction between Chapter VI and Chapter VII is not the same as that between peacekeeping and peace enforcement—a self-styled Chapter VI mission must be peacekeeping, but a Chapter VII operation can be either peacekeeping, peace enforcement, or both.

15. John F. Kennedy, Commencement Address at American University in Washington, 10 June 1963, in 1963 Public Papers of the Presidents of the United States, pp. 459, 464.

16. For a recent consideration of Kant's thesis, see Michael W. Doyle, "Liberalism and World Politics," American Political Science Review 80 (1986): 1151–69.

17. See, in this context, the forward-looking statement issued by the Security Council after its meeting at the level of heads of state and government, in Note by the President of the Security Council, 31 January 1992, UN Doc. S/23500.

18. See Vienna Convention on the Law of Treaties, supra chapter 2 note 3, art. 31(3)(b), 1155 UNTS, p. 340.

19. Questions of Interpretation and Application of the 1971 Montreal Convention Arising from the Aerial Incident at Lockerbie (Libya v. U.S.), Provisional Measures, 1992 ICJ 114 (Order of 14 April 1992) (denying request for provisional measures, but leaving final status of economic sanctions undecided); Application of the Convention on the Prevention and Punishment of the Crime of Genocide (Bosnia and Herzegovina v. Yugoslavia), Provisional Measures, 1993 ICJ 3 (Order of 8 April 1993) (ordering Serbia to take measures to prevent genocide, but reserving a decision on Bosnia's request to nullify sanctions). See also Thomas M. Franck, "The 'Powers of Appreciation': Who is the Ultimate Guardian of UN Legality?" *American Journal of International Law* 86 (1992): 519–23; W. Michael Reisman, "The Constitutional Crisis in the United Nations," *American Journal of International Law* 87 (1993): 83–100.

20. For a more complete discussion of the political significance of Security Council resolutions, see Sally Morphet, "Resolutions and vetoes in the UN Security Council: their relevance and significance," *Review of International Studies* 16 (1990): 341–59.

21. 1989 Index to the Proceedings of the Security Council, UN Doc. ST/LIB/SER.B/S.26, and press releases from United Nations Information Center.

22. See David D. Caron, "The Legitimacy of the Collective Authority of the Security Council," *American Journal of International Law* 87 (1993): 552, 577–88 (describing the ability of the permanent members of the Council to block modification of Council action through the "reverse veto").

23. Interview with Yasushi Akashi, 19 March 1993.

24. F. Y. Chai, "Consultation and Consensus in the Security Council," in *Dispute Settlement Through the United Nations*, edited by K. Venkata Raman (Dobbs Ferry, NY: Oceana Publications, 1977) pp. 517, 552–60.

25. On informal groups in the Council, see Sydney D. Bailey, *The Procedure of the UN Security Council* (Oxford: Clarendon Press, 1988), pp. 142–45.

26. Article 11(2) states that the Assembly must refer "any question on which action is nec essary" to the Council. The International Court of Justice, in *Certain Expenses of the United Nations (Article 17, paragraph 2, of the Charter)*, 1962 ICJ 151, 164–65 (July 20), interpreted this provision to mean that the Assembly need refer to the Council only proposals for enforcement action under Chapter VII, thereby upholding broad powers for the Assembly.

27. GA Res. 377A, UN GAOR, 5th Sess., Supp. No. 20, p. 10, UN Doc. A/1775, 1950. The resolution, passed in the early months of the Korean War, was a U.S. initiative to respond to the Soviet veto by removing actions to the Assembly, where the U.S. enjoyed wide support. The resolution thus interpreted Article 27(2) of the Charter, by which any negative votes of permanent members do not constitute vetoes for "procedural matters," to cover the transfer of these issues to the Assembly.

28. SC Res. 119, 31 October 1956, UN SCOR, 11th Year, Res. and Dec., p. 9, UN Doc. S/INF/11/Rev. 1.

29. The Cyprus mission (UNFICYP) was funded by voluntary contributions, a practice that ended with Security Council Resolution 831 of 27 May 1993.

30. United States General Accounting Office, United Nations: How Assessed Contributions for Peacekeeping Operations Are Calculated, August 1994, GAO/NSIAD–94–206, pp. 11–16.

31. Philippe Manin, "Article 12, Paragraphe 1," in *La Charte des Nations Unies*, supra chapter 2 note 30, pp. 295, 297–301. This appears to be true even when the Council is exercising enforcement action, as seen in the Assembly's recommendation to the Council that it lift the arms embargo on Bosnia-Herzegovina. GA Res. 48/88, para. 17, UN GAOR, 48th Sess., Supp. No. 49, pp. 40, 42, UN Doc. A/48/49, 1993.

32. Interview with Nana Sutresna, 25 February 1993.

33. Letter dated 5 October 1990 from the President of the Security Council addressed to the Secretary-General, 5 October 1993, UN Doc. S/21847.

34. For an excellent discussion of the process, see Enid C. B. Schoettle, "Financing UN Peacekeeping," in *Keeping the Peace in the Post-Cold War Era: Strengthening Multilateral Peacekeeping* (New York: The Trilateral Commission, 1993), pp. 17, 21–33, 44–46.
35. See GA Res. 48/229, UN GAOR, 48th Sess., Supp. No. 49, p. 316, UN Doc. A/48/49, 1993; GA Res. 47/217, UN GAOR, 47th Sess., Supp. No. 49, p. 272, UN Doc. A/47/49, 1992.
36. See, for example, GA Res. 47/138, UN GAOR, 47th Sess., Supp. No. 49, p. 214, UN Doc. A/47/49, 1992; 1992 UN Election Report, supra chapter 2 note 53.
37. For a recent examination, see James S. Sutterlin, "The UN Secretary-General as Chief Administrator," in *The Challenging Role of the UN Secretary-General: Making "The Most Impossible Job in the World" Possible,* edited by Benjamin Rivlin and Leon Gordenker (Westport, CT: Praeger, 1993), pp. 43–59. For a complete legal study of this role, see "The Role of the Secretary-General as Chief Administrative Officer of the United Nations," 1982 *United Nations Juridical Yearbook* 189, UN Doc. ST/LEG/ SER.C/20, UN Sales No. E.89.V.1, 1989.
38. Two recent essays on the changing duties of the office are Inis L. Claude, Jr., "Reflections on the Role of the UN Secretary-General"; and Leon Gordenker, "The UN Secretary-Generalship: Limits, Potentials, and Leadership," in *The Challenging Role of the UN Secretary-General,* supra note 37, pp. 249–60, 261–82.
39. For excellent studies contrasting the visions of the Secretary-General adopted by the League of Nations and United Nations, see Leon Gordenker, *The UN Secretary-General and the Maintenance of Peace* (New York: Columbia University Press, 1967), pp. 4–29; Rovine, supra chapter 2 note 48, pp. 201–07; and Stephen M. Schwebel, *The Secretary-General of the United Nations: His Political Powers and Practice* (Cambridge, MA: Harvard University Press, 1952), pp. 3–48.
40. Paul C. Szasz, "The Role of the U.N. Secretary-General: Some Legal Aspects," *New York University Journal of International Law and Politics* 24 (1991): 161, 191; see also Abi-Saab (1978), supra chapter 2 note 60, pp. 195–98.
41. Franck (1985), supra chapter 2 note 48, p. 117. The literature on the subject is vast. For excellent studies, see id. pp. 117–60; Thomas M. Franck, "The Good Offices Function of the UN Secretary-General," in *United Nations, Divided World,* supra chapter 2 note 66, pp. 79, 86–90; Vratislav Pechota, "The Quiet Approach: A Study of the Good Offices Exercised by the United Nations Secretary-General in the Cause of Peace," in *Dispute Settlement Through the United Nations,* supra note 24, pp. 577–676; and sources cited in note 38.
42. Dag Hammarskjold, Statement on His Re-Election to a Second Term, Before the General Assembly, 26 September 1957, reprinted in *Servant of Peace,* supra chapter 2 note 86, pp. 148, 150.
43. Introduction to the Annual Report of the Secretary-General on the Work of the Organization, 16 June 1960–15 June 1961, UN GAOR, 16th Sess., Supp. No. 1A, pp. 1, 7, UN Doc. A/4800/Add.1, 1961. For other descriptions of Hammarskjold's vision, see Gordenker (1967), supra note 39, pp. 72–80; Abi-Saab (1978), supra chapter 2 note 60, pp. 1–5; Rovine, supra chapter 2 note 48, pp. 327–340; and two full-length treatments of Hammarskjold: Brian Urquhart, *Hammarskjold* (New York: Alfred A. Knopf, 1972); and Mark W. Zacher, *Dag Hammarskjold's United Nations* (New York: Columbia University Press, 1970).
44. Franck (1985), supra chapter 2 note 48, p. 134.
45. For perceptive further thoughts on the Secretary-General's relationships with other actors in the UN, see Gordenker (1993), supra note 38.
46. For a recent study, see Donald J. Puchala, "The Secretary-General and His Special Representatives," in *The Challenging Role of the UN Secretary-General,* supra note 37, p. 81–97.
47. Cf. Young (1967), supra chapter 1 note 22, pp. 83–89.

48. Interview with Iqbal Riza, 28 October 1993.
49. Interview with UNTAC provincial director, 12 March 1993.
50. UN Charter, art. 101(3).
51. For a good review of this problem with respect to first-generation operations, see Robert C. R. Siekmann, *National Contingents in United Nations Peace-Keeping Forces* (Dordrecht: Martinus Nijhoff, 1991), pp. 64–97.
52. See Theodor Meron, *The United Nations Secretariat: The Rules and the Practice* (Lexington, MA: Lexington Books, 1977), pp. 93–116.
53. See Franck (1985), supra chapter 2 note 48, pp. 126–27; Schwebel, supra note 39, pp. 92–103.
54. GA Res. 906, UN GAOR, 9th Sess., Supp. No. 21, p. 56, UN Doc. A/2890, 1954.
55. See, for example, GA Res. 34/22, UN GAOR, 34th Sess., Supp. No. 46, p. 16, UN Doc. A/34/46, 1979 (Cambodia issue in 1979).
56. Interview with Paul Szasz, 4 December 1992.
57. GA Res. 48/88, supra note 31, para. 17.
58. SC Res. 837, 6 June 1993, and SC Res. 885, 16 November 1993.
59. As Under Secretary-General for Peacekeeping Operations Kofi Annan expressed in his frustration over Security Council resolutions on Bosnia, "Forget the resolutions. . . . We know where we want to go. Let's figure out how to get there." Brian Hall, "Blue Helmets, Empty Guns," *The New York Times Magazine*, 2 January 1994, pp. 19, 38.
60. Law Concerning Cooperation for United Nations Peace-Keeping Operations and Other Operations, 15 June 1992, translated in 32 ILM 215 (1993). For example, the law precludes participation in the monitoring of cease-fires, disarmament, and demobilization, unless approved by a separate law. Id. art. III(3), annex art. II.
61. "U.N. Bosnia Commander Wants More Troops, Fewer Resolutions," *The New York Times*, 31 December 1993, p. A3. General Briquemont shortly thereafter quit UNPRO FOR out of frustration; some speculate that he was pushed out.
62. SC Res. 145 (S/4405), 22 July 1960, UN SCOR, 15th Year, Res. and Dec., p. 6, UN Doc. S/INF/15/Rev.1.
63. For an excellent recent study, see Virginia Page Fortna, *Regional Organizations and Peacekeeping: Experiences in Latin America and Africa* (Washington, DC: Henry L. Stimson Center Occasional Paper No. 11, 1993). For details on the sharing of responsibilities between UNOMIL and the ECOWAS force, see Report of the Secretary-General on Liberia, 9 September 1993, UN Doc. S/26422.
64. See David Wippman, "Enforcing the Peace: ECOWAS and the Liberian Civil War," in *Enforcing Restraint*, supra chapter 2 note 17, pp. 157–203.
65. See, for example, *An Agenda for Peace*, supra chapter 1 note 11, pp. 17–18.
66. For further thoughts on the importance of these institutions and economic reconstruction generally, see Alvaro de Soto and Graciana del Castillo, "Obstacles to Peacebuilding," *Foreign Policy* 94 (Spring 1994): 69–83.

Chapter 4

1. Treaty of Peace between the Principal Allied and Associated Powers and Germany (Treaty of Versailles), 28 June 1919, arts. 10–13, 15, 16, 225 Consol. T.S. 189, 198–201.
2. The critical loopholes in the Covenant include Articles 12(1) (permitting war after three months); 12(2) (requiring Council report within six months of submission of dispute); 15(7) (permitting war if Council decision not adopted unanimously, excluding the disputants); and 15(8) (precluding Council action over issues within the domestic jurisdiction of the parties).
3. F. P. Walters, *A History of the League of Nations* (London: Oxford University Press, 1952), pp. 93–94, 127, 138.

4. F. S. Northedge, *The League of Nations: its life and times 1920–1946* (Leicester: Leicester University Press, 1986), p. 72.
5. Treaty of Versailles, art. 45, 225 Consol. T.S. p. 213.
6. Treaty of Versailles, part III section IV, annex, art. 35, 225 Consol. T.S. p. 222.
7. Treaty of Versailles, part III section IV, annex, art. 19, 225 Consol. T.S. p. 219.
8. See Letter from Eric Drummond, Secretary-General of the League of Nations, to Harold Nicolson, British diplomat (15 December 1919) (League of Nations Archive No. 11/2475/2432), in which Drummond notes that the League's Legal Adviser, Joost van Hamel, believed that sovereignty rested with Germany although it was "in abeyance for fifteen years." Drummond himself referred to the situation as "a new international legal conception—namely, a territory over which there is no sovereignty."
9. Walters, supra note 3, pp. 239–41; Hurst Hannum, *Autonomy, Sovereignty, and Self-Determination: The Accommodation of Conflicting Rights* (Philadelphia: University of Pennsylvania Press, 1990), pp. 391–94. See generally Sarah Wambaugh, *The Saar Plebiscite, with a Collection of Official Documents* (Cambridge, MA: Harvard University Press, 1940), pp. 73–103.
10. Saar Basin Governing Commission, Report presented by the Greek Representative, M. Caclamanos, and adopted by the Council of the League of Nations, 20 September 1920, *LNOJ* 1 (1920): 400, 403.
11. Id.
12. Saar Basin: Enquiry into the Administration of the Territory, *LNOJ* 4 (1923): 930–32.
13. Wainhouse, supra chapter 1 note 2, pp. 21–23; Wambaugh (1940), supra note 9, pp. 92, 100.
14. Wainhouse, supra chapter 1 note 2, pp. 25–29; Walters, supra note 3, pp. 589–93.
15. Wambaugh (1940), supra note 9, pp. 265–67, 295.
16. Treaty of Versailles, art. 102, 225 Consol. T.S. p. 247.
17. Id. art. 103, 225 Consol. T.S. pp. 247–48; see Méir Ydit, *Internationalised Territories: From the "Free City of Cracow" to the "Free City of Berlin"* (Leyden: A. W. Sythoff, 1961), pp. 194–97. On the guarantee concept, see Hans L. Leonhardt, *Nazi Conquest of Danzig* (Chicago: University of Chicago Press, 1942), pp. 290–97.
18. Constitution of the Free City of Danzig, art. 49, *LNOJ* Special Supp. No. 7 (1922): 11–12; Convention Between Poland and the Free City of Danzig, 9 November 1920, art. 6, 6 LNTS 189, 193. See also Leonhardt, supra note 17, pp. 26–30; Ian F. D. Morrow, "The International Status of the Free City of Danzig," *British Year Book of International Law* 18 (1937): 114–26.
19. Advisory Opinion, Consistency of Certain Danzig Legislative Decrees with the Constitution of the Free City, 1935 PCIJ (ser. A/B) No. 65, p. 41. See also Ydit, supra note 17, pp. 218–23; Leonhardt, supra note 17, pp. 125–64.
20. Walters, supra note 3, p. 794. See also Leonhardt, supra note 17, pp. 307–38; and the scathing critique in Ydit, supra note 17, pp. 216–23.
21. Hannum, supra note 9, p. 378.
22. This list does not include plebiscites organized by the Principal Allied and Associated Powers of World War I that were not overseen by the League of Nations. For a discussion, see Plebiscites Held Since 1920 Under the Control or Supervision of International Organizations, Memorandum prepared by the Secretariat, 20 February 1957, UN Doc. A/C.4/351; and Sarah Wambaugh, *Plebiscites Since the World War, with a Collection of Documents*, 2 vols. (Washington, DC: Carnegie Endowment for International Peace, 1933).
23. Peace Treaty between Lithuania and the Russian Socialist Federal Republic, and Protocol, 12 July 1920, art. 2, 3 LNTS 105, 125; cf. art 2, Remark 1, where the two sides agree that the final Lithuanian-Polish boundary will be negotiated between those two states.
24. The Dispute between Lithuania and Poland, Report by M. Hymans, Acting President of the Council of the League of Nations, 28 October 1920, Procès-Verbal of the Tenth

Session of the Council, held in Brussels, 20th October, 1920–28th October, 1920, Annex 127, pp. 281, 283, 1920.

25. For further details, see Wambaugh (1933), supra note 9, pp. 298–330, 547–56; Walters, supra note 3, pp. 105–09, 140–43, 398–400.

26. Report by Viscount Ishii on the Request Addressed by the Supreme Council of the Principal Allied Powers to the Council of the League of Nations to Find a Solution of the Question of Upper Silesia, adopted by the Council on August 29th, 1921, LNOJ 2 (1921): 1220–26.

27. Convention Concerning Upper Silesia, March 15, 1922, 16 Martens Nouveau Recueil 645; see also Wambaugh (1933), supra note 22, vol. 1, pp. 249–61.

28. See Walters, supra note 3, pp. 406–08, 447–48; see also Advisory Opinion, Access to German Minority Schools in Upper Silesia, 1931 PCIJ (ser. A/B) No. 40, p. 4.

29. Convention Concerning the Territory of Memel, 8 May 1924, annexes II and III, 29 LNTS 85, 109–115; see also Ydit, supra note 17, pp. 48–50.

30. Treaty of Peace, 24 July 1923, art. 3(2), 28 LNTS 11, 17.

31. Question of the Frontier between Turkey and Iraq: Decision of the Council, 16 December 1925, LNOJ 7 (1926): 187–92. Treaty Between the United Kingdom and Iraq and Turkey Regarding the Settlement of the Frontier Between Turkey and Iraq, 5 June 1926, 64 LNTS 379. See also Wambaugh (1933), supra note 22, vol. 1, pp. 538–44.

32. Dispute between Columbia and Peru: Appeal of the Columbian Government under Article 15 of the Convenant: Draft Report of the Council, provided for in Article 15, Paragraph 4, of the Covenant, submitted by the Committee of the Council, 18 March 1933, LNOJ 14 (1933): 516–23.

33. Agreement Between Colombia and Peru Relating to the Procedure for Putting into Effect the Recommendations Proposed by the Council of the League of Nations in the Report It Adopted on March 18th, 1933, 25 May 1933, 138 LNTS 251.

34. See Ydit, supra note 17, pp. 59–62; Walters, supra note 3, pp. 536–40.

35. Question of Alexandretta and Antioch, 27 January and 29 May 1937, LNOJ 18 (1937): 118–23, 329–33.

36. Walters, supra note 3, pp. 742–45.

37. Treaty of Peace with Italy, 10 February 1947, art. 21(1), 49 UNTS 3, 137.

38. SC Res. 16, 10 January 1947, UN SCOR, 2nd Year, Res. and Dec., p. 1, UN Doc. S/INF/2/Rev. 1 (II). The Council approved the plan for Trieste before the formal conclusion of the Peace Treaty with Italy.

39. Id. Annex VI, 49 UNTS pp. 186–97.

40. Memorandum of Understanding Between the Governments of Italy, the United Kingdom of Great Britain and Northern Ireland, the United States of America and Yugoslavia Regarding the Free Territory of Trieste, 5 October 1954, 235 UNTS 99.

41. For a thorough account, see Ydit, supra note 17, pp. 231–72.

42. GA Res. 181, UN Doc. A/519, p. 131, 1947.

43. Statute for the City of Jerusalem (Draft Prepared by the Trusteeship Council), UN TCOR, 2nd Sess., Third Part, Annex, p. 4, UN Doc. T/118/Rev.2, 1948.

44. Id. art. 12(2), p. 9.

45. Id. arts. 4(1), 14–24, 35–37, pp. 6, 10–14, 19–23. For a comparison of the Jerusalem and Trieste regimes, see Ydit, supra note 17, pp. 294–97.

46. For an excellent discussion, see Ydit, supra note 17, pp. 273–315.

47. Communiqué on the Moscow Conference of the Three Foreign Ministers, 27 December 1945, sec. III, reprinted in Department of State Bulletin 13 (1945): 1027, 1030.

48. GA Res. 112, UN Doc. A/519, p. 16, 1947.

49. GA Res. 195, UN Doc. A/810, p. 25, 1948.

50. For further background, see Wainhouse, supra chapter 1 note 2, pp. 323–42.

51. GA Res. 376, UN GAOR, 5th Sess., Supp. No. 20, p. 9, UN Doc. A/1775, 1950.

52. Moreover, the Commissions, though approved by a political organ of the UN, were quite small and consisted wholly of representatives of governments, under their instructions, rather than UN officials. Wainhouse, supra chapter 1 note 2, p. 339.

53. SC Res. 39, 20 January 1948, UN SCOR, 3rd Year, Res. and Dec., p. 2, UN Doc. S/INF/2/Rev.1 (III).

54. SC Res. 47, 21 April 1948, UN SCOR, 3rd Year, Res. and Dec., p. 3, UN Doc. S/INF/2/Rev.1 (III).

55. For further background, see Wainhouse, supra chapter 1 note 2, pp. 357–71; Evan Luard, A History of the United Nations, Volume 1: The Years of Western Domination, 1945–1955 (New York: St. Martin's Press, 1982), pp. 278–94.

56. GA Res. 2145, UN GAOR, 21st Sess., Supp. No. 16, p. 2, UN Doc. A/6316, 1966.

57. GA Res. 2248, UN GAOR, 5th Special Sess., Supp. No. 1, p. 1, UN Doc. A/6657, 1967.

58. Among best discussions of ONUC are Abi-Saab (1978), supra chapter 2 note 60; Urquhart, supra chapter 3 note 43, pp. 389–589; and Rajeshwar Dayal, Mission for Hammarskjold: The Congo Crisis (Princeton, NJ: Princeton University Press, 1976); see also Rosalyn Higgins, United Nations Peacekeeping 1946–1967, Documents and Commentary, vol. 3 (London: Oxford University Press, 1980); United Nations, The Blue Helmets: A Review of United Nations Peace-keeping, 2nd ed. (New York: United Nations, 1990, UN Sales No. E.90.I.18), pp. 215–59; and Evan Luard, A History of the United Nations, Volume 2: The Age of Decolonization, 1955–1965 (New York: St. Martin's Press, 1989), pp. 217–316.

59. First report of the Secretary-General on the implementation of Security Council resolution S/4387 of 14 July 1960, 18 July 1960, UN SCOR, 15th Year, Supp. for July, August and September 1960, p. 16, UN Doc. S/4389.

60. See Abi-Saab (1978), supra chapter 2 note 60, pp. 39–53.

61. See, for example, 12 August 1960 ONUC Memorandum, supra chapter 2 note 80, pp. 65, 70.

62. Id. p. 70.

63. Abi-Saab (1978), supra chapter 2 note 60, pp. 133–47, 165–68; Luard (1989), supra note 58, pp. 276–83.

64. SC Res. 169 (S/5002), 24 November 1961, UN SCOR, 16th Year, Res. and Dec., p. 3, UN Doc. S/INF/16/Rev.1.

65. This view seems to be accepted by Bowett, supra chapter 1 note 24, pp. 196–98.

66. Complete discussions on the subject include Arthur H. House, The U.N. in the Congo: The Political and Civilian Efforts (Washington, DC: University Press of America, 1978); and Harold Karan Jacobson, "ONUC's Civilian Operations: State-Preserving and State-Building," World Politics 17 (1964): 75–107.

67. SC Res. 143 (S/4387), 14 July 1960, UN SCOR, 15th Year, Res. and Dec., p. 5, UN Doc. S/INF/15/Rev.1.

68. SC Res. 145 (S/4405), 22 July 1960, UN SCOR, 15th Year, Res. and Dec., p. 6, UN Doc. S/INF/15/Rev.1.

69. Memorandum by the Secretary-General on the Organization of the United Nations Civilian Operation in the Republic of the Congo, 11 August 1960, UN SCOR, 15th Year, Supp. for July, August and September 1960, p. 60, UN Doc. S/4417/Add.5 [hereinafter 11 August 1960 ONUC Civilian Operation Memorandum].

70. House, supra note 66, p. 189.

71. Id. pp. 196–243; Jacobson, supra note 66, pp. 92–93; 21 September 1960 ONUC Report, supra chapter 2 note 80, p. 194.

72. 11 August 1960 ONUC Civilian Operation Memorandum, supra note 69, p. 61.

73. Id.; see also Aide-memoire dated 24 and 25 July 1960 on assistance to the Congo, for the Prime Minister of the Republic of the Congo, 20 August 1960, UN SCOR, 15th Year, Supp. for July, August, and September 1960, p. 104, UN Doc. S/4447, which notes:

[The consultants' role] obviously does not mean that [they] get any responsibility or executive authority in relation to any activities within the Congolese administration, but only that, while serving the United Nations in the administration of its own Technical Assistance activities as approved by the Government, they would form a panel on which the Government may draw for advice on specific questions as it might see fit.

74. 21 September 1960 ONUC Report, supra chapter 2 note 80, p. 194.

75. Brian Urquhart, Remarks to Council on Foreign Relations Study Group on Collective Involvement in Internal Conflicts, 16 December 1992.

76. Dag Hammarskjold, Statement on UN Operations in the Congo before the General Assembly, 17 October 1960, UN GAOR, 15th Sess., Plenary Meetings, vol. 1, pp. 741, 742, UN Doc. A/PV.906, reprinted in Servant of Peace, supra chapter 2 note 86, pp. 319, 323.

77. Jacobson, supra note 66, pp. 96–98, 105–06.

78. Letter dated 20 August 1960 from the First Deputy Minister for Foreign Affairs of the Union of Soviet Socialist Republics to the Secretary-General, 20 August 1960, UN SCOR, 15th Year, Supp. for July, August, and September 1960, p. 102, UN Doc. S/4446.

79. House, supra note 66, pp. 425–28.

80. See 11 August 1960 ONUC Civilian Operation Memorandum, supra note 69, pp. 62–64; 12 August 1960 ONUC Memorandum, supra chapter 2 note 80, pp. 66, 68.

81. See, for example, Perez de Cuellar's recitation in his Report of the Secretary-General on the Work of the Organization, UN GAOR, 45th Sess., Supp. No. 1, pp. 5–6, UN Doc. A/45/1, 1990.

82. The political background to UNTEA is well described in Franck (1985), supra chapter 2 note 48, pp. 76–82; and Luard (1989), supra note 58, pp. 327–47; see also William J. Durch, "UN Temporary Executive Authority," in The Evolution of UN Peacekeeping, supra chapter 2 note 8, pp. 285–98.

83. Agreement Between the Republic of Indonesia and the Kingdom of the Netherlands Concerning West New Guinea (West Irian), 15 August 1962, art. 5, 437 UNTS 274, 276. See also Franck (1985), supra chapter 2 note 48, p. 79 (criticizing the accord as "an arbitrary disposition of people and territory by power politics reminiscent of the 1878 Congress of Berlin").

84. West Irian Agreement, art. 18, 437 UNTS p. 282.

85. GA Res. 1752, UN GAOR, 17th Sess., Supp. No. 17, p. 70, UN Doc. A/5217, 1962.

86. Report of the Secretary-General regarding the act of self-determination in West Irian, 6 November 1969, UN GAOR, 24th Sess., Annex, Agenda item 98, pp. 2, 20, UN Doc. A/7723.

87. Id.

88. GA Res. 2504, UN GAOR, 24th Sess., Supp. No. 30, p. 3, UN Doc. A/7630, 1969.

89. UN Charter, arts. 1(2), 73, 76; GA Res. 850, UN GAOR, 9th Sess., Supp. No. 21, p. 28, UN Doc. A/2890, 1954 (recommending dispatch of UN missions to oversee process of choice on future status); Declaration on the Granting of Independence to Colonial Countries and Peoples, GA Res. 1514, UN GAOR, 15th Sess., Supp. No. 16, p. 66, UN Doc. A/4684, 1960.

90. Enhancing the effectiveness of the principle of periodic and genuine elections: Report of the Secretary-General, 19 November 1991, UN Doc. A/46/609, pp. 27–28 [hereinafter 1991 UN Election Report].

91. See, for example, Report of the United Nations Plebiscite Commissioner for the Trust Territory of Togoland under British Administration, 5 September 1956, UN Doc. A/3173 and Add. 1.

92. See Gregory H. Fox, "The Right to Political Participation in International Law," Yale Journal of International Law 17 (1992): 539, 570–590; 1991 UN Election Report, supra note 90, pp. 6–7.

93. Manila Accord Between the Philippines, the Federation of Malaya and Indonesia, 31 July 1963, para. 10, 550 UNTS 343, 346.

94. Annual Report of the Secretary-General on the Work of the Organization, 16 June 1963–15 June 1964, UN GAOR, 19th Sess., Supp. No. 1, pp. 26–27, UN Doc. A/5801, 1964.

95. For further discussion, see Luard (1989), supra note 58, pp. 348–56.

96. Note by the Secretary-General concerning the appointment of his Personal Representative to Bahrain and the terms of reference of his mission, 28 March 1970, UN SCOR, 25th Year, Supp. for January, February, and March 1970, p. 175, UN Doc. S/9726.

97. SC Res. 278, UN SCOR, 25th Year, Res. and Dec., p. 7, UN Doc. S/INF/25.

98. For further information, see Report of the Personal Representative of the Secretary-General in Charge of the Good Offices Mission, Bahrain, 30 April 1970, UN SCOR, 25th Year, Supp. for April, May, and June 1970, Annex I, p. 166, UN Doc. S/9772; Erik Jensen, "The Secretary-General's Use of Good Offices and the Question of Bahrain," *Millenium* 14 (1985): 335–48; Edward Gordon, "Resolution of the Bahrain Dispute," *American Journal of International Law* 65 (1971): 560–68.

99. Treaty of Peace with Italy, art. 23 and Annex XI, 49 UNTS pp. 139, 214.

100. GA Res. 289, UN Doc. A/1251, p. 10, 1949.

101. For further details, see John Wright, *Libya: A Modern History* (Baltimore: Johns Hopkins University Press, 1982), pp. 60–76; Majid Khadduri, *Modern Libya: A Study in Political Development* (Baltimore: Johns Hopkins University Press, 1963), pp. 111–79; and Adrian Pelt, *Libyan Independence and the United Nations: A Case Study of Planned Decolonization* (New Haven, CT: Yale University Press, 1970).

102. GA Res. 390, UN GAOR, 5th Sess., Supp. No. 20, p. 20, UN Doc. A/1775, 1950.

103. GA Res. 617, UN GAOR, 7th Sess., Supp. No. 20, p. 9, UN Doc. A/2361, 1952.

Chapter 5

1. Letter dated 10 April 1978 from the representatives of Canada, the Federal Republic of Germany, France, the United Kingdom of Great Britain and Northern Ireland and the United States of America to the President of the Security Council, 10 April 1978, UN SCOR, 33rd Sess., Supp. for April, May and June 1978, pp. 17–19, UN Doc. S/12636.

2. Report of the Secretary-General submitted pursuant to paragraph 2 of Security Council resolution 431 (1978) concerning the situation in Namibia, 29 August 1978, UN SCOR, 33rd Year, Supp. for July, August, and September 1978, pp. 33, 34, UN Doc. S/12827 [hereinafter UNTAG Plan].

3. SC Res. 435, 29 September 1978, UN SCOR, 33rd Year, Res. and Dec., p. 13, UN Doc. S/INF/34.

4. Agreement Among the People's Republic of Angola, the Republic of Cuba, and the Republic of South Africa, 22 December 1988, 28 ILM 957.

5. Virginia Page Fortna, "United Nations Transition Assistance Group," in *The Evolution of UN Peacekeeping*, supra chapter 2 note 8, pp. 353, 363–65.

6. For more details on UNTAG, see *The Blue Helmets*, supra chapter 4 note 58, pp. 341–88; Fortna, "United Nations Transition Assistance Group," supra note 5, pp. 353–87; and National Democratic Institute for International Affairs, *Nation Building: The U.N. and Namibia* (Washington, DC: National Democratic Institute of International Affairs, 1990). In addition, General Assembly Resolution 45/75, UN GAOR, 45th Sess., Supp. No. 49A, pp. 104, 105, UN Doc. A/45/49, 1990, asked the Secretary-General to prepare a detailed report on UNTAG. This report, a draft of which this author obtained, will be exceptionally useful to policymakers and scholars if it is finished and made public.

7. Draft UNTAG Report, supra note 6, pp. 88–89, 100–114.

8. UNTAG Plan, supra note 2, p. 35 (noting UNTAG will "[s]upervis[e] and control all aspects of the electoral process").
9. See Draft UNTAG Report, supra note 6, p. 173 (discussing exchange of letters between Ahtisaari and the Administrator-General, published in the Extraordinary Official Gazette on 13 October 1989, clarifying Ahtisaari's powers).
10. National Democratic Institute, supra note 6, p. 57.
11. Interview with Paul Szasz, 4 December 1992.
12. National Democratic Institute, supra note 6, pp. 74–75.
13. Report of the Secretary-General on the Work of the Organization, UN GAOR, 45th Sess., Supp. No. 1, p. 2, UN Doc. A/45/1, 1990.
14. Procedure for the establishment of a firm and lasting peace in Central America (Esquipulas II Agreement), supra chapter 2 note 11.
15. Letter dated 3 March 1989, cited in Letter Dated 5 April 1989 from the Secretary-General addressed to the President of the General Assembly, 5 April 1989, UN Doc. A/44/210.
16. Letter dated 6 July 1989 from the Secretary-General Addressed to the President of the General Assembly, 6 July 1989, UN Doc. A/44/375.
17. GA Res. 43/24, UN GAOR, 43rd Sess., Supp. No. 49, p. 27, UN Doc. A/43/49, 1988.
18. GA Res. 44/10, UN GAOR, 44th Sess., Supp. No. 49, p. 18, UN Doc. A/44/49, 1989; SC Res. 637, 27 July 1989, UN SCOR, 44th Year, Res. and Dec., p. 19, UN Doc. S/INF/45.
19. Fortna, *Regional Organizations and Peacekeeping*, supra chapter 3 note 63, pp. 8–9.
20. For more details, see the reports of the Secretary-General on ONUVEN: A/44/642 (17 October 1989), A/44/834 (7 December 1989), A/44/917 (31 January 1990), A/44/921 (22 February 1990), and A/44/927 (30 March 1990).
21. Observation by the United Nations of Elections to be Held in a Member State, Memorandum to the Under-Secretary-General for Special Political Affairs, 1982 *United Nations Juridical Yearbook* 188, UN Doc. ST/LEG/SER.C/20, UN Sales No. E.89.V.1, 1989. The Legal Counsel's advice concerned any election "which concerns only [one] State" and suggested the Secretary-General could become involved if the Security Council or General Assembly gave its authorization.
22. Letter Dated 5 April 1989, supra note 15, p. 2. See also Stoelting, supra chapter 2 note 31, pp. 378–80.
23. Letter Dated 5 April 1989, supra note 15, p. 2.
24. For more information, see The Blue Helmets, supra chapter 4 note 58, pp. 389–401; Brian D. Smith and William J. Durch, "UN Observer Group in Central America," in *The Evolution of UN Peacekeeping*, supra chapter 2 note 8, pp. 436–62.
25. Letter dated 5 October 1990 from the President of the Security Council Addressed to the Secretary-General, UN Doc. S/21847. See also Stoelting, supra chapter 2 note 31, pp. 381–83.
26. GA Res. 45/2, UN GAOR, 45th Sess., Supp. No. 49A, p. 12, UN Doc. A/45/49, 1990.
27. See the reports of the Secretary-General, Notes by the Secretary-General, UN Docs. A/45/870 (14 December 1990), A/45/870/Add.1 (22 February 1991).
28. GA Res. 45/257B, UN GAOR, 45th Sess., Supp. No. 49A, p. 1, UN Doc. A/45/49/Add.1, 1991; see also GA Res. 45/257A, UN GAOR, 45th Sess., Supp. No. 49A, p. 48, UN Doc. A/45/49, 1990.
29. See Domingo E. Acevedo, "The Haitian Crisis and the OAS Response: A Test of Effectiveness in Protecting Democracy," in *Enforcing Restraint*, supra chapter 2 note 17, pp. 119–55.
30. See 1991 UN Election Report, supra chapter 4 note 90, p. 25; 1992 UN Election Report, supra chapter 2 note 53, pp. 15–16; Stoelting, supra chapter 2 note 31, pp. 391–92.
31. See 1992 UN Election Report, supra chapter 2 note 53, pp. 15–16 (qualifying earlier criteria for election missions and proposing "potential international disruption" as more appropriate standard). See also Mélida N. Hodgson, "When to Accept, When to

Abstain: A Framework for U.N. Election Monitoring," *New York University Journal of International Law and Politics* 25 (1992): 137–73.

32. San Jose Agreement on Human Rights, 26 July 1990, reprinted in United Nations, *El Salvador Agreements: The Path to Peace* (New York: United Nations, 1992), p. 7, UN Doc. DPI/1208–92614–July 1992–5M.

33. SC Res. 729, 14 January 1992, UN SCOR, 47th Year, Res. and Dec., p. 1, UN Doc. S/INF/48.

34. SC Res. 832, 27 May 1993.

35. For the UN's official reports, see the many periodic reports of the Secretary-General on ONUSAL, for example, UN Docs. S/23037–A/45/1055 (16 September 1991), S/23222–A/46/658 and Corr.1 (15 and 29 November 1991), S/23580–A/46/876 (19 February 1992), S/23999 and Add.1 (26 May and 19 June 1992), S/24066–A/46/935 (5 June 1992), S/24833 and Add.1 (23 and 30 November 1992), S/25006 (23 December 1992), S/25812 and Adds. 1–3 (21, 24, 25 May 1993), S/26371 (30 August 1993), S/26581 (14 October 1993), S/26606 (20 October 1993), S/26790 (23 November 1993), S/1994/179 (16 February 1994), S/1994/304 (16 March 1994), S/1994/375 (31 March 1994), S/1994/536 (4 May 1994), S/1994/561 and Add. 1 (11 and 18 May 1994), S/1994/1000 (26 August 1994); and S/1994/1212 and Add.1 (31 October and 14 November 1994). For one early assessment, see David Holiday and William Stanley, "Building the Peace: Preliminary Lessons from El Salvador," *Journal of International Affairs* 46 (1993): 415–38.

36. For the report, see Letter Dated 29 March 1993 from the Secretary-General Addressed to the President of the Security Council, 1 April 1993, Annex, UN Doc. S/25500.

37. See, for example, Americas Watch, *El Salvador: Peace and Human Rights: Successes and Shortcomings of the United Nations Observer Mission in El Salvador (ONUSAL)* (New York: Americas Watch, 1992), pp. 14–18, 23–25.

38. See Theo van Boven, "The Security Council: The New Frontier," *International Commission of Jurists: The Review* 48 (1992): 12–23.

39. SC Res. 690, 29 April 1991, UN SCOR, 46th Year, Res. and Dec., p. 35, UN Doc. S/INF/47. The settlement plan appears in: The Situation Concerning the Western Sahara: Report of the Secretary-General, 18 June 1990, UN Doc. S/21360, and The Situation Concerning Western Sahara: Report by the Secretary-General, 19 April 1991, UN Doc. S/22464.

40. See, for example, The Situation Concerning Western Sahara: Reports of the Secretary-General, UN Docs. S/26185 (28 July 1993)(containing compromise proposal in Annex I), S/26797 (24 November 1993), S/1994/283 (10 March 1994), S/1994/819 (12 July 1994), and S/1994/1257 (5 November 1994).

41. See William J. Durch, "United Nations Mission for the Referendum in Western Sahara," in *The Evolution of UN Peacekeeping*, supra chapter 2 note 8, pp. 406–34.

42. SC Res. 696, 30 May 1991, UN SCOR, 46th Year, Res. and Dec., p. 37, UN Doc. S/INF/47; SC Res. 747, 24 March 1992, UN SCOR, 47th Year, Res. and Dec., p. 85, UN Doc. S/INF/48. The settlement, or Acordos de Paz para Angola, may be found in Letter dated 17 May 1991 from the Chargé d'Affaires a.i. of the Permanent Mission of Angola to the United Nations addressed to the Secretary-General, 17 May 1991, UN Doc. S/22609.

43. Further Report of the Secretary-General on the United Nation as Angola Verification Mission (UNAVEM II), 25 November 1992, UN Doc. S/24858, p. 6.

44. SC Res. 864, 15 September 1993. For further details, see the many reports of the Secretary-General on UNAVEM II, for example, UN Docs. S/23191 (31 October 1991), S/23671 and Add.1 (3 and 20 March 1992), S/24556 (9 September 1992), S/24858 and Add.1 (25 and 30 November 1992), S/25140 and Add.1 (21 and 25 January 1993), S/25840 and Add.1 (25 and 27 May 1993), S/26060 (12 July 1993), S/26434 (13 September 1993), S/26872 and Add.1 (14 and 15 December 1993), S/1994/100 (29 January 1994), S/1994/374 (31 March 1994), S/1994/611 (24 May 1994), S/1994/740 and

Add.1 (20 and 29 June 1994), S/1994/865 (22 July 1994), S/1994/1069 (17 September 1994), S/1994/1197 (20 October 1994), and S/1994/1376 (4 December 1994).

Chapter 6

1. For further readings on the history of modern Cambodia, see David P. Chandler, *The Tragedy of Cambodian History: Politics, War, and Revolution since 1945* (New Haven, CT: Yale University Press, 1991); Ben Kiernan, *How Pol Pot Came to Power: A History of Communism in Kampuchea* (London: Verso, 1985); and Federal Research Division, Library of Congress, *Cambodia: A Country Study*, edited by Russell R. Ross (Washington, DC: U.S. Government Printing Office, 1990).

2. The Khmer Rouge years are well documented in the following works in English: *Cambodia 1975–1978: Rendezvous with Death*, edited by Karl D. Jackson (Princeton, NJ: Princeton University Press, 1989); Nayan Chanda, *Brother Enemy: The War after the War* (San Diego: Harcourt Brace Jovanovich, 1986); Elizabeth Becker, *When the War was Over: The Voices of Cambodia's Revolution and its People* (New York: Simon & Schuster, 1986); Michael Vickery, *Cambodia: 1975–1982* (Boston: South End, 1984); François Ponchaud, *Cambodia: Year Zero*, translated by Nancy Amphoux (New York: Holt, Rinehart and Winston, 1978); and Chandler (1991), supra note 1.

3. Karl D. Jackson, "The Khmer Rouge in Context," in *Cambodia, 1975–1978*, supra note 2, p. 3.

4. Analysis prepared on behalf of the Sub-Commission by its Chairman of materials submitted to it and the Commission on Human Rights under decision 9 (XXXIV) of the Commission on Human Rights, 30 January 1979, UN Doc. E/CN.4/1335.

5. Id. p. 3.

6. GA Res. 34/22, UN GAOR, 34th Sess., Supp. No. 46, p. 16, UN Doc. A/34/46, 1979.

7. Declaration on Kampuchea, In Report of the International Conference on Kampuchea, New York (13–17 July 1981), Annex I, p. 7, UN Doc. A/CONF.109/5, UN Sales No. E.81.I.20.

8. See Kishore Mahbubani, "The Kampuchean Problem: A Southeast Asian Perception," *Foreign Affairs* 62 (Winter 1983/84): 407, 418.

9. For an analysis of the PRK, see Michael Vickery, *Kampuchea: Politics, Economics and Society* (London: F. Pinter, 1986).

10. From 1979 to 1988, the margin of votes in favor of the annual Cambodia resolution increased steadily from 70 to 103. For an excellent analysis of the state of play in the mid-1980s, see M. R. Sukhumbhand Paribatra, "Can ASEAN Break the Stalemate?" *World Policy Journal* 3 (1985): 85–106.

11. For background, see Justus M. van der Kroef, "Cambodia: The Vagaries of 'Cocktail' Diplomacy," *Contemporary Southeast Asia* 19 (1988): 300–320.

12. See Letter dated 28 July 1988 from the Permanent Representative of Indonesia to the United Nations addressed to the Secretary-General, 28 July 1988, Annex I, UN Doc. A/43/493–S/20071; Letter dated 22 February 1989 from the Chargé d'affaires a.i. of the Permanent Mission of Indonesia to the United Nations addressed to the Secretary-General, 22 February 1989, Annex, UN Doc. A/44/138–S/20477 and Corr.1.

13. See Michael Leifer, "Power-Sharing and Peacemaking in Cambodia?" *SAIS Review* 12 (Winter–Spring 1992): 139, 143–44.

14. Organization of Work, Text adopted by the Conference at its 4th plenary meeting, on 1 August 1989, Paris Conference on Cambodia Document CPC/89/4, p. 3.

15. Interview with David Lambertson, 26 February 1993.

16. For the Evans plan, see Australian Department of Foreign Affairs and Trade, *Cambodia: an Australian Peace Proposal: Working Papers prepared for the Informal Meeting on Cambodia, Jakarta, 26–28 February 1990* (Canberra: Australia Government Publishing Service, 1990).

17. Summary of Conclusions of the Meeting of the Five Permanent Members of the Security Council on the Cambodian Problem, Paris, 15–16 January 1990, p. 1, reprinted in *The New York Times*, 17 January 1990, p. A6.

18. Statement of the Five Permanent Members of the Security Council of the United Nations on Cambodia, in Letter dated 30 August 1990 from the Permanent Representatives of China, France, the Union of Soviet Socialist Republics, the United Kingdom of Great Britain and Northern Ireland and the United States of America to the United Nations addressed to the Secretary-General, 31 August 1990, Annex, Appendix, UN Doc. A/45/472–S/21689 [hereinafter Framework Document].
19. Id.
20. Leifer, supra note 13, pp. 145–47; see also Robert S. Ross, "China and the Cambodian Peace Process: The Value of Coercive Diplomacy," Asian Survey 31 (1991): 1170–85.
21. See Muthiah Alagappa, "Regionalism and the Quest for Security: ASEAN and the Cambodian Conflict," Journal of International Affairs 46 (1993): 439–67.
22. Letter dated 8 January 1991 from the Permanent Representatives of France and Indonesia to the United Nations addressed to the Secretary-General, 11 January 1991, Annex II, UN Doc. A/46/61–S/22059.
23. For further political background, see Leifer, supra note 13, pp. 145–52.
24. The Paris accords may be found at 31 ILM 180 (1992). They consist of (1) a Final Act, summarizing the work of the Paris Conference; (2) the Comprehensive Settlement Agreement; (3) the Agreement Concerning the Sovereignty, Independence, Territorial Integrity and Inviolability, Neutrality and National Unity of Cambodia, on Cambodia's future status; and (4) the Declaration on the Rehabilitation and Reconstruction of Cambodia. For a complete legal study, see Ratner (1993), supra chapter 2 note 37.
25. UN Charter, art. 78.
26. Cambodia: A Country Study, supra note 1, pp. 222, 224.
27. Comprehensive Settlement Agreement, art. 3.
28. Id. Annex 1, Sec. A, para. 2.
29. Id. arts. 8–11, 21–22; Annex 1, Sec. C; Annex 2.
30. Interview with Rafeeudin Ahmed, 26 February 1993.
31. Comprehensive Settlement Agreement, Annex 1, Sec. B.
32. Id. Annex 1, Sec. B, para. 1.
33. Id. Annex 1, Sec. B, para. 2.
34. Id. (stipulating that agencies "will comply with any guidance provided by [UNTAC]").
35. Id. Annex 1, Sec. B, para. 3.
36. Id. Annex 1, Sec. B, para. 4.
37. Interview with UNTAC senior adviser, 5 March 1993; comment of UNTAC senior military officer, 5 March 1993.
38. Comprehensive Settlement Agreement, art. 13.
39. Id. Annex 1, Sec. D, para. 3.
40. Id. Annex 3, paras. 8 and 9. For background on the controversy over ethnic Vietnamese in Cambodia, see Ratner (1993), supra chapter 2 note 37, p. 20; Nayan Chanda, "Wounds of History," Far Eastern Economic Review, 30 July 1992, pp. 14–16.
41. Comprehensive Settlement Agreement, art. 15.
42. Ratner (1993), supra chapter 2 note 37, pp. 6 n.24, 25–26.
43. Comprehensive Settlement Agreement, art. 16.
44. Id. Annex 1, Section E.
45. Fourteen thousand of these were refugees eligible for such status under international law and living in a refugee camp under the supervision of UNHCR, and more than 350,000 were considered "displaced persons," Cambodians not granted such status in Thailand and living since the early 1980s in camps controlled by the factions and assisted by the United Nations Border Relief Operation.
46. Comprehensive Settlement Agreement, Annex 4, Part III.
47. Declaration on the Rehabilitation and Reconstruction of Cambodia, 23 October 1991, 31 ILM 203 (1992).

48. See Ratner (1993), supra chapter 2 note 37, pp. 22–25, for a discussion of the sovereignty question.
49. Comprehensive Settlement Agreement, art. 6 (emphasis added).
50. See, for example, Chet Atkins, "Cambodia's 'Peace': Genocide, Justice and Silence: The Return of the Khmer Rouge Serves Neither Diplomacy nor Humanity," The Washington Post, 26 January 1992, p. C4 (opinion column by U.S. Congressman); Ben Kiernan, "The Inclusion of the Khmer Rouge in the Cambodian Peace Process: Causes and Consequences," in Genocide and Democracy in Cambodia: The Khmer Rouge, the United Nations and the International Community, edited by Ben Kiernan (New Haven, CT: Yale University Southeast Asia Studies, 1993), pp. 191–272.
51. David P. Chandler, A History of Cambodia, 2nd ed. (Boulder, CO: Westview Press, 1992), p. 1.
52. See generally Ross, supra note 20.
53. Elizabeth Becker, "Up from Hell," The New Republic, 17 February 1992, pp. 32, 34–35 (reviewing Chandler (1991), supra note 1).

Chapter 7

1. For the most detailed official information on this subject, see the periodic reports of the Secretary-General on Cambodia: UN Docs. S/23870 and Corrs.1 and 2 (1 May 1992), S/24090 (12 June 1992), S/24286 (14 July 1992), S/24578 (21 September 1992), S/24800 (15 November 1992), S/25124 (25 January 1993), S/25289 (13 February 1993), S/25719 (3 May 1993), S/25784 (15 May 1993), S/25913 (10 June 1993), S/26090 (16 July 1993), S/26360 (26 August 1993), S/26529 (5 October 1993), S/26546 (7 October 1993), S/26649 and Add.1 (27 October and 3 November 1993), and S/1994/645 (31 May 1994). Unless otherwise noted, all statistics in this chapter are derived from these reports or UNTAC press documents.
2. See Minutes, Clarification of Certain Principled Views to Act as the Basis of our Views and Stance, 6 February 1992 (document obtained by author from UNTAC and reliably attributed to senior Khmer Rouge leadership).
3. Interview with UNTAC civil administration component and information/education division officials, 3 and 10 March 1993.
4. Interview with State of Cambodia official, 17 March 1993.
5. Interviews with UNTAC civil administration and electoral component officials, 8 March 1993; interview with FUNCINPEC official, 18 March 1993.
6. Interviews with UNTAC civil administration component and information division officials, 3 and 6 March 1993.
7. Interview with member of Sihanouk's personal staff, 19 March 1993.
8. See, for example, "Radio Details Sihanouk Reconciliation Plan," FBIS, East Asia Daily Report, 4 March 1993, p. 42 (Sihanouk statement broadcast on Khmer Rouge radio).
9. Interview with James Schear, 10 December 1993.
10. Interviews with UNTAC civil administration component service chief and Kampot province officials, 10 and 11 March 1993.
11. The term is taken from William Shawcross, Sideshow: Kissinger, Nixon and the Destruction of Cambodia, rev. ed. (New York: Simon & Schuster, 1987).
12. Interviews with Indonesian officials, 23–25 February 1993.
13. Interview with Rafeeudin Ahmed, 26 February 1993.
14. SC Res. 717, 16 October 1991, UN SCOR, 46th Year, Res. and Dec., p. 39, UN Doc. S/INF/47; Report of the Secretary-General on Cambodia, 30 September 1991, UN Doc. S/23097; Comprehensive Settlement Agreement, art. 9; Annex 2, art. I, para. 1.
15. On January 8, 1992, in response to increased publicity and concerns about the dangers of unexploded mines in Cambodia, the Council passed Resolution 728, UN SCOR, 47th Year, Res. and Dec., p. 38, UN Doc. S/INF/48, expanding UNAMIC's mandate to include training in mine clearance and initiation of a mine-clearance program.

16. Discussions with officials at U.S. Mission to the United Nations, February 1992, and interviews with diplomats in Singapore and Jakarta, 22–25 February 1993.

17. Report of the Secretary-General on Cambodia, 19 February 1992, UN Doc. S/23613.

18. The Special Representative's personal staff also included a group of special assistants, who handled matters directly reaching Akashi, such as high-level political decisions, UNTAC's relationship with the SNC and Prince Sihanouk, visiting dignitaries, and reports to, and requests for views from, Headquarters. These aides maintained constant contact with New York and drafted the reports issued by the Secretary-General to the Security Council.

19. SC Res. 745, 28 February 1992, UN SCOR, 47th Year, Res. and Dec., p. 39, UN Doc. S/INF/48.

20. GA Res. 46/222A, UN GAOR, 46th Sess., Supp. No. 49A, p. 12, UN Doc. A/46/49/Add.1, 1992.

21. GA Res. 46/222B, UN GAOR, 46th Sess., Supp. No. 49A, at 13, UN Doc. A/46/49/Add.1, 1992.

22. GA Res. 47/209A, UN GAOR, 47th Sess., Supp. No. 49 (Volume I), p. 255, UN Doc. A/47/49, 1992; GA Res. 47/209B, UN GAOR, 47th Sess., Supp. No. 49 (Volume II), p. 19, UN Doc. A/47/49, 1993; GA Res. 48/255, 1994.

23. Interviews with UNTAC civil administration and military component officials, 3 and 16 March 1993.

24. Interview with UNTAC Phnom Penh province official, 8 March 1993.

25. Interview with Rafeeudin Ahmed, 26 February 1993.

26. Interviews with UNTAC officials responsible for administration, 8 and 18 March 1993.

27. Interviews with western diplomat and UNTAC officials, 3, 6, and 8 March 1993.

28. Interview with State of Cambodia official, 17 March 1993.

29. See, for example, "Control of Troop Pullout, SNC Role Viewed," FBIS, East Asia Daily Report, 22 June 1992, p. 36 (Khmer Rouge radio statement).

30. See Comprehensive Settlement Agreement, Annex 2, art. III (lacking any explicit linkage provisions).

31. See the Secretary-General's Reports of 12 June, 14 July, 21 September, and 15 November 1992, UN Docs. S/24090, S/24286, S/24578, and S/24800.

32. SC Res. 792, 30 November 1992, UN SCOR, 47th Year, Res. and Dec., p. 44, UN Doc. S/INF/48.

33. Hans Vriens, "A nasty moment," Far Eastern Economic Review, 11 June 1992, p. 24.

34. Interview with UNTAC Force Commander Lieutenant General John Sanderson, 16 March 1993.

35. Nayan Chanda, "UN divisions," Far Eastern Economic Review, 23 July 1992, pp. 8–9; interview with UNTAC human rights component official and UNTAC special assistant, 3 and 8 March 1993.

36. Nate Thayer, "Martial Races," Far Eastern Economic Review, 25 March 1993, p. 30. Although these men were demobilized, they met the very broad definition of "foreign forces" that the SNC adopted on October 20, 1992. UNTAC Report on the Operations of the Strategic Investigation Teams on Investigation of the Presence of "Foreign Forces" in Cambodia, 9 December 1992, Annex A, p. 2. Vietnam rejected that definition and denied that the men in question had any ties to it. As a legal matter, the SNC's definition, albeit accepted by all four factions, cannot be viewed as authoritative since Cambodia is only one of the parties to the Paris accords. See also Andrew Ghosh, "Holiday in Cambodia: The U.N.'s strategic dead-end," The New Republic, 28 June 1993, pp. 21–25 (describing difficulties of identifying Vietnamese forces).

37. Nayan Chanda, "Strained ties," Far Eastern Economic Review, 17 December 1992, pp. 26–28.

38. Interviews with members of UNTAC electoral component and provincial human rights officer, Kampot, 4 and 11 March 1993.

39. Interview with UNTAC CIVPOL official, 18 March 1993.
40. Second Progress Report of the Secretary-General on the United Nations Transitional Authority in Cambodia, 21 September 1992, UN Doc. S/24578, pp. 6–7.
41. Interview with UNTAC civil administration component official, 3 March 1993.
42. See Comprehensive Settlement Agreement, art. 6.
43. Interviews with UNTAC civil administration component officials, 5 and 10 March 1993.
44. Interviews with Russian diplomats, 10 and 15 March 1993.
45. Stan Sesser, "Report from Cambodia," *The New Yorker*, 18 May 1992, pp. 43, 56–59; interviews with UNTAC civil administration component officials, 5 and 10 March 1993.
46. Interview with UNTAC civil administration foreign affairs service official, 8 March 1993.
47. Interview with UNTAC civil administration defense service official, 10 March 1993.
48. Interview with UNTAC civil administration public security service official, 5 March 1993.
49. Interview with UNTAC civil administration finance service official, 16 March 1993.
50. Interviews with UNTAC civil administration finance service officials, 3, 16, and 17 March 1993.
51. Interview with civil administration information service official, 10 March 1993.
52. Interview with UNTAC civil administration specialized control service official, 15 March 1993.
53. Interviews with UNTAC civil administration investigations service official and UNTAC special assistant, 10 and 19 March 1993.
54. See Nayan Chanda, "Easy scapegoat," *Far Eastern Economic Review*, 22 October 1992, p. 18.
55. Interviews with UNTAC provincial officials in Kompong Thom, Phnom Penh, and Kampot, 2, 8, and 14 March 1993.
56. Interviews with UNTAC civil administration component officials, 3 and 8 March 1993.
57. "Request to Oust Provincial Governor Rejected," FBIS, East Asia Daily Report, 12 January 1993, p. 43.
58. Interview with UNTAC Battambang province official, 12 March 1993.
59. Fourth Progress Report of the Secretary-General on the United Nations Transitional Authority in Cambodia, 3 May 1993, UN Doc. S/25719, p. 14; Nate Thayer, "Shot to Pieces," *Far Eastern Economic Review*, 20 May 1993, pp. 10–11.
60. Fourth Progress Report of the Secretary-General, supra note 59, pp. 23, 26–27.
61. United Nations Electoral Law for the Conduct of a Free and Fair Election of a Constituent Assembly for Cambodia, 1992, 12 August 1992. UNTAC amended the law several times and also promulgated implementing regulations for the conduct of the campaign.
62. See, for example, "Khieu Samphan Addresses Election Law," FBIS, East Asia Daily Report, 10 August 1992, p. 36; "Voter Registration 'Not Fair' in Three Respects," FBIS, East Asia Daily Report, 24 December 1992, p. 15 (later statement of Sihanouk broadcast on Khmer Rouge radio).
63. The accords required that, to vote, a person be born in Cambodia or have a parent born in Cambodia. Comprehensive Settlement Agreement, Annex 3, para. 4. The electoral law required that a voter be either born in Cambodia to a parent born in Cambodia, or born elsewhere to a parent whose parent was born in Cambodia. UN Electoral Law, supra note 61, para. 3.
64. Interviews with UNTAC senior official and electoral component official, 8 March 1993.
65. See Gordon Fairclough, "Civics Classroom," *Far Eastern Economic Review*, 13 May 1993, p. 23.
66. Nate Thayer and Rodney Tasker, "Voice of the People," *Far Eastern Economic Review*, 3 June 1993, pp. 10–11 (citing UNTAC Human Rights component director Dennis McNamara).
67. Id.; "Akashi Declares Election Campaign 'Success' Despite Violence," FBIS, East Asia Daily Report, 20 May 1993, p. 27.

68. Victor Mallet, "Cambodian Elections: Polling Stations in the Battleground," *The Financial Times,* 19 May 1993, p. 7.
69. See, for example, "Khieu Samphan Issues Statement on Election," FBIS, East Asia Daily Report, 14 May 1993, p. 42 (Khmer Rouge radio calling election a "stinking election farce").
70. Letter dated 2 June 1993 from the Secretary-General addressed to the President of the Security Council, 2 June 1993, UN Doc. S/25879, Annex.
71. Freeness and fairness of the Cambodian elections, Statement by the Special Representative of the Secretary-General, in Report of the Secretary General on the Conduct and Results of the Elections in Cambodia, 10 June 1993, UN Doc. S/25913, Annex II, pp. 7, 9. Akashi's qualified statement contrasts with the unequivocal endorsement the Special Representative for Eritrea gave after Eritrea's April 1993 referendum, which he called "free and fair at every stage." Text of announcement on the Referendum in Eritrea, cited in Enhancing the effectiveness of the principle of periodic and genuine elections: Report of the Secretary-General, UN Doc. A/48/590, 18 November 1993, p. 10 [hereinafter 1993 UN Election Report].
72. See Mary Kay Magistad, "Cambodian Rulers Cited in Anti-Voting Violence," *The Washington Post,* 10 June 1993, p. A29.
73. Interview with UNTAC human rights component official, 15 March 1993.
74. Interview with UNTAC officials in Kampot, 11 March 1993.
75. See Standard Minimum Rules for the Treatment of Prisoners, ESC Res. 663C, UN ESCOR, 24th Sess., Supp. No. 1, p. 11, UN Doc. E/3048, 1957.
76. See, for example, Asia Watch, *Cambodia: Human Rights Before and After the Elections* (New York: Asia Watch (Division of Human Rights Watch), 1993), pp. 25–35.
77. See Nayan Chanda, "Theatre of cruelty," *Far Eastern Economic Review,* 24–31 December 1992, p. 11. The SNC ratified the International Covenant on Civil and Political Rights; the International Covenant on Economic, Social, and Cultural Rights; the Convention against Torture and Other Forms of Cruel, Inhuman and Degrading Treatment or Punishment; the Convention on the Elimination of All Forms of Discrimination against Women; the Convention on the Rights of the Child; and the Convention relating to the Status of Refugees and its Protocol. Second Progress Report of the Secretary-General, supra note 40, p. 3.
78. Directive 93/1, from the Special Representative of the Secretary-General establishing procedures for the Prosecution of persons responsible for Human Rights Violations, 6 January 1993.
79. For further information, see Stephen P. Marks, "Forgetting 'The Policies and Practices of the Past': Impunity in Cambodia," *The Fletcher Forum* 18 (Summer/Fall 1994): 17, 32–35.
80. Commission on Human Rights Res. 1993/6, UN ESCOR, Commission on Human Rights, 49th Sess., Supp. No. 3, p. 50, UN Doc. E/CN.4/1993/122.
81. For a report on the small number who did not wish to return, see Jay Solomon, "Going nowhere," *Far Eastern Economic Review,* 17 September 1992, p. 56.
82. Interview with UNTAC repatriation component official, 17 March 1993; see also Rodney Tasker, "Empty Dreams," *Far Eastern Economic Review,* 1 April 1993, p. 22.
83. The economic adviser, who also ran the financial control service of the civilian administration component, assumed charge of the rehabilitation component midway in UNTAC's mandate.
84. For background, see William Branigin, "Phnom Penh Said to Undercut U.N. Effort to Save Forests," *The Washington Post,* 3 February 1993, p. A22.
85. Susan Cunningham, "Cambodia: After a Brief Respite, Logging is Cutting its Way Back," *The Bangkok Post,* 24 August 1993, Inside Indochina Section, p. 3.
86. See, for example, United Nations Transitional Authority in Cambodia, *The Secretary-General's Consolidated Appeal for Cambodia's Immediate Needs and National Rehabilitation* (Phnom Penh: UNTAC, 1992), pp. 24–25.

87. Interviews with UNTAC military and rehabilitation component officials, 16 and 17 March 1993; see also "Khieu Samphan Office on UN Chief's Aid Appeal," FBIS, East Asia Daily Report, 27 April 1992, pp. 34, 35 (calling UN aid plan "contrary to the Paris agreement").
88. Interview with UNTAC rehabilitation component official, 16 March 1993.
89. Interview with UNTAC rehabilitation component official, 17 March 1993.
90. Interview with UNTAC special assistant, 4 March 1993.
91. Interview with Akashi, 19 March 1993.
92. Prince Sihanouk spoke on behalf of a deadlocked SNC regarding the bans on exportation of logs and gems and a loan from the Asian Development Bank, both of which were opposed by the Khmer Rouge members of the SNC. "Meeting Discusses Various Issues," FBIS, East Asia Daily Report, 23 September 1992, p. 19; "Sihanouk Agrees to Sign Reconstruction Loans," FBIS, East Asia Daily Report, 14 January 1993, p. 28; interview with Akashi, 19 March 1993.
93. See, for example, SC Res. 840, 15 June 1993 (endorsing the results of the election and calling upon all parties to comply with its results).
94. Constitution of the Kingdom of Cambodia, arts. 7–9 (21 September 1993).
95. See generally A continued United Nations human rights presence in Cambodia: Report of the Special Representative of the Secretary-General, Mr. Michael Kirby (Australia), on the situation of human rights in Cambodia, submitted in accordance with Commission resolution 1993/6, 24 February 1994, UN Doc. E/CN.4/1994/73 and Add.1.
96. SC Res. 880, 4 November 1993.
97. William Branigin, "U.N. Ends Cambodia Operation; Mission Successful Despite Flaws," The Washington Post, 27 September 1993, p. A12 (at least 21 killed as of Akashi's departure on 26 September 1993).

Chapter 8

1. For an excellent analysis of this question with respect to the entire United Nations, see W. Kendall Stiles and Maryellen MacDonald, "After Consensus, What?: Performance Criteria for the UN in the Post-Cold War Era," Journal of Peace Research 29 (1992): 299–311.
2. Interview with UNTAC human rights provincial officer, Battambang, 12 March 1993.
3. Interviews with UNTAC provincial director and FUNCINPEC official, 11 and 18 March 1993.
4. For a gloomy assessment one year after the elections, see Nate Thayer and Nayan Chanda, "Things Fall Apart . . . ," Far Eastern Economic Review, 19 May 1994, pp. 16–19; Henry Kamm, "Despite U.N.'s Effort, Cambodia is Chaotic," The New York Times, 4 July 1994, pp. A1, A4.
5. For a similar contextual appraisal, see Michael Doyle and Nishkala Suntharalingam, "The UN in Cambodia: Lessons for Complex Peacekeeping," International Peacekeeping 1 (1994): 117–43.
6. See Jeffrey Clark, "Debacle in Somalia: Failure of the Collective Response," in Enforcing Restraint, supra chapter 2 note 17, pp. 205, 221–28.
7. Interviews with members of UNTAC information/education division, 6 and 10 March 1993.
8. Interview with Western diplomat, 6 March 1993.
9. Interview with UNTAC information/education official, 6 March 1993.
10. Interviews with State of Cambodia and resistance party officials, 17 and 18 March 1993; see also Nayan Chanda, "Easy scapegoat," supra chapter 7 note 54.
11. Interview with UNTAC senior official, 8 March 1993.
12. Interviews with UNTAC human rights component and Phnom Penh province officials, 10 March 1993.
13. Interviews with UNTAC civil administration component official, 4–5 March 1993.
14. See Nate Thayer, "Moaners beware," Far Eastern Economic Review, 5 November 1992, p. 27.

15. Interviews with UNTAC special assistants, 4, 8, and 10 March 1993.
16. Interviews with Singaporean and Indonesian officials, 22–25 February 1993.
17. Interview with Akashi, 19 March 1993.
18. Id.
19. Interview with UNTAC senior adviser, 5 March 1993.
20. See Doyle and Suntharalingam, supra note 5, p. 143 n.43 (quoting Akashi: "I cannot afford not to succeed.").
21. Interview with Akashi.
22. Interview with senior Western diplomat, 6 March 1993.
23. Interviews with UNTAC special assistant, senior civil administration component official, civil administration service chief, and human rights component official, 3, 10, and 15 March 1993.
24. Interview with UNTAC Phnom Penh province official, 8 March 1993.
25. Interviews with UNTAC provincial directors, 8 and 12 March 1993.
26. Interviews with UNTAC provincial directors, 8, 9, and 11 March 1993.
27. Interview with UNTAC rehabilitation component official, 17 March 1993.
28. Interview with Liberal Democratic Party official, 17 March 1993.
29. Interview with UNTAC senior human rights component official, 15 March 1993; see also van Boven (1991), supra chapter 2 note 88; David P. Forsythe, "The UN Secretary-General and Human Rights: The Question of Leadership in a Changing Context," in The Challenging Role of the UN Secretary-General, supra chapter 3 note 37, pp. 211–32.
30. Report of the Secretary-General on Cambodia, 19 February 1992, UN Doc. S/23613, p. 5.
31. Interviews with UNTAC information/education division official and provincial director, 6 and 12 March 1993.
32. Interviews with UNTAC special assistant and senior human rights component official, 10 and 15 March 1993.
33. Interview with UNTAC electoral component official, 19 March 1993.
34. Interviews with UNTAC human rights component officials, 3 and 15 March 1993.
35. Interviews with UNTAC civil administration component officials, 3, 8, and 10 March 1993.
36. Chanda, "UN divisions," supra chapter 7 note 35, p. 8.
37. Interviews with UNTAC human rights component officials, 3 and 15 March 1993. Compare Doyle and Suntharalingam, supra note 5, pp. 130–31 (distinguishing between actions UNTAC could take on its own and those requiring active cooperation of the factions).
38. Interviews with provincial human rights officer and special prosecutor, 13 and 15 March 1993.
39. SC Res. 766, 21 July 1992, UN SCOR, 47th Year, Res. and Dec., p. 41, UN Doc. S/INF/48; 783, 13 October 1992, id. p. 42; 792, 30 November 1992, id. p. 44; 810, 8 March 1993; 826, 20 May 1993; 835, 2 June 1993; 840, 15 June 1993; 860, 27 August 1993; and 880, 4 November 1993.
40. SC Res. 792, supra note 39, paras. 10, 12; Chanda, "Strained ties," supra chapter 7 note 37.
41. Interview with Akashi, 19 March 1993.
42. Interview with UNTAC repatriation component official, 17 March 1993.

Chapter 9

1. Such a recipe would include Boutros-Ghali's list in An Agenda for Peace, supra chapter 1 note 11, pp. 14–15: a clear and practicable mandate; the cooperation of the parties in implementing that mandate; the continuing support of the Security Council; the readiness of Member States to contribute the military, police and civilian personnel, including specialists, required; effective United Nations command at Headquarters and in the field; and adequate financial and logistic support.

2. Note by the President of the Security Council, 3 May 1994, UN Doc. S/PRST/1994/22 (identifying six "factors, among others. . . . [to] be taken into account").

3. U.S. Department of State, *The Clinton Administration's Policy on Reforming Multilateral Peace Operations, May 1994* (unclassified version of directive).

4. Id. pp. 3–4 (favoring peace enforcement only if threat to world peace is "significant").

5. See, for example, John Chipman, "Managing the Politics of Parochialism," in *Ethnic Conflict and International Security,* edited by Michael E. Brown (Princeton, NJ: Princeton University Press, 1993), pp. 237–63.

6. McDougal, Lasswell, and Reisman, supra chapter 2 note 51, pp. 191–92.

7. Declaration of Principles on Interim Self-Government Arrangements, 13 September 1993, Annex II, para. 3(d), 32 ILM 1527, 1536.

8. For a sample of recent essays on these questions, see *Emerging Norms of Justified Intervention: A Collection of Essays from a Project of the American Academy of Arts and Sciences,* edited by Laura W. Reed and Carl Kaysen (Cambridge, MA: American Academy of Arts and Sciences, 1993); Stephen John Stedman, "The New Interventionists," *Foreign Affairs* 72 (Winter 1993): 1–16; Richard Falk, "Intervention Revisited: Hard Choices and Tragic Dilemmas," *The Nation,* 20 December 1993, pp. 755–64; Michael Mandelbaum, "The Reluctance to Intervene," *Foreign Policy* 95 (Summer 1994): 3–18.

9. See, for example, Reports of the Special Committee on Peace-keeping Operations, 4 June 1992, UN Doc. A/47/253, and 25 May 1993, UN Doc. A/48/173; Special report of the Special Committee on Peace-keeping Operations, 31 August 1992, UN Doc. A/47/386; Implementation of the recommendations contained in "An Agenda for Peace": Report of the Secretary-General, 15 June 1993, UN Doc. A/47/965–S/25944; and 1994 Secretary-General Peacekeeping Report, supra chapter 1 note 18.

10. See *An Agenda for Peace,* supra chapter 1 note 11, pp. 8–9; Brian Urquhart, "For a UN Volunteer Military Force," *The New York Review of Books,* 10 June 1993, pp. 3–4; "A UN Volunteer Military Force–Four Views," *The New York Review of Books,* 24 June 1993, pp. 58–60 (responses to Urquhart's proposal); "A UN Volunteer Force–The Prospects," *The New York Review of Books,* 15 July 1993, pp. 52–56 (more responses). To its credit, the General Assembly has given heightened attention, in words at least, to the nonmilitary aspects of peacekeeping through its annual resolution entitled "Comprehensive review of the whole question of peace-keeping in all their aspects." See, for example, GA Res. 48/42, UN GAOR, 48th Sess., Supp. No. 49, p. 115, 1993.

11. Keith B. Richburg, "U.N. Force Reasserts Clout in Somalia," *The Washington Post,* 7 July 1993, p. A27 (comments of U.S. Army Colonel Ed Ward).

12. For an excellent proposal for restructuring the Secretariat, see Brian Urquhart and Erskine Childers, "Towards a More Effective United Nations: Two Studies," 1991 *Development Dialogue* (1991): 1–93. For two recent proposals on UN financing, see Ford Foundation, *Financing an Effective United Nations: A Report of the Independent Advisory Group on U.N. Financing* (New York: The Ford Foundation, 1993), and Schoettle, supra chapter 3 note 34. See also Joachim W. Müller, *The Reform of the United Nations,* 2 vols. (New York: Oceana Publications, 1992) (describing reform process in late 1980s through the "Group of 18").

13. Among the best are Urquhart and Childers, supra note 12.

14. For a review of structural changes undertaken by Boutro-Ghali, see Restructuring and efficiency of the Secretariat: Report of the Secretary-General, 29 September 1993, UN Doc. A/48/428.

15. Interviews with Brian Urquhart and Martti Ahtisaari, 25 November and 4 December 1992.

16. Interviews with Kofi Annan and Iqbal Riza, 17 November 1992 and 28 October 1993.

17. See 1994 Secretary-General Peacekeeping Report, supra chapter 1 note 18, p. 9 (describing relation between DPKO and DPA).

18. See id. p. 10 (endorsing this concept).
19. See Urquhart and Childers, supra note 12, pp. 20–35.
20. See 1992 UN Election Report, supra chapter 2 note 53, and 1993 UN Election Report, supra chapter 7 note 71.
21. GA Res. 46/137, UN GAOR, 46th Sess., Supp. No. 49, p. 209, UN Doc. A/46/49, 1991.
22. See 1992 UN Election Report, supra chapter 2 note 53, p. 16, and 1993 UN Election Report, supra chapter 7 note 71, pp. 16–21, in which the Secretary-General discusses the evolving guidelines for UN electoral involvement.
23. Interview with Martti Ahtisaari, 4 December 1992.
24. See 1994 Secretary-General Peacekeeping Report, supra chapter 1 note 18, p. 11.
25. For reports from 21 states on their mostly military training, see Training for peace-keeping: Note by the Secretary-General, 14 December 1993, UN Doc. A/48/708.
26. Interview with UNTAC military component official, 16 March 1993.
27. I thank Stephen Heder for originally mentioning this idea. Compare W. Michael Reisman, "Preparing to Wage Peace: Toward the Creation of an International Peacemaking Command and Staff College," American Journal of International Law 88 (1994): 76–78.
28. Interview with UNTAC provincial director, 8 March 1993.
29. In 1993, in its most detailed position on this question, the General Assembly simply reiterated that training "is primarily the responsibility of Member States" and endorsed a very limited role for the Secretariat. GA Res. 48/42, supra note 10, paras. 45–51.
30. For recent proposals in this regard, see Amnesty International, Peace Keeping and Human Rights (New York: Amnesty International USA, 1994).
31. Interviews with officials at the UN Centre for Human Rights, 7–8 December 1992; see also David P. Forsythe, supra chapter 8 note 29, pp. 211, 225–27. Indeed, Secretary-General Waldheim moved the Centre to Geneva in order to remove it from the political and media spotlight of the UN's political center.
32. Interviews with officials from UN Centre for Human Rights.
33. Vienna Declaration and Programme of Action, 25 June 1993, Part II, paras. 13–16, 32 ILM 1661, 1675; GA Res. 47/127, UN GAOR, 47th Sess., Supp. No. 49, p. 201, UN Doc. A/47/49, 1992; GA Res. 48/129, UN GAOR, 48th Sess., Supp. No. 49, p. 248, UN Doc A/48/49, 1993.
34. GA Res. 48/141, UN GAOR, 48th Sess., Supp. No. 49, p. 261, UN Doc. A/48/49, 1993.
35. Some of these have been mentioned by the Special Committee on Peace-keeping Operations in recent reports, for example, 1992 Report of the Special Committee on Peace-keeping Operations, supra note 9, p. 26; in An Agenda for Peace, supra chapter 1 note 11, p. 21; and by the General Assembly, for example, in GA Res. 48/42, supra note 10, para. 14.
36. The Deputy Special Representative for Namibia, Cedric Thornberry, began, but as of this date had not completed, a comprehensive report on UNTAG that combined elements of both types of reports. Draft UNTAG Report, supra chapter 5 note 6.
37. For more on these groupings, see Peter R. Baehr and Leon Gordenker, The United Nations: Reality and Ideal (New York: Praeger, 1984), pp. 51–60.
38. Report on the Saar Basin Governing Commission, supra chapter 4 note 10, p. 403.
39. UNEF II Rules, supra chapter 2 note 1, p. 91. See also Franck (1985), supra chapter 2 note 48, pp. 170–74 (background on UNEF II).
40. See, for example, GA Res. 48/124 and 48/131, supra chapter 2 note 36.
41. Final Document, in Tenth Conference of Heads of State or Government of Non-Aligned Countries, Jakarta, 1–6 September 1992: Basic Documents (Jakarta: PT Gramedia Pustaka Utama, 1992), pp. 23–24. Other parts of the Final Document, however, for example, id. p. 17, reaffirmed the NAM's position on sovereignty.
42. Interviews with Isslamet Poernomo and Nana Sutresna, 24 and 25 February 1993.
43. Interview with Kofi Annan, 17 November 1992.

44. Interview with Nana Sutresna, 25 February 1993.
45. See Final Document, supra note 41, pp. 23–26 (under the heading "Restructuring, Revitalization, and Democratization of the United Nations").
46. See Reisman (1993), supra chapter 3 note 19, pp. 98–99 (relying on Article 12(2) of the Charter, which requires the Secretary-General, with the consent of the Security Council, to notify the General Assembly of issues the Council is considering). See also 3 May 1994 Note by the President of the Security Council, supra note 2, para. 4 (favoring monthly consultations).
47. See GA Res. 47/62, UN GAOR, 47th Sess., Supp. No. 49, p. 25, UN Doc. A/47/49, 1992; GA Res. 48/26, UN GAOR, 48th Sess., Supp. No. 49, p. 29, UN Doc. A/48/49, 1993. For some of the proposals, see Question of Equitable Representation on and Increase in the Membership of the Security Council: Report of the Secretary-General, 20 July 1993, UN Doc. A/48/264.
48. See Leo Muray, "Enlarging the UN Security Council," Contemporary Review 263 (1993): 182–85.
49. Xinhua News Agency Report, 30 September 1992 (available through NEXIS Asia-Pacific All News file); Question of Equitable Representation on and Increase in the Membership of the Security Council: Report of the Secretary-General, 26 July 1993, A/48/264/Add.1, p. 8 (Indonesian submission to Secretary-General).
50. For a critique of current proposals for reform of the Council and increased Assembly involvement as failing to address the legitimacy of Security Council action, see Caron, supra chapter 3 note 22, pp. 566–76.
51. See John MacKinlay and Jarat Chopra, A Draft Concept of Second Generation Multinational Operations 1993 (Providence, RI: Thomas J. Watson Jr. Institute for International Studies, 1993); James S. Sutterlin, Military Force in the Service of Peace, Aurora Papers No. 18 (Ottawa: Canadian Centre for Global Security, 1993).
52. Interview with UNTAC electoral component official, 8 March 1993.
53. See Doyle and Suntharalingam, supra chapter 8 note 5, pp. 130–31.
54. For a proposal to stretch consensual peacekeeping even more, see Elgin Clemons, "No Peace to Keep: Six and Three-Quarters Peacekeepers," New York University Journal of International Law and Politics 24 (1993): 107, 139–41.
55. Interview with James Schear, 24 May 1993.
56. An Agenda for Peace, supra chapter 1 note 11, pp. 19–21; Ford Foundation, supra note 12. See also Paul Lewis, "United Nations Is Finding Its Plate Increasingly Full but Its Cupboard Is Bare," The New York Times, 27 September 1993, p. A4; Analysis of the financial situation of the United Nations: Report of the Secretary-General, 18 October 1993, UN Doc. A/48/503 [hereinafter 1993 Financial Situation Report]; Financing an effective United Nations: A Report of the Independent Advisory Group on United Nations Financing: Report of the Secretary-General, 2 November 1993, UN Doc. A/48/565 (response to Ogata-Volcker report).
57. See Paul Lewis, "The Peacekeeper in Chief Needs More Soldiers," The New York Times, 4 March 1994, p. A4.
58. See 1993 Financial Situation Report, supra note 56, pp. 8–10, 23–24.
59. Interviews with UNTAC electoral component officials, 8 and 16 March 1993.
60. See 1993 Financial Situation Report, supra note 56, p. 10. The Ford Foundation study recommends a $400 million fund, Ford Foundation, supra note 12, pp. 18–19; and Boutros-Ghali $800 million, 1994 Secretary-General Peacekeeping Report, supra chapter 1 note 18, p. 14.
61. See An Agenda for Peace, supra chapter 1 note 11, p. 21; Ford Foundation, supra note 12, pp. 12–13, 20–21.
62. See The Clinton Administration's Policy on Reforming Multilateral Peace Operations, supra note 3, p. 6.
63. GA Res. 48/218B, 1994.

64. See William Branigin, "Missteps on the Path to Peace: Problems Mount and Budgets Soar," *The Washington Post*, 22 September 1992, pp. A1, A14; Public Law 103–317, 26 August 1994, Titles V and VII (appropriating approximately $1.2 billion to pay off U.S. arrearages as of 1994, but falling short of amount needed to fund 1995 bills).

65. Boutros-Ghali seemed to be highlighting this prospect by the middle of 1994. See Letter dated 7 July 1994 from the Secretary-General addressed to the President of the Security Council, 19 July 1994, UN Doc. S/1994/845 (warning of a "financial collapse").

Chapter 10

1. Brian Urquhart, "International Peace and Security: Thoughts on the Twentieth Anniversary of Dag Hammarskjold's Death," *Foreign Affairs* 60 (Fall 1981): 1, 3. See also Brian Urquhart, "Who Can Police the World?" *The New York Review of Books*, 12 May 1994, pp. 29, 33.

2. Interview with UNTAC senior official, 8 March 1993.

3. For reflections on this idea, see Helman and Ratner, supra chapter 2 note 40. In a May 1994 press conference, Boutros-Ghali noted that the UN has offered personnel to help govern such failed states, but added that "unless there is the agreement of the Member States . . . we will be accused of neocolonialism." UN Press Release SG/SM/5297, 25 May 1994.

4. For some of the growing body of commentary on this question, see Hall, supra chapter 3 note 59; Comments of W. Michael Reisman on panel entitled "A Constitutional Crisis at the United Nations? Checks and Balances for the Security Council after the Cold War," at the Annual Meeting of the American Branch of the International Law Association, New York, 28 October 1993.

5. As the UN's commander in Bosnia stated in December 1993, "There is a fantastic gap between the resolutions of the Security Council, the will to execute those resolutions and the means available to commanders in the field." "U.N. Bosnia Commander Wants More Troops, Fewer Resolutions," supra chapter 3 note 61.

6. See Stedman, supra chapter 9 note 8.

7. I appreciate insights from Kishore Mahbubani on the idea of an exhausted people.

8. Interviews with Horacio Boneo and Martti Ahtisaari, 11 November and 4 December 1992.

B·I·B·L·I·O·G·R·A·P·H·Y

The following bibliography is divided into sources concerning the United Nations and related topics and those concerning Cambodia and UNTAC. Except for a handful of book-length publications, it does not include official documents of international organizations or governments, which are identified in the footnotes. Where the footnotes include citations to several separately authored chapters of one book, only the book and its editor(s) are listed. Finally, for newspapers or news weeklies, only the name of the periodical is noted, except for lengthy or noteworthy essays in weekly magazines.

A. UNITED NATIONS, INTERNATIONAL LAW, AND RELATED SUBJECTS

Books and Articles

Abi-Saab, Georges. *The United Nations Operation in the Congo 1960–1964*. Oxford: Oxford University Press, 1978.

———. "La deuxième génération des opérations de maintien de la paix." *Le Trimestre du Monde* 1992/4 (November 1992): 87–97.

Americas Watch. *El Salvador: Peace and Human Rights: Successes and Shortcomings of the United Nations Observer Mission in El Salvador (ONUSAL)*. New York: Americas Watch, 1992.

Amnesty International. *Peace Keeping and Human Rights*. New York: Amnesty International USA, 1994.

Baehr, Peter R., and Gordenker, Leon. *The United Nations: Reality and Ideal*. New York: Praeger, 1984.

Bailey, Sydney D. *How Wars End: The United Nations and the Termination of Armed Conflict 1945–1964 Volume I*. Oxford: Clarendon Press, 1982.

———. *The Procedure of the UN Security Council*, 2nd ed. Oxford: Clarendon Press, 1988.

Bar-Yaacov. Nissim. *The Handling of International Disputes by Means of Inquiry*. New York: Oxford University Press, 1974.

Beigbeder, Yves. *International Monitoring of Plebiscites, Referenda and National Elections: Self-determination and Transition to Democracy*. Dordrecht: Martinus Nijhoff Publishers, 1994.

Beitz, Charles R. "Recent international thought." *International Journal* 43 (1988): 183–204.

Boutros-Ghali, Boutros. "L'Onu en Première Ligne." *Politique Internationale* 57 (Autumn 1992): 143–49.

Bowett, Derek W. *United Nations Forces: A Legal Study*. New York: Frederick A. Praeger, Publishers, 1964.

Brierly, J. L. *The Law of Nations: An Introduction to the International Law of Peace*, 6th ed. Edited by Sir Humphrey Waldock. Oxford: Clarendon Press, 1963.

Burton, John W. "Resolution of Conflict." *International Studies Quarterly* 16 (1972): 5–29.

Caminos, Hugo, and Lavalle, Roberto. "New Departures in the Exercise of Inherent Powers by the UN and OAS Secretaries-General: The Central American Situation." *American Journal of International Law* 83 (1989): 395–402.

Caron, David D. "The Legitimacy of the Collective Authority of the Security Council." *American Journal of International Law* 87 (1993): 552–88.

Cassese, A., ed. *United Nations Peace-Keeping: Legal Essays*. Alphen aan den Rijn: Sijthoff & Noordhoff, 1978.

Chipman, John. "Managing the Politics of Parochialism." Chap. 12 in *Ethnic Conflict and International Security*. Edited by Michael E. Brown. Princeton, NJ: Princeton University Press, 1993.

Claude, Inis L. Jr. *Swords into Plowshares: The Problems and Progress of International Organization*, 4th ed. New York: Random House, 1971.

Clemons, Elgin. "No Peace to Keep: Six and Three-Quarters Peacekeepers." *New York University Journal of International Law and Politics* 26 (1993): 107–41.

Cordier, Andrew W., and Foote, Wilder, eds. *Public Papers of the Secretaries-General of the United Nations: Dag Hammarskjold 1958–1960*. New York: Columbia University Press, 1974.

Cot, Jean-Pierre, and Pellet, Alain, eds. *La Charte des Nations Unies*, 2nd ed. Paris: Economica, 1991.

Damrosch, Lori F. "Politics Across Borders: Nonintervention and Nonforcible Influence over Domestic Affairs." *American Journal of International Law* 83 (1989): 1–50.

————, ed. *Enforcing Restraint: Collective Intervention in Internal Conflicts*. New York: Council on Foreign Relations Press, 1993.

Dayal, Rajeshwar. *Mission for Hammarskjold: The Congo Crisis*. Princeton, NJ: Princeton University Press, 1976.

de Soto, Alvaro, and del Castillo, Graciana. "Obstacles to Peacebuilding." *Foreign Policy* 94 (Spring 1994): 69–83.

Diehl, Paul F. "When Peacekeeping Does Not Lead to Peace: Some Notes on Conflict Resolution." *Bulletin of Peace Proposals* 18 (1987): 47–52.

————. "Peacekeeping Operations and the Quest for Peace." *Political Science Quarterly* 103 (1988): 485–507.

————. *International Peacekeeping*. Baltimore: Johns Hopkins University Press, 1993.

Diehl, Paul F., and Kumar, Chetan. "Mutual Benefits from International Intervention: New Roles for United Nations Peace-keeping Forces." *Bulletin of Peace Proposals* 22 (1991): 369–75.

Dobbie, Charles. "A Concept for Post-Cold War Peacekeeping." *Survival* 36 (Autumn 1994): 121–48.

Doyle, Michael W. "Liberalism and World Politics." *American Political Science Review* 80 (1986): 1151–69.

Durch, William J., ed. *The Evolution of UN Peacekeeping: Case Studies and Comparative Analysis*. New York: St. Martin's Press, 1993.

Evans, Gareth. *Cooperating for Peace*. St. Leonards: Allen & Unwin, 1993.

Falk, Richard. "Intervention Revisited: Hard Choices and Tragic Dilemmas." *The Nation*, 20 December 1993, pp. 755–764.

Foote, Wilder, ed. *Servant of Peace: A Selection of the Speeches and Statements of Dag Hammarskjold, Secretary-General of the United Nations 1953–1961*. New York: Harper and Row, 1962.

Ford Foundation. *Financing an Effective United Nations: A Report of the Independent Advisory Group on U.N. Financing*. New York: The Ford Foundation, 1993.

Fortna, Virginia Page. *Regional Organizations and Peacekeeping: Experiences in Latin America and Africa*. Washington, DC: Henry L. Stimson Center Occasional Paper No. 11, 1993.

Fox, Gregory H. "The Right to Political Participation in International Law." *Yale Journal of International Law* 17 (1992): 539–607.

Franck, Thomas M. *Nation Against Nation: What Happened to the U.N. Dream and What the U.S. Can Do About It*. New York: Oxford University Press, 1985.

————. "The Emerging Right to Democratic Governance." *American Journal of International Law* 86 (1992): 46–91.

————. "The 'Powers of Appreciation': Who Is the Ultimate Guardian of UN Legality?" *American Journal of International Law* 86 (1992): 519–23.

Ghébali, Victor-Yves. "Le développement des opérations de maintien de la paix de l'ONU depuis la fin de la guerre froide." *Le Trimestre du Monde* 1992/4 (November 1992): 67–85.

Goodrich, Leland M., Hambro, Edvard, and Simons, Anne P. *The Charter of the United Nations: Commentary and Documents*, 3rd rev. ed. New York: Columbia University Press, 1969.

Gordenker, Leon. *The UN Secretary-General and the Maintenance of Peace*. New York: Columbia University Press, 1967.

Gordon, Edward. "Resolution of the Bahrain Dispute." *American Journal of International Law* 65 (1971): 560–68.

Gottlieb, Gidon. *Nation Against State: A New Approach to Ethnic Conflicts and the Decline of Sovereignty.* New York: Council on Foreign Relations Press, 1993.

Goulding, Marrack. "The Evolution of United Nations Peacekeeping." *International Affairs* 69 (1993): 451–64.

Gurr, Ted Robert. *Minorities at Risk: A Global View of Ethnopolitical Conflicts.* Washington, DC: United States Institute of Peace Press, 1993.

Haas, Ernst B. "Regime Decay: Conflict Management and International Organizations, 1945–1981." *International Organization* 37 (1983): 189–256.

Hall, Brian. "Blue Helmets, Empty Guns." *The New York Times Magazine,* 2 January 1994.

Halperin, Morton H. "Guaranteeing Democracy." *Foreign Policy* 91 (Summer 1993): 105–122.

Halperin, Morton H., and Scheffer, David J. *Self-Determination in the New World Order.* Washington, DC: Carnegie Endowment for International Peace, 1992.

Hannum, Hurst. *Autonomy, Sovereignty, and Self-Determination: The Accommodation of Conflicting Rights.* Philadelphia: University of Pennsylvania Press, 1990.

Harrelson, Max. *Fires All Around the Horizon: The U.N.'s Uphill Battle to Preserve the Peace.* New York: Praeger Publishers, 1989.

Helman, Gerald B., and Ratner, Steven R. "Saving Failed States." *Foreign Policy* 89 (Winter 1992–93): 3–20.

Henkin, Louis. "International Law: Politics, Values and Functions." *Recueil des Cours* 216 (1989 IV): 13–416.

Higgins, Rosalyn. *The Development of International Law Through the Political Organs of the United Nations.* London: Oxford University Press, 1963.

———. *United Nations Peacekeeping 1946–67: Documents and Commentary,* 4 vols. London: Oxford University Press, 1969, 1970, 1980, 1981.

———. "The New United Nations and the Former Yugoslavia." *International Affairs* 69 (1993): 465–83.

Hodgson, Mélida N. "When to Accept, When to Abstain: A Framework for U.N. Election Monitoring." *New York University Journal of International Law and Politics* 25 (1992): 137–73.

Holiday, David, and Stanley, William. "Building the Peace: Preliminary Lessons from El Salvador." *Journal of International Affairs* 46 (1993): 415–38.

House, Arthur H. *The U.N. in the Congo: The Political and Civilian Efforts.* Washington, DC: University Press of America, 1978.

Iklé, Fred Charles. *How Nations Negotiate.* New York: Harper and Row, 1964.

Jacobson, Harold Karan. "ONUC's Civilian Operations: State-Preserving and State-Building." *World Politics* 17 (1964): 75–107.

James, Alan M. "Unit Veto Dominance in United Nations Peace-Keeping." Chap. 3 in *Politics in the United Nations System.* Edited by Lawrence F. Finkelstein. Durham, NC: Duke University Press, 1988.

———. *Peacekeeping in International Politics.* New York: St. Martin's Press, 1990.

Jennings, Sir Robert, and Watts, Arthur, eds. *Oppenheim's International Law,* 9th ed. Harlow: Longman, 1992.

Jensen, Erik. "The Secretary-General's Use of Good Offices and the Question of Bahrain." *Millenium* 14 (1985): 335–48.

Kamminga, Menno T. *Inter-State Accountability for Violations of Human Rights.* Philadelphia: University of Pennsylvania Press, 1992.

Keohane, Robert O. "Realism, Neorealism and the Study of World Politics." Chap. 1 in *Neorealism and Its Critics.* Edited by Robert O. Keohane. New York: Columbia University Press, 1986.

Keohane, Robert O., and Nye, Joseph S. *Power and Interdependence: World Politics in Transition.* Boston: Little, Brown, 1977.

Khadduri, Majid. *Modern Libya: A Study in Political Development.* Baltimore: Johns Hopkins University Press, 1963.

Lalande, Serge. "Somalia: Major Issues for Future UN Peace-keeping." Paper prepared for International Colloquium on New Dimensions of Peace-keeping, Graduate Institute of International Studies, Geneva, 10–11 March 1994.

Lall, Arthur. *Modern International Negotiation: Principles and Practice.* New York: Columbia University Press, 1966.

Leonhardt, Hans L. *Nazi Conquest of Danzig.* Chicago: University of Chicago Press, 1942.

Leurdijk, Dick A. "Fact-Finding: The Revitalization of a Dutch Initiative in the UN." *Bulletin of Peace Proposals* 21 (1990): 59–69.

Luard, Evan. *A History of the United Nations,* 2 vols. New York: St. Martin's Press, 1982, 1989.

Luck, Edward C. "Making Peace." *Foreign Policy* 89 (Winter 1992–93): 137–55.

MacKinlay, John, and Chopra, Jarat. "Second Generation Multinational Operations." *The Washington Quarterly* 15 (Summer 1992): 113–31.

———. *A Draft Concept of Second Generation Multinational Operations 1993.* Providence, RI: Thomas J. Watson Jr. Institute for International Studies, 1993.

Makinda, Samuel M. *Seeking Peace from Chaos: Humanitarian Intervention in Somalia.* Boulder, CO: Lynne Rienner Publishers, 1993.

Mandelbaum, Michael. "The Reluctance to Intervene." *Foreign Policy* 95 (Summer 1994): 3–18.

Maynes, Charles William. "Containing Ethnic Conflict." *Foreign Policy* 90 (Spring 1993): 3–21.

McDonald, Robert. *The Problem of Cyprus,* Aldelphi Paper No. 234. London: International Institute for Strategic Studies, 1989.

McDougal, Myres S., Lasswell, Harold D., and Miller, James C. *The Interpretation of Agreements and World Public Order: Principles of Content and Procedure.* New Haven, CT: Yale University Press, 1967.

McDougal, Myres S., Lasswell, Harold D., and Chen, Lung-Chu. *Human Rights and World Public Order.* New Haven, CT: Yale University Press, 1980.

McDougal, Myres S., Lasswell, Harold D., and Reisman, W. Michael. "The World Constitutive Process of Authoritative Decision." In *International Law Essays: A Supplement to International Law in Contemporary Perspective.* Edited by Myres S. McDougal and W. Michael Reisman. Mineola, NY: The Foundation Press, 1981.

Meron, Theodor. *The United Nations Secretariat: The Rules and the Practice.* Lexington, MA: Lexington Books, 1977.

Miller, E. M. "Legal Aspects of the United Nations Action in the Congo." *American Journal of International Law* 55 (1961): 1–28.

Morphet, Sally. "Resolutions and Vetoes in the UN Security Council: Their Relevance and Significance." *Review of International Studies* 16 (1990): 341–59.

Morrow, Ian F. D. "The International Status of the Free City of Danzig." *British Year Book of International Law* 18 (1937): 114–26.

Müller, Joachim W. *The Reform of the United Nations,* 2 vols. New York: Oceana Publications, 1992.

Muray, Leo. "Enlarging the UN Security Council." *Contemporary Review* 263 (1993): 182–85.

National Democratic Institute for International Affairs. *Nation Building: The U.N. and Namibia.* Washington, DC: National Democratic Institute for International Affairs, 1990.

Northedge, F. S. *The League of Nations: its life and times 1920–1946.* Leicester: Leicester University Press, 1986.

Novicki, Margaret A. "A New Agenda for the OAU: Salim Ahmed Salim." *Africa Report* (May/June 1992): 36–39.

O'Brien, Conor Cruise, and Topolski, Feliks. *The United Nations: Sacred Drama.* New York: Simon & Schuster, 1968.

Padilla, David, and Houppert, Elizabeth. "International Election Observing: Enhancing the Principle of Free and Fair Elections." *Emory International Law Review* 7 (1993): 73–132.

Pelt, Adrian. *Libyan Independence and the United Nations: A Case of Planned Decolonization.* New Haven, CT: Yale University Press, 1970.

Peterson, M. J. *The General Assembly in World Politics.* Boston: Allen & Unwin, 1986.
Raman, K. Venkata, ed. *Dispute Settlement Through the United Nations.* Dobbs Ferry, NY: Oceana Publications, 1977.
Ramcharan, B. G. "The Good Offices of the United Nations Secretary-General in the Field of Human Rights." *American Journal of International Law* 76 (1982): 130–41.
Reed, Laura W., and Kaysen, Carl, eds. *Emerging Norms of Justified Intervention: A Collection of Essays from a Project of the American Academy of Arts and Sciences.* Cambridge, MA: American Academy of Arts and Sciences, 1993.
Reisman, W. Michael. "Private Armies in a Global War System: Prologue to Decision." *Virginia Journal of International Law* 14 (1973): 1–55.
———. "Sovereignty and Human Rights in Contemporary International Law." *American Journal of International Law* 84 (1990): 866–76.
———. "The Constitutional Crisis in the United Nations." *American Journal of International Law* 87 (1993): 83–100.
———. "Preparing to Wage Peace: Toward the Creation of an International Peacemaking Command and Staff College." *American Journal of International Law* 88 (1994): 76–78.
Rikhye, Indar Jit. *The Theory and Practice of Peacekeeping.* New York: St. Martin's Press, 1984.
Rikhye, Indar Jit, and Skjelsbaek, Kjell, eds. *The United Nations and Peacekeeping: Results, Limitations and Prospects: The Lessons of 40 Years of Experience.* New York: St. Martin's Press, 1991.
Rivlin, Benjamin. "Regional Arrangements and the UN System for Collective Security and Conflict Resolution: A New Road Ahead?" *International Relations* 11 (1992): 95–110.
Rivlin, Benjamin, and Gordenker, Leon, eds. *The Challenging Role of the UN Secretary-General: Making "The Most Impossible Job in the World" Possible.* Westport, CT: Praeger, 1993.
Roberts, Adam. "The Crisis in UN Peacekeeping." *Survival* 36 (Autumn 1994): 93–120.
Roberts, Adam, and Kingsbury, Benedict, eds. *United Nations, Divided World.* Oxford: Clarendon Press, 1988.
Rovine, Arthur W. *The First Fifty Years: The Secretary-General in World Politics 1920–1970.* Leyden: A. W. Sythoff, 1970.
Rubin, Jeffrey Z., ed. *Dynamics of Third Party Intervention: Kissinger in the Middle East.* New York, Praeger, 1981.
Sabki, Hisham M. *The United Nations and The Pacific Settlement of Disputes: A Case Study of Libya.* Beirut: Dar el-Mashreq, 1970.
Schachter, Oscar. "The Twilight Existence of Nonbinding International Agreements." *American Journal of International Law* 71 (1977): 296–304.
Schoettle, Enid C. B. "Financing UN Peacekeeping." In *Keeping the Peace in the Post-Cold War Era: Strengthening Multilateral Peacekeeping.* New York: The Trilateral Commission, 1993.
Schwebel, Stephen M. *The Secretary-General of the United Nations: His Political Powers and Practice.* Cambridge, MA: Harvard University Press, 1952.
Sherry, George L. "The United Nations, International Conflict, and American Security." *Political Science Quarterly* 101 (1986): 753–71.
Siekmann, Robert C. R. *National Contingents in United Nations Peace-Keeping Forces.* Dordrecht: Martinus Nijhoff, 1991.
Skjelsbaek, Kjell. "Peaceful Settlement of Disputes by the United Nations and Other Intergovernmental Bodies." *Cooperation and Conflict* 21 (1986): 139–54.
Sohn, Louis. *Case on United Nations Law,* 2nd ed. Brooklyn, NY: The Foundation Press, 1967.
Stedman, Stephen John. "The New Interventionists." *Foreign Affairs* 72 (Winter 1993): 1–16.
Stiles, Kendall W., and MacDonald, Maryellen. "After Consensus, What?: Performance Criteria for the UN in the Post-Cold War Era." *Journal of Peace Research* 29 (1992): 299–311.

Stoelting, David. "The Challenge of UN-Monitored Elections in Independent Nations." *Stanford Journal of International Law* 28 (1992): 371–424.

Sutterlin, James S. *Military Force in the Service of Peace,* Aurora Papers No. 18. Ottowa: Canadian Centre for Global Security, 1993.

Szasz, Paul C. "The Role of the U.N. Secretary-General: Some Legal Aspects." *New York University Journal of International Law and Politics* 24 (1991): 161–98.

Tenth Conference of Heads of State or Government of Non-Aligned Countries, Jakarta, 1–6 September 1992: Basic Documents. Jakarta: PT Gramedia Pustaka Utama, 1992.

Tessitore, John, and Woolfson, Susan, eds. *A Global Agenda: Issues Before the 48th General Assembly of the United Nations.* Lanham, MD: University Press of America, 1993.

Touval, Saadia. *The Peace Brokers: Mediators in the Arab-Israeli Conflict, 1948–1979.* Princeton, NJ: Princeton University Press, 1982.

———. "Why the U.N. Fails." *Foreign Affairs* 73 (September/October 1994): 44–57.

Touval, Saadia, and Zartman, I. William, eds. *International Mediation in Theory and Practice.* Boulder, CO: Westview Press, 1985.

United Nations. *The Blue Helmets: A Review of United Nations Peace-keeping,* 2nd ed. New York: United Nations, 1990, UN Sales No. E.90.I.18.

United Nations Office of Legal Affairs. *Handbook on the Peaceful Settlement of Disputes.* New York: United Nations, 1992, UN Sales No. E.92.V.7, UN Doc. OLA/COD/2394.

Urquhart, Brian. *Hammarskjold.* New York: Alfred A. Knopf, 1972.

———. "International Peace and Security: Thoughts on the Twentieth Anniversary of Dag Hammarskjold's Death." *Foreign Affairs* 60 (Fall 1981): 1–16.

———. "The United Nations System and the Future." *International Affairs* 65 (1989): 225–31.

———. *Ralph Bunche: An American Life.* New York: W.W. Norton & Company, 1993.

———. "For a UN Volunteer Military Force." *The New York Review of Books,* 10 June 1993, pp. 3–4; responses in 24 June 1993, pp. 58–60, and 15 July 1993, pp. 52–56.

———. "Who Can Police the World?" *The New York Review of Books,* 12 May 1994, pp. 29–33.

Urquhart, Brian, and Childers, Erskine. "Towards a More Effective United Nations: Two Studies." *Development Dialogue* 1991 (1992): 1–93.

van Boven, Theo. "The Role of the United Nations Secretariat in the Area of Human Rights." *New York University Journal of International Law and Politics* 24 (1991): 69–107.

———. "The Security Council: The New Frontier." *International Commission of Jurists: The Review* 48 (1992): 12–23.

van Haegendoren, Geert. "International Election Monitoring." *Belgian Review of International Law* 20 (1987): 86–123.

Väyrynen, Raimo. "The United Nations and the Resolution of International Conflicts." *Cooperation and Conflict* 20 (1985): 141–71.

Wainhouse, David W. *International Peace Observation: A History and Forecast.* Baltimore: Johns Hopkins University Press, 1966.

———. *International Peacekeeping at the Crossroads: National Support—Experience and Prospects.* Baltimore: Johns Hopkins University Press, 1973.

Walters, F. P. *A History of the League of Nations,* 2 vols. London: Oxford University Press, 1952.

Wambaugh, Sarah. *Plebiscites Since the World War, with a Collection of Documents,* 2 vols. Washington, DC: Carnegie Endowment for International Peace, 1933.

———. *The Saar Plebiscite, with a Collection of Official Documents.* Cambridge, MA: Harvard University Press, 1940.

Webster, Donovan. "One Leg, One Life at a Time." *The New York Times Magazine,* 23 January 1994.

Weiss, Thomas G., and Kessler, Meryl A. "Resurrecting Peacekeeping: The Superpowers and Conflict Management." *Third World Quarterly* 12 (1990): 124–46.

White, N. D. *Keeping the Peace: The United Nations and the Maintenance of International Peace and Security.* Manchester: Manchester University Press, 1993.

Whomersky, C. A. "The International Legal Status of Gdansk, Klaipeda and the former East Prussia." *International and Comparative Law Quarterly* 42 (1993): 919–28.

Wright, John L. *Libya: A Modern History.* Baltimore: Johns Hopkins University Press, 1982.

Ydit, Méir. *Internationalised Territories: From the "Free City of Cracow" to the "Free City of Berlin."* Leyden: A. W. Sythoff, 1961.

Young, Oran R. *The Intermediaries: Third Parties in International Crises.* Princeton, NJ: Princeton University Press, 1967.

——. "Intermediaries: additional thoughts on third parties." *Journal of Conflict Resolution* 16 (1972): 51–65.

Zacher, Mark W. *Dag Hammarskjold's United Nations.* New York: Columbia University Press, 1970.

Zartman, I. William, and Berman, Maureen. *The Practical Negotiator.* New Haven, CT: Yale University Press, 1982.

Zimmern, Alfred. *The League of Nations and the Rule of Law 1918–1935.* London: MacMillan, 1939.

Newspapers
The New York Times.
The Washington Post.

B. CAMBODIA.

Books and Articles
Alagappa, Muthiah. "Regionalism and the Quest for Security: ASEAN and the Cambodian Conflict." *Journal of International Affairs* 46 (1993): 439–67.

Amer, Ramses. "The United Nations' Peacekeeping Operation In Cambodia: Overview and Assessment." *Contemporary Southeast Asia* 15 (1993): 211–231.

Asia Watch. *Political Control, Human Rights, and the UN Mission in Cambodia.* New York: Asia Watch (Division of Human Rights Watch), 1992.

——. *Cambodia: Human Rights Before and After the Elections.* New York: Asia Watch (Division of Human Rights Watch), 1993.

Australian Department of Foreign Affairs and Trade. *Cambodia: an Australian Peace Proposal: Working Papers prepared for the Informal Meeting on Cambodia, Jakarta, 26–28 February 1990.* Canberra: Australia Government Publishing Service, 1990.

Becker, Elizabeth. "Kampuchea in 1983: Further From Peace." *Asian Survey* 24 (1984): 37–48.

——. *When the War was Over: The Voices of Cambodia's Revolution and its People.* New York: Simon & Schuster, 1986.

——. "Up From Hell." Review of *The Tragedy of Cambodian History: Politics, War, and Revolution Since 1945,* by David P. Chandler. *The New Republic,* 17 February 1992, pp. 32–37.

"Cambodia: Elections in the Killing Fields." Chap. 8 in *Life, Death and Aid: The Médecins Sans Frontières Report on World Crisis Intervention.* Edited by François Jean. London: Routledge, 1993.

Carney, Timothy, and Choo, Tan Liam. *Whither Cambodia?: Beyond the Election.* Singapore: Institute of Southeast Asian Studies, 1993.

Chanda, Nayan. *Brother Enemy: The War after the War.* San Diego: Harcourt Brace Jovanovich, 1986.

——. "Civil War in Cambodia?" *Foreign Policy* 76 (Fall 1989): 26–43.

Chandler, David P. *The Tragedy of Cambodian History: Politics, War, and Revolution since 1945.* New Haven, CT: Yale University Press, 1991.

——. *A History of Cambodia,* 2nd ed. Boulder, CO: Westview Press, 1992.

——. *Brother Number One: A Political Biography of Pol Pot.* Boulder, CO: Westview Press, 1992.

Doyle, Michael W., and Suntharalingam, Nishkala. "The UN in Cambodia: Lessons for Complex Peacekeeping." *International Peacekeeping* 1 (1994): 117–43.
Federal Research Division, Library of Congress. *Cambodia: A Country Study.* Edited by Russell R. Ross. Washington, DC: U.S. Government Printing Office, 1990.
Foreign Broadcast Information Service, East Asia Daily Report.
Ghosh, Andrew. "Holiday in Cambodia: The U.N.'s strategic dead-end." *The New Republic,* 28 June 1993, pp. 21–25.
Hannum, Hurst. "International Law and Cambodian Genocide: The Sounds of Silence." *Human Rights Quarterly* 11 (1989): 82–138.
Jackson, Karl D., ed. *Cambodia 1975–1978: Rendezvous with Death.* Princeton, NJ: Princeton University Press, 1989.
Kiernan, Ben. *How Pol Pot Came to Power: A History of Communism in Kampuchea.* London: Verso, 1985.
————. "The Inclusion of the Khmer Rouge in the Cambodian Peace Process: Causes and Consequences." In *Genocide and Democracy in Cambodia: The Khmer Rouge, the United Nations and the International Community.* Edited by Ben Kiernan. New Haven, CT: Yale University Southeast Asia Studies, 1993.
Leifer, Michael. "Power-Sharing and Peacemaking in Cambodia?" *SAIS Review* 12 (Winter–Spring 1992): 139–53.
McAuliff, John and McDonnell, Mary Byrne. "Ending the Cambodian Stalemate." *World Policy Journal* 7 (1989/90): 71–105.
Mahbubani, Kishore. "The Kampuchean Problem: A Southeast Asian Perception." *Foreign Affairs* 62 (Winter 1983/84): 407–25.
Marks, Stephen P. "Forgetting 'The Policies and Practices of the Past': Impunity in Cambodia." *The Fletcher Forum* 18 (Summer/Fall 1994): 17–43.
Paribatra, M. R. Sukhumbhand. "Can ASEAN Break the Stalemate?" *World Policy Journal* 3 (1985): 85–106.
Peang-Meth, Abdulgaffar. "The United Nations Peace Plan, the Cambodian Conflict, and the Future of Cambodia." *Contemporary Southeast Asia* 14 (1992): 33–46.
Ponchaud, François. *Cambodia: Year Zero.* Translated by Nancy Amphoux. New York: Holt, Rinehart and Winston, 1978.
Ratner, Steven R. "The Cambodia Settlement Agreements." *American Journal of International Law* 87 (1993): 1–41.
Ross, Robert S. "China and the Cambodian Peace Process: The Value of Coercive Diplomacy." *Asian Survey* 31 (1991): 1170–85.
Sesser, Stan. "Report from Cambodia." *The New Yorker,* 18 May 1992.
Shawcross, William. *Sideshow: Kissinger, Nixon and the Destruction of Cambodia,* rev. ed. New York: Simon & Schuster, 1987.
————. "A New Cambodia." *The New York Review of Books,* 12 August 1993, pp. 37–41.
Smith, R. B. "Cambodia in the Context of Sino-Vietnamese Relations." *Asian Affairs* (London) 16 (1985): 273–87.
Sutter, Valerie O. *The Indochinese Refugee Dilemma.* Baton Rouge, LA: State University Press, 1990.
Thomas, Trisha. "Into the Unknown: Can the United Nations Bring Peace to Cambodia?" *Journal of International Affairs* 44 (1991): 495–515.
Van der Kroef, Justus M. "Cambodia: The Vagaries of 'Cocktail' Diplomacy." *Contemporary Southeast Asia* 19 (1988): 300–320.
Vickery, Michael. *Cambodia: 1975–1982.* Boston: South End, 1984.
————. *Kampuchea: Politics, Economics and Society.* London: F. Pinter, 1986.

Newspapers
The Bangkok Post.
The Far Eastern Economic Review.
The Financial Times.

I·N·T·E·R·V·I·E·W·S

A Word on Methodology

Interviews were used to supplement the research in parts I, II, and IV of this book and as a primary resource for chapters seven and eight in part III, the Cambodia case study. In those chapters, interviews are cited for those facts regarding UNTAC not generally available in the public realm as well as those perspectives on UNTAC attributable to the persons interviewed.

In most cases, interviewees' names are provided only in the following list, rather than in the individual endnotes, an approach most interviewees preferred in order not to have their remarks directly attributed to them. In those cases where interviewees agreed to speak on the record for all or part of their conversations, names are included in the appropriate endnotes. The bulk of the Cambodia-related interviews were conducted during a month-long trip to Southeast Asia in February and March 1993.

Judgments as to the credibility of all the interviewees are based on the author's own assessment in light of his knowledge and experiences. In my case, these experiences included service as legal adviser to the U.S. delegation to the Paris Conference on Cambodia from 1989-91, a position in which I worked closely on the development of U.S. government policy for the idea of UNTAC, directly participated in many negotiating sessions among the interested states and Cambodian factions (in Paris, Jakarta, New York, and Beijing), and served as one of a group of drafters of the Paris accords. For another three years, I followed the peace process at the State Department and the Council on Foreign Relations, conducting the interviews listed below and reading a wide range of publicly available sources on the peace process.

For those instances in which there was any possibility of disagreement over facts, I corroborated the statements of interviewees, although I often cite only the interviewee who made a particular point most fully and clearly. I assume, of course, full responsibility for the conclusions formed from these interviews.

List of Persons Interviewed

Interviewees are identified according to the position they held at the time of the interview and the location of the interview.

Rafeeuddin Ahmed, Executive Secretary and Under Secretary-General, United Nations Economic and Social Commission for Asia and the Pacific, Bangkok, Thailand

Salman Ahmed, Assistant Provincial Electoral Officer, Kompong Thom Province, UNTAC, Kompong Thom, Cambodia

Martti Ahtisaari, Chairman, Bosnia Working Group, International Conference on the Former Yugoslavia, Geneva

Yasushi Akashi, Special Representative of the Secretary-General, UNTAC, Phnom Penh, Cambodia

Christine Alfsen-Norodom, Rehabilitation and Economic Affairs, UNTAC, Phnom Penh, Cambodia

Hédi Annabi, Department of Peacekeeping Operations, United Nations, New York

Kofi Annan, Assistant Secretary-General for Peacekeeping Operations, United Nations, New York

Dewi Anwar, Researcher, Indonesian Institute of Sciences, Jakarta, Indonesia

Anthony Banbury, Human Rights Officer, Battambang Province, UNTAC, Battambang, Cambodia

Bantarto Bandoro, Head, Department of International Affairs, Centre for Strategic and International Studies, Jakarta, Indonesia

Elizabeth Becker, Journalist, Washington, D.C.

Jamel Benyamed, Chief of Provincial Coordination, Civil Administration Component, UNTAC, Phnom Penh, Cambodia

Horacio Boneo, Director, Electoral Assistance Unit, United Nations, New York

Timothy Carney, Director of Information and Education, UNTAC, Phnom Penh, Cambodia

Bernard Constantin, Chief, Public Security Service, Civil Administration Component, UNTAC, Phnom Penh, Cambodia

Ibrahim Deria, Financial Control Officer, Kampot Province, UNTAC, Kampot, Cambodia

Dr. Bruce Eshaya Chauvin, Medical Coordinator, International Committee of the Red Cross, Phnom Penh, Cambodia

Nicholas Etheridge, Resident Representative of Canada to the Supreme National Council, Phnom Penh, Cambodia

Eric Falt, Press Spokesman, UNTAC, Phnom Penh, Cambodia

Gustave Feissel, Director, Department of Political Affairs, United Nations, New York

Mary Fiske, Political Officer and Special Assistant to the Special Representative, UNTAC, Phnom Penh, Cambodia

Georges Gabore, Provincial Director, Ratanakiri Province, UNTAC, Phnom Penh, Cambodia

Georges Germanos, Provincial Director, Kampong Thom Province, UNTAC, Kampong Thom, Cambodia

Jose L. Gomez del Prado, Chief, ad interim, Advisory Services, Technical Assistance and Information Branch, UN Centre for Human Rights, Geneva

Dominique Guéret, Chief, Defence Service, Civil Administration Component, UNTAC, Phnom Penh, Cambodia

Osman Hassan, Electoral Officer, Kampot Province, UNTAC, Kampot, Cambodia

Stephen Heder, Deputy Director of Information and Education Rights, UNTAC, Phnom Penh, Cambodia

Michael Honnold, Economic Officer, Mission of the United States of America to the Supreme National Council of Cambodia, Phnom Penh, Cambodia

Ieng Mouly, Secretary-General of the Khmer People's Liberation Front, Phnom Penh, Cambodia

Janos Jelen, Deputy Provincial Director, Siem Reap Province, UNTAC, Siem Reap, Cambodia

Wojciech Kaluza, Chief, Foreign Affairs Service, Civil Administration Component, UNTAC, Phnom Penh, Cambodia

Ataul Karim, Political Adviser to the Special Representative, UNTAC, Phnom Penh, Cambodia

T. Kawakami, Senior Political Officer and Special Assistant to the Special Representative, UNTAC, Phnom Penh, Cambodia

Moncef Khane, Officer-in-Charge, Battambang Province, UNTAC, Battambang, Cambodia

Khieu Kanharith, Vice Minister, Council of Ministers, State of Cambodia, Phnom Penh, Cambodia

Rolf Knuttson, Political Officer, Department of Political Affairs, United Nations, New York

Tommy T. B. Koh, Ambassador-at-Large, Ministry of Foreign Affairs, Republic of Singapore

Vishakan Krishnadasan, Legal Adviser, UNTAC, Phnom Penh, Cambodia

Kusnadi Pudjiwinarto, Director for Asia and the Pacific, Department of Foreign Affairs, Jakarta, Indonesia

Mochtar Kusuma-Atmadja, Jakarta, Indonesia

Andrew Ladley, Assistant to the Director of Elections, UNTAC, Phnom Penh, Cambodia

David Lambertson, Ambassador of the United States of America to the Kingdom of Thailand, Bangkok, Thailand

Roger Lawrence, Economic Adviser to the Special Representative and Director of Rehabilitation, UNTAC, Phnom Penh, Cambodia

Antony Lydon, Provincial Director, Kampot Province, UNTAC, Kampot, Cambodia

Gianni Magazzeni, Special Assistant to the Under Secretary-General, United Nations, Geneva

Kishore Mahbubani, Deputy Permanent Secretary, Ministry of Foreign Affairs, Republic of Singapore

Michael Maley, Deputy Director of Elections, UNTAC, Phnom Penh, Cambodia

Stephen Marks, Deputy Director of Human Rights, UNTAC, Phnom Penh, Cambodia

Georg Mautner-Markhof, Chief, Special Procedures Section, UN Centre for Human Rights, Geneva

Dominique McAdams, Deputy Chief Electoral Officer, UNTAC, Phnom Penh, Cambodia

Thomas McCarthy, UN Centre for Human Rights, Geneva

Dennis McNamara, Director of Human Rights, UNTAC, Phnom Penh, Cambodia

Hocine Medili, Director of Administration, UNTAC, Phnom Penh, Cambodia

Viji Menon, Deputy Director, Ministry of Foreign Affairs, Republic of Singapore

Youri Miakotnykh, Ambassador of the Russian Federation to the Supreme National Council of Cambodia, Phnom Penh, Cambodia

Craig Mokhiber, Legal Officer, UN Centre for Human Rights, Geneva

Nana Sutresna, Ambassador-at-Large, Department of Foreign Affairs, Jakarta, Indonesia

Arne Nyberg, Chief, Complaints and Investigation Service, Civil Administration Component, UNTAC, Phnom Penh, Cambodia

Ok Serei Sopheak, Vice President, Liberal Democratic Party, Phnom Penh, Cambodia

Herbert Okun, Political Adviser, International Conference on the Former Yugoslavia, Geneva

Thomas Pickering, United States Ambassador to the Republic of India, Washington, D.C.

Rajeev Pillay, Deputy Resident Representative, UNDP, Phnom Penh, Cambodia

Mark Plunkett, Special Prosecutor, UNTAC, Phnom Penh, Cambodia

Jean-Noel Poirier, Special Assistant to the Deputy Special Representative, UNTAC, Phnom Penh, Cambodia

Gérard Porcell, Director of Civil Administration, UNTAC, Phnom Penh, Cambodia

Anatoly Poujay, Political Officer and Special Assistant to the Special Representative, UNTAC, Phnom Penh, Cambodia

Iqbal Riza, Assistant Secretary-General for Peacekeeping Operations, United Nations, New York

Brigadier General Klaas Roos, Police Commissioner, UNTAC, Phnom Penh, Cambodia

Stephane Rousseau, Human Rights Officer, Siem Reap Province, UNTAC, Siem Reap, Cambodia

Behrooz Sadry, Deputy Special Representative of the Secretary-General, UNTAC, Phnom Penh, Cambodia

Lieutenant General John Sanderson, Force Commander, UNTAC, Phnom Penh, Cambodia

James Schear, Consultant to the Special Representative of the Secretary-General for Cambodia, Washington, D.C.

Sina Than, Office of Prince Sihanouk, Royal Palace, Phnom Penh, Cambodia

Richard Solomon, Ambassador of the United States of America to the Republic of the Philippines, Washington, D.C.

Mark Storella, Political Counselor, Mission of the United States of America to the Supreme National Council of Cambodia, Phnom Penh, Cambodia

Sun Yuxi, Political Counselor, Embassy of the People's Republic of China to the Supreme National Council of Cambodia, Phnom Penh, Cambodia

Peter Swarbrick, Special Assistant to the Special Representative, UNTAC, Phnom Penh, Cambodia

Paul Szasz, Legal Adviser, International Conference on the Former Yugoslavia, Geneva

Kazuo Tateishi, Chief, Specialized Control Service, Civil Administration Component, UNTAC, Phnom Penh, Cambodia

Nathanial Thayer, Reporter, Far Eastern Economic Review, Phnom Penh, Cambodia

Judy Thompson, Deputy Chief Electoral Officer, UNTAC, Phnom Penh, Cambodia

Charles Twining, Chief, Mission of the United States of America to the Supreme National Council of Cambodia, Phnom Penh, Cambodia

Brian Urquhart, Senior Fellow, The Ford Foundation, New York

Veng Sereyvuth, FUNCINPEC Party, Phnom Penh, Cambodia

Eduardo Vetere, Provincial Director, Phnom Penh Province, UNTAC, Phnom Penh, Cambodia

Sergio Vieira de Mello, Director of Repatriation and UNHCR Representative, UNTAC, Phnom Penh, Cambodia

Dieter Von Sampson, Provincial Director, Kampong Cham Province, UNTAC, Phnom Penh, Cambodia

Agnes Wagenaar, Human Rights Officer, Kampot Province, UNTAC, Kampot, Cambodia

I·N·D·E·X

K

L